# A SHORT HISTORY OF GERMANY

# A SHORT

# HISTORY OF GERMANY

BY

ERNEST F. HENDERSON

VOLUME I

9 A.D. TO 1648 A.D.

New York

THE MACMILLAN COMPANY

LONDON: MACMILLAN & CO., LTD.

1902

*All rights reserved*

Norwood Press

J. S. Cushing & Co. — Berwick & Smith

Norwood Mass. U.S.A.

DEDICATED

BY GRACIOUS PERMISSION

TO

His Royal Highness

PRINCE HENRY OF PRUSSIA

ON THE OCCASION OF

HIS VISIT TO AMERICA

# PREFACE

GERMANY stands in the centre of Europe, and on her soil all the great international struggles have been fought, —the Thirty Years' War, the early campaigns of the Spanish Succession War, the Seven Years' War, the gigantic wars against Napoleon. It is the custom for modern educators to recommend the study of the history of France as a guiding thread through the intricacies of general European history; but is this choice justifiable? The two great, omnipresent factors of the whole mediæval period are the Papacy and the Empire; the Empire was German from the ninth to the nineteenth century, —from the days of Charlemagne until the days of Francis II., —and the Empire interfered in the affairs of the Papacy and of Italy far more than did France. When we come to the period of the Reformation, surely Luther and his kind were more prominent than the French reformers, and the Emperor Charles V. had more to do with the affairs of Europe than any of the French kings. In the Thirty Years' War, larger interests were at stake than in the Huguenot struggles, and the German Peace of Westphalia necessitated a recasting of the whole map of Europe. Louis XIV., it is true, gave the tone to the high society of his age, and French was almost universally spoken and written at the German courts; but this influence was neither very deep nor very beneficial. Nor can it be denied that the French Revolution produced great results for Europe. Yet its effects, as far as Germany was concerned, have been overrated; the liberation of the serfs would probably have been accomplished without it, while constitutional government, popular representation, and trial by jury had still to wait for half a century.

If we look for striking personalities and events, the reigns of Frederick the Great and of William I. were of supreme importance to Europe, and, as was not the case with Louis XIV. and Napoleon, their acquisitions were of a permanent character. All in all, it has seemed to me that I could engage in no more thankful occupation than in writing the history of Germany; the more so as German treatments of the subject presuppose more knowledge than is usually to be found in the American reader, and as no other American writer has ever attempted the task. The work of Lewis, founded on an antiquated German text-book, does not fulfil the most modest demands.

My warm thanks are due to Professor Sumner, of the Massachusetts Institute of Technology, for valuable suggestions; to my brother, Mr. H. G. Henderson, for stylistic revision; and to my wife for the detection of errors in the proof. The tables in Lindner's *Deutsche Geschichte* have made it easier for me to draw up my own chronological view; while Putzke's valuable school atlas has been of assistance in the matter of maps. For a complete bibliography of German history, the reader is referred to Dahlmann-Waitz, *Quellenkunde*, and to the *Jahresbericht der Geschichtswissenschaft*.

E. F. H.

WASHINGTON, D. C.,
February 13, 1902.

# CONTENTS

CHAPTER                                                               PAGE

I. The Early Germans . . . . . . . . 1

II. The Rise and Fall of the Carolingians . . . . 22

III. The Relations between Church and State under the Saxon and Franconian Emperors . . . . 49

IV. The Popes and the Hohenstaufens . . . . 76

V. The Age of Chivalry . . . . . . . . 102

VI. The Kings from Different Houses . . . . . 122

VII. The Rulers of the House of Luxemburg . . . 146

VIII. The Teutonic Order and the Hanseatic League . . 172

IX. The Era of the Church Councils . . . . . 203

X. German Life on the Eve of the Reformation . . 228

XI. Martin Luther and the Emperor Charles V. . . . 251

XII. Friends and Allies of the Reformation . . . . 285

XIII. Anabaptism and Civil War . . . . . . 308

XIV. The Emperor's Wars and the Protestant Party in Germany . . . . . . . . . 333

XV. Charles V. at War with the Protestant Princes . . 363

XVI. The Roman Catholic Reaction . . . . . 395

XVII. The Beginning of the Thirty Years' War . . . 422

XVIII. The Career of Wallenstein, the Intervention of Foreign Powers, and the Peace of Westphalia . . . 450

CHRONOLOGICAL TABLE . . . . . . . . 499

INDEX . . . . . . . . . . . 509

# MAPS

FACING PAGE

Germany in the Middle Ages . . . . . . . 151

Trade Map of the Hanseatic League, 1400 . . . . . 191

Central Europe in 1477 A.D. . . . . . . . . 229

Germany in 1648 A.D. . . . . . . . . . 489

# A SHORT HISTORY OF GERMANY

## CHAPTER I

### THE EARLY GERMANS

LITERATURE: In Bruno Gebhardt, *Handbuch der deutschen Geschichte,* there is a useful but dry treatment of the period covered by this chapter. See Tacitus, *Germania,* and the extracts from the Salic Law translated in Henderson, *Select Historical Documents of the Middle Ages,* a work compiled with the idea of laying a foundation for the present history. The most attractive treatment of these early times is that of Freytag, *Bilder aus der Deutschen Vergangenheit,* as good from a historical as from a literary standpoint. Kaufmann's *Deutsche Geschichte,* reaching to the reign of Charlemagne, is excellent. Hauck's *Kirchengeschichte Deutschlands* cannot be too highly praised, but only extends to 1125 A.D.

THE remains of lake-dwellings found beneath the surface of the water, the belongings of the dead rendered up by recently discovered tombs, a few comments of Roman writers on a people with whom their armies had come into hostile contact, a detailed description, finally, by the hand of Tacitus, of Germany and the Germans as they were in his day, — such are the sources from which modern historians have reconstructed the first period in a great nation's history.

No idle whim drove our forefathers out into the lakes and caused them to erect their houses on posts driven into the mud. Here alone in a wild age could they find refuge from beasts of prey and from the greed of man ;

The lake-dwellers.

here they could readily supply themselves with fish, while not debarred from making hunting expeditions to the shore.   None too restricted was the area of these watery homes, for in some of the settlements the superstructures rested on no less than from twenty to thirty thousand posts.   One enemy, indeed, could not be avoided, for almost every one of the buildings of which the ruins remain ended by being burnt to the water's edge.   Charred and broken the piles stand there to this day, while from the mud at their base have been extracted many a tool and weapon — chisels of bone, axes and saws of stone, daggers and arrowheads made from the stag's horn or the tooth of the wild boar.

Ancient
graves.

The first traceable information concerning the Germans was brought to southern Europe by a Marseilles merchant named Pytheas, who, in the days of Alexander the Great, visited the shores of the Baltic and discovered great quantities of the useful product known as amber.   From this period, the fourth century before Christ, seem to date many of the graves that have furnished such interesting relics.   The age of stone and bone implements was passing into an age of bronze and iron.   A certain striving for elegance and luxury becomes evident — we find necklaces of amber beads, of ivory, and of colored stones, while bits of yellow ochre lead to the inference that paint was not unknown as a means of personal adornment.   Owing to the great number of graves laid open, and to the richness and variety of their contents, the museums of Germany are full to overflowing with these implements and trappings of prehistoric man.   From the tomb discovered near Hallstatt in the Salzkammergut in 1846 there have been taken six thousand objects of various kinds, while with regard to the human remains themselves, the interesting fact is made apparent that about one-half of the bodies had been burned, one-half buried in their natural state. Strangely enough, in these old burial places, bodies laid to rest in oaken coffins have been found to be better preserved than those in stone chests. The tombs themselves are of every size and shape, the largest measuring some two hundred and fifty feet in length, by thirty-five to forty in height; some are regular chambers of stone covered each with an enormous slab; one such discovered near Luneburg measures some eighteen by fourteen feet.

These graves furnish information of more than antiquarian interest. The fact that the wives and servants of great personages were immolated with them is proved beyond dispute; one group has been found consisting of a single upright figure surrounded by eight others in a crouching position. Bones of animals mixed with those of human beings lead to the assumption that war-horses, also, followed their masters to Walhalla. The shape and material of the implements and utensils, the uses for which they were evidently intended, the character, finally, of the ornamentation, all throw light on the civilization of the time. Where razors and combs are found we can infer that attention was paid to personal appearance; while the curious urns with human face discovered in West Prussia point to an interesting attempt at symbolical and artistic expression. Eyes and nose are clearly marked, the cover of the urn is the top of the head, while in the ears hang bronze rings with drops of amber, and around the neck circlets of bronze and iron. Another class of inferences can be drawn from the fact that implements made from a certain kind of stone are found miles away from places where such stone abounds; an extensive trade in such objects must have been carried on, and, indeed, traces can be found of the very workshops in which they were doubtless manufactured.

*Ancient customs.*

Leaving the antiquarian's field for more solid ground, we find various items of interest in the works of Latin authors. Cæsar, Strabo, and Tacitus all mention the Germans as spreading out toward the south. To this they were driven by pressure from the rear, as also by insufficiency of territory resulting from superficial and extravagant methods of agriculture. Much that we hear is mere rumor, as when Pliny gravely asserts that the dwellers on the Baltic islands have horses' hoofs, and ears large enough to cover their bodies.

Of the clashes at arms with the Germans, Roman writers have more to say. In the days of the Consul Marius the flood-gates of the North seemed opened, and the Cimbrians and Teutons rushed in, making the Romans tremble for their very capital. A few details of the two great battles fought by Marius, one in southern France and one in northern Italy, have come down to us: how the barbarians were completely outwitted by superior tactics, allowing the Romans to fall upon them simultaneously in front and rear; how the burning sun of the South helped to weaken the power of resistance of the children of the North; and how, in both cases, defeat meant utter annihilation. On the field of Aquæ Sextiæ none were left but the faithful German dogs, who mounted guard over the bodies of the slain.

The first great organizer among the Germans was a certain Ariovistus with whom Cæsar came in contact; Roman discipline eventually prevailed, Ariovistus was worsted, and, after the flight of the formidable leader, a short era of friendliness and peace ensued. Germans entered the Roman service and even came to form the imperial body-guard, learning valuable lessons of strategy which they were afterward able to turn to telling account. Differences arose between Augustus and the tribe of the Sigambrians, who, joining with others, made an inroad into

Gaul, defeated the legate, and even secured a Roman eagle. Peace was eventually restored, but the emperor, determined that his provinces should never again be exposed to such danger, prepared for an invasion of Germany on a large scale. Year after year he sent his stepsons, Drusus and Tiberius, to tame this stubborn people. Fortresses were built, of which one, the Saalburg near Homburg, has remained to our own day, and is about to be reconstructed on the old lines; a canal was dug through which Roman fleets swept from the Rhine to the Yssel, passing thence through the Zuyder Zee, then an inland lake, into the North Sea.

A few years later, 9 A.D., came the crucial conflict for land and liberty. It was then that the Cheruscan leader, Hermann or Arminius, fell on the Roman proconsul, Varus, in the Teutoburg Forest, destroying his splendid army. "Varus, Varus, give me back my legions!" was the wail of the distracted emperor when he heard the disheartening news. He dismissed his body-guard and forbade the city to all German visitors. With a few unimportant expeditions the long series of Roman aggressions closed, and Tacitus does not hesitate to call Arminius "the undoubted liberator of Germany."

From now on, for several generations, there was peace, and the great Roman historian learns to love and honor the country about which he writes. Within the compass of a few pages he gives us a wonderful picture of the Germans of his day; he, the aristocrat, writhing under the imperial yoke, feels strangely drawn toward this simple and innocent people, this "special, unmixed race, like only to itself." *The Germania of Tacitus.*

Tacitus tells of a land full of "bristling" woods and "uncanny" marshes, but rich in cattle, which lacked, however, "a peculiar stately character" and the "proud adornment of its brows." To have a numerous herd was the "joy of the German, his favorite, his only, source of wealth." The settlements were made, not in towns as with the Romans, but in open spaces near fountains or groves; the houses stood by themselves — possibly, suggests the historian, through dread of fire, but probably because the people knew no better. Each village had its common pasturage and distributed its arable land in lots or parcels, prescribing rigidly to all its members what land should lie fallow, what crops should be raised, and when and how the seed should be sown.

The "marks," as they were called from the broad boundary line drawn around them, over which no stranger could come without blowing his horn, were populated by large groups of kinsmen or clans. Strong as in the old patriarchal days were the ties of family; the head of the clan commanded and watched over all the rest, and the Romans wondered at seeing chieftains as anxious to redeem their nephews from captivity as though they were their own sons. Justice was administered in the court of the "hundred," or district containing some hundred families with their slaves and dependants, and the "*centenarius*" or hundred-man, who opened and closed the "moot," remained for centuries the acknowledged mouthpiece of the old Germanic liberties.

The
German
warrior.

The German men as described by Tacitus were a strange mixture of high-mindedness and brutality. Loyalty and bravery were cardinal virtues. Each chieftain was surrounded by a war-band of chosen youths, who were to cover and defend him and to sacrifice their own heroic deeds to his glory; the chieftain fought for victory, the war-band for the chieftain. If, on the one hand, it was disgraceful for a leader to be outdone in bravery by any of his followers, it betokened, on the other, the ineffaceable shame of a lifetime to have deserted a leader or to have thrown away the shield in battle.  To supplement these virtuous ideals it must be stated that reverence for old men and hospitality to strangers are mentioned among the characteristics of the ancient Germans.  To refuse shelter to one asking it was considered a crime, and when a man's own stores were exhausted, he accompanied his guest to the house of a neighbor.  For persons of distinction entertainments were inaugurated: naked youths would disport themselves in the sword dance among upturned blades and sharpened spear-heads; "pleasure it gave to the lookers-on, pleasure, too, to those who performed," which is more remarkable.  When a chieftain died he was honored to the utmost in his burial, his body being burned amid the fumes of the richest and rarest of woods.

The reverse of the picture is highly unedifying.  When not on the war-path the chieftains were wont to lie about like lazy dogs, leaving the care of the fields and all other peaceful labors to the women and slaves.  For their own part they passed their time in gambling and in drinking a concoction which was new to the Roman historian, and of which he did not approve, but which we of wider experience have no difficulty in designating as a kind of beer brewed from barley.  For successive days and nights these carouses would continue, to the accompaniment of the falling dice, the desire of winning amounting to a frenzy.  On one casual throw the players would stake all their earthly possessions, yes, even the liberty of their own persons.  Voluntarily the loser submitted to be bound and to be handed over to a neighboring tribe in exchange for merchandise.  "Stubbornness in a wrong cause," is the verdict of Tacitus; but he adds that the Germans themselves consider it pride in keeping the word once pledged.

No less anomalous than the position of these sottish yet courageous chieftains was that of the German women.

*The German in time of peace.*

Legally considered they were chattels, like the slaves, and the very name "Weib" has come down in grammar as *The German women.* of the neuter gender. Their marriage contracts were regular sales, the union not being lawful unless the bridegroom could prove by witnesses that he had paid the required sum. It was a token of subjection when the free, waving hair was bound into a braid and knot.

Yet Tacitus has much to say about the honor and respect shown to these same women, and about their helpfulness and strength of character. They, with their children, stood by in the battles, exhorting or chiding as the case might demand. " In them," writes Tacitus, " each man sees his holiest witnesses — those best fitted to award him his meed of praise. To his wife or mother he brings his wounds, which they are not afraid to look upon and count. . . . History tells how, by their prayers, the tide of many a wavering and half-despaired-of battle has been turned." The marriage relation was respected, and polygamy only allowed among the princes, who for state reasons might make family alliances. Infidelity was punished by severe and public scourging: "there among the Germans," writes Tacitus, " vice is not laughed at, and to do evil with evil doers is not scoffingly called 'being up to date.' "

*The Roman wall.* With the last page of the *Germania* the curtain falls for a long period of years, but we can trace developments from the final outcome. The Romans definitively abandoned an aggressive policy and built away at their protecting wall, a monumental fortification, second only in conception and execution to the great wall of China. There are sections of this *Limes* or *Pfahlbau* which must have been fifty feet broad at the base and as high as sixteen feet. The whole was some three hundred miles in length, flanked by hundreds of camps and towers, the latter near enough to each other to permit of communicating signals by lighting

fires at night or by raising and lowering beams by day.
Behind the wall was a moat, in front a waste stretch of
land which Germans might only cross when escorted by
Roman soldiers.

Meanwhile, within the precincts of the Roman Empire
itself, numerous Germans had been allowed to settle;
whole tribes at last were given tracts of land, receiving the
official title of *fœderati*, or allies, and engaging to fight the
battles of their adopted country.    Their influence made
itself felt in every direction ; many individuals rose to
honor and distinction in the state service, and allied themselves in marriage with the noblest families of the capital.
The Romans, for their own part, found pleasure in the
general appearance and cast of countenance of the foreigners; it became the fashion to imitate them, and the Roman
ladies took to wearing blond wigs, or to smearing their own
hair with the reddish oil which the German warriors used
when they decked themselves for battle.    Of such moment
did the Emperor Honorius consider the matter, that he
issued an edict against the practice.    Even with the Germans who remained at home the Romans maintained a
certain amount of intercourse and commerce.    German
traders, indeed, were subject to stern restrictions, and were
only allowed to approach the *Limes* at stated points, but
the Roman merchants penetrated into the very heart of
Germany.    Essentially Roman products, such as statues of
Jupiter, not to speak of numberless imperial coins, have
been found in Freienwalde and in the Lausitz — as far
north, indeed, as modern Sweden.    The Emperor Tiberius
is known to have looked upon the German turnip as a
delicacy, while the grain of which the *Schwarzbrod* is made
is referred to in a decree of the year 301.    About the same
time, too, we hear of German smoked meats, beyond a
doubt the famous Westphalian hams.    Other staples were

Intercourse
of Romans
and Ger-
mans.

furs, goose feathers, sausages, antlers, human hair, and pomatum.

The Christianizing of the Goths.

Roman culture, to some extent at least, penetrated in the wake of the traders, while Roman Christianity, in the form of the Arianism just then in vogue in the Eastern Empire, found its way to the tribe of the Goths. Toward the end of the third century the latter had made an inroad into the empire and had carried away captive two Greeks from Cappadocia. To these exiles there was born in 311 A.D. a son named Ulfila or Wulfila, a gifted boy who made himself equally familiar with the Greek, the Gothic, and the Latin languages. As he grew up and regained his liberty he embraced that form of the Christian religion in favor at Constantinople, was consecrated bishop at Antioch, and returned as missionary to the scenes of his youth. Here, after making a number of converts, he incurred the enmity of Athanarich, king of the Visigoths, and was obliged to flee to Roman soil, where he founded a haven of rest in Mœsia. He labored and taught for many years, occasionally journeying to Constantinople, where we find his name in the records of a council in 360 A.D., as one of the subscribers to the Arian creed. When, twenty-one years later, he died, his loss was widely felt, and no less a person than the Emperor Theodosius walked in his funeral procession.

The Bible of Wulfila.

Of all Wulfila's services to his people and to posterity, one of the greatest was the translation of the Bible into the Gothic tongue, a large fragment of which work, including nearly the whole New Testament, is known as the Silver Codex and is preserved in the library of the university at Upsala, a treasure beyond price, the oldest existing monument of German learning and letters. To us, indeed, it has a value that is more than philological and literary, for from it we glean historically almost all that we know of the culture of the Germans during the whole fourth century. There are native words for many a Biblical term that show a fair degree of civilization: "smiths" are distinguished from "carpenters," "buildings" from "tents." Jars and kettles, dishes, chests, and baskets seem to have been in common use, as also threshing-flails and millstones. Gardeners cultivated their gardens, deeds were drawn up and sealed. Yet the written language of the Goths must have been very imperfect, for we know that Wulfila was obliged to extend the alphabet, supplying the deficiencies from the Greek and Latin. Fondly and faithfully the old bishop labored over his task; but in the midst of his work the thought came to him that the warlike doings in the Book of Kings might not edify his rude hearers, so he quietly left it out.

All this time, while the Goths were being guided toward Christianity and civilization, and while Roman armies and Roman society were growing more and more Germanized, a great and important change was coming over the face of northern Europe. The marvellous prolificness of the Germans, added to their lack of intensive methods of cultivating the soil, precipitated the movement known as the wandering of the nations. Already, in the third century, the fifty or more tribes whose names are mentioned by Tacitus had merged and coalesced into larger associations, which had gradually pressed forward to the very borders of Roman territory. The final impetus came from the rear, when, about 375 A.D., the fierce Asiatic tribe of the Huns crossed the Volga and entered on their career of conquest and intimidation. With the Visigoths, whom they drove before them, was that Alaric who was later to sack Rome. There is no need here to follow in detail the different migrations of the tribes, or to trace the rise and fall of each small monarchy; of the eight Teutonic kingdoms

The wandering of the nations.

founded on Roman soil in the fifth and sixth centuries, four, those of Odoacer and Theodoric, of the Burgundians, and of the Vandals, were quickly to wane and fall; two, those of the Visigoths in Spain and the Lombards in Italy, were to endure for a few centuries, while only two, that of the Anglo-Saxons in Britain and that of the Franks in Gaul, were to show real and lasting vitality.

Manner of settlement on Roman ground.

It must not be supposed of these wandering German conquerors that, wherever they came, they utterly stamped out the Roman civilization. On the contrary, the two peoples often settled down peacefully side by side, the newcomers merely claiming for themselves a certain fixed share, one-third or two-thirds of each estate. In this there was no great hardship to the Romans, for, according to the same principle, armies of so-called allies had often been quartered on them. For the student of institutions, nothing can be more instructive than to trace the gradual fusion of the two civilizations: the Romans gave language, literature, and law, as well as many of their time-honored customs, to their invaders; the latter brought in new principles of government and a new conception of liberty and personal rights.

The question suggests itself, why Germany was not emptied, and rendered desolate by this constant pouring forth of peoples. In point of fact the migrators rarely constituted the whole of their tribe; remnants, for instance, of Goths who remained behind on the Black Sea while their fellows invaded Italy could still be found in the seventeenth century. It was the surplus population, as a rule, that was anxious to be gone; and their exodus, not infrequently, took place with the solemn sanction of a general assembly. Nor was the break with the parent stock considered final; individuals might still hold land in their old settlements. Long after his conquest of the north coast of Africa, Genseric, the Vandal king, received a deputation from his former home in Silesia, urging that he and his followers should renounce their old possessions. The request was refused on the plea that no one could be secure against a change of fortune.

Far, then, from being depopulated, Germany's store of warriors seemed to the Romans fairly inexhaustible; "they increase, but we decrease," wrote Salvianus in the fifth century, while Paul, the son of Warnefried, who outlived the last invasions, contrasts his own desolate land with crowded Germany, and surmises that the ice and snow of the North are more favorable to propagation than the climate of poor, plague-ridden Italy.

The Franks, especially, never lost touch with their own and with kindred German peoples, — an important fact, when we consider the enervating effect of purely Roman influences on Goths and Visigoths, Burgundians and Vandals. These Franks were the founders of a new Germany; and with them our history will concern itself almost exclusively; they had begun their career of expansion about the year 400 A.D., at which time, unlike the Goths, they were still heathen. We hear of them, a little later, in northern Gaul, and in the present Holland and Belgium, roughly divided into two great groups, the Salians and Ripuarians, each group in turn consisting of many different tribes. It was Clovis, a Salian Frank of the family of Meroveus, who, by extensive conquests, and especially by the base murder of all possible rival princes, first consolidated these lands into a strong kingdom. He captured and put to death Syagrius, that enterprising Roman governor who, after the fall of the Western Empire, had continued to administer in his own name a large part of Gaul. He lopped off many of its provinces from the once powerful Visigothic kingdom of Toulouse, and carried off the treasures which Alaric had gathered together in Rome. He

*The tribe of the Franks.*

defeated the Allemanni in a memorable battle, and their
former lands along the Main and the Neckar became
known by the name of Franconia, with the principal city
of Frankfort, or ford of the Franks. The Burgundians
were partially, in the next generation wholly, subdued.

But Clovis was more than a conqueror, he was also a far-
seeing statesman; no wiser political move was ever made
than when, in 496 A.D., he determined to become a Christian,
and to adhere to the form of religion authorized by Rome,
as opposed to that spread by the Eastern church. Many
writers have, with justice, attributed the fall of the other
Germanic kingdoms to mutual hatred of the Arians and
the orthodox. Clovis, on the contrary, rallied around him
the entire clergy of Gaul, with all their wealth and influence. His biographer, the Bishop of Tours, lauds him to
the skies as the champion of the true faith, and even when
commenting on a treacherous murder, which the king himself had instigated, declares that thus the Lord laid low
his enemies, as a reward for walking in His ways and
doing what was pleasing in His sight.

The conversion took place publicly and with dramatic
effect. The king had registered a vow that, should he
prove successful in the battle of Tolbiacum against the
Allemanni, he would yield to the entreaties of his Burgundian wife and accept her God. After the battle, with a
number of his followers, he received baptism; and the proud
Sigambrian knelt at the feet of Remigius of Rheims, and
meekly bowed his head while the bishop bade him burn
what he had adored and adore what he had burned. It
must not, however, be supposed that this act was the result
of any mere sudden impulse. Clovis was well prepared for
it, and had well weighed its future consequences. He had
always desired to win the support of the church, and had
already allowed his infant sons to be baptized. The story

The con-
version of
Clovis.

has been often told of how at a distribution of booty he had interfered to save a sacred vessel for a Christian bishop; his design had been defeated, for his warriors were far from looking upon him as an absolute despot, but with his own hand he had afterward killed the man who thwarted him. The results of the conversion proved in the end more far-reaching than even Clovis could have foreseen; the way had been opened for a close alliance between the Roman Papacy and the Frankish kingdom. Had the Franks remained heretics in the eyes of Rome, the imperial crown could never have been placed on the head of Charlemagne. As for Clovis himself, he had found a watchword that legitimatized, as it were, his position: "I cannot endure it," he said of the Visigoths, "that these Arians should possess a part of Gaul. Let us, with God's help, set forth and conquer them and add their land to our kingdom!" *Results of the acceptance of Christianity.*

The Franks were able in a way to give their own stamp to the Christianity they adopted, and their Christ became the model of a warrior-leader. Clovis regretted that he and his followers had not been present to avenge the Crucifixion, and good Bishop Gregory praises the utterance. The miracles recorded in Merovingian times consist largely of saintly intervention in the midst of battle, and of similar godlike performances. Old heathen rites continued to be performed under the guise of Christian ceremonial; and saints' images, like idols, were carried round as a protection against fire, illness, and death. It was a change of name, but not of substance; Siegfried's dragon became the dragon of St. George, while the virtues of the old goddesses were transferred to the Virgin Mary.

For two and a half centuries after the death of Clovis the dynasty of the Merovingians continued to reign over the Franks; but only twice, and for brief spaces of time, were all the different lands united under one hand. The *The Merovingian kings.*

usual law of succession demanded that the father should provide equally for all of his sons ; the kingdom accordingly was riven, and sundered, and a premium set on fratricide and intrigue. Two more bloodthirsty women than those guardians of princes, Brunhilda and Fredegunda, would be hard to find in all history.

It is strange to note in these early times how the power of the kings was marked and estimated by purely external tokens, by wealth and display, or even by the length of the royal locks. The gold of the conquered Romans gave a chance for unaccustomed luxury, and monarchs vied with each other in reckless extravagance. King Chilperich had a dinner service of gold and precious stones, while one single dish of the many owned by King Gunthram weighed 470 pounds. Queen Fredegunda's son, at the age of two, possessed four wagon loads of silks and ornaments, while no less than fifty such accompanied the Princess Raguntha, who in 584 A.D. was sent to the Visigoths in Spain. The scale was often turned in favor of a candidate to the throne by the amount of his treasure, so that the relative who seized a dead king's belongings increased his chances of succeeding to the throne.

The long wavy hair was a distinguishing feature of this dynasty, and their particular pride and joy. We can see it still on all the coins and seals of the time, and we know from old chroniclers that he who lost his curls was debarred from the throne until they grew again. A distracted mother once chose death for her two sons rather than that they should suffer such indignity.

Decline of the Merovingian dynasty.

As time went on the Merovingian kings became more and more feeble and enervated ; we hear of vicious acts committed in earliest youth. The wonder is that the race did not sooner die out; its scions, at last, had not strength of mind even for the crimes and bloodshed that lend a shuddering interest to the reigns of their ancestors. They became the type for all future ages of *rois fainéants*, of shadowy, do-nothing kings. All the power had come into the hands of the chief officers of the household, the mayors of the palace, who for years and generations conducted the business of ruling. Einhard, the friend and biographer of Charles the Great, has preserved a most vivid picture of the weakness of the declining dynasty. He tells how the feeble king, content with the royal name, and with the waving hair and long beard, sat on the throne and played the part of ruler; how he received the envoys of foreign powers, and delivered to them, as if on his own authority, the answers which had been dictated to him, and which he might not dare to change.

No wonder that the practice of the Christian religion, St. Colum-
which especially needed the fostering care of wise rulers, banus.
began to decline. So degenerate did the church become that Columbanus, the Irish missionary who sought these regions at the end of the sixth century, was forced to write home that "the love of mortification was scarcely to be found even in a few places." What man could do to stem the disorders Columbanus did. A member of that church of St. Patrick which had developed its own teachings in antagonism to Rome, he was a perfectly fearless, nay relentless, reformer. When still a youth he had determined to go forth into the world and preach the gospel, and had sprung over the prostrate form of his mother when she tried to bar his egress, declaring that he never wished to look upon her face again. With twelve comrades he had crossed over to the Continent, where his fiery enthusiasm won him many followers. Even bishops turned to him for guidance and powerful nobles placed their children under his care. His courage was unbending; he braved the heathen in the very act of sacrificing, and once poured on the

ground the libation the Allemanni were about to offer to their god.  He labored incessantly for fifty years, but at last was expelled from the land on the plea that his method of calculating Easter differed from that of the Gallic clergy !

Columbanus founded three monasteries and drew up a rule for their guidance — so severe, indeed, that the pain of scourging was prescribéd for an unguarded cough.  More lasting than his own foundations was that of one of his disciples, St. Gall, who, at one of the loveliest points of the lake of Constance, established a settlement where, through-out the darkest of the Dark Ages, learning and art shone forth like a beacon light.

Meanwhile in other fields the spirit of order had been at work among the Frankish people.  A form of local govern-ment had been established for all the different parts of the kingdom, and a code of laws drawn up, simple yet com-prehensive, and readily sufficing for all the ordinary matters of daily life.  Just as in modern times we see states divided into counties and townships, so the Merovingian land fell naturally into the canton (*civitas* or *gau*) and the hundred. In the latter the people still chose their *centenarius* or hun-dred-man, but the chief official in the district was now the king's count, who took for his maintenance one-third of the revenue drawn from fines and taxes.  The count it was who now at regular stated intervals came to the spot on the village green where the hundred court was to be held, ascended the throne that was placed there for him, and hung up his shield on a post or tree to show that the solemn proceedings were about to begin.  Those charged with crime and their accusers were brought before him, though very different were the proceedings from those of a modern trial.  The merits of the case itself were not gone into ; the plaintiff brought the charge, the defendant fur-nished, not witnesses, but a number of kinsmen and neigh-

bors who were willing to swear that they did not consider
him guilty.   Or, again, resort might be had to the judgment   The ordeal.
by ordeal or to trial by combat, the count, apparently assisted by priests, conducting the proceedings.   Under the
Merovingian and Carolingian rulers a number of ordeals
were in vogue, but none was more common than that of
forcing the suspected person to seize with his bare hand a
stone suspended by a string in a caldron of boiling water.
If the water burnt his hand, the voice of God was believed
to have spoken against him, and he was handed over to the
law to suffer the penalty for his crime.

It is difficult to put one's self in the attitude of these
simple, superstitious people; it is all too evident that only
fraud on the part of the priest could save the victim from
injury.   Yet in every case of ordeal the burden of proof
lay with the accused; in every case the commonest laws of
nature would have had to be reversed before he could be
declared innocent.   Women as well as men were forced to
walk a certain distance with red-hot irons in their hands,
or to cross barefoot over glowing ploughshares.   In the
ordeal by cold water the victim was bound and thrown into
a tank, where, if he sank, he was punished; if he floated,
he went free.   Was the whole system a bit of priestly jug-
glery, to show their power of working miracles?

The ordeal or the combat over, the man who had suc-   The Salic
cumbed was obliged to submit to the penalty prescribed by   Law.
the law of his own tribe or province.   These laws were
early committed to writing — in the Latin language — and
are among the most interesting records of the past.   They
seem to have been drawn up originally in answer to a need
of regulating the relations of the conquerors to the subjected Romans.   Most famous of all is the Salic Law, which
dates from the time of Clovis, and takes us down the whole
scale of punishments, from the fine required for the murder

of a bishop to that claimed for abusive epithets, like witch, perjurer, spy, fox, or hare. Wounds were rated according to their length, depth, and relative position, and according to the amount of blood that flowed from them; and the sum was increased tenfold, with the fee of a doctor in addition, if the blow had been struck below the waist. It is curious to note that crimes with the Franks were not offences against the state, but purely against the individual and his friends: " If any one shall have dug up and plundered a corpse already buried, and it shall have been proved on him, he shall be outlawed until the day when he comes to an agreement with the relatives of the dead man, and they ask for him that he be allowed to come among men." And again, " If any one's father have been killed, the sons shall have half the compounding money ( *Wergeld*) ; and the other half, the nearest relatives . . . shall divide among themselves."

Poetic thoughts in old laws.

Through these old laws, as well as through the oldest legal formulas that have been preserved, there often runs a vein of poetry, while some situations are painted in the most dramatic language. The guilty man, says an old curse, shall be outlawed so far as fire burns and earth grows green, so far as " the hawk flies through the long spring day with the wind resting under his two wings." According to the Salic Law the offender who has not wherewith to pay his fine is first to renounce all his property, " and he shall afterward go into his house, and shall collect in his hand dust from the four corners of it, and shall afterward stand upon the threshold, looking inward into the house. And then, with his left hand, he shall throw over his shoulders some of that dust on the nearest relative that he has. . . . And after that, in his shirt, without girdle and without shoes, a staff in his hand, he shall spring over the hedge." A dismal picture of renunciation and ruin! But not more moving than the account in the Frisian Law of the three cases of necessity, in which the mother can lay hands on the heritage of her child: "when the child is captive and in chains in the north over the sea or in the south over the mountains;" "when years of scarcity come and fierce hunger stalks over the land and the child would die of starvation;" "when," finally, "the child is stark naked or homeless, and the misty dark night and the icy cold winter rise over the palings, and all men hasten to house and home, and the wild beast seeks the hollows of the trees and the caves of the mountains, there to eke out his existence; when the child, under age, weeps and bemoans its bare limbs and bewails that it has no roof, and that its father who should protect it against the cold winter and fierce hunger is lying so deep down in the darkness under earth and oaken planks, covered and held fast by four nails: then the mother may alienate and sell her child's inheritance!"

The alliterative form in many of the old laws shows a joy in sweet sounds, and we know from other evidence that the Germans were already in the habit of singing popular melodies. Tacitus tells how they "filled the valleys and wooded heights with the echoes of gleeful song," though the Emperor Julian wonders how they can enjoy their own music, which seems to him "not unlike the croaking of violently shrieking birds." A later, still severer, critic was a certain Deacon John, who inveighs against the German rendering of the noble Gregorian chants: "when they try," he says, "to sing the mild melody with their own modulations and trills, the barbaric wildness of their thirsty throats emits harsh tones with a certain natural resonance, as if heavy wagons with confused noise of thunder were driving along over logs." Interesting animadversions, in the youth of their race, on the most musical people the world has known!

Popular melodies.

# CHAPTER II

## THE RISE AND FALL OF THE CAROLINGIANS

LITERATURE : *The Life of Charlemagne*, by Einhard, a contemporary, is of great interest. The Capitulary of 802, in Henderson's *Select Documents*, should be read in connection with the founding of the Holy Roman Empire. The most scholarly and complete work on the whole period is Mühlbacher, *Deutsche Geschichte unter den Karolingern.* Von Löher, *Kulturgeschichte der Deutschen im Mittelalter*, is valuable. Of lives of Charlemagne in English one of the best is that by Davis.

The mayors of the palace.

IN the seventh century we find three different divisions of the Frankish kingdom : Austrasia, Neustria, and Burgundy — each with its own petty Merovingian king and its own mayor of the palace. After frequent civil wars the mayor of Neustria, Pepin of Héristal, succeeded at Testry, in 687 A.D., in subduing the mayor of Austrasia, who happened at the time to be administering also the affairs of Burgundy. A significant date this 687, for by this battle unity was restored to the Franks, and the power concentrated in the hands of Pepin and his descendants. Pepin, we are told, "arranged all things and returned to Austrasia," leaving his own son as major-domus of Neustria.

Strong men were needed if the work of Clovis were not to be undone ; but the new rulers proved a warlike race for the next four generations, showing no weak member until after the days of Charles the Great. Each in turn — Pepin of Héristal, Charles Martel, Pepin the Short, and Charles the Great himself — put down with an iron hand revolts of the conquered tribes, finding in time new powers to reckon with, like the dukes of Bavaria, the Lombards and the popes in Italy, the Avars in the present Austria, the Moors in Spain, or the untamed Saxons at home.

Most alarming of all because it threatened the downfall of the whole civilization of the West, was the war-cloud that approached from the South, where the devoted followers of Mohammed, ever since the Hegira, or flight to Mecca, in 622 A.D., had been steadily advancing and conquering everything in their way. Marvellous had been their progress from the sands of Arabia, along the whole northern coast of Africa, across the straits of Gibraltar, which were named after one of their generals, through Spain and Aquitaine, and well into Gaul. In one of the great battles of the world, fought near Poictiers in 732 A.D., Charles Martel — the dealer of heavy, hammer-like blows — drove them back, owing his victory largely to his own skill and bravery, but also to discords in the enemy's camp and to the ready response with which his call to arms was met in all the heterogeneous parts of the Frankish kingdom. Few details of the battle are known; but contemporaries place the enemy's losses at wild, extravagant figures, and the victory was in so far decisive that the Mohammedans ceased to assume the offensive and were soon driven out of Aquitaine. *Charles Martel and the Arabs.*

From this war date the beginnings of the great feudal system that prevailed in Europe down into the 19th century, for in order to equip his nobles with horses Charles sequestered large estates of the church and granted out the usufruct. The recipients of these so-called benefices made certain agreements which placed them in the position of vassals. They took an oath of fidelity, and gradually acquired privileges and, especially, immunity from the interference of the royal justices. Their holdings came to be known by the name of *feuda*, or fiefs, whence the name feudal system. *Beginning of the feudal system.*

A radical measure, this seizure of ecclesiastical lands, and one that has only been resorted to at great crises in the world's history. In spite of his great service to Christendom, the church could never forgive Charles's act of violence, and he died in bad repute, at least with his Gallic clergy. A pious bishop of Orleans, who was said to have descended into hell in the good company of an angel, declared that he had seen him there. The monks of St. Wandrille, in the monastery chronicle, bewail that their good lands have gone for the purchase of spurs and saddles; while a legend relates that once, when Charles's tomb was opened, diabolical fumes were seen to escape.

St. Boniface, the Romanizer of the German church.

Yet this same prince had been the constant friend and protector of the warmest advocate and most zealous servant the church of Rome had ever possessed, the English missionary Winfred, or Boniface, to whom he had given a letter of safe-conduct addressed to all the nobles of his land, and whom he had allowed to map out the whole Frankish territory into ecclesiastical provinces. Boniface founded the monastery of Fulda, became the first archbishop of Mainz, and completely Romanized the German church, so that it conformed in even the most petty observances. He once declared that without this support from Charles he could neither have governed his priests and monks, nor prevented the exercise of pagan and idolatrous rites.

This new and close union with Rome was of vast importance for the future. The eternal city had often been the goal of pious pilgrimages, a hunting ground for sacred relics. But never before had the popes attained to the exercise of any considerable influence within Frankish territory. Gregory the Great had adopted the humblest tones even to the murderess Brunhilda, whom he begged to protect his missionaries on their way to England. Now the German people were to be folded closely in Rome's embrace, not to be liberated until the time of the Reformation.

For the literary culture of Germany Boniface also did his part. Fulda became a home of letters, and many of the monks and nuns who at his bidding came from England were in turn the founders of new monasteries and thus of new intellectual centres. Boniface himself wrote a grammar and a number of poems, and could not refrain from interspersing verses even in his letters to the Pope. Not merely in spiritual matters was he applied to, but also in those relating to pure diction. The account of a vision that he has left us in one of his letters does as much credit to his poetic imagination and his powers of expression as to his sanctity.

All this while the position of the mayors of the palace, although they had assumed the rank and title of dukes, was, to say the least, anomalous; yet the people had sanctioned it and had wished for no change of dynasty. They still set store by their feeble kings, and once when Grimoald, Charles Martel's great-uncle, had tried to place his own son on the throne, he had forced a revolt that cost him his life. But by the time of Pepin, Charles's son, the complexion of affairs was altered, and nobles, clergy, and people alike were desirous of a change. Pepin, eager for a sanction that would command respect, sent to the Pope, in 752 A.D., and propounded the riddle on which the fate of nations rested, "With regard to the kings of the Frankish kingdom, who possessed no more royal power, was this right or no?" And Pope Zacharias answered in similar oracular terms, "Rather should he have the name of king who has the power than he to whom no royal power remains."

Then Pepin allowed himself to be chosen and done homage to by the people, and to be consecrated by the primate

*Pepin as king of the Franks.*

Pepin and
the see of
Rome.

Boniface. Mindful of this religious side to his elevation, he signed himself henceforth as "king by the grace of God," and when the next Pope, Stephen IV., announced his intention of coming over the Alps, he dutifully went to meet him at St. Maurice, taking with him his little boy of twelve, the future Charlemagne. Afterward, in St. Denis, Stephen solemnly anointed the new king and his two sons, and placed a diadem on the head of the queen. "What was done for none of your ancestors has been done for you," he later wrote, ". . . through our humility the Lord has anointed you king." By solemn papal fiat the crown was declared hereditary, and a curse pronounced on whoever should presume to choose a king from any other line. The two potentates then concluded an alliance which was to last "until the consummation of the ages."

Through his friendly union with the Roman pontiff, a great field of activity had been opened up for the newly made king. As champion of the church, he descended upon Italy, where the Lombards were threatening the power of the papal see. Wresting whole districts from their hands, notably the Pentapolis and the Ravenna exarchate, he handed them over to the Pope, and this gift, known as the "donation of Pepin," laid the foundation for the temporal greatness of the Roman see.

The conquests of
Charles the
Great.

Never have two men better supplemented each other's work than in the case of Pepin and Charlemagne. What the one began the other carried to completion, until, by perfectly natural steps, the crown of the Frankish kingdom merged into that of the Holy Roman Empire. For posterity, indeed, Pepin has remained far in the background, whereas Charlemagne has been the hero of all the ages. Whenever antiquity has been found desirable for a law or for an institution, it has been dated back to his reign; innumerable writings are spiced with anecdotes about him.

The image of his banner-bearer, Roland, became the accepted emblem of civic jurisdiction; the greatest emperors paid their reverence at his tomb. It was his coffin that Napoleon carried off to Paris, as the token of a whole dead empire; his crown, and his alone, that the Corsican coveted.

It is more as a lawgiver and administrator than as a conqueror that Charles has lived in the memory of the people, and it is with that side of his activity and with his dominating personality that we are here most concerned. We shall, therefore, follow him not too closely on his military career, as he rode along on his charger from one confine of his domains to the other, adding mile on mile until twelve thousand ultimately stood to his credit. In his forty-six years of rule he engaged in some sixty warlike expeditions, and the wonder is that he found time and inclination for his many works of peace. At the end of his reign he could look around on magnificent results. The Lombard kingdom in Italy, after a checkered life of two centuries, had been brought to an end, and the iron crown rested on his own head; the last free German tribes had been drawn within the limits of the Frankish kingdom; the last remnants of heathenism had gone down before the sword and the laws of the determined conqueror. A Bavarian duke had been brought to bay, had been shorn as a monk, and thrust in a cloister, while his land had been parcelled out as a Frankish province.

In the present Austria the fierce Avars had been put to rout; little had availed them their huge chain of "rings," or strong-walled fortresses; a death-blow had been struck to their pride as a people, while the booty they had stolen from the Eastern Empire had been carried off as a rich prize. Some of it came to England as a gift to the king of Wessex. A part of Spain, too, the land between the Pyrenees and the Ebro, had been won for the empire, while, in the North, the Danes and the Slavs had felt the weight of the imperial displeasure.

In the broad plains between the Rhine and the Elbe had been waged the fiercest and longest of all the wars, and, after thirty-three years of heroic resistance, the heathen Saxons had been forced to bow their necks forever under the yoke of a Christian king. With unheard-of fury this contest had raged, and Charles had been reduced to the severest of all measures, to wholesale massacre; for the stern old Saxon race, with a native aristocracy so proud that to marry beneath one's rank meant death, was fighting for gods and for freedom.

But this king knew no half-measures. His will was to be law, and death and the cross of Christ were the only alternatives he offered. He felled the mighty Irmensäule, the sacred tree of Wotan, and carried off the treasure heaped up in the neighboring temple. He forced baptism on his captives at the point of the sword, and made them pay their tithes to the church and keep the Sabbath holy; so strict were the laws he passed that for converts to eat meat in Lent was a capital crime, unless the offender could gain the absolution of a Christian priest. To avenge two of his commanders, who had been defeated on the Weser, he caused forty-five hundred of the enemy who had fallen into his hands to be executed in a single day. At the end of the war whole districts, bereft of their inhabitants, lay waste or were left to the Slavs; tribe after tribe and clan after clan were transplanted to other parts of the kingdom; and to this day Sachsbach, Sachsenberg, and other places in Thuringia and Hesse preserve the name and the memory of these first unwilling colonists. Forever crushed was the spirit of opposition; and two generations later a Saxon poet could liken Charles to one of the old apostles, declaring that he had brought the Saxon people to the gates of heaven.

Charles's expeditions into Italy brought him into personal contact with various popes, and he continued for most part the close and friendly relations that had been inaugurated by his father.  By his order, all the correspondence that Pepin had had with Rome was collected and copied, and is still preserved.  It concerns of course the Lombards, their common enemy, but also those important questions upon which the Eastern and Western church differed so radically as never to be able to come to an agreement — the iconoclastic controversy, namely, and the dogma of the procession of the Holy Ghost from the Son as well as from the Father.

Charles the Great and Pope Adrian I.

Charles had begun his reign by acceding to the wish of his mother, Bertrada, and taking to wife a daughter of the Lombard king, Desiderius.  Pope Stephen IV. had been furious, and had written a most vehement letter, in which he spoke of the Lombards as propagators of leprosy and a horribly faithless and ill-odored people.  Charles had afterward repudiated his wife, and become the warmest ally of Adrian I., at whose behest he had made war on Desiderius. In the midst of this conflict, at Easter, 773, he had made a pilgrimage to Rome, where he was received with pomp and rejoicing.  The youth of the city had come out to meet him with palms and olive branches, and the Pope had received him in state at St. Peter's.  Over the grave of the apostle they had sworn mutual fidelity, and Charles had solemnly ratified the donation once made by Pepin to the church.  He had taken the title, " Patrician of Rome." In 781 the Pope had personally baptized Charles's eldest son, and when, in 795, Adrian died, tears of real sorrow were shed by the Frankish king.  He caused to be prepared the memorial tablet that now stands embedded in the wall near the chief entrance of St. Peter's.

Adrian's successor, Leo III., had continued the friendly

intercourse, and had sent Charles the keys of St. Peter's
tomb and the banner of the city of Rome. There stands
to this day in the Lateran palace a picture of St. Peter
laying his hands on the heads of the two chief potentates
of Christendom, and granting to the one victory, to the
other long life. Charles, for his part, considered himself
the patron, protector, and censor of the papacy : " Admon-
ish the Pope " — so he instructs his envoy — " to lead an
honest life, and especially to observe the sacred decrees of
the church." He himself makes rules for good order in
the bishoprics and monasteries, and passes laws against the
keeping of falcons, hawks, and conjurers by bishops, abbots,
and abbesses, and the writing of sentimental ditties by
nuns. Frequently he admonishes the clergy to read the
service with due reverence, or to see that the children
of their parishioners duly learn their letters ; he inveighs
against the laying aside of shoes during the divine service,
and insists on the use of altar-cloths. Choir practice was
often held in his presence, and he took pains to have German singers trained in Rome, being shocked to find how
superior in this respect the Italians were to his own people.
The reed organ had recently been invented in Constantinople, and he ordered instruments to be sent to him in order
that they might be copied by native workmen.

With such an interest in the affairs of the church and of
the papacy, it is not surprising that when Leo came to
Saxony as a fugitive with a tale of outrageous treatment
at the hands of the Romans, Charles constituted himself
judge and avenger. He received the Pope with great honor
in the midst of his troops, and the court poet describes the
occasion. We are in a perfect atmosphere of fluttering
standards and sounding trumpets, while Charles, conspic-
uous for his height, rides round on a mighty war-horse
resplendent in glittering armor. He leads the Pope to the

church and afterward to a splendid feast, where the hall is adorned with rich carpets and with hangings of purple and gold.

In Rome the form of a trial was gone through. Leo ascended a pulpit, and, with the Bible in his hand, cleared himself of all charges against him. His enemies were then deported beyond the Alps. He himself showed his gratitude by the most important single act committed in the Middle Ages — the placing, namely, of an imperial crown on the head of the Frankish king. The scene took place in St. Peter's on Christmas morning, which, according to the then reckoning, was also the first day of the new year — 800 A.D. It all came on Charles in the nature of a surprise, and he declared to Einhard that, had he known of Leo's intention, he would have remained away. The Pope, whose interest in the matter was to establish a jurisdiction that could forever rid him of his enemies, had stepped forward as the king was rising from prayer at the tomb of St. Peter, and the people had greeted the act with warm acclamations, calling down long life and victory on the new Augustus, the crowned of God.

Charles's reluctance was doubtless real, for his sudden coronation as king of the Romans gave rise to numerous difficulties that might better first have been removed. For the dignity he was called to enjoy was not merely a revival of the so-called empire of the West, but a distinct menace to the power of the emperor of the East. No single chronicler of the time speaks of him as the successor of Romulus Augustulus, but all regarded him as the direct heir of the last Byzantine prince. That throne was considered vacant, as an infamous woman occupied it at the time. Only after twelve years of acrid negotiation was a treaty concluded with Nicephorus, the successor of Irene.

It is not unlikely, too, that Charles objected to the prominent part assumed by the Pope. He may have foreseen the proud claims that were later to be put forth, although at the moment there was no cause to fear, for Leo was humility itself, being the first to fall down and "adore" the new emperor.

The pro-
gramme of
the new
empire.

At all events, the emperor was well aware of the importance of his new position. The long capitulary, or series of laws, issued in 802 A.D., is his official programme, as it were — nothing less than the expression of his ideal of an empire. At the head of all things he stands himself, his chief duty being to provide for the welfare of his subjects. Every man in his realm has, in a new form of oath, to plight his troth to him. In his hands are justice, morality, and religion. His empire is to be a haven of rest where all discords are to cease, and no one to infringe on another's rights. In his personal care are all the churches of God, all widows, orphans, and strangers, "for the Emperor himself, after God and His saints, has been constituted their protector and defender."

Extent of
the empire.

The territory over which Charles's rule extended embraced modern France and a part of Spain, as well as Holland and Belgium. Of what is now Germany but about one-half was included within his boundaries, the land beyond the Elbe being occupied by Slavic tribes; on the other hand are to be reckoned in modern Austria, Bohemia, and Moravia, and more than two-thirds of Italy. The distances were great and the roads and means of transport poor; yet often at the call of some distant province Charles travelled the length and breadth of his domains. He was frequently in Italy, frequently on the farthest confines of his Saxon lands.

Was it possible to make such varied elements, peoples of so many tongues and such opposite customs and ideals, submit to any one central form of government? Charles tried it, and for the term of his own life at least succeeded in his endeavors. The newly conquered lands were divided into counties, each under its own count; regular courts were held, definite duties required of the people, and church tithes imposed. The borders of the empire were protected by "marches," stretches of land studded with fortresses and garrisoned by Frankish troops, over whom was a "margrave," with extended powers.

Charles was determined to keep the threads of power firmly in his own hand, and to know just how his lands were administered; he despatched supervisors in all directions whose duty it was to report on the work and efficiency of all the different officials. *The missi dominici.*

These *missi dominici*, or king's messengers, prototypes of the later justices itinerant in England, went forth two by two from the royal court, a clergyman and a layman being paired together. Arrived in the special districts appointed for their activity, they called assemblies, inquired into the manner of administering affairs, listened to the representations of men chosen from the people, and heard the appeals of individuals who complained of denial of justice. In addition to this it devolved on the *missi*, as the emperor's representatives, to receive the oath of fealty from all who had come to man's estate. Over the relics of a saint the subject swore to be true to the monarch as a vassal to his lord, so far as God gave him intelligence. Another of the duties of the envoys was to see that military service was actually performed by those from whom it was due. As a rule every able-bodied man was obliged to serve for a certain number of days, and to appear in camp equipped at his own expense. This, in the case of poor men, was manifestly impossible, and a law was passed that several might join together in fitting out one common representative. Even then, military service was the bane of this

otherwise mild rule.   Many, in despair, gave up their freedom and became the serfs of their more fortunate neighbors.    Thus the large landowners developed into petty
potentates, and a whole social revolution worked itself out.
The ultimate fall of the Carolingian dynasty is attributable in large part to the fact that the kings could no longer
rely directly on their subjects, but were often at the mercy
of powerful *seigneurs*.   The real lord of the peasant was
the man from whom he held his land.

The capitu-
laries.
At the end of their year of service the *missi dominici*
brought their reports to Charles, who made them the
basis of instructions for the next year's envoys.    Many
such instructions have been preserved, and afford some of
the best glimpses into the methods of administration.
They are called capitularies, because of their chapters or
headings.   They concern all branches of the service, the
management of the emperor's private estates, as well as of
the public lands.   Indeed, there was no distinction under
this greatest of autocrats.    Whatever revenues came in
from tolls and customs, from spoils of war, from tribute,
gifts, and payments for protection, from lordless lands, and
from his own farms, were disposed of according to his will.
Yet with regard to these same private estates, he kept the
most rigid reckoning, and is said even to have counted the
eggs as they arrived for use in the palace.

No one who has not read these capitularies can appreciate their attention to detail ; among thousands of directions for the welfare of the state they give the proper food
for hens, the plants, by name, that are to be in the kitchen
garden, the kinds of apples that must be grown.    The
juice is no longer to be pressed from the grapes, as
formerly, by treading them with the naked feet, while it
is decreed that the gardener's house can be made more
ornamental by trailing it over with green vines.    The

prices of food and clothing had been discussed in the Diet of 808 A.D., and a capitulary determines that a cloak of the best fur may be sold for thirty shillings, but that an ordinary one is not to cost more than ten. The value of the shilling had been previously fixed at the twentieth part of a pound; new coins had been issued — twelve pence to the shilling — and refusal to accept them, as far, at least, as Slavs were concerned, had been declared punishable with flogging. Against usury, "when one demands back more than one gave — when, for example, one lends ten shillings, and then claims more," strict penalties were decreed.

Many of Charles's capitularies concern the matter of education. He had learned in Italy to venerate the culture of his own and of past ages, and it became a fixed purpose with him to rouse in his own Franks an appreciation of art and of civilization. He gathered around him the great men of his time, often calling them, as in the case of Peter of Pisa and Alcuin of York, from distant countries. He took lessons himself, as did all his family, while a regular school was established in the palace for the sons of nobles. "We are seeking most zealously," he writes to his prelates, "to foster the sciences, which, through the carelessness of our forefathers, have almost fallen into oblivion, and we invite, through our own example, as far as in us lies, to the eager study of the free arts." Latin he himself spoke fluently, Greek not so well, and writing was an art or accomplishment to which, with all his efforts, he could personally not attain. He kept his tablets under his pillow, so Einhard tells us, and frequently rose in the night to practise forming his letters; but his stiffened fingers would lend themselves to no such petty work. We learn, nevertheless, that he was able to compose a grammar of his mother tongue, and that he gave German names to the four winds and the twelve months, besides ordering a collection to be

*Charles the Great and the advancement of learning.*

made of old German national songs. Numerous were the manuscripts, both of heathen and of Christian writers, that he caused to be carefully copied, — a document badly penned roused his anger to the utmost, — and, as grateful scholars know, the utterly illegible scrawls of Merovingian state documents gave place under his influence to the clear and regular characters that are known as the Carolingian minuscule.

The clergy as teachers.

Frequently did Charles enjoin upon his clergy the cultivation of a literary style, even criticising such of their letters as came to his notice. He bids them be not merely chaste in their manner of living, but also to train themselves in the use of language; to edify the people, not merely by their outward appearance, but also by proficiency in reading. "As a regular course of life," he writes, "brings about purity of morals, so may constant teaching and learning regulate and beautify the powers of speech."

The emperor ordered, and frequently repeated the charge, that priests should consider it their duty to teach all people the Lord's Prayer, and the Athanasian as well as the Apostles' creed. Whoever refuses to learn them "shall be punished with blows and made to fast on bread and water until he shall have thoroughly learned all," and "women shall be made amenable through strokes of the whip or through fasting." Besides this religious instruction it was evidently intended that the clergy should open schools in the different villages; a law provides that "every one shall send his son to learn his letters, and the child shall remain at it with all industry until he shall have been instructed."

The learned men at court.

The chief teacher of the day was the learned Alcuin. He it was who founded an academy, in the Athenian sense, where the emperor himself and his chief courtiers discoursed on learned subjects. In order the better to keep up the illusion they adopted the names of great men of old;

Charles himself was David, and Alcuin Horace, while Angilbert, the chief epic poet of his age, was hailed by the name of Homer. Alcuin was the head of the royal schools and main adviser in all points concerning the spread of learning. In such of his letters as have come down to us he shows a mental power and an independence of spirit that are worthy of all admiration. As friend to friend he writes to Charles, as likely as not opposing some intention of the latter; or, again, he rebukes the royal princes for some unseemly action. In old age, indeed, religious scruples assailed the brilliant scholar and made him question the morality of reading the heathen poets; he feels called upon to warn his pupils against the seductive charms of Virgil.

The poet Angilbert began an epic with Charles himself for a theme; passages have come down to us on the building of Aix; there is also a spirited picture of a royal hunt, and a lively description of the meeting of Pope and emperor at Paderborn.

We hear more of literary men at Charles's court than we do of designers and painters, yet decorative art had already reached a certain stage of development. Scratched on sword hilts and on other objects we can trace the first faint beginnings of an attempt at ornamentation, and see how in each succeeding epoch new motives or patterns come into vogue. The earliest of such decorations are interwoven bands with dots, then spiral lines, and finally the shapes of beasts and birds and the outline of the human form. Crude indeed were these early efforts; there existed a formal type for all beasts, and another for all birds. But already, in the time of the Carolingians, we can find new elements; the Italian influence is readily perceptible in the little scenes that illuminate the pages of breviaries and other books. Dainty lamps and candlesticks come in, and

*The progress of art.*

especially characteristic are the Italian ovules and acanthus leaves. In the use of their colors the artists were little at home; all was still formal, with no thought of truth to nature. The monk Gottschalk, who made a beautiful Bible for Charles, employed various hues perfectly arbitrarily — rose-color when dealing with martyrs, gold to signify virgin purity, and silver to betoken married life. Other manuscripts of the time are full of green horses, bright red rocks, and men and women with blue hair.

Death of Charles and coronation of Louis.

All in all, however, this reign was a glorious renaissance. But what was to become of the Holy Empire on the death of the capable head? A division document is known to have been drawn up in 806, according to which the land is to be divided into shares for the emperor's three sons; but, strangely enough, of the imperial dignity itself there is not so much as a word. Was the crown imposed against Charles's will not to pass to his descendants?

The death of two sons in succession altered the problem and rendered division unnecessary. The old emperor himself, in the cathedral at Aix, placed the crown on the head of the only survivor and soon afterward concluded his own busy and useful life. All depended on the personality of his successor. Was he brave and strong, or would he yield to others; if the latter, what were the influences under which he was likely to fall? How little men knew Louis the Pious, the first regular bigot on the Frankish-German throne!

Disintegration of the empire.

The history of the century that followed on the death of Charles the Great is one long study in the process of disintegration. Not a single great undertaking characterizes the reign of Louis the Pious, nothing is added to the edifice already reared. For a few years the prosperity of the empire continues from the impetus that Charles had given it, but then the decline begins. The weak monarch falls completely under the influence of the clergy, fasting and praying, and making lamentable confessions of his own worthlessness. Numberless were his visits to churches and monasteries, constant his interrogating of his own conscience. He allows Pope Stephen IV. to cross the Alps and crown him, though Charlemagne with his own hands had already performed that act. He had grown so superstitious that the falling in of a gallery over which he was accustomed to pass seemed a premonition of death, and with the help of his clerical friends he sets his house in order. The deed known as the division of 817 gives a share of the empire to each of his three sons, but constitutes one of them emperor, the other two merely kings. Thus was preserved the unity that the church required; there was to be one pope and one emperor, as there was one sun and one moon, one spiritual and one secular sword.

A second marriage, with Judith, the proud daughter of the Guelphs, brought Louis into conflict with his former friends, and made the court a hotbed of deceit and intrigue. The fruit of the union was a boy known in history as Charles the Bald, and called, even by a contemporary, the "new Benjamin." His mother was determined that the shares of the older sons should be curtailed, and that her son should be appanaged with a kingdom. The clergy felt slighted that the document of division, drawn up so solemnly and with their aid, should so readily be laid aside. The older brothers refused to have their portions curtailed, and entered into open rebellion. Lothar, the future emperor, was declared already coregent. A reaction took place in favor of Louis, but the continued intrigues by the party of Charles the Bald precipitated a new revolt. And now for the first and last time in papal history, a vicar of St. Peter crosses the Alps and plays an active part on the field of battle — that

*The advent of Charles the Bald.*

particular field, indeed, owing to the Pope's conduct, has gone down to posterity as the " Field of Lies."

The penance at Soissons.

The army of the father lay opposed to that of the sons, near Colmar, in Alsace.   The Pope, Gregory IV., crossed over and demanded to see the emperor.  He was well received and remained several days, being allowed to pass freely to and fro among the soldiers.   The night after his return to the rebel camp, the greater part of the imperial troops went over to the enemy.   Louis himself, as well as Judith and Charles the Bald, were made prisoners.  For the son of Charles the Great what deep humiliations! Louis was compelled this time to drink the cup of bitterness to the very dregs, to regularly bow his neck beneath the yoke.   A Diet at Compiègne declared that through this man's short-sightedness and neglect the empire had sunk so low as to be regarded by its enemies with mockery and derision.   He is adjudged, therefore, to have forfeited the temporal rule.   Then openly, on the steps of the church of St. Medard, at Soissons, the son of Charlemagne was obliged to confess, not once, but four times, that he had offended God, given umbrage to the church of Christ, and brought confusion upon the people.   A list of other sins was thrust into his hand, for which he was told to ask forgiveness; among them were sacrilege and murder and some public acts of which the clergy disapproved.   Surely no monarch, not even Henry IV., ever fell to quite such depths; Agobard of Lyon, writing at this time, speaks of him tersely as "the emperor that was!"

End of the reign of Louis the Pious.

The severity with which Louis had been treated brought about a revulsion of feeling; he lived to be restored to power and to see a still grander assembly of bishops reverse the proceedings at Soissons.   Still, his reign ended in a general atmosphere of family discord, civil war, and social ruin. The once glorious Frankish kingdom was nearing the verge of destruction. All the contemporary writings that exist — reports of bishops, protocols of diets, visions declared to have been seen by saints, not to speak of chronicles, annals, and letters — give forth one continuous wail of complaint. " They love bribes and not justice," says one writer, referring to the leading personages of the time. The counts are accused of conniving at crime; the territorial lords, of falsifying measures; the clergy are charged with simony, extravagance, and neglect of duty. To add misery to demoralization, there came year after year of bad harvest and of plague. Einhard, in his description of the translation of a saint's relics, makes the devil gloat over all the harm he has done, and moralize about the prevalent injustice and iniquity. Then Einhard himself bursts forth: " Ah, how deep is our age sunken, when not good men, but evil demons, are our preceptors."

All this time, like moths fretting a garment, external enemies were rending and tearing at the confines of the empire. The Bulgarians oppressed its Slavic subjects; the Saracens from Africa and Spain harassed its southern coast; while the Northmen or Vikings had already begun those depredations which were to make them lords of the north coast of France, of the steppes of Russia, of southern Italy, and of all of England.

*The coming of the Northmen.*

Out from the stormy coasts of Norway, in those small, stanch boats, — one of which has been so miraculously preserved to us in the bowels of the earth, — they took their way, making for the mouths of the different rivers of the Frankish kingdom, and burning and slaying in all directions. They did not hesitate to attack even great cities like Hamburg and Paris, and to wring tribute from the grandsons and great-grandsons of Charles the Great.

Year after year, for the better half of a century, these depredations continued, until the Treaty of Clair-sur-Epte,
in the year 911, handed over to the troublesome guests
the present Normandy.

The wars of the sons of Louis the Pious.

Of the four sons of Louis the Pious three survived him;
the death of one, Pepin of Aquitaine, had greatly simpli-
fied the situation. Here was a real, existent kingdom that
could be bestowed on the landless Charles the Bald. But
the war of the sons against the father had been but the
prelude to a bitter struggle among the brothers themselves.
The eldest, Lothar, claimed as emperor a supremacy that
Louis and Charles were not willing to grant. At the battle of Fontenoy, in 841 A.D., the latter were victorious, and
in the following year they sealed by an oath at Strassburg
their intention to hold out together for their rights. The
wording of this agreement has come down to us in the pages
of the historian Nithard, who took part in the battle of
Fontenoy, and whose vanity in ascribing the victory to his
own deeds of valor may be pardoned in view of his services
in preserving such valuable records.

Here in this document of Strassburg we have the first
great literary landmark to show that, from the fusion of
the Franks and the Romans, two new nationalities, the
French and the Germans, in the narrower sense of the
term, had resulted. In order to be understood by the followers of his brother, Louis the German has to swear his
oath in a language that is not German and no longer Latin,
while Charles repeats the oath in the German tongue.

The Treaty of Verdun.

Lothar eventually yielded to the strength of the alliance
against him, and on an island in the River Saone, not far
from Mâcon, the three brothers came together to make one
of the most momentous arrangements ever consummated
by three individuals. It was decided to divide equally
among them all the lands that had belonged to the empire

of Charles the Great, and a body of one hundred and twenty men was appointed to map out and measure the territory, and to calculate the income from the different estates and bishoprics. The task was lightened by the fact that Bavaria as a whole already belonged to Louis, Aquitaine to Charles, and Italy to Lothar.

By August, 843, the survey was ended and the whole arrangement was ratified by the famous Treaty of Verdun. To Lothar, who retained the imperial name as a mere title of honor, was given the so-called middle kingdom, extending from the North Sea down through Italy. All to the west of him, in an almost straight line from Ghent to Arles, went to Charles; while Louis's possessions were, roughly speaking, bounded on the west by the Rhine. As an instance of the care with which the division was made we are told that a small district on the left bank of the river, including the town of Worms, was added to the German's share because of the abundance of wine, which doubtless served to balance other deficiencies.

It must not be supposed that even after the signing of the treaty an era of peace like the dew of heaven descended upon the land. One of Charles's vassals ran away with Lothar's daughter, and after this matter had been arranged a new dispute arose in which Charles and Lothar sided against Louis the German. It was difficult, indeed, to maintain law and order, the more so as the Treaty of Verdun had arbitrarily sundered existing divisions, such as church dioceses or even the lands of one and the same great noble. Quarrels and violence ruled the day; "innocent blood is shed unavenged, the fear of kings and of laws has departed from men, with closed eyes the people are approaching hell-fire," says a writer of the time.

All the same the Treaty of Verdun was for the Germans the birthday of their nation. He to whose lot it had fallen

*The Treaty of Mersen.*

to become its ruler was, fortunately, the strongest and most capable of the grandsons of Charles the Great. In numerous battles Louis defeated the Bohemians, and a new enemy, the Moravians. When his brother Lothar's son, Lothar II., died childless in 869, he made a fight for a fair share of Lorraine, and dispossessed Charles the Bald, who had already taken possession. By the Treaty of Mersen, 870 A.D., a line was drawn from north to south which coincided pretty nearly with natural race distinctions. By his energy and determination Louis had made the Rhine Germany's stream, not Germany's boundary. Nor was he content with merely increasing his territory, but did his best to preserve law and order, calling upon the clergy to aid his endeavors. Acts of synods have been preserved in which penalties were decreed for different crimes, and a system of judicial procedure established; the nobles were not to oppress the common people, while a serf accused of the murder of a priest was to prove his innocence by the ordeal of the red-hot ploughshares.

The deposition of Charles the Fat.

Owing to a succession of deaths the whole Frankish empire, as Charles the Great had possessed it, was reunited under one of Louis the German's sons. But the hand of Charles the Fat was too feeble to hold the reins of government for more than a moment. He was ill in body as well as in mind, was frequently attacked by epilepsy, and suffered tortures from an aching head. He paid the Normans to leave him alone, closing with them a most unworthy treaty; but he incurred thereby the hatred of the thousands of brave men who, for ten months, relying on his coming, had been defending Paris against the fierce enemy. The needs of the time demanded an able-bodied and a whole-souled man; this the people came to realize, and they fell away from their emperor, who crawled off to his estates in Swabia to die. Had the suffering and weak-spirited monarch not gone willingly, he would have been compelled to go by force, for the bastard Arnulf of Carinthia, grandson of Louis the German, was already on the march with an army of Bavarians and Saxons, Thuringians, Franks, and Swabians. Charles the Fat had sent an embassy to meet him, and to conjure him, by a bit of the true cross of Christ which they carried with them for the purpose, to be mindful of the oath of fealty once sworn. At the sight of the holy token Arnulf had been moved to tears, but nothing could change his resolution. He allowed himself now to be raised on the Frankish throne, his election denoting, as has been well said, the first independent action of the German secular world. The nobles, eager for a warrior at their head, had brought it about.

Arnulf, too, was looked upon for a while as head of the whole Carolingian empire, and, though born out of wedlock, as a lawful descendant of Charles the Great. But a reaction had set in against the whole idea of universal rule. In Italy and in France, in Upper and in Lower Burgundy, local kings, set up by the people, came to the fore, and Arnulf was wise enough to sanction the new development. He took up zealously the practical duties of a ruler, and defeated the Normans in an important battle on the River Dyle. He made, too, an expedition to Rome, and forced the imperial crown from the timid hand of Pope Formosus.

*The end of the German Carolingian line.*

With the death of Arnulf's son, Louis the Child, who barely attained to man's estate, the German branch of the Carolingian line came to an end. It had waned and lost power after the manner of the Merovingians, and for a time it seemed likely that the heads of the different stem-duchies would follow the general trend, and set themselves up as independent rulers. What civilization remained in these disordered times was kept alive in the monasteries. For that if for nothing else we owe the church a debt of gratitude.

Civilization in the monasteries. Throughout all the years of political anarchy the cloister was looked upon as a quiet refuge where the individual could give himself up, not only to pious contemplation and to learning, but also to the practice of many a useful art and accomplishment. By the ninth century the wise rule of St. Benedict had superseded all others, and according to its precepts the brethren were to busy themselves at certain hours with manual occupations. Unless a brother grew too proud of his skill and the idea happened to come into his head that he was conferring a favor on his monastery, his activity was to be unrestricted.

Many were the spheres within which the monks were called upon to labor. They made clearings in the forests and tilled the lands, so that wherever a monastery was founded the neighborhood began to assume a friendlier character. The cloister precincts contained many buildings and for various purposes. More than forty such are shown in the plan for St. Gall, which was drawn up under Abbot Gozbert in 820, and is still exhibited to interested visitors. Besides the abbot's stately house with its own kitchen and storeroom, there are schools for outsiders, hospices for travellers, infirmaries and dispensaries. The artisans and common workmen had their own abodes, hidden from the main edifices by hedges and walls, while a building was set apart for the letting of blood, which played so large a part in mediæval medicine. It is not impossible, in fact is known to have been the case in an English monastery, that the brothers were bled all round at stated intervals to tame their unruly passions.

Each such Benedictine monastery, in short, was a little world in itself, separated often from the outer life by palisades and intrenchments, moats and turreted walls.

Masons and carpenters, tailors and shoemakers, weavers and brewers, dwelt therein, and the people from the surrounding districts far and near came to wonder and gape at the busy workers and to carry home the new ideas.  If illness broke out in the vicinity, the monks were the great healers, and distributed their medicines free to those who sought them.  If strangers came, they were the guests of the monks; and traders from a distance often journeyed to buy books or other products of monastic industry.

The monastery schools were always of two kinds, one for those who later expected to join the order and who were obliged to wear its frock, the other for the sons of neighboring nobles and freemen.  Writing, reading, and arithmetic were the chief subjects taught; and very small children were made to imitate the letters of the alphabet by crossing and curving their fingers.  The discipline was severe and consisted mainly in flogging; in St. Gall, in 937, a pupil, hoping to escape this punishment, set fire to the school, whereby the flames did great damage.

The monastery schools.

A chief occupation of the monks of St. Benedict was the copying of old manuscripts, and it must not be forgotten, in estimating their services to the world, that to them, and to them only, we owe the preservation of the ancient classics.  The greatest care was bestowed on making the letters and illuminating the initials, and many a tenth-century manuscript is still clear and legible.  It is sad to note that some of the copyists found their task irksome; one occasionally comes upon expressions written on the margin, of relief that darkness has at last fallen, or of thankfulness that the whole is ended.  Yet the joy of seeing the monastery library grow under their efforts must have atoned for much labor.

Various, as has been said, were the arts practised by the monks.  Beautiful illustrations were made for breviaries,

The monks as artists.

which were bound in leather, and sumptuously adorned. Here, too, were wrought gold and silver chalices, shrines, crucifixes, and candelabra. One and the same monk often displayed a variety of talents. In the time of Charles the Fat, St. Gall could count among its members a certain Totilo, famous as a preacher and teacher, a writer of poems, and composer of music, yet able to turn his hand at will to painting, sculpture, or architecture. Charles cursed those who had made a monk out of such a man, regretting that his own court should have lost him as an ornament. Much of Totilo's work has perished in the course of these last thousand years, but a dypticum, or set of folding tablets, has happily been preserved. Here, beautifully carved in ivory, we have Christ surrounded by angels, while near him are the four evangelists, and a series of allegorical figures intended to represent the sun and the moon, the sea, and the earth.

# CHAPTER III

## THE RELATIONS BETWEEN CHURCH AND STATE UNDER THE SAXON AND FRANCONIAN EMPERORS

LITERATURE : For a whole series of important documents on the struggle for the right of investiture see Henderson, *Select Documents*. Giesebrecht, in his *Deutsche Kaiserzeit*, gives a very extended and interesting treatment of the subject ; he is admirably supplemented by Hauck in the third volume of his *Kirchengeschichte*. The article *Investiturstreit* in Herzog's *Realencyclopedie* is excellent. See also Manitius, *Deutsche Geschichte*, 911-1125.

IN an age when there was practically no increase of territory, no war, excepting internal revolts, no foreign policy, it is difficult to find a thread through the mazes of German history. The development of the royal power forms an attractive theme, but our materials are too scant for its worthy treatment. We know that the election of Conrad I., in 911 A.D., saved the country from falling apart into five independent duchies ; but we know, too, that Conrad's dealings with the autocratic dukes ended in failure, and that at his death, in preference to keeping the royal dignity in his own family, he turned the choice of the princes on his chief rival, Henry of Saxony. The latter, by wise military reforms, by conciliating the dukes, by conquering the invading hordes of the wild Hungarians, brought things to such a pass that the coronation of his son Otto I., in 936, was a veritable triumph of concord. The three archbishops, of Mainz, of Treves, and of Cologne, placed on him the royal insignia — the sword, the mantle, the sceptre, the staff, and the diadem — and anointed him

*The kings and the heads of the duchies.*

with the holy oil; while the heads of four duchies — Lorraine, Franconia, Swabia, and Bavaria — served as marshal, cup-bearer, seneschal, and chamberlain. But, nevertheless, a great part of Otto's long reign was occupied in putting down revolts. In vain he changed the persons of the heads of the duchies — they all refused to become mere tools of his will. As a last resort he turned to the bishops and abbots for support, and formed with them an alliance that was greatly to influence the future course of history.

The kings and the bishops.

In the reign of Charlemagne the clergy had been humble and dutiful; no forged donation of Constantine, no false Isidorian decretals, had as yet furnished a basis for extravagant claims. In the reign of Louis the Pious Gregory II. had interfered in favor of Lothar I., but he had acted more as an adviser than as one with authority. It was reserved for Nicholas I., in the matter of the divorce of Lothar II., to promulgate the all-might of Rome, to threaten Germans with ban and excommunication, and to summon foreigners before his judgment seat.

Between Conrad I. and the church there had been a firm alliance; it was by the efforts of an archbishop that he had been raised to the throne; a bishop, Salamo of Constance, was his chief adviser. A synod, held at Hohenaltheim in 916, at which a papal legate was present, had spoken a threefold curse against those who should break their oath of fealty, and had declared treasonable undertakings against the king to be punishable with lifelong imprisonment in a monastery.

Otto the Great and the bishops.

But these same ecclesiastical influences had widened the breach between Conrad and the dukes, and Henry I., whose policy was one of conciliation, had begun his reign by repulsing the Archbishop of Mainz. Conrad had not been able, Henry did not care, to go to Rome and negotiate with the Pope for the restoration of the imperial dignity. Church and state had little in common.

Under Otto I. there was again a change. The failure of his attempt to bring the duchies into the hands of men who would do his will led once more to a favoring of the clergy, while holding them, indeed, with a strict hand. Otto allowed the different cathedral chapters to choose their own bishops, but subject always to his own final approval. He was sure thus of having about him men whom he could trust, and he drew them still closer by obliging them to come to him for the sign of their office, the shepherd's crook or staff. In the matter of endowment he was generous in the extreme, as were all of his successors down to the time of the great struggle in the following century. It was thus that mere church dignitaries became powerful princes and pillars of the throne — the immense advantage being that, with sacerdotal celibacy a rule of the church, these holdings could never become hereditary, but could always be regranted at the pleasure of the crown. In the meantime great services were required and performed; as holders of fiefs the bishops and abbots sent their regular contingents of vassals to the army, as members of the royal chancery much of the business of the court was in their hands. Even in their own sphere they were not unrestricted; Otto drew them before his own tribunals and disposed arbitrarily of church funds.

Otto's interference in the politics of Italy brought him into closer contact with the Papacy. He had been called in by a helpless woman, Adelaide, heiress to part of the land, who was being oppressed by Margrave Berengar of Ivrea, and whom he not only freed from her persecutor but also made his own wife. Later still a new call came against this same Margrave Berengar, this time from the Pope. Such was the chain of circumstances by which Rome came within *Otto the Great and the popes.*

the circle of interest of the German kings and a new direction was given to their policy.

The condition of the Papacy during the middle years of the tenth century was such as to cry aloud to heaven for betterment. An infamous but powerful woman, Marozia, had been the paramour of one Pope, had caused the fall and death of another, and had finally placed her illegitimate son, a boy of twenty, on the chair of Peter, whence he was cast out by his own brother, Alberich, who became the head and ruler of Rome. Alberich's mantle descended on Octavian, a mere boy, who, however, was soon chosen Pope, under the name of John XII., thus combining in his own person the secular and spiritual headship of the eternal city. He it was who, when his lands were threatened with invasion by Berengar, sent an appeal to the powerful ruler of Germany, offering to revive, in his honor, the old custom of the imperial coronation, which had been in abeyance for more than a generation. In February, 962 A.D., Otto received the crown in St. Peter's, from the young Pope's hand; — not altogether trusting his host and benefactor, for he had given orders to his sword-bearer to watch with weapon drawn, even while he knelt by the grave of the apostle. John was furthermore obliged to swear by St. Peter's holy bones that he would not make common cause with the enemies against whom he had applied for aid.

Deposition of Pope John XII.

The precaution proved not unnecessary; the young Pope felt crushed and oppressed by the greatness of his visitor. He sent propitiatory envoys, not only to Berengar's son Adalbert, whom he welcomed in Rome, but even to the heretical Greek emperor. The letters to the latter were intercepted; it remained to be seen how the Northern hero would take such perfidy. His first step was to march into Rome and make the people swear to submit all future papal elections to the confirmation of himself and of his son.  At a synod which was called in St. Peter's, and over which the emperor presided, the most damning charges were brought against the head of the church.  He was proved to be sacrilegious, unchaste, a brigand : he had drunk the devil's health, — at least, so the charges ran, — and had invoked heathen gods while playing dice ; he had chosen a ten-year-old boy to be bishop of Todi, and had given a deacon his consecration in a horse's stall.  Otto himself accused him of being a perjured traitor, and of conspiring with the enemies of the empire.

The matter did not end here.  John was declared deposed, and soon died, but the Romans refused to accept the Pope whom Otto chose, and elected a cardinal-deacon, Benedict.  It was only after a siege of the city, which ended in famine and capitulation, that Benedict was induced to appear in an assembly and beg for mercy.  He came clad in the papal robes and holding the bishop's staff ; he was led out, stripped of his pallium ; his staff was broken in pieces, and he was carried off to Hamburg to die in captivity.  These measures had been drastic, but they proved efficacious ; some of the following popes were sober, honest Germans, and the end of Otto's reign marks a complete imperial supremacy over the church.

Otto II. died too young, and Otto III. was too unaffect-  Otto III.
edly pious to enter into new conflicts.  The latter was a man possessed of two strong but absolutely contradictory passions, the one for imperial magnificence, the other for abject asceticism.  Throned on the Aventine, surrounded by a host of obsequious officials, he went so far as to sign himself " emperor of all emperors," and to deck himself in wondrous garments ; but again, as a pilgrim, barefoot in the coarsest of sackcloth, he approached holy places, or retired for a fortnight at a time to a cave or a cloister, and

humbly called himself "servant of the apostles." He
descended into the tomb of Charles the Great, to pay his
reverence to the illustrious dead. To his bishops he was
more than generous, deeding to them whole counties,
involving them deeper and deeper in secular cares and
interests, teaching them to serve two masters, God and
mammon, Pope and emperor.

**Henry II. and Conrad II.** With the popes there was no further interference until
the reign of Henry III. Henry II. had been most churchly
minded, and, after his death, was regularly canonized as a
saint. He had treated his own clergy with great generosity,
with some severity, and at times with a sort of playfulness.
He was in despair, he said, at the rich gifts Bishop
Meinwerk of Paderborn induced him to make to that
bishopric; a charter or deed is extant which begins by asserting that there are two sides to man's nature, a manly
commanding and a womanly obedient : outwardly seeming
to slumber but inwardly awake, and following out this
thought he, the Emperor, has made these gifts to Paderborn ! Just what he meant would be difficult to say.

Conrad II. had enjoyed a magnificent coronation in Rome
at the hands of Pope John XIX., the occasion being graced
by the presence of King Rudolph of Burgundy, Abbot
Odilo of Cluny, and King Canute of England. But under
this same Pope, a mere layman who had been chosen for
political reasons by the counts of Tusculum, the papacy
begins to sink back into the slough from which Otto the
Great had raised it. Europe was scandalized by a proposition said to have emanated from John himself to abandon
the papal rights in the East to the Patriarch of Constantinople for a round sum of money.

**The char- acter of Henry III.** Unfortunately for pleasure-loving popes there was developing at this very moment, in the important monastery
of Cluny, a decided tendency toward asceticism and a de-

termination to reform the government of the church. Its most triumphant product was to be Pope Gregory VII., but its influence was already widely felt when the young Henry III., in 1037 A.D., succeeded to the German crown. He was a pious, God-fearing man, a warm opponent, even to his own detriment, of the besetting sin of simony, or selling of church preferments to the highest bidder; so strong an advocate of peace and good-will among his nobles that he frequently at the celebration of mass rose up before the high altar and uttered eloquent exhortations. On the field of battle he had often been seen to kneel and pray; like Otto III., he went on pilgrimages, and even allowed his royal back to be scourged by fanatic priests.

Such was the man who was called upon to confront a situation of affairs hitherto unheard of even in Rome. There had been cases of rival popes, but here were three at a time; while into the whole complication there entered the most trivial and unworthy of motives: The crime of Simon, the selling of the gift of the Holy Spirit, had reached the worst stage of its development. *Three claimants of the papacy.*

Through the gold of the Tusculan counts, Benedict IX., a mere boy, but the best representative the family could muster, was raised upon the papal chair. He proved a monster of vice, but the Romans bore with him for years, hoping for amendment. At last, in 1045 A.D., a portion of the citizens rose against him, drove him out, and, in the following year, John, bishop of the Sabine district, was recognized as his successor. Silvester III., as he called himself, was little better than Benedict, for he too had bought his election. A conflict ensued in which Benedict carried off the victory.

Benedict was not averse to resigning the Papacy, — it was said, indeed, that he was most anxious to settle down and lead a respectable married life, — but he and his friends had risked too much capital for him to retire empty-handed. Doubtless, no one would have cared for the papal dignity as a mere matter of speculation, but a purchaser was found in the person of an honest man filled with ambition to cleanse and reform the church. John Gratian, who took the name of Gregory VI., paid a thousand pounds of silver for the opportunity to carry out his philanthropic ideas.

Henry III. and the three popes.

All this was an abomination in the nostrils of right-thinking men, and Henry III. was called upon to raise his hand and sweep away the vast web of defilement. Even on purely political grounds the state of affairs cried aloud for interference. Henry with an army marched to Italy, and in synods held at Sutri and at Rome procured the deposition of all three popes. Silvester was relegated to a monastery, Benedict was publicly stripped of the tokens of his dignities, while Gregory VI., forced to decree his own fall, was exiled to Germany. With the latter there went as companion the monk Hildebrand, the man beyond all others who was to build up a strong, pure Papacy, and to resent all royal interference in church matters. In the terrible wrestling of papal and imperial claims, he was to bring his rival to the most abject penance.

For the moment the triumph of Henry III. was absolute; the great ascetic and reformer, Damiani, proclaimed that next to God it was this emperor who had snatched Rome from the maw of the insatiable dragon and driven out the money-changers from the temple. Like King Josias of old, he had cast down the false altars and destroyed the idols. The vacant pontifical throne was bestowed by Henry on a German, the bishop of Bamberg, who took the name of Clement; while the Romans agreed, as in the days of Otto, to submit to the emperors the confirmation of future popes-elect. On Clement followed quickly Poppo of Brixen as

Damasus II., and Bruno of Toul as Leo IX., both directly appointed by the emperor — the latter, indeed, his near relative and a German by birth.

In Leo IX. the church had found a head who almost for the first time in its history convinced the world that he really meant to exercise a wide rule. A determined reformer, he held his synods as kings had held their diets: compelled bishops, Germans as well as Italians, either to cleanse themselves of charges or to renounce their sees; and proclaimed war to the death on simony and sacerdotal marriage. He was a pope well able to awaken popular sympathy, handsome and with pleasing voice. Indefatigable in the exercise of his duties, he would travel hundreds of miles to hold a synod; his journeys occupied a great part of his time, one visit to Germany lasting as long as six months.

The reforms of Pope Leo IX.

By efforts such as these the people gained a new conception of the high priest of Christendom, and the German bishoprics were bound closer to the Papacy than ever before. Leo demanded that each of the archbishops should appear personally in Rome at least every third year, and regular reports were required from the monasteries. Yet even now some of the clergy resented the papal interference. In Leo's very presence the Archbishop of Mainz refused to end the mass because the Pope had criticised the singing and ordered the removal of one of his deacons. The Bishop of Frisingen had a grievance so serious that he would rather, he said, have his own throat cut than that Leo should remain in office.

This Pope inquired too closely into the matter of episcopal elections, although no one could as yet have been conscious whither such interference was to lead, for with the autocratic Henry III. he remained on the best of terms. The emperor was so completely master of the situation that when Leo died, in 1054, he kept the matter of a successor open for months, and then appointed another of his own relatives, Victor II.

It seemed, indeed, as though the imperial supremacy were safely and lastingly established; yet soon a shadow fell over the house of Franconia that changed all things, gave the clergy and nobles a chance for independence, and allowed the Papacy not only to emancipate itself, but to claim jurisdiction over wide stretches of German land. Henry III. died suddenly in the prime of life, leaving a child as heir, with no strong member of the family, but only a weak woman, to act as guardian.

The very next Pope was chosen hastily without regard to German interests; the election was not even announced to the Empress Agnes until months had passed. At the Roman court there began to be mutterings against all interference of laymen in ecclesiastical affairs. Humbert, one of Pope Stephen's cardinals, ventured to say plainly that lay investiture was a species of simony, that the ring and the staff were spiritual, not secular symbols, and that no one appointed by a king was a real bishop, while the idea of a woman interfering in such matters was simply preposterous.

On the death of Stephen, in 1058, the right of the German regent to nominate a pope was acknowledged again, but only because the reform party was in desperate straits, the Roman nobles having revolted and set up a pope of their own. The whole was a clever move on the part of the monk Hildebrand, who now makes his entry on the stage on which he is so long to be the principal figure, and who succeeded in gaining the acceptance of his own candidate. That the tendency of his party was toward emancipation from the German yoke is shown by the famous decree concerning papal elections that was passed in a synod at Rome in 1059. The cardinals and clergy of the city were to form the whole conclave; laymen were to play no part. Matters were not yet ripe for an absolute denial of the rights so recently accorded to the emperor, but the wording was so ambiguous, the recognition so half-hearted, that the clause was capable of almost any interpretation. Moreover, scant as the concessions were, they were only incorporated in that version of the document that was intended for German eyes; we have a papal rendering, the one designed for Europe at large, in which they are absolutely lacking.

As yet the Papacy had the strength of its convictions; it had prestige, but it had no great resources, no powerful ally in arms. In Hildebrand's mind, however, there was forming the idea of a bold alliance. A generation earlier, brave Norman knights returning from the Holy Land had taken service with the Lombard princes against the Greeks and Saracens in Apulia. On the strength of their representations as to the wealth and agreeableness of the land, Norman settlers had come to Italy in great numbers, and a career of conquest had been inaugurated which reached its climax when the blue-eyed, fair-haired giant, Robert Guiscard, became master of Calabria. It is true these Normans had been the bitterest enemies of the Papacy, and had even taken prisoner in battle the august person of Leo IX. But Hildebrand, in 1058 A.D., journeyed to meet and make friends with Count Richard of Aversa, who lent him three hundred fighters to help him batter down the castles of recalcitrant Roman nobles. In the following year Pope Nicholas II. himself, in the presence of Hildebrand and Cardinal Humbert, interviewed Richard and Robert, and solemnly invested the former with Aversa, the latter with Apulia, Calabria, and Sicily. These were lands that by no stretch of the imagination could be held to belong to the Papacy; yet, in return for his inexpensive

*The Normans as allies of the Papacy.*

gift, Nicholas was allowed to dispose of the whole military force of the Normans, they taking oath to uphold his honor and the rights and possessions of St. Peter.

In Milan at this time a revolutionary party had come to the fore, desirous of civic power, but wise enough to write upon their shields the watchword of reform, and to choose for their special objects of attack the married priests and simonistic clergy. The allies of the Papacy were increasing in number. Hildebrand went to Milan as papal legate and gave his hearty support to this "Pataria," or rag-mob; they, in turn, proved a counterpoise to the power of the archbishop, who, as his appointment came from the German court, adhered to the imperial party.

Capture
of the
young king,
Henry IV.

In Germany, during all this time, there was discord instead of the much needed unity. Early in 1061 a party among the bishops met in a synod, renounced the Roman decree of 1059 concerning papal elections, condemned the person of the Pope, cancelled all his acts, and ordered that his name be wiped off the records of the church. On the death of Nicholas there resulted a schism; the Hildebrandine party chose Alexander II., the party of the empress, Honorius II. In the neighborhood of Rome there was fighting between the adherents of the two men; the cause of Honorius was in the ascendant, when events in Germany bereft him of nearly all his followers. The most radical, although the most bloodless, of revolutions had taken place. The heads of the discontented party, Archbishop Anno of Cologne, Bishop Gunther of Bamberg, the Margrave of Meissen, and others, having formed a plan to seize the young king's person, prepared a gayly decorated vessel and enticed him on board at Kaiserswerth. As the boat receded from the shore a deep gulf opened up between the old policy and the new; the young king, indeed, panic-stricken, leaped into the quick stream and was rescued with great difficulty, but in no other direction was there any resistance. The empress retired to a monastery; Henry himself came under the tutelage, first of Anno of Cologne, whose severity made him moody and morose, then under that of Adalbert of Bremen, who by ill-judged complaisance weakened his moral fibre.

To judge by his actions as a whole, Henry was a passionate and somewhat unsteady character, though able to arouse devotion in the lower classes. Probably never in the whole course of history have more opposing statements been made about one man. That he was the monster his enemies depict him is now no longer believed; still less can we trust the panegyrics that flowed from the pen of his devoted friends. Yet our sympathies may well go out to him, for never did ill-luck and failure more persistently dog a man's path; far out over the grave did the curse of the church pursue him, and for years even his dead bones could find no rest.

*Character of Henry IV.*

A dispute regarding the incumbent of the Milan archbishopric precipitated this most bitter of all conflicts, Hildebrand, of course, supporting the candidate of the Pataria. The matter was doubly important from the fact that the latter league now embraced many other of the north Italian cities. In the very year that this matter reached its climax the all-powerful monk ascended the pontifical throne, taking the name of Gregory in memory of the sixth pope of that name, whom he had once accompanied to Germany. One of the last acts of the dying pope, Alexander, had been to hurl the ban of the church against five of Henry's councillors. From the latter's point of view, no more ill-timed moment for a quarrel could possibly have been found, a revolt having broken out among his own Saxon nobles that threatened his liberty if not his life.

*Beginning of the conflict with Gregory VII.*

It was an old feud, this with the Saxons, due, it would seem, in the final instance, to a jealousy of the ruling house of Franconia.   These proud people could never forget that during more than a century the rulers of Germany had been men of their own tribe.   And this young Franconian came among them, they said, like a master among his slaves, refused to regrant their duchy to the old and popular line of Billung, and built mighty fortresses in the Harz Mountains the better to crush them down. Indeed, everywhere there had arisen walls, ramparts, and towers, ostensibly against the savage Wends.   In one of these castles, the Harzburg, Henry was surrounded, and only escaped by letting himself down with a rope from the window and fleeing through the winter night.   The struggle went through various stages, and the king's attitude to the Pope fluctuated accordingly.   When at the lowest depths, with not an ally, Henry wrote a submissive letter, promising obedience in the Milan affair and the avoidance of intercourse with his excommunicated followers.   " We have sinned against heaven and against thee," he tells Gregory, " and are no more worthy to be called thy son."   His situation was indeed desperate ; the princes at large had been horrified at the disclosure of a pretended plot in which the king was concerned, to murder one of their number, Rudolf of Swabia.   But the accuser, who was to have proved his case by the ordeal of battle, became a maniac before the day appointed.   The Saxons, too, ruined their cause by the unhallowed vindictiveness with which they pillaged the royal tombs on the Harzburg, wantonly desecrating the bones of Henry's brother and of his infant son.   The tide of feeling changed, many princes came back to their allegiance, the battle of Homburg on the Unstrut quelling the whole revolt.

This was the time that Gregory chose for one of his

most autocratic letters to the king, charging him with having failed to keep his promises of submission, and with continuing to practice simony and lay investiture in spite of the papal command — a command which, if obeyed, would have withdrawn the bishops from the royal obedience and made them independent heads of principalities within the confines of the empire.

It has been noted by one of Gregory's biographers that he knew no bounds where "justice" was concerned, and that his idea of justice often consisted in overthrowing the precedents of ages. This was the Pope: a little pale man of fifty, but so eloquent that he caused his listeners to think that a heavenly spirit was speaking to them, who made St. Peter what he has since become for the whole Roman Catholic world — a lord and emperor second only to God Himself. And he, Gregory, as St. Peter's vicar, claimed all the honor and obedience that was due to the apostle, claimed that the bishops of Christendom should obey his will without questioning, and that in the moment of disobedience all allegiance of their flocks should cease. And if the clergy, how much more the laity! He, the Pope, is the ultimate ruler; a king who acts counter to his decrees is no longer king. Compared to apostolic prerogatives, he declares, all royal power is but ashes and spray. The founders of kingship were tyrants who, driven on by the devil in blind lust and insupportable presumption, strove to raise themselves above their equals. The foundation of the priesthood, on the other hand, rests on the providence of Almighty God; for His own glory he has created it; in His mercy He has given it to the world; its head is Christ, and the least of its members is greater than the mightiest ruler.

Gregory's letter of December, 1075, has been designated as the ultimatum of the Papacy; on the manner of its re-

Exalted
claims of
Gregory
VII.

Deposition
of Gregory
VII.

ception depended war or peace. Henry chose the former. He hastily summoned a council of bishops to Worms, where, amid feverish excitement, judgment was passed on the head of the church. "Since thou hast defiled thy life and conversation with such manifold infamy," they wrote to Gregory, "we renounce the obedience which we never promised to thee, and which we shall not in future at all observe." Henry's language was even more violent; he calls himself "king not through usurpation, but through the holy ordination of God," and speaks of Gregory as "Hildebrand, at present not pope but false monk." "As if we," he cries, "had received our kingdom from thee; as if the kingdom and the empire were in thine and not in God's hand!" He traces the steps by which the Pope has ascended the throne of peace, by perfidy, bribery, favor, and the sword, and bids him descend and relinquish his usurped eminence: "I, Henry, king by the grace of God, together with all our bishops, do say to thee, Descend, descend, unto everlasting damnation!" The king's fatal mistake was that he did not emphasize his words by appearing with an army in Italy.

Anathema-
tizing of
Henry IV.
Gregory for his part could find no more fitting form in which to express his horror and abomination than a vehement address to the apostle Peter himself: "Hear thy servant," he prays, "whom thou hast nourished from infancy"; "the wicked hate me," he continues, "for my faithfulness to thee." He is sure that by St. Peter's own wish and favor the power has been bestowed upon him of binding and loosing in heaven and on earth": "through thy power and authority, in the name of Almighty God, Father, Son, and Holy Ghost, I withdraw from Henry the king, son of Henry the emperor, who has risen against thy church with unheard-of insolence, the rule over the whole kingdom of the Germans, and over Italy!" He

absolves all Christians from their oath of fealty and forbids any one to serve Henry as king. By the token of this anathema the world is to know beyond the shadow of a doubt that " thou art Peter, and upon this rock the Son of the living God hath built His church, and the gates of Hell shall not prevail against it ! "

For the first time the regenerated Papacy had rallied its full forces; for the first time its vaunted absolutism was pitted against the sovereignty of a great throne. Nor did Gregory rely on the power of the ban alone; he cast out his nets among the discontented bishops and princes of which Germany was full, and drew in a rich haul. He sent an open letter to all the upholders of the faith, reviewing the course of the quarrel from the beginning, justifying his own acts and appealing for aid. When Henry attempted to call a national council at Worms, he found that the general defection was becoming alarming, and that many of those who had been most violent against the Pope were now listening to his overtures.

The Saxon rebellion was fanned into new flame; a number of South German princes began to form a threatening alliance and to talk of electing a rival king; the bishops, having to choose between the power which had raised them to what they were and the princes whose equals they had become, declared for the latter. Henry had taken up his position at Oppenheim, separated by the Rhine from the arbiters of his fate. He was ready for any humiliation, and daily sent envoys begging his enemies to name their conditions, but to leave him the royal title and insignia. He would better his mode of life, he would answer to the princes, if need be, for every act of government. Not a manly attitude, but the needs of the moment were great.

*Ultimatum of the German princes to Henry.*

The ultimatum of the princes was severe enough, but

stopped short of deposition. They declared that the throne would be forfeit in case within a year and a day Henry should have failed to obtain the papal absolution. The Pope was to be invited to come to Augsburg and discuss affairs with the princes — in other words, in the heart of his own dominions to sit in judgment on the king! Henry in the meantime was to take up his abode in Spires, to refrain from all public acts, and to abandon the citizens of Worms, who had furnished his chief support.

Henry's determination to seek the Pope's pardon.

Like a criminal under pledge of good conduct, Henry lived in Spires, avoiding all intercourse with the world and deprived of all the consolations of religion. But in quiet he had taken his measures : above all it was necessary to sunder the union of the Pope and the princes ; this meeting in Augsburg meant lasting degradation for German kingship. It must not, it should not, take place. The first step was for Henry to obtain for himself, at any cost, the papal absolution. This could be done by appealing, as it were, from the Pope as ally of the princes to the Pope as high priest of the Christian religion. The whole teaching of the church required that a sinner who turned and repented should have pardon, and the outward form of repentance was sufficient for the simple and literal mind of that day. An age that insisted upon the actual shedding of tears and on actual corporal prostration when humility was in order, or on refusal and modest flight behind the altar in the case of elevation to a church office, was not going to be too severe on a king ready to kneel in sackcloth and ashes, or to stand barefoot in the winter snows.

Henry sent an envoy to Rome to announce that he was coming as a penitent. Gregory pretended to doubt his sincerity, and started on his journey to Augsburg. In Mantua, however, he was met by the news that the king had

already crossed the Alps.  The Pope retraced his steps
and took refuge in the castle of Countess Matilda of Tuscany — that pillar of the church who signed herself in life
" Matilda, if anything, then so by the grace of God," but
whose tomb stands in St. Peter's, among those of the
popes, with the proud inscription, " Champion of the
Apostolic See."

The scene that now took place in Canossa is one that The days at<br>Canossa. must appeal strongly to the imagination even at a distance of centuries : the high precipitous hill guarded by
its triple wall and surmounted by a palace, a church, and
a monastery ; the blue peaks of the Apennines in the distance; the snow-covered landscape; the king in penitential
garb and bare feet standing before the rigidly closed door.
The mental struggle that went on, indeed, was rather in
the mind of Gregory than of Henry.  The Countess Matilda
and also the Abbot of Cluny beset him with tearful entreaties and implored him to relent.  He attempted at
first to make the condition that Henry should renounce
the royal crown and name; he remained obdurate for three
long days, on each of which the king presented himself
with woful mien.  At last the demands even of inexorable
justice seemed to have been fulfilled, and the head of Christendom gave way.  Beyond a doubt his political triumph
would have been greater could he have sat in the midst
of the princes at Augsburg and taken his revenge for the
day of Sutri; but this Henry had forestalled.  Through
the mediation of the Countess Matilda, Henry signed certain general agreements relative to the German princes ;
then the gate of Canossa was thrown open, and the king
entered, accompanied by his excommunicated councillors,
who were included in the amnesty.  All the penitents
threw themselves weeping on the ground ; the spectators
too were melted to tears and Gregory's own eyes moist-

ened.    The absolution was administered in due form, the
Eucharist partaken of, and the apostolic blessing crowned
the work of peace.    Henry rode away a humble victor, but
none the less victorious because of his humility.

Renewal
of the ban.
The cause of the church had now been separated from
that of the rebellious princes, but the latter were more
fiercely hostile than before.    They raised up a rival king
in the person of Rudolph of Swabia, who expressly renounced the right of investing bishops for which Henry
had always fought.    But even this did not at once win
Gregory; for three years he maintained neutrality, summoning both kings to appear before him.    He seems really
to have longed for peace, for the German church was coming into sore straits.    Only when he found that he could
not be arbiter, that his whole influence, indeed, rested on
his being a partisan, did he once more take sides.    There
was no doubt as to how to choose ; Henry had paid no
attention to his measures against lay investiture, but had
calmly annulled elections and publicly invested whom he
pleased.    Rudolph had been more pliant; his army, too,
had just won a victory over that of Henry at Flarcheim.
A renewal of the decree against investiture, in 1080, was
followed by a second hurling of the ban.    Once more St.
Peter is bidden to incline his ears to a whole list of the
enormities of this "Henry whom they call king," who
"did raise his heel against thy church and strive, by casting me down, to subjugate it."    His crime is disobedience,
"which is the crime of idolatry."    In the apostle's name
the power and dignity of kingship is granted to Rudolph
for his humility, obedience, and truthfulness.    More clearly
than ever does Gregory in this prayer show that his aim is
universal rule.    The world is to know that if ye (Peter
and Paul) can bind and loose in heaven, "so ye can on
earth take away empires, kingdoms, principalities, duchies,

margravates, counties, and all possessions of men, and grant them to any man ye please according to his merits."

But Gregory was claiming too much; even among good, pious, and churchly men there were many who would not follow him in this theory of St. Peter's omnipotence. The second ban harmed nobody but its promulgator; few could see that the king had in any way deserved such severity. "Nobody," writes the papal-minded Gebhard of Salzburg, "considers us worth listening to." Nineteen bishops, assembled at Mainz, threw all the blame of the civil war on Gregory. A synod at Brixen not only declared him deposed, but even appointed his successor, Clement III. Gregory's straits.

All Gregory's efforts to raise up allies were in vain. William the Conqueror of England, once strongly under papal influence, would not interfere. Robert Guiscard was hastily loosed from the ban that his depredations upon holy property had brought down upon him, but even then could give no assistance. Rudolph of Swabia was slain in battle. Henry, unmolested, could lead his Pope in triumph to the very gates of Rome. Entry was, indeed, a different matter; not for three years was it successfully accomplished. Gregory then took refuge in the castle of St. Angelo, and when Henry demanded the imperial crown he refused to give it until the king should do penance and be loosed from the ban. When the nobles urged the Pope to the contrary he is said to have offered to let down the crown by a string from the castle wall if Henry would dispense with the consecration! He was completely at bay. "Help!" he wrote in an encyclic letter, "lend support to your father and mother, as you hope through them to achieve forgiveness of sins, blessing, and grace in this world and the world to come!"

The Roman nobles, at last worn out by Gregory's obdurateness, and experiencing more harm than good from his Death of Gregory VII.

ally, Robert Guiscard, determined to abandon him and allow Henry to enter the city. The proud judge of Canossa, the man who had considered himself second in rank to none but St. Peter, was now deposed by a Roman synod: Clement III. was acknowledged pope, and on Easter Day, 1084 A.D., crowned Henry and his queen with the imperial crown. Gregory fled to Salerno, but his race was run. For the fifth time he reiterated the ban against Henry: with the hand of death already upon him he refused him absolution — that, he said, should only be granted to those who believed that in him, Gregory, as rightful Pope, was vested the power of the apostles, Peter and Paul. "I have loved justice and hated iniquity, therefore I die in exile," were his last recorded words.

The death of Gregory did not bring peace either in Italy or in Germany. His party chose first Victor III., who shortly died, and then Urban II., the inspirer of the crusades. The polemical writings of the next few years outnumber and outvie in bitterness those that had gone before: the old antagonism of view seemed only to have deepened and broadened. Is the Pope really above the emperor even in secular matters? Are the bishops more subject to their temporal or to their spiritual head? In many, if not the majority, of German sees there were rival incumbents: many refused intercourse with those anathematized by Gregory.

The Countess Matilda.

The rallying-point for all the discordant elements in Italy was the Countess Matilda of Tuscany. From purely political motives, and at the instigation of Pope Urban, she now married the son of Guelph of Bavaria, Henry's bitter enemy. The countess was forty, the bridegroom seventeen, and the union was never consummated; the only bond was the common determination to drive Henry from his throne. They corrupted the young Prince Conrad, caused him to rise against his father and to receive independently the crown of Italy. There was nothing this woman would have left undone to further the interests of the Papacy. When she died she left to it all her lands, though many of them were fiefs of the empire, thus starting a new conflict that went on for a century.

Henry's chief foes henceforward were they of his own household. At that council of Piacenza that first broached the subject of a crusade his wife appeared, instigated it is said by Matilda, and made most loathsome charges. Soon after, the second son, Henry, who had been declared heir to the throne after Conrad's defection, left the camp by night and joined his father's enemies. The climax was reached when this same prince, pretending to seek a reconciliation and offering to escort the emperor to a diet, decoyed him instead to a castle near Bingen and kept him like a common prisoner. Discouragement and discomfort did their work; utterly broken, Henry agreed to abdicate and to surrender the insignia of empire. He asked for absolution from the ban and confessed to a papal legate that from first to last he had sinned against the Roman church. The comfort he received was but cold; only in Rome, the legate said, could the sentence be reversed.

The young Henry V. was now recognized as king by the Diet of Mainz, and an embassy was despatched to Rome to invite the Pope to Germany. Henry IV. made a last attempt to regain his throne, but died in the endeavor; twice his body was dug up by order of the church before it found rest in an unconsecrated chapel near Spires; not for five years did Rome remove her curse. To such extremities had the struggle for the investiture reduced the head of the empire.

As for Henry V. it remained to be seen how he would act when confronted with the problems that had troubled

*Wretched ending of Henry IV.*

*Henry V. and Paschal II.*

his father. He had been called to the throne by that
father's enemies, and with the understanding that he
should reverse the former policy. Yet this question of
investiture could not be thrust aside; like the trail of
a serpent, it poisoned everything. It was as impossible
for Henry V. to give up inalienable rights as it had been
for Henry IV.; he too became involved in a long struggle
with the Papacy, which had once more vehemently proclaimed that the clergy disgraced their calling when as
vassals they laid their consecrated hands in the blood-
stained hand of a layman.

In the year 1111 Henry crossed the Alps and approached Rome with an immense army. He had sent
envoys to tell of his willingness to treat on the old subject
and to demand the imperial crown. They arrived at a
time when Pope Paschal II. was almost friendless; he
had looked around for the traditional allies of the Papacy,
but the Normans were enjoying the excitement of the
crusades, and could not respond to his call. It was under
these circumstances that Paschal proposed the most
remarkable, the most startling, solution of the difficulty
that had ever yet been evolved. The church was to
return to the Arcadian simplicity of its early days; the
bishops were to give up their principalities, fiefs, and
jurisdictions, and the empire to take back all the lands
and rights which, since the time of Charlemagne, had
come into the hands of the clergy. The latter were to
content themselves with tithes and pious offerings; but, on
the other hand, their nomination, election, and investiture
were to be entirely free. To give splendor and emphasis
to the occasion, both acts, the renunciation and the imperial coronation, were to take place on one and the same
day.

Once more this struggle for the investiture gave rise

to a never-to-be-forgotten scene — a scene that wiped out, indeed, that shameful humiliation at Canossa. On the day appointed, Henry entered St. Peter's magnificently escorted. He was determined that the odium of what was about to happen should fall on the Pope, and declared that for his own part he had no wish to rob either bishops or abbots. Then Paschal read the church's renunciation, and a tumult arose, fiery, unquenchable. The Pope, in the very citadel of the apostle, was loudly accused of heresy and other crimes. Not one of the clergy, it seemed, was willing to give up his imperial fiefs. The king grew impatient at the long delay, declared that the Pope had broken his compact, and demanded back the full and free right of investiture as enjoyed by his forefathers. The penalty of refusal was a bitter one for the successor of a Gregory VII. — nothing short, indeed, of the arrest and carrying off of Paschal and his cardinals. They were taken for safety to a neighboring hospice, and, in the midst of heavy fighting, were finally removed from the city.

For weeks this captivity lasted, and the poor pontiff's soul was racked by news of anarchy in Rome and by fears of a fresh schism. When flesh and blood could no longer stand it, he at last gave way, renouncing, without equivalent, everything the king demanded, especially that right in defence of which Gregory VII. and Urban II. had filled all Europe with war and tumult. In the camp before Rome, on April 12, 1111 A.D., a document to this effect was placed in Henry's hands, and on the day following the coronation ceremony was performed. With hostages in his train the emperor withdrew triumphant.

Was this the solution of the long war? Could any one for a moment have believed that the Papacy would continue grovelling in the dust? The wonder is, not that the Pope and the Gallic clergy should have repudiated

*Capture of the Pope and cardinals.*

*Paschal repudiates his concessions.*

these forced concessions, but that a year should have
elapsed before they did so; then, indeed, the anathema was
hurled with all force at this Henry, this second Judas,
who, by treachery, perjury, and desecration had forced
Paschal to sign the deed.

Thus again the question of the investiture became the
centre of a fierce conflict; again, too, Germany was rav-
aged by enemies who tried to dethrone the emperor.  A
chronicler assures us that men raged against each other
with bestial delight, that the clergy could scarcely count
on their bare lives, that fields lay waste and villages in
ruins, that churches had ceased to celebrate the service of
the mass.

It was indeed high time for a settlement; a new antipope had been elected under Henry's auspices and new
schism introduced into all the bishoprics.   For a moment
it seemed as if peace might be achieved at the Council of
Rheims in 1119, but the new Gregorian pope, Calixtus II.,
was seized with a panic after the treaty of peace had
actually been drawn up, and the council ended with a
more formal promulgation than ever of the ban against
Henry and his Pope.  Hundreds of candles were lighted
and simultaneously extinguished, symbolic of the thrusting into perpetual darkness of the wretch who was bur-
dened with the awful curse of Rome.

The
Concordat
of Worms,
1122 A.D.

In Germany the war dragged slowly on, but ever since
that eventful proposition of Paschal II. there had been
germinating an idea that was now at last to bear fruit.
Was it not possible, after all, to render unto Cæsar the
things which were Cæsar's and unto God the things that
were God's ?   The cloud lifted on the eve of what promised to be a bloody battle, and after much negotiation
there resulted what is known as the famous Concordat of
Worms.

There were to be two investitures : one on the part of the emperor with the sceptre as the symbol of temporal power, the other on the part of the Pope with the pastoral staff and ring. Elections were to be held in the presence of the emperor, and in Germany proper the function in which he was especially interested was to precede the ecclesiastical act. In Italy and Burgundy the order was to be reversed.

Where lay the victory? It would be hard to say. Calixtus indeed was proud of his work, and caused the text of the document to be placed as an inscription in one of the apartments of the Vatican. The world at large gave way to unbounded rejoicing that the long and desperate struggle was over.

In the Rhine meadows near Worms, in the presence of a crowd so great that the city had been found incapable of containing it, the reconciliation of state and church after their war of fifty years was concluded in all form. The papal legate publicly extended to the emperor the kiss of peace, the ban was loosed, and the body and blood of Christ partaken of in common. The old contentions were laid aside, but the future was to show whether or not there was room in Europe for two claimants to world rule.

# CHAPTER IV

## THE POPES AND THE HOHENSTAUFENS

LITERATURE : For the relations of Frederick Barbarossa with Popes Adrian IV. and Alexander III., see Henderson, *Select Documents.* For treatment of whole period, see Henderson, *History of Germany in the Middle Ages*, — founded mainly on the Jahrbücher, — which contains also a bibliography. Prutz, Toeche, Winkelmann, and Schirrmacher are the main authorities.

Lothar and Innocent II.

" THE king comes before the gates, first swearing due honor to the city. He then is made the vassal of the Pope, and takes the crown which he bestows." Such was the inscription under a painting in the audience hall of the Lateran in which King Lothar, Henry V.'s successor, was represented as kneeling before Pope Innocent II. The special occasion was doubtless the investiture with the estates of the Countess Matilda, which this Saxon king was weak enough to accept as a fief, after claiming them in full ownership. He was to pay for their use a hundred pounds of silver.

Lothar could never have gone so far as this motto implies ; but he was too yielding, too fond of a compromise. He and the Pope were vastly afraid of offending each other and thus reopening the old conflict, an attitude for which the German nation on the whole was grateful. " He left behind him such a memory of his time," writes the annalist of *Pöhlde*, " as will be blest until the end of the world," while we know from another source that " quiet and abundance prevailed, and peace between church and state." So far did this complaisant spirit go, that Lothar at Liège

76

performed the service of marshal for Innocent, leading his horse by the bridle after holding the stirrup for him to mount. When a question arose as to the feudal ownership of Apulia, which was to be conferred on Rainulf of Alife, — the Pope held the point, the emperor the shaft, of the banner of investiture!

Lothar's title at home was disputed by one of that house of Hohenstaufen that was to play such a brilliant and tragic rôle for more than a century; for his own part he formed an alliance by marriage with the Guelphs of Bavaria, thus inaugurating the unhallowed struggle of Guelph and Ghibelline — just why the Hohenstaufen were so called is not known — which in a different form was to be fought out in the cities of Italy. As a rule Ghibelline came to mean imperial and Guelph papal, though there were times when the two terms denoted little more than blind, malignant opposition. At Lothar's death in 1137, the Guelph, Henry the Proud of Bavaria, was pitted against Conrad of Hohenstaufen, and, though the latter was the choice of the princes, a bitter struggle ensued, which did not end on the death of the rival candidate, but was continued with various fortunes for nearly ten years. *Guelph and Ghibelline.*

In the midst of these dissensions and mishaps the news came that Edessa, the stronghold of the Christians in Syria, had fallen. St. Bernard of Clairvaux appeared in person before Conrad, and, after several attempts to make the king take the cross, was at last successful. On the feast of St. John, 1146 A.D., the monk rose up in the cathedral at Spires and gave vent to a burst of overwhelming eloquence. Conrad was moved to tears and declared that the Lord Himself had spoken. Delighted with his success, Bernard seized the standard from the altar and bestowed it on the king as leader of the crusading hosts. But of all the great expeditions none ended more wretchedly than this second *The second crusade.*

crusade. Jealousy, treachery, and disaster dogged Conrad's steps, and when, sick at heart, he returned to Germany, it was only to become involved in new struggles with the Guelphs.

The *Decretum Gratiani*.

The Papacy, too, had suffered greatly in prestige by the failure of the crusade it had inaugurated, but it did not cease to put forward new claims and pretensions. Toward the end of Conrad's reign these claims found a lasting form in a collection of canon law, the *Decretum Gratiani*, which was to control the life of the church for centuries. It is full of sentences from that famous forgery of the ninth century attributed to Isidore of Seville; it rings with assumptions of papal omnipotence. And more and more the popes were striving to become the first princes as well as the first bishops of Christendom. They commenced to surround themselves with retinues of nobles as well as of clergy, and the imperial diadem with which Hildebrand had crowned Nicholas II. was now regularly worn with the mitre. It professed to be the crown of Constantine.

Accession of Frederick Barbarossa.

It was well for Germany that a brilliant and determined man now came to the throne. The empire was to succumb in the end to the Papacy, but it would have succumbed miserably and weakly had it not been for Frederick Barbarossa. To him it is due that the war of the popes and Hohenstaufens became a war of gods and Titans. Around his name cluster some of the most glorious traditions of German history.

Inextricably interwoven with Frederick's struggles with the Papacy are his dealings with the cities of northern Italy. Ever since Charlemagne conquered and Otto the Great recovered Lombardy, the Germans had maintained their claims to sovereignty. Those claims were now to be enforced and legalized, but the free communes that had grown up since then were to prove very different antagonists from the

Berengars and Lamberts of earlier times. The citizens, whose houses were actual castles, had drawn into their own hands all the jurisdictions, tolls, and revenues, had conquered stretches of surrounding territory, and were on the alert for further conquests at the expense of smaller towns.

Frederick, at the time of his election, was thirty years of age, small, fair-complexioned, with reddish hair and beard. Endowed by nature with great capacities, he was likewise extremely ambitious. On the very day after the election he informed Pope Eugene III. of his intention to restore to its pristine glory the empire " bestowed upon him by God." By God, not by man. He promised love and respect for the Pope's person, but, unlike his predecessors, demanded neither sanction nor confirmation. Difficulties began almost at once with the important city of Milan. Frederick had sent a letter ordering the inhabitants to cease their persecution of the little towns of Lodi and Como, but the missive had been received with scorn and the royal seal trampled under foot. In the autumn of 1154 the king crossed the Alps and mustered his army in the Roncaglian fields near Piacenza. All of the Lombard cities, Milan included, seem to have taken the oath of allegiance, and gifts were sent from all quarters — ostriches, parrots, lions, and rare silks. But treacherous conduct was discovered on the part of the Milanese consuls, and the ban of the empire was spoken over the devoted city.

*Frederick Barbarossa and Milan.*

The first duty, however, seemed to be to march to Rome and secure the imperial coronation, which had been promised by Pope Adrian IV. On the way the disobedient city of Tortona was levelled to the ground. Adrian advanced to Sutri, but a disagreement at once arose because of the king's refusal to hold the stirrup for the Pope, who had ridden up to the royal tent. Either this holding of the stirrup, or else no kiss of peace! Adrian withdrew in

*Adrian and Frederick.*

anger.  The question was hotly discussed, and several cardinals followed their master; but, finding that the papal
claim was grounded in precedent, Frederick yielded.   On
reaching Rome he showed his devotion to the Pope by
seizing his enemy, Arnold of Brescia.   The coronation
day ended, indeed, in a bloody tumult, and eight hundred
Romans are said to have fallen.

**Submission of Milan.**  The negotiations with Milan went on for some years,
but at last, in 1158, Frederick recrossed the Alps with one
of the largest armies that ever a head of the Holy Roman
Empire had led into Italy.   Now came a sad time of reckoning for the valiant commune.   The conditions of pardon
were hard: the rebuilding of Como and Lodi, an oath of
allegiance, a fine, the right of the emperor to maintain a
castle within the city walls and to appoint the consuls or
rulers, finally the delivery of three hundred hostages, fifty of
whom were to be taken to Germany.   The submission was
made with all the dramatic formalities customary in the
Middle Ages.  The twelve consuls of the city humbled themselves before the emperor, who awaited them in his camp,
seated on his throne.   They approached barefoot, with
ropes around their necks, through two long lines of German
soldiery, and delivered up their swords to symbolize the
surrender of all the weapons in Milan.   The humiliating
ordeal ended with the unfurling of the imperial banner
from the top of the cathedral.

**The Italian communes.**  This war with the Italian cities was a conflict of two
utterly incongruous principles: the liberalism of communi-
ties which, long left to themselves, had wrought out their
own prosperity, and an imperialism that had begun to claim
its root in the old traditions of Rome.   On the one hand
the golden lion of Durazzo, on the other the code of Justinian.   The Archbishop of Milan himself, after the submission of the city, addressed Frederick as follows: " Know

that all the right of the people to make laws has been vested in thee. Thy will is law, according to the saying. 'What pleases the prince has the vigor of law.'" Yet how little, in reality, did the precepts of the sixth suit the needs of the twelfth century!

Frederick had clearly recognized the value to himself of the renaissance in Roman Law that was taking place at Bologna; he now enlisted the services of a number of doctors of the new university and set them to formulating the imperial rights, or *regalia*, in Italy. He began with the communes, but he intended afterward, in a similar manner, to adjust his relations to the Normans and the Papacy. His commission reported that the throne might justly claim the tolls and taxes from public roads, rivers, and harbors; the product of mines, salt works, and the like; the estates of felons, and the half of treasure trove. The emperor might call in an emergency for horses, transport wagons, or ships, and even levy an extraordinary war tax. He was to have the right of building his own palaces in cities where such had formerly stood, and, finally, of appointing the chief civic magistrates. *The regalia, or royal rights.*

Thus armed with the majesty of the law, Frederick set about his task of making northern Italy submit to leading strings; his officials collected revenue to the amount of some million marks; everywhere he set up his own *podestàs* in opposition to the local authorities. Disaffection at once became rife; Genoa maintained that she had grown rich from her shipping and not from her imperial fiefs, and, although the claim was moderated, took care to strengthen her fortifications. Crema had to submit to one of the most terrible sieges in history, a single incident of which will here suffice. Frederick caused a movable tower, the advance of which had been checked, to be literally festooned with the persons of hostages and captives, who were let *Annihilation of Milan.*

down in baskets and thus exposed to the missiles of their own friends. There was no faltering; almost all were killed, and the city itself was eventually given over to pillage and flame.

But the fate of Milan was hardest of all. The people refused to accept the emperor's new officials because the treaty of 1158 had expressly permitted the Milanese to have their own consuls. Frederick maintained that the new Roncaglian decrees had abrogated all old agreements. He laid waste the fields and vineyards and cut off every avenue of supply; the crowded city could at last hold out no longer and sent eight of its consuls to surrender the keys and the tokens of their own dignity. Never were people more thoroughly humbled and abased; hundreds of the proudest nobles were made to approach in the pouring rain, barefooted, with ashes strewn upon their heads, and to kiss the emperor's feet and cry for mercy. The mast of the sacred *caroccio*, the last rallying point in all battles, was lowered before him, and the city's banner removed. All the standards of the army were given over. Frederick and his princes decreed that the city should be blotted from the face of the earth, that within a week the inhabitants must withdraw to four appointed spots in the vicinity, there to make new settlements. In the ruins, Lodi, Como, and Cremona, bitter enemies of old, were allowed to riot at will. "A second Troy has perished," writes Godfrey of Viterbo; while Frederick in his triumph signs his public documents, "Roman Emperor, crowned of God, great and peace-bringing; glorious Triumpher and continual Increaser of the Empire."

Frederick Barbarossa and Adrian IV.
From a German point of view the question of the Lombard cities seemed happily and finally settled; the emperor's officials ruled absolutely, showing themselves, indeed, tyrannical and oppressive, and, above all, extortionate. Frederick

himself was too busy, during these years, in asserting his position regarding the Papacy, to look too closely into administrative matters.

With Adrian IV., the only Englishman who ever sat on the throne of Peter, a trivial incident had reopened the old quarrels. In a letter regarding the capture of a bishop by a highwayman, whom Frederick had taken no steps to punish, Adrian casually spoke of the empire as a "benefice" which he had seen fit to "confer" on the emperor. In his answering manifesto the latter tells how the papal envoys, "as if inflated with the mammon of unrighteousness, out of the height of their pride, from the summit of their arrogance, in the execrable elation of their swelling hearts, did present to us a message in the form of an apostolic letter, the tenor of which was that we should always keep it before our mind's eye how the lord Pope had *conferred* upon us the distinction of the imperial crown, and that he would not regret it if our Highness were to receive from him even greater *benefices*." After some more mockery and invective against this "message of paternal sweetness," Frederick goes on to give an eloquent assertion of his own theory of the imperial power. It is his by election of the princes and from God alone; it is one of the two necessary swords to which Christ subjected the world; did not St. Peter himself say, "Fear God, honor the king"? The Pope's assumption is a lie; the honor of the empire has remained glorious and undiminished *since the founding of Rome and the establishment of the Christian religion*, and this emperor wishes it known beyond the shadow of a doubt that he would rather incur danger of death than submit to shame and disaster. In his letter to the Pope the incident of the picture in which the Emperor Lothar figured as a vassal was not forgotten. The Pope was fain in the end to explain away his objectionable utterance by means of a convenient sophistry.  By *beneficium* he had not meant the technical feudal term for *benefice*, but simply a benefit — and surely a pope was conferring a benefit on an emperor by crowning him !

It may be that, after all, Adrian's breaches of etiquette were due to his being a blunt Briton ; for he soon committed another offence that was taken almost equally ill, by addressing the emperor in the second person singular and putting his own name before that of Frederick.  Still again he roused the imperial ire by sending a personal letter through the hand of a minor official.  Relations were decidedly strained at the time of the Pope's death in 1159.

Alexander III. and the rival popes. The choice of a successor seemed to be a challenge of the most outspoken kind.  Alexander III. was not only a man known as a political opponent of the emperor, but as Chancellor Roland he had been the bearer of that very letter about *benefices* that had so angered Frederick.  His whole manner on that occasion had been haughty and insolent.  No wonder that Frederick almost hanged the envoys sent by Alexander to announce his accession, and that he took advantage of a schism among the cardinals to recognize another as pope.  The synod of Pavia, of 1160 A.D., which was indeed nothing but an assembly of German and Lombard bishops, pretended to review the whole question of the election from the beginning, and declared for Victor IV.  In his opening address, the emperor had vindicated his right to hold the council by appealing to the examples of Constantine, Theodosius, and Justinian, of Charlemagne and Otto the Great.  After the fateful decision, he received Victor at the door of the cathedral, held the stirrup for him to dismount, and led him to the altar.  The anathema was hurled at " Chancellor Roland " and the bishops who had consecrated him, and was naturally returned in kind.

Little could Frederick have known that this enemy

whom he thought to annihilate was a man of the stamp of Gregory VII.; it was this same Alexander who later humbled Henry II. of England in the matter of the murder of Thomas Becket. And the emperor's cause was weakened still more by the death in 1164 of his own pope; many who had supported Victor were not willing to acknowledge Paschal III. Yet Frederick and many of his clergy and nobles took a solemn oath at Würzburg to fight the fight to the bitter end, never to acknowledge Roland or a pope chosen by his party. All that oaths can do this oath was meant to accomplish: the Diet of Würzburg engaged in case of Frederick's death to elect no one who would not renew it; the temporal and spiritual lords promised to impose it on their vassals and to consider all recusants as enemies of the empire. *The oath of Würzburg.*

This new Justinian was very sure of his cause. He took this occasion to glorify the empire by the canonization of its founder, Charlemagne; the bones were raised from the tomb and placed in a golden shrine. He might well have occupied himself, as he was frequently implored to do, by redressing the wrongs of the Lombard cities; but his main idea was to reach Rome and strike at the heart of the opposition. In July, 1167, he seemed at the goal of his desires; after much fighting the Leonine city fell into his hands, St. Angelo was besieged, Santa Maria in Torre set fire to, and an entrance thus forced into the interior of St. Peter's. After a skirmish in those holy halls themselves the opposition ceased and the church of the chief of the apostles was in the emperor's hands. Pope Paschal was solemnly enthroned; Alexander escaped from the city. The inhabitants agreed to abandon him, and the senate took the oath of fealty. *Conquest of Rome.*

Here was a triumph without equal, but it was followed like a flash by the hardest blow of fate the emperor had *Pestilence breaks out.*

ever experienced — a blow that marks a turning-point in
his career. On the first day of August, amid general
rejoicing, he and his empress had worn their crowns in a
grand assembly at St. Peter's. On the day following the
weather changed; a violent thunderstorm was succeeded
by a deadly heat; the mists of the Campagna rose to battle
for Alexander. A pestilence broke out in the camp and
also in the city; death was wafted on every current of
air. The emperor hastened to reach the Tusculan hills, but
many of his soldiers were too ill to move; his losses were
simply enormous — a contemporary places them at twenty-
five thousand in a single week. High and low sank alike
beneath the scourge.

The people of the twelfth century saw in Frederick's
mishap nothing less than a judgment of God. Thomas
Becket, in one of his letters, breaks forth into a perfect
hymn of praise. He likens the emperor to Sennacherib,
who was struck down while opposing Hezekiah: "The
Lord has crushed the hammer of the godless, and, if they
do not come to their senses will shortly crush the rest"
(meaning his own king); John of Salisbury implies that
Frederick had better consider Italy a lost land.

The victory
of the
Lombard
League.

The time had at last come for the Lombard cities to
avenge the wrongs inflicted by the imperial officials.
During the five years that succeeded the terrible vengeance
of 1162, the sufferings of the banished Milanese had been
intense; a horrible burden of taxation had pressed the life
blood out of the wretched people. Every rod of land,
every hearth, every span of oxen, had to pay its inexorable
tribute; swine and poultry were requisitioned for the private tables of the officials. No wonder the annals of the
city name the record of taxable objects the "book of pain
and mourning"!

Already before Frederick reached Rome the bow had

stretched to breaking, and in quiet the beginnings had been made of the famous Lombard League. From the first it took sides with Alexander, but its most daring act of insubordination was the leading back of the Milanese to the scene of their former glory. All the cities lent a hand, and like magic the walls arose from their ruins; a bas-relief of the time, representing the happy return, is still to be seen.

As for the former conqueror, his position became desperate. An appeal was sent to Germany for reënforcements, but they were too late in coming. Attacks on Milan and on Piacenza failed, and at last, with few followers, he prepared to fly from Italy. At Susa he was shut in, and would have been taken, had not a faithful chamberlain counterfeited his person.

*Frederick's desperate straits.*

The Pope and the Lombard League continued to prepare for the final struggle that was sure to come; a new city was founded and strongly fortified. It was to be a common rallying place for all the forces, and was named Alessandria in honor of the Pope.

In the long interval that elapsed before Frederick's return strong efforts were made to bring about a reconciliation with the church. Frederick was bound by the Würzburg decrees, but he went so far as to send an envoy to Italy with the astounding proposition that he for his own person should recognize no Pope at all, "save Peter and the others in heaven," but that his son Henry, the young king of the Romans, should acknowledge Alexander and receive the imperial coronation.

Frederick's first act on entering Italy in 1174 was to wreak vengeance on Susa, which was soon a heap of ashes. But Alessandria, situated in a swampy plain and surrounded by massive earthen walls, proved an effectual stumbling-block. Heavy rains came to the rescue of the

*The return to Italy and the battle of Legnano.*

city, and the imperial tents and huts were all but sub-
merged. The besieger at last burnt his own battering
rams and movable towers, and retreated to Pavian territory.
On the failure of long negotiations he prepared for a decisive battle, and sent a strong appeal for aid to his most
powerful vassal, Henry called the Lion, Duke of Saxony
and Bavaria and brother-in-law of Richard Plantagenet.
On the refusal of this mighty prince hung the fate of
the campaign; no threats could move him, no entreaties
availed. Frederick went into the battle of Legnano fore-
doomed to defeat. He was wounded and thrown from
his horse; his army mourned him as dead, but he finally
reached Pavia after days of adventurous flight. Legnano
was thoroughly decisive; by the advice of his nobles
Frederick determined to abandon the policy he had pursued for so many years and to make his peace. This
could be done to the greater advantage, inasmuch as the
cities believed that reënforcements were surely on the
way from Germany, and were, moreover, disunited among
themselves. The treaty of Venice was far from being the
dictate of a conquering power.

The peace
of Venice.
Many of its clauses were in the form of a compromise: a
truce of six years with the Lombard cities, during which
time a peace was to be arranged; a continuance on the
emperor's part in the enjoyment of the revenues from the
estates of Matilda for fifteen years, when it was hoped
the differences would have been adjusted by commissioners;
a truce with other allies of the Pope, such as the emperor
of Constantinople and the king of Sicily. There were to
be mutual recognitions of each other's dignities on the part
of Pope and emperor.

The pageant
at Venice.
Now that the peace was to become an accomplished fact,
all concerned united in arranging a worthy pageant;
Venice and the emperor seem to have shared the expense.

When on Sunday, July 24, 1177, Frederick landed on the Lido, he was met by cardinals whom Alexander had sent to release him from the ban. The Doge, the patriarch of Grado, and a crowd of lesser dignitaries furnished a brilliant escort with their gondolas and barks. On the piazzetta the emblem of the lion of St. Mark's floated from tall masts, and a platform with a throne for the Pope had been erected at the door of the church. A dense crowd of all nationalities and of all ranks filled the square, to witness the outward and visible sign of an imperial surrender at discretion. No fitter setting for such a scene could have been found the whole world over, and Frederick, in spite of his small stature, must have played his part with becoming dignity. When he landed, his mantle of royal purple was still around him; he threw it off as he advanced to the foot of the papal throne, then knelt on the ground before his old enemy and kissed his feet. The world looks to-day on the exact spot where this occurred, and three marble slabs have been placed to commemorate it. On the following day a friendly meeting was held and the conversation was amicable and gay.

The peace with the Lombard cities was duly arranged, and was signed at Constance in 1183. The emperor retained some show of sovereignty, but the real advantage was on the other side; the League was recognized as a lawful power, the consuls were to be chosen by the cities but invested by the crown; the ordinary revenues, jurisdictions, and right of fortification and defence were to remain with the towns. One characteristic episode ended the struggle of so many years: Frederick was determined that the city of Alessandria, so long from its very name a thorn in the flesh, should technically cease to exist. The demand was granted, and it was agreed that the name should be changed to Cæsarea in honor of the emperor himself. We

*Settlement of difficulties.*

still have the treaty which binds all the inhabitants to quit the city and remain away until led back by an imperial envoy. Then all the males were to swear fidelity to Frederick and his son.

**Crusade of Frederick Barbarossa.** Frederick's further relations with the popes were not altogether smooth; and once his son, Henry VI., as king of the Romans, led a regular plundering expedition through the domains of Urban III., who in turn incited a small rebellion in Germany. But on the whole it may be said that the questions at issue were unimportant, and Frederick finally showed his zeal for the church in the most convincing way. At the Diet of Mainz, in 1188, in the midst of wild excitement, he and his younger son took the cross, while thousands of knights, following the example of their gray-haired sovereign, also assumed the votive emblem. On May 11, 1189, the crusading army started on its way; on that day the crowds assembled at Ratisbon looked for the last time on their beloved emperor. In the river Saleph, not far from Seleucia, he found his death while seeking refreshment in the cool waters after a hot day's march. According to the legend so beloved in the fatherland, he sits in the heart of the Kyffhäuser Mountain, waiting for the time when his country shall need him. Then, like a second Messiah, he will come again.

**Henry VI. and Sicily.** With the marriage and accession of Henry VI., a new and fatal element comes into the struggle for supremacy between empire and Papacy. His bride was Constance, last descendent and heiress of the Norman kings. Not only did this marriage and the successful assertion of the claim to Sicily greatly increase the resources of the Hohenstaufens, but the Papacy awoke to the fact that its own possessions were now threatened as much from the South as from the North, held fast, as it were, in a strong vise. Whatever the special occasions of the quarrels that ensued, this one never healing grievance must be kept in view. We shall soon see the shadows deepen all along the line; we shall see an almost comedy-like trifling of the heads of Christendom give place to the dark episodes of the greatest of mediæval tragedies, as a climax to which royal blood is shed on the scaffold, and the whole original structure of the mediæval empire falls to the ground in a heap of ruins.

Henry VI. inherited his father's stature and cast of countenance, his iron will, his power of forming grand conceptions, and also his cruel severity; we hear of rebels being skinned alive, crowned with redhot crowns, or covered with pitch and ignited. Fortune more than once stood him in good stead, as when the lion-hearted Richard of England fell into his hands, and, by the magnitude of his ransom, enabled him to carry out his plans for the conquest of Sicily; yet in general his successes were due to his own courage and perseverance. His scope of conquest was all-embracing; for the first time a German emperor came forward in the Orient — to quote a Byzantine chronicler — as "lord of lords and king of kings." The Emperor Alexius was reduced to such straits that he had to impose the so-called "German tax" on all his provinces — a measure so odious that it was repealed, and an attempt made to raise money by confiscating the holy utensils of the churches. As a last resort the tombs of the Greek emperors were plundered and the bodies stripped of their ornaments.

*Character and achievements of Henry VI.*

With the popes there were differences but, as yet, no open break; indeed, at his imperial coronation in 1191, Henry went so far as to kiss, as though making a cross, the brow, mouth, chin, breast, and two cheeks of the aged Celestine III. He had, indeed, to withstand a league of the Pope, the Lombard cities, the Sicilians, and his own empress Constance, and also, because of Celestine's opposition, to renounce the projected coronation of his infant son. Henry died on the point of embarking on a great crusade, for which he had brought together some sixty thousand men; but Celestine declared that, for taking captive a crusader, in the person of Richard of England, he had *ipso facto* incurred the ban, and long refused to have him buried in consecrated ground.

Philip, Otto IV., and Innocent III.

Frederick II., Henry's son, grew up in Palermo more of a Sicilian than a German. His uncle, Philip of Hohenstaufen, had intended to temporarily assume the German crown as his guardian; but, in view of the troubled times, accepted it in his own right, becoming involved in a long war with a rival king, Otto IV., the son of the now humiliated Henry the Lion. To the papal throne there had come, in 1198, Innocent III., the worthy peer of Alexander III. He it was who later forced King John of England to pay a yearly tribute for his crown. For years he fed the flame of civil war in Germany, first turning the scale in favor of Otto, then promising to crown Philip, and finally, after Philip's murder by Otto of Wittelsbach, taking Otto IV. once more completely under his wing and teaching him, like a pedagogue, the art of ruling. "Do not be backward in making concessions," he writes, "do not be sparing of promises, but also keep them faithfully. . . . Thou must educate thyself to the dignity and the bearing of a king." The news of Otto's unanimous acceptance by the princes, he wrote, had cured him of an illness; then he casually mentioned a number of concessions "which thou altogether must grant without making difficulty." Among them were the imperial privileges sanctioned, after fifty years of warfare, by the Concordat of Worms, and the suzerainty over Sicily.

Innocent crowned Otto emperor in 1209, but soon found him making common cause with Sicilian rebels, and accused him of stretching out his hand for that crown. "If thou dost continue in thine obstinacy, we cannot help but punish thee with the anathema," he wrote a year later, and on hearing that Otto had actually crossed the boundary of Sicilian territory, carried his threat into execution. He wrote to the German princes that he had been deceived in this man as God Himself had once been deceived in Saul, and worked upon their feelings by declaring that Otto, brought up in England, would try to reduce them to the miserable state of the English barons. God had reproved Saul, he wrote again, and had substituted "one younger than he," who had obtained and held the kingdom.

As the "one younger than he" who was to succeed this modern Saul, Innocent had fixed upon Frederick of Sicily, of whom his mother at her death had appointed him guardian; it was true the dreaded union of Germany and Sicily would thus be accomplished, but Innocent considered that he held this youth completely under his thumb. It would be possible to bind him by all sorts of promises and agreements. Without fear for the future he therefore enlisted the services of Philip Augustus of France, who placed large sums at the young prince's disposal. The English court was equally zealous in sustaining Otto IV., and thus was brought about the first great international complication in the history of Europe. It culminated in the battle of Bouvines, fought in 1214 A.D., where Philip Augustus thoroughly routed Otto's English and German forces, sending to Frederick as a promising token one of the imperial eagles. It was a death blow to the house of Brunswick, and Frederick was soon formally acknowledged as head of the German nation. *The battle of Bouvines.*

In person, like his immediate ancestors, Frederick was not imposing. According to one account he was "red, bald, and short-sighted," while a Mohammedan historian opines that as a slave he would not have brought a hundred drachmæ. He had grown up among Saracens and had imbibed many of their tastes, to the detriment of his morals as well as his orthodoxy. He kept a harem like any Oriental potentate, and the popes succeeded first and last in citing a goodly number of his heretical acts and utterances. But in his love of art, science, and literature, in his views on philosophy and on the duties of a monarch, he was far in advance of the Christians of his age; he tells us himself that he spent his spare moments in reading; we have a work on falcons from his hand; and we know that with clear common sense he ridiculed the belief in ordeals or judgments of God. The laws that he passed for Sicily were far in advance of the age and contain the germs of modern legislation.

The outbreak of Frederick's great quarrel with the Papacy is usually ascribed to his failure to perform a crusading vow, which in the excitement of the moment he had taken on the day of his coronation. But will this account for the inordinate hatred of one pope after another? Doubtless they wished him to undertake the crusade, but rather to get rid of him than from unadulterated zeal for the cause. This young man was making his Sicilian kingdom too powerful, he was interfering too much with the Lombard communes. Year after year he postponed his promised journey, though in 1225 A.D. he married Iolanthe, daughter of John of Brienne and heiress of Jerusalem. By the Treaty of San Germano, drawn up in July, 1225, Frederick bound himself to the Pope by promises more definite than any he had yet given. He agreed to cross to the Holy Land in August, 1227, with a thousand knights, a hundred transport ships, and fifty galleys, and to maintain these forces for a period of two years. He was also to furnish sums amounting to about eleven million francs of modern coin. Should he fail to cross, or to provide the knights and the money, he was to be *ipso facto* under the ban, and his kingdom of Sicily was to pay the forfeit. Already before the day appointed there had been a falling-out with the Pope because of Frederick's renewed interference with the affairs of the Lombard League. "Take care," the Pope wrote, in a long letter of reprehension, "that God do not annihilate thee and wipe out thy race." Already the conception was forming that this was a "viper brood," to be relentlessly pursued from one generation to another.

Honorius died before the term agreed upon, but his successor, Gregory IX., was peremptory in requiring the fulfilment of the promise. The ships came together at Brindisi, where thousands of pilgrims awaited them. But the heat of a southern summer, joined to poor accommodations, brought about a pestilence of which many died. Frederick himself was taken with fever, and resigned his enterprise at the eleventh hour, though whether he was quite sincere is open to doubt. Gregory maintained that the illness was feigned, and would listen to no excuse, but declared the emperor under the ban, and forbade the Sicilians to pay him further taxes. In fact, his hatred went to the most incredible lengths; for when Frederick, though still under the ban, nevertheless undertook the crusade, he, the Vicar of God, sent monks to preach against him, and *wrote to the head of the infidels asking him not to surrender!* Frederick maintained, ten years later, that he still had this intercepted letter in his hands.

Frederick II. and Gregory IX.

This crusade of Frederick II., though bloodless, had greater results to show than any but one of its predecessors. By the Treaty of 1229, arranged by negotiation, the sultan of Egypt agreed to surrender Jerusalem and an

The crusade accomplished.

important strip of seacoast. Before a crowd of pilgrims, in the church of the Holy Sepulchre, Frederick placed the crown of Jerusalem on his own head. But on that very day the *clavegeri*, or papal troops, had wrested from him his mainland provinces in southern Italy; he hastened home, routed his enemy, and reduced the Pope to terms. In August, 1230 A.D., he was loosed from the ban, and a year later Gregory acknowledged him as king of Jerusalem and confirmed the treaty with the Saracens.

Further hostilities with Gregory IX.

All this was but prelude to a fiercer struggle that broke out nine years later with this same Pope. The causes were Frederick's bestowal of Sardinia on his son Enzio, and a new Lombard war which had resulted for the Emperor in the victory of Cortenuova. By papal decree all his subjects were released from allegiance and his body given over to Satan. Both parties issued manifestoes to the world at large which leave nothing to be desired in point of vehemence. " Princes, take heed," writes Frederick, " people, listen to your own cause ! . . . Run for water for the protection of your own houses when that of your neighbor is on fire ! "

Gregory's letter, especially, is a model of invective. A furious beast, it declares, has come up from the sea with feet like a bear, teeth like a lion, and limbs like a leopard. She only opens her mouth to blaspheme the name of the Lord. The old story is repeated, which we meet in so many papal letters, of Frederick being an ungrateful son to Mother Church; all the old grievances pass in review: the vow so often deferred, the plague in Brindisi, which is ascribed to the emperor's bad management, the favoring of Saracens in Jerusalem. Then comes the most damning, and possibly the most true, of all the charges. This king, says Gregory, maintains from the throne of pestilence "that the whole world has been deceived by three impostors —

Moses, Mohammed, and Christ; of whom two died honorably, the third on a cross." A most serious charge in an age when burnings for heresy were already becoming popular.

As the struggle went on Gregory stooped to conspire for the election of an anti-king, but, failing in this, decided to call a general council of the church for Easter Day, 1241. Frederick was asked to suspend hostilities, and to grant the prelates a safe-conduct, but refused on the ground that the Pope was only seeking time to strengthen his forces. It was altogether a time of strain and excitement, for the Tartars or Mongols, under the grandson of the great Timour, were ravaging the Eastern dependencies of the empire, and had defeated Duke Henry of Silesia at Liegnitz. Frederick ordered every one of his German male subjects with an income of over three marks of silver to take to arms. Gregory maintained that the danger had been purposely exaggerated, and that the army was destined for use against the Papacy. Wits of the time said that the khan meant to destroy the empire, but had asked Frederick what office the latter could fill at his, the khan's, court. The emperor had answered that he knew something about birds, and would take the position of falconer. The great Oriental leader, it was further asserted, in despair at the discords of Christians, had in reality come to make peace between Pope and emperor.

The conflict of church and state had indeed reached a stage where no blow was too ponderous, no means too unprecedented. The Pope repeatedly preached crusades against Frederick, offering the same remission of sins to those who would take up arms as to those who went as pilgrims to Jerusalem. Gregory is even charged with having used the funds which the faithful had already subscribed for the liberation of Palestine in crushing this personal enemy. Frederick's measures were no less radical:

*The capture of the prelates.*

a Genoese fleet had been chartered to carry prelates to the
Pope's great council at Rome; the emperor had issued a
warning that all who attended would do so at the risk of
their lives. These shiploads of cardinals, bishops, abbots,
and Lombard deputies he considered fair prey. Enzio,
the emperor's natural son, assisted by Pisan ships, fell in
with the Genoese fleet off the island of Monte Cristo in
April, 1241, gave them battle with such effect that two
thousand men, among them an archbishop, found their
deaths in the waves of the Mediterranean, and carried off
as prizes some hundred high ecclesiastics. They were
incarcerated at Melfi and Naples, and held as hostages,
the last of them not being liberated until after some years
had elapsed.

**Death of Gregory IX.** This blow was followed up by the taking of Tivoli and
by an advance on Rome. But death at this juncture most
inopportunely snatched Gregory away. Frederick was warring against the person of the Pope, not the institution
of the Papacy, and he waited to see what effect the new
election would have on his affairs. He waited long and
vainly, for the cardinals could come to no agreement. He
wrote to remind them of their duty in the style in which
his correspondence with the late Pope had given him facility, calling them sons of Belial, troop of perdition, the
laughing-stock of nations: "Like serpents you cling to
earth instead of rising to heaven. You each want the
tiara, and no one will leave it to the other." He is said to
have advocated, in a pamphlet written by his chancellor,
that the Papacy should be done away with altogether, or
that he himself should be made Pope.

**Innocent IV.** When, after two years, Sinobaldo Fiesco ascended the
papal throne, as Innocent IV., it seemed as though the
struggle had at last reached its end. A peace treaty was
drawn up and signed by which Frederick was to be loosed

from the ban, and, in certain questions, notably regarding the Lombard cities, the Pope and cardinals were to be arbiters. But difficulties and misunderstandings arose ; Innocent felt that the Papacy was not receiving its due, and took a sudden determination to fly beyond the emperor's reach. At Lyons he issued a summons to a general council, and received a deputation from Germany, with whom he agreed to put through the election of a new king.

At the third session of the council that was opened at Lyons, in 1245 A.D., and at which a hundred and fifty prelates were present, sentence was passed on Frederick and he was declared forever deposed from the throne of the empire. In his boundless self-partiality Innocent asserted later that he could remember no case that had ever been more carefully and deliberately tried by experienced and holy men. Their sessions had been secret, it is true, but some had undertaken the rôle of plaintiff, others that of defendant. The formal act of accusation calls Frederick the prince of tyranny and destroyer of the universe, and recommends that he, drunken with the blood of so many saints, be given over to everlasting ignominy; the name of this Babylonian, *and of his offspring*, is to be wiped out eternally, inasmuch as he is boundlessly merciless and cruel !

*Final anathematizing of Frederick II. by Innocent IV.*

When the act was read, Thaddeus of Suessa, Frederick's legal representative, rose in solemn protest; he had already declared that the council was not universal, and had been told that it was as much so as the ambushes of the emperor would allow. He now proclaimed that this was the day of wrath, of misery, and of anguish. And, indeed, the end of all things seemed at hand. The empire that had been so glorious was crushed to earth. To gain means to carry on his struggle, Frederick had been obliged to deed away its most cherished privileges, which there was no hope of

*A struggle to the death.*

ever regaining.  Its crown was now to be bandied about and despised and rejected by German princes; unworthy foreigners were to wear it, one of whom, Alfonso of Castile, never dared to show his face within his own domains. And the last scions of the proud Hohenstaufen dynasty, so great in peace if not in war, were to be pursued like vermin, to be preached against and prayed against as worse than infidels, and, finally, to be literally extirpated by the Sicilian henchman of the papacy.  Ably did Innocent follow up his declaration to the council of Lyons, "Until our last breath we and our cardinals will maintain the struggle for the cause of God and of the church."

**End of the reign of Frederick II.**  Frederick's last years were spent like a lion at bay.  The rival kings in Germany, first Henry Raspe, who fattened on the papal generosity, and then William of Holland, occupied the full attention of his son Conrad; the emperor himself was constantly in the field against the papal adherents in Italy.  He returned one day from a hunting expedition to find his camp near Parma a heap of ashes, and many of his soldiers captive.  Constant attempts were made against his life, and the Pope rewarded those would-be assassins who were fortunate enough to escape alive. Frederick's own chancellor and most cherished friend, Peter de Vigne, is believed to have offered him a poisoned cup; the betrayed monarch ordered his eyes to be pierced with glowing irons, and the blinded wretch beat out his own brains against the pillar of a church.

**Death and burial.**  The final blow was the capture by the Bolognese of the capable and beloved Enzio, who was to remain incarcerated for the next score of years.  Frederick himself fell a victim to dysentery while still in the field.  In his tomb in Palermo he was able at last to rest long and well, for when the grave was opened in the eighteenth century the body was in a perfect state of preservation, save that the nose had been crushed by the weight of a superimposed coffin.

Conrad IV. abandoned Germany in 1252, and fought with his brother Manfred for their common Sicilian heritage until his death, two years later. Manfred, for a time, became reconciled to the Pope, accepted the lieutenancy of Sicily, and held the bridle of Innocent's palfrey at Naples. But the proud spirit of his race again asserted itself; he fled to Lucera, where the Saracens received him with open arms, aiding him to gain a victory over the papal troops and to have himself crowned king at Palermo. *The last of the Hohenstaufens.*

But Clement IV. signed a treaty in 1265 with Charles of Anjou, brother of the king of France, transferring to him all rights over the Sicilian kingdom, and the great reckoning with Manfred took place at Benevento in the following year. Manfred was slain after deeds of such valor that the French knights themselves carried stones to mark his place of burial; but a papal legate ordered the body exhumed and thrown into the waters of the Volturno. *Charles of Anjou.*

Thus had the race of Barbarossa dwindled, until no one was left but Conradin's son, the young Conradin, a boy of fifteen, who had been brought up by his uncles in Bavaria. Fugitives from Benevento came to offer him the crown of Sicily; six thousand knights rallied round him, and he crossed the Alps as liberator of Italy. Yet Clement IV. likened him more justly to a lamb going to the slaughter. At Tagliacozzo he was defeated; after a week's flight he was betrayed by a Frangipani, a former Ghibelline, to Charles of Anjou. On the latter rests the direct responsibility of that cruel execution in the market-place of Naples; but the real murderer was the claimant to the crown of Constantine and to the chair of Peter, who stirred no finger in his behalf. *Execution of Conradin.*

# CHAPTER V

## THE AGE OF CHIVALRY

LITERATURE: Prutz, *Kulturgeschichte der Kreuzzüge*, contains much information. In August Sach, *Deutsches Leben in der Vergangenheit*, are many chapters on this period. See also Freytag and von Löher. Richter, *Deutsche Kulturgeschichte*, is a similar work to Sach. Alwin Schultz, *Das höfische Leben*, describes the material side of knighthood. Scherer's *German Literature* should also be consulted.

Character of the period.

FOR the greater part of a century and a quarter the House of Hohenstaufen, like an eagle returning to the charge, had been bruising its wings against an enemy with supernatural resources. But there is another aspect to the whole period that we cannot afford to pass over; in many ways it was the brightest time that Germany was to know for five hundred years. The court was brilliant and magnificent; the festival that Frederick Barbarossa gave at Mainz in 1184, in honor of the knighting of the heir to the throne, outdid anything the chroniclers had ever seen. The princes were growing powerful within settled boundaries; knights jousted and tourneyed, practised leaping full-armed upon their chargers, or busied themselves in acquiring the latest French accomplishments; burghers worked away at their counters, gradually developing commercial greatness and civic liberty; monks and missionaries increased in numbers and activity, and found congenial fields for enterprise in reclaiming and colonizing Slavic lands; in law and medicine there was a general awakening, and also in learning and art. Castles and churches were built that have lasted to this day, while the literature furnished two undying epics; lyric poets sang as they were not to sing again until the days of Goethe. Material prosperity kept pace with the intellectual growth; the rich began to clothe themselves in velvets, silks, and satins, to sit on divans, sleep on mattresses, pour their wine from carafes, and flourish coats of arms with fields of azure, gules, and rampant beasts. The poor, too, found the ordinary articles of diet cheaper and far more varied. Rice and Indian meal were introduced.

If we seek for the cause of all this movement and activity, we shall find that the chief impulse was given by the crusades, a term which is here used to denote, not merely the eight well-known invasions of the Holy Land, but also the countless minor expeditions that filled two whole centuries. Twice a year fleets went out from Marseilles, Genoa, and Venice, and we hear of single ships carrying as many as a thousand passengers. *Influence of the crusades.*

What must it have been for a narrow-minded, poverty-stricken German to come suddenly out into this chaos of races, languages, and religions! From the Italians he could learn naval tactics and many secrets of trade; from the French, who predominated in Syria, the more polite arts; and from the infidel himself many a good, sturdy virtue.

We are too apt thoughtlessly to acquiesce in the ecclesiastical view of the bloodthirsty Oriental who stood in the way to prevent innocent Christians from proceeding barefoot to the tomb of Christ. Were these Mohammedans so wicked and were our pilgrims so utterly without guile? We know positively that many of the latter, up to the moment of taking the cross, had been robbers and cut-throats, that others had gone merely to escape poverty and a burden of debt. The kind of excitement that drew them was the excitement of newly discovered gold-fields. Re- *Culture of the Mohammedans.*

cently deciphered historical sources of the Mohammedans have changed the conventional picture. These heathen, whom the church proclaimed to be raging so furiously, found time to be shocked beyond measure at the gambling, drinking, and worse excesses that went on in the Christian army. The taverns along the road were dens of vice; the frivolous way in which oaths and compacts were made and broken is held up to execration, not only by the Arabs, but by the better-minded crusaders themselves. And, as to cruelties exercised on helpless prisoners, we hear of nothing more absolutely wanton than the crucifixion of the captives in Edessa or the sending to the Greek emperor by Bohemund of Antioch of a whole cargo of sliced-off noses and thumbs. It was one thing for Christian knights to band together to obtain toleration for their new religion; but to send an expedition to the holy city of Mecca for the express purpose of seizing the bones of the dead prophet was blind and heartless desecration. What a broadening effect it must have had on these invaders later to find that men could lead moral, useful, and generous lives without ever having heard of the Church of Rome!

Broadening of the mental horizon. What Europe in general and Germany in especial gained from these Oriental wars cannot be overestimated. The geographical horizon was widened in all directions; guide-books that showed the different stopping-places on the route were eagerly devoured; pilgrims from different localities interchanged views and experiences. And as new needs arose efforts were made to meet and overcome them. On the first crusade, coins of all sorts were carried along and sold for what they would bring; later, drafts and letters of credit were invented and a general coin adopted, the Saracen besant, that could be used for all occasions. For nearly a hundred years no offence was taken at the fact that these coins were dated from the Hegira and adorned with mottoes of praise to Allah and Mohammed. When the church at last forbade such emblems, the merchants contented themselves with keeping the same appearance and the same Arabic letters, but making them spell Christian texts!

It must not be supposed that trade was confined to lands conquered by the Christians, or that it went on only in the intervals of peace. On the contrary, the seaports of Syria were an outlet for the commerce of the whole East, and so brisk was the interchange of commodities that the church frequently interfered, and even found it necessary to issue fiery edicts against the sale of weapons and supplies to the enemy in time of war. It was in these days that many of our most common articles of daily use first found their way to the West, — drugs and spices, dyes, incense, sandalwood, Tyrian silks, camels'-hair garments, not to speak of fruits and oil. It is natural that many of the new words that at this time came to be common to the European languages should refer to commercial products; tariff, bazaar, muslin from Mosul, damasks from Damascus. The "arabesque" becomes a well-known form of ornamentation, while amulets, talismans, elixirs, grow to be familiar terms. "Rosaries" are taken over from Buddhism and applied to Christian use, while heraldry is the gainer, not only of new terms, but also of the Byzantine cross. Mohammedry becomes "mummery," while "assassin" is one of the deadly tribe of hasheesh eaters. It is to these times that the use of Arab numerals — nine digits and a cipher — dates; it matters little whether they came in by way of Spain or Palestine. Commercial activity called for quicker methods of reckoning, and the more convenient system, long in vogue with the Saracens, was rapidly adopted, after the middle of the twelfth century, in all parts of Europe.

*Commercial activity.*

The increase in the volume of commerce was enormous; not only were the religious orders of knighthood great traders and bankers, but the merchants of Genoa, Pisa, and Venice had quarters in all the Syrian towns, where they lived under their own laws and were accorded every possible trading privilege. The liveliest intercourse was kept up with the neighboring centres of industry, especially with Damascus, itself a terminus for the caravan trade with the Persian Gulf; Christian shippers did not hesitate even to sell other Christians as slaves in return for the much-prized Oriental products. Germany, of course, her seaports being so distant, took little direct part in this trade; but the castles of her nobles were decked out with every Oriental comfort, and their gardens filled with new plants and trees.

Fostering of a national sentiment.
For Germany one important result of the spirit of criticism and comparison aroused by the crusades, was the fostering of a feeling of nationality. It is now that in the literature we find the first expression of love for the fatherland, and joy at returning to it after long wanderings. Walter of the Vogelweide doubtless voiced the sentiments of thousands when he praised the virtue, the true love, and the plenteous delight to be found in his own country: "Oh, that I may dwell long therein!" is his sudden and hearty outburst. It is always a sign, too, of national self-appreciation when the heroes of the past are drawn from the mists of oblivion and made the objects of reverence and devotion. Charles the Great is now brought into prominence both as a lawgiver and a man. The *Chanson de Roland*, which dealt with the unfortunate Spanish expedition, was translated into German and eagerly and widely read; while Frederick Barbarossa, well knowing how popular such an act would be, caused the bones of the founder of the empire to be exhumed and enshrined and himself canon-

ized.   The gifts that were made on this occasion still adorn the wonderful chapel that Charles had built at Aix.

For the church in general, and the German church as well, the crusades, so long as they were in any way successful, denoted an increase in power, prosperity, and prestige.   The Papacy had been allowed to assume the headship of the whole movement; there were times when the response of Christendom to its appeals for men and money was more than enthusiastic.   But also in another way there was an actual increase in material wealth.   Many a knight and noble, in order to secure ready money for his expedition, sold or pledged his estates to a neighboring bishopric or monastery.   Too often, instead of returning, he died on the way, or disappeared for years from view.   A favorite theme in the literature of the time is this Christian warrior, who spends a good part of his life as a captive among the infidels, undergoes most thrilling experiences, and is at last set free by the loving daughter of his Saracen captor.   In the meantime the church will have been enjoying his revenues.

*Increase in the power of the church.*

It may safely be said, then, that never were the ecclesiastical coffers so full as in the earlier days of the crusades, never were her general commands more implicitly obeyed, never were more love and reverence shown for her buildings, her emblems, and her ritual.   Those who had taken the cross wore it on the front of their garments while accomplishing their vow, on their backs when returning home, and once again on their breasts when consigned to their last rest.   Even Frederick II., when his coffin was opened, was found to have the sacred emblem conspicuously attached to his imperial robe.

This idea of the Bible or the sword, this belief that the blood of a heretic was pleasing in the sight of God, had seized on high and low.   Crusades were preached, not only against the Turks and Saracens of Palestine, but also against the Jews, the Moors of Spain, the Waldensians of Italy, the Albigensians of southern France, the Wends and Stedingers of Germany. Such skill with the sword as should enable a man worthily to smite God's enemies, wherever they might be found, became as much a Christian virtue as unselfishness or humility.

Divergent religious opinions.

But, as has been intimated, familiar intercourse with those holding alien beliefs, and the growing perception that the dreaded infidels might, after all, have brave and noble qualities, gave rise to a great deal of independent thought. Men began to reason about the supremacy of the Papacy, and the justification for its claims. The circumstance is significant, that, in his greatest of all mediæval poems, Wolfram von Eschenbach introduces us to a Christian brotherhood, entirely outside of the accepted priestly hierarchy, and makes his knights of the Holy Grail answerable only to Heaven. What would Gregory VII. or Innocent III. have said to such an association, claiming as it did that the highest of all earthly honors was to become the Grail's king! As the thirteenth century progresses it shows more and more enlightenment, and at the same time an ever increasing divergence of religious opinion. The poet Freidank doubts if, after all, heretics and heathen are to end in hell-fire. Walter of the Vogelweide thinks Christians, Jews, and Mohammedans serve all the same God, while Frederick II., as we have seen, is openly accused of declaring the head of the Christian religion an impostor.

The early Inquisition.

But in proportion as its enemies increased, so too did the church gird itself for the conflict, and the age of chivalry is, likewise, one of inquisitions and of burnings at the stake. Pope Innocent III. was a mighty heretic hunter. The Lateran Council of 1215 passed new and stricter rules, and crimes which a generation before were dismissed with a simple "let him go to the devil," were now punished by a horrible death. Committees were appointed to inquire into men's inmost beliefs. In some districts the people were obliged, at stated intervals, to prove their orthodoxy ; houses were searched for hidden heretics, and trials held over dead bodies. In Strassburg, in 1212 A.D., eighty men and women were subjected to the ordeal of glowing iron, and all but a few found guilty, and executed. In Verona sixty persons were burned at one time. The laws of Innocent IV. provided that even those who recanted should be imprisoned for life, and their children and grandchildren be legally dead, unless they could prove that they had aided in bringing to justice these same progenitors. The very dwellings of heretics were to be torn down, and Innocent's successor, Alexander IV., decreed the same fate for the houses of those who had harbored heretics, or even of neighbors who could not prove that they *had not* so done.

In Germany the fortunes of the Inquisition are mainly connected with the name of one man, Conrad of Marburg, to whom the popes intrusted unheard-of powers for the rooting out of pestilential opinions. Priests and monks were placed under his jurisdiction, inasmuch as his tribunal was declared competent in all cases where heresy was concerned; he might preach crusades against the recalcitrant, and offer absolution from sins to all who would join the hunt — a privilege expressly extended to murderers who might enlist in the good cause. This same Conrad of Marburg was father confessor to that Landgravine of Thuringia who is known in history as St. Elizabeth, and with whose name are connected such a host of pretty miracles. The landgrave disapproved of her charities, it was said, and found her once with a basket of bread under her arm ; but when

Conrad of Marburg.

the lid was removed nothing was to be seen but a pile of sweet-smelling roses. In connection with Conrad she appears in another light: as a conscientious disciple who, do what she would, could never satisfy her stern mentor. He could scarcely be brought to forgive her, we are credibly told, for having missed one of his sermons; while for another offence, of no greater magnitude, he caused her to be soundly scourged. When the landgrave died, Elizabeth left the Wartburg and settled in the vicinity of Marburg, so as to be near Conrad; the latter made her dismiss her favorite serving-maids and keep repulsive creatures around her person.

Pursuit of heretics.

In his pursuit of heretics Conrad was aided by a certain John, the one-eyed and one-handed, and also by a monk, Dorso, one of that order of *Domini canes*, or sleuth-hounds of the Lord, which had just been founded and given extensive privileges at Rome, with the understanding that they were to act as guardians of the faith. These two particular men had themselves been heretics, but had returned to the fold with a rabid hatred of their former associates. They professed to be able to tell from a man's exterior to what pernicious sect he belonged, and they laid it down as a fixed principle that better a hundred innocent persons should perish than one guilty one escape. The assurance and zeal of the inquisitors imposed at first upon the common people and induced them to permit the persecutions and burnings; still other friends were made by a judicious distribution of the lands of the victims; while the cause of the Emperor Frederick II. was itself in too great jeopardy to admit of his interfering on the side of mercy.

End of the Inquisition.

Under these favoring circumstances, Conrad of Marburg and his friends became so courageous that they dared to accuse even venerable prelates and persons of the highest rank. Even Frederick's elder son, that unfortunate Henry who was later denied the succession, became an object of their suspicion, while against a Count of Sayn the accusation was soberly brought that he had been seen in the act of riding upon a crab. This very Count of Sayn forced matters to a climax by appealing to a Diet of the empire and by sending directly to Rome to Pope Gregory IX. himself. The latter expressed surprise at the lengths to which his representative had gone, but before he could interfere the Germans had found a way of their own for freeing themselves from the thraldom of the Inquisition. An uprising had taken place against the whole spirit of the institution, and Conrad and his subordinates had been murdered, though not in time to prevent the slaughter of thousands of Frisians, against whom a crusade had been preached. The final blow to the Inquisition was given by the Diet of Frankfort of 1234, which decreed that henceforth offences against the faith should be tried in the regular courts, with the ordinary means of defence. Four extra sessions were to be held monthly, over which the young king was to preside in person.

This rise of heretical sects and the church's intolerance toward them is one dark shadow on the history of the time. A brighter side is the new impulse given to chivalry by the crusades, and the rise of a general order of knighthood, with its code of virtues and observances, and its new and fascinating literature. There had been a time when any man whose trade was war, and who fought on horseback, with one or more followers, could call himself a *miles*, or knight, and hold his *feudum*, or fief. That was now to change. Closer contact with other countries, and especially with France, where the institution was more fully developed, had led to a different determination of rank, and to the adoption of the *ordo militaris*, or rule of knightly conduct. "Polite society," as we should call it to-day,

*A general order of knighthood.*

became narrowed to those of good birth, who had undergone the ceremony of " knighting," or initiation.  Doubtless the religious orders in Palestine served largely as a model, for this order, too, prided itself on its Christianity and on its ability to fight.  Certain courtly graces were indispensable, and also a reverence for woman — like that due to a patron saint.

German chivalry never emancipated itself from French influence; the names that refer to the tourney and other knightly sports are all taken from that language.  French, too, are the dishes on the well-ordered table, the materials for the courtly garments, the more elegant of the dances.  French formalism, even, passed over to Germany, and men troubled themselves about their manners and about points of etiquette as they did about their sins.  Great stress was laid on how to meet and greet, or how to enter and leave a room.  Godfrey of Strassburg, in order to be edifying, weaves into his poem of *Tristan* a long dissertation as to whether it is better to speak, or simply to make a silent bow.

Duties of a knight.

There was much that was admirable even in this conventional knighthood, for the whole system rested on a basis of sincerity and fidelity.  To his liege lord the knight was to be a true vassal, to aid him in the administration of justice, to take part in his wars and in his feuds, to repair to his court whenever summoned — even if to some mere festivity.  On receiving his fief he swore to be " faithful, devoted, and willing," laid his hands in the hands of his lord, or sealed his vow with a kiss.  He might bring no charges in court that affected his master's life, limb, or honor; he was bound to furnish pecuniary aid, if needed, for ransom, for the marriage of the eldest daughter, or for knighting of the eldest son.  Altogether his conduct was to be courtly: — *höfisch* is the German term, and *höflich* is still the word for all that is pretty and polite.

There were duties toward others besides the lord. For God, for his country, for justice, or for honor, the knight was to be ready to sacrifice his life without so much as a moment's hesitation; he was to protect the helpless with his heart's blood and be true to the death to his friend or to his lady. That he should have such a lady was one of the rules of the game; he became her vassal and knelt to her as he knelt to his lord. In her service all his jousts were fought, at her feet he laid all his prizes. Her banner, veil, or garland, or even her linen undergarment, would be fastened to his helm or spear, a constant token of his devotion.

The requisite as to good birth grew more and more severe with time; descent from three generations of knights or from three generations of men who might have been knights had they so chosen — for many never were initiated — became a *sine qua non;* indeed, the rule was later extended to sixteen quarterings of the shield. The tournament regulations of the time provide that he who attempts to enter the lists with imperfect lineage shall atone by public disgrace — as a hedge-knight be made to ride the barrier. Similar was the punishment for those found to be tainted with heresy, to have committed treason, deserted from the army, broken their oath, or borne false witness. *Perfect lineage.*

One priceless mirror of these times we have in the splendid poem of *Parsifal*, a study not only in the externals, but also in the ideals of knighthood. A purer, more beautiful, character than that of the hero has never been conceived, and the reader is allowed to assist, as it were, at its development toward perfection. A boy of ancient lineage, with a face like an angel and the tenderest of hearts, is brought up in seclusion, away from the clang of arms, by a mother who fears she may lose him as she has already lost her husband. But knights whom he chances to meet in the forest, and *Parsifal the ideal knight.*

whom he takes for gods, fire his imagination; he must and will away to the court of King Arthur, and he forces his mother to give him a horse. Hoping, however, that ridicule will dishearten him with the project, she decks him out in the garments of a fool, herself falling dead with grief after he has left her. The youth, raw and untutored, does mean and unchivalrous acts, but learns from Gurnemanz, one of Arthur's followers, the rules of the order of knighthood. The wonderful skill of the poet, Wolfram von Eschenbach, of whom his own contemporaries said "never did mouth of layman speak better," is shown by the way in which, all through the long poem, what is conventional is contrasted with what is spiritual. Gawain is the exponent of the one type of knight, brave and correct in all his doings; Parsifal, of the other. But the latter has first to free himself from the shackles of this same conventionality: Gurnemanz has told him that a well-behaved knight never asks troublesome questions; so when in the mysterious mountain of Monsalvat he sees the terrible pain of Amfortas, the bloody lance, the mystic power of the Holy Grail, he omits to show the interest of ordinary human sympathy. Though received the day before with the honors of a king, he is now ignominiously dismissed, and a mocking laugh rings out from one of the receding towers. To Arthur's court Kundry, the messenger of the Grail, follows him, denouncing him as false and dishonored; for the first time he learns that one word of sympathy would have freed Amfortas from his pain.

The purification of Parsifal.
Now begins the long process of atonement and purification; Parsifal wanders forth in absolute despair, no longer believing in a God, but determined to the last to be true to his wife, Condwiramur, and to be strong in battle. His one thought is to reach the mountain of Monsalvat and make good his fault; a pious hermit whom he meets in the magic calm of a Good Friday, tells him that only through faith in

God, through pity and humility, can the Grail be found.
With hope in his heart he continues his wanderings, performing generous and brave deeds, and being received back
with honor at the court of Arthur. Here Kundry reappears,
and, worshipping at his feet, tells him the Grail has appointed him lord and king. Constancy and fidelity are the
virtues which have brought about his salvation; these are
the ideals of a true knight.

Not only the poems, romances, and chronicles of these
times, but even the dry legal documents, bear witness to
the spirit of chivalry. In the charters of privileges, in the
deeds of gift, where people signed according to their rank,
the title of knight assumes a leading importance; those
who have a right to bear it, seldom, if ever, omit it, and its
owner has the place of honor next to the king's count and
banner-bearer. Even princes, if the ceremony of knighting
have not been performed, are on a lower plane; while,
strangely enough, doctors of law are, *ipso facto*, knights.

*Importance of title of knight.*

The ceremony of knighting was considered such an
epoch in the life of a layman as the consecration by the
bishop in that of an ecclesiastic; it usually took place at
some festival or on the eve or morrow of a battle. The
knighting of the young King Henry VI., in 1184, was made
the occasion of the grandest rejoicings in the history of the
Middle Ages, seventy thousand knights being entertained
by Frederick Barbarossa in his own great camp. Not for
a hundred years, declares a poet, will the occasion be forgotten. The actual ceremony itself consisted of a blow
struck with the flat of a sword across the shoulders of the
kneeling candidate, in token that this was the last insult of
man he might ever bear in silence. At the same time there
was taken the vow of obedience to the laws of chivalry, a
step so important that the record of it was placed on the
tombstones of the dead.

*Ceremony of knight-ing.*

Preparation for knighthood.

As with every other calling in the Middle Ages, the preparation for knighthood was very long and very thorough, and the youth who was destined to become a "courtly man" went through various stages of apprenticeship. In his seventh year he was sent to the castle of some great noble, where for seven years he performed the duties of a page, and learned the elements of good manners. Some of the rules of conduct to be observed at such a lord's table have been handed down, and serve, although trivial matter in themselves, to illustrate the spirit of the times. As forks had not yet been invented, it was not forbidden to take the food from the plates with the fingers, which, however, were not to be put into the mustard-pot or other general dishes. When helping one's self from the latter, a spoon was to be used or a crust of bread, but one that had not already been in the mouth. No leaning of the elbows on the table was allowed, no blowing into the food to cool it, no using of the tablecloth for other than the regular purposes, no picking of the teeth with the points of the knives.

The squire.

As the page grew older he became a squire, often leaving the home of his first master to seek other service. He was now instructed in the use of weapons, in the art of hunting with falcons and greyhounds, in singing, dancing, and polite intercourse with women. After being dubbed a knight his daily occupation was the necessary training for the joust and tournament. As endurance was the chief object, this training consisted in running, jumping, and taking long walks; leaping into the saddle was a feat much affected and extremely difficult, on account of the heavy armor.

The joust.

The joust was a simple encounter between two knights armed with spears, and was entered into by any two strangers who felt inclined for adventures. Redoubtable champions would travel from land to land, fighting every one who came in their way. The man of quality was recognized at once by the finer points and special polite observances of the sport. The chief object was to thrust the spear at the adversary when in full gallop, so as either to unhorse him, or, more usually, to shiver the weapon; a good jouster could break some fifty lances in the course of a day. The blows were good or bad according to what part of the shield they struck; and to wound the horse, or to let one's own steed trample on a fallen foe, was unpardonable awkwardness. The conflict was to cease the moment one of the antagonists raised the visor of his helm.

The chief and climax of all knightly encounters was the tourney or tournament, in which hundreds and even thousands took part at a time, and which closely resembled a battle; these encounters, indeed, formed a regular part of military training, just as do the manœuvres, reviews, and sham battles of to-day, and they gave the only opportunity to the prince or lord of judging the valor of his knights and promoting the deserving. It would be difficult to understand, otherwise, how violent was the opposition when the church took upon itself to forbid tourneys. *The tournament.*

The giver or arranger of a tournament would divide the participants into two sides, each under its own leader. The day began with certain conventional evolutions, after which the knights singled out their special antagonists. The roughest form of the pastime was the so-called sword-war, in which, with mighty thrusts and slashes, the adversaries sought to cut off each other's helm-plumes, to split their wooden shields, or to strike their swords from their hands and thus render them defenceless. The ultimate aim of such encounters was to take as many prisoners as possible, and afterward demand a heavy ransom. Even in

an ordinary joust the steed and armor of him who was unhorsed fell to his conqueror.   Besides such general booty
there were often special prizes consisting of horses, dogs,
or falcons.   The Margrave of Meissen, for one of his tour-
naments at Nordhausen, had a tree erected with leaves of
gold and silver, which were distributed among the knights
according to their deeds of valor.

Features of<br>the tourna-<br>ment.    A favorite feature of the tournament was the disguised
or masquerading knight, who with visor down and clad in
some remarkable garment — snow-white or pea-green —
would enter the lists at a critical moment.   Or a dozen
horsemen, garbed exactly alike, would sweep over the crest
of a neighboring hill and turn the tide of victory.   Such
incidents added to the interest, and doubtless were often pre-
arranged.   Some of the disguises were expressly designed
to raise a laugh, as when knights of tried valor fought in
the skirts of women.   Ulrich von Lichtenstein rode
through the land as Frau Venus, challenging all comers.

The church<br>and the<br>tourna-<br>ment.    There was a very serious side to these encounters, that
justified the church in its attitude toward them.   We hear
of sixty and even a hundred knights falling dead in a day
from wounds, heat, and exhaustion; Ulrich von Lichtenstein tells of a tournament, in which he himself took part,
that lasted for twelve hours; on this arena bitter enemies
fought out their old quarrels.   Not once, but a hundred
times, papal bulls were issued regarding the matter; it was
made a law of the church that those who fell in such a
contest might not be buried in consecrated ground, and
many a woman went as a pilgrim to Rome to gain a dispensation for her dead husband.   Occasionally, indeed, as
when Innocent III. tried to win all Europe for his last
crusade, general concessions were made to the knights, and
permission accorded to hold the much-desired meetings.

Besides his jousts and tourneys, the knight had to be

ready at any time, either on his own account or on behalf
of the helpless and oppressed, to take part in the judicial
duel or trial by combat.   All through the age of chivalry,
all through the twelfth and thirteenth centuries, recourse
was had to this means of proving guilt or innocence; it was
the usage of the ordinary county courts.   A favorite artifice,
not only of the author of *Lohengrin*, but also of other poets
of the time, is to present a disconsolate heroine with no
one to fight in her defence, until at last some unknown
champion makes his appearance, just as the allotted term
of grace is about to expire.

Trial by
combat.

If this ordeal of battle went against the accuser, he was
subject to the same punishment that would have been inflicted on the defendant.   The duels were held in enclosed
spaces from which the combatants could not escape; before
the conflict, both parties heard mass, and over the sacred
relics each swore to the justice of his cause.   The struggle
was begun on horseback, but, so soon as one of the participants lost his saddle, was continued on foot and with the
sword.   At the last moment, when one had the other at
his mercy, it was customary to remit the death-stroke if the
vanquished man would confess his guilt, or, as the case
might be, withdraw his charge.

Should a woman prefer, she might fight in her own
defence, and not the least curious of ancient legal remains
are the provisions for such a combat.   The man is to stand
waist deep in a circular pit, with a club in his right hand
with which he may hit his antagonist; but he may not
chase her nor even support himself against the edge.   She
for her part has a heavy stone tied in the end of a veil;
she is further allowed, if she can seize his head from behind,
to bend it back and throttle him.   Should her veil become
entwined about his free arm, he may draw her down into
the pit.

Women
as com-
batants.

Devotion to
women.

It may be that such regulations date already from a time when the devotion to woman was waning. At the beginning of the thirteenth century the poet Reinmar of Zweter had still been able to compare a beautiful lady to the Holy Grail on which only the pure in heart might gaze. But soon into this *Minnedienst*, or love service, there began to creep exaggerations and extravagances. Ulrich von Lichtenstein tells us in his memoirs how, although the disease was considered contagious, he mingled with lepers to gain his lady's sympathy; how he drank of the water in which she had bathed her hands; how he had his lip cut because it projected too far for her taste; how, finally, he sent her his finger in a rich receptacle because she had mocked at the trifling nature of a wound he had gained in her honor. And all this Ulrich does simply and solely because he wishes to be in the fashion; he has a wife at home with whom he is on the best of terms and who has presented him with a numerous progeny.

Occasionally such extravagances met with deserved ridicule, as when the friends of a Reinmar von Hagenau twitted him with having sung the praises of one lady so long that she must have grown quite ancient. A certain Tannhuser, who died about 1270, complains of having been asked to capture salamanders, moon-reflections, and the like, and to stop the Rhine from flowing by Coblenz; he declares that his whole fortune has gone in serving ladies and in baths twice a week.

Discomforts of knighthood.

It is a wonder that knights could joust and play, and make love so merrily, when we consider how, after all, the greater part of their lives were spent. Behind their thick bare walls, throughout the cold winter months, they played their games of chess, drank their cups of wine, and listened to tales of the crusades sung by the wandering minstrel. For the woman it was still worse. Is it mere chance that in the poems of the time the maiden is always looking out of the window as the knight comes winding up the glen? Then there was constant danger from the assaults of enemies. In every one of the castles of the time there is the donjon tower, the last despairing resort in case of need; in many there is the "pitch-nose" through which boiling tar can be poured on the heads of the besiegers; while below is the dark, damp dungeon, in which captives were literally left to rot.

With the interregnum, as the period that followed on the fall of the Hohenstaufen dynasty is called, the demoralization of poverty began to set in. The age of chivalry is over, the age of the robber-knight has begun. Commerce and industry work a social revolution; the burgher becomes the important man in the state; military tactics change, and there is no longer room for a set of men whose chief merit was bearing the burden of a now useless armor.

*Decline of knighthood.*

# CHAPTER VI

## THE KINGS FROM DIFFERENT HOUSES

AUTHORITIES: The chief authority is Lindner's *Deutsche Geschichte unter den Hapsburgern und Luxemburgern*. Prutz, *Staatengeschichte des Abendlandes im Mittelalter*, is a useful résumé. Riezler, *Die literarischen Widersacher der Päpste*, tells at length about the *Defensor Pacis*. See also Creighton's *History of the Papacy*.

The election of Rudolph of Hapsburg.

AT the time of the execution of Conradin the uppermost thought in many minds was that vengeance must be taken for the cruel deed — vengeance against the Papacy, or at least against its henchman, Charles of Sicily. Legends had arisen as to how, from the scaffold, the brave young prince had thrown his gauntlet far out into the crowd, and how an eagle had wetted its wings in the blood of the last Hohenstaufen. The troubadours had taken up the theme; one of them wonders that he still has power to depict the calamity, that the mere thought of it does not strike him dead. "How can the Germans continue to live," he cries, "bearing in their hearts the memory of this loss. The best has been taken and only disgrace harvested!"

But the pressing problems of the moment occupied too much attention. How to get rid of this anarchy, of these petty foreign kings! At last, in 1272, Pope Gregory X., who found himself in danger of worse thraldom under the Anjevins than ever under the Hohenstaufens, took matters into his own hands. On the death of Richard of Cornwall, the rival of Alfonso of Castile, he wrote to the German electors that if they did not speedily choose a head of the empire, he and his cardinals would impose one upon them.

Obeying his behest, they gave their votes for Rudolph, Count of Hapsburg. The most striking phenomenon of the period which this reign inaugurated is the frequent change of rulers and of dynasties; but connected with this are two features of great interest: the growth and assumption of power of the seven electors, and the rise of a popular and literary, as well as of an imperial, opposition to the Papacy. We shall first sketch the incidents in the reigns of the rulers from Rudolph to Louis of Bavaria, and then take up in detail these main lines of development.

Of the six different kings, from four different houses, that ruled in the seventy years between 1273 and 1346, the one that has left the chief impression on German history was Rudolph of Hapsburg. We even know how he looked, which cannot be said of the others, for the marble image on his tombstone is one of the most carefully executed of monuments. Begun long before the king died, the sculptor is said to have visited him at frequent intervals to note and change the wrinkles that appeared in his face. He was tall and gaunt, with a Roman nose, and with curls that covered his ears. In character he was renowned for cleverness, astuteness, and firmness, but also for zeal in increasing his boundaries. "Sit still on Thy throne, O Lord," once prayed the Bishop of Basel, "or the Count of Hapsburg will shove Thee off!" There was a gravity about this pale face that was supposed to denote great virtue, which gravity and which pallor were handed down to a long line of descendants.

Personality of Rudolph of Hapsburg.

It has often been supposed that Rudolph was chosen "king of the Romans" rather for his insignificance than for any other qualities, but such is not the case. He could boast, indeed, of no compact principality, like Saxony, Brandenburg, Bavaria, Bohemia, or the Palatinate; but in other respects he was reputed one of the richest men of his time, and his lands stretched from the Alpine passes well into Alsace. He was a relative of the Hohenstaufens and had supported them to the best of his ability, accompanying Conradin at least as far as Verona on his last fatal march. All this spoke greatly in his favor; still more so the fact that he had many eligible daughters, and that three of the electors were in search of wives. Six of these women were advantageously married, the seventh entering a nunnery; and when in his old age Rudolph wished to make an alliance with Burgundy, he had no one left to sacrifice on the altar of Hymen but himself. At the age of sixty-six he wedded a princess of fourteen!

The struggle with Ottocar of Bohemia.

Rudolph's great achievement, the overthrow of King Ottocar of Bohemia and the confiscation of Austria, proved of private more than of public benefit, enabling him, as it did, to provide an appanage for his family, which they have held down to the present day. The struggle had been one for supremacy, inasmuch as Ottocar denied the validity of Rudolph's election; it had been long and fierce, for the Bohemian had a strong following and the revenues of many lands. Ottocar had once been reduced to submission and had agreed to do homage; but his friends declared that, during the performance of this act, which was to be in private, Rudolph had purposely let fall the walls of his tent and displayed his enemy upon his knees. The tables turned, indeed, and there came a time when, to use the words of a contemporary chronicle, "all the family of King Rudolph ran to confessors, arranged their affairs, forgave their enemies, and received the communion; for a mortal danger seemed to hang over them." But these troubles ended with that scene on the Marchfeld near Dornkrut, where Ottocar, defeated and deserted, still refused to submit, but rather fought on with the strength and spirit of a giant until unhorsed and mortally wounded.

To the disgrace of the Germans, his seventeenth wound was inflicted after he was already captive. Dante, writing his immortal poem a few years later, gives this hero a prominent place in purgatory.

On the whole, Rudolph's reign may be considered distinctly beneficial to Germany, and he left a memory that was revered for centuries. Much that he attempted remained unaccomplished, but he was firm in his endeavors to put down crime, and is known to have included as many as twenty-nine robbers in one sweeping sentence of death. He did his best, also, to stop private feuds, but with no great success. What could one expect of an age in which there was absolutely no conception of such a thing as "breach of the peace"? Not for two whole centuries was any general law passed making it a crime to take private vengeance for the infliction of wrongs.

False Fredericks and false Conradins.

Quiet and peace did not return at once; whole classes of men found their cherished hopes not fulfilled. There was no lack of minor revolts, while strange delusions seized upon the people. False Fredericks and false Conradins cropped up on all sides, the exposure of the one seeming not to deter the rest. A certain Dietrich Holzschuh, the most famous of all, was from the first recognized in Cologne as an arrant impostor. He was imprisoned for a while, then brought into the market-place, crowned with tinsel, and seated on a ladder in lieu of a throne. But this was the beginning, not the end, of his experiences. With half of his hair torn out, and with mud-spattered garments, but stoutly maintaining that he was Frederick II., Dietrich was finally driven from the city, but took refuge in the neighboring Neuss. Here he gave, it was said, convincing proofs of his identity to Frederick's old soldiers, and was encouraged to set up his court, which was visited from far and near. Such rumors were spread

of his power and wealth that the Marquis of Este sent a
special envoy to inquire into the matter.   Princes were
summoned before the new mercy-seat, and Rudolph was
ordered to come and do homage for his royal office.   Dietrich later moved to Wetzlar, before which town the king
appeared in force, demanding his surrender.   He was
finally brought into camp chained to the stirrup of Marshal
Pappenheim's horse, was tortured, then burnt at the stake.

Adolphus
of Nassau
and Albert
of Austria.

Rudolph's successor, Adolphus of Nassau, was a young,
almost poverty-stricken nobleman, who was noted chiefly
for his fighting qualities, and who had more than once
consented to act as a paid *condottiere*.   Once on the throne,
which he achieved by bribery, his chief idea seemed to be
to gain for himself a dynastic appanage like that of the
Hapsburgs — a step to which he was driven, indeed, by
the fact that the crown, as such, was almost without revenues.   But this endeavor led him into shifty ways and
into acts of downright violence.

In the background was always the stern figure of Albert
of Austria, the son of Rudolph, who regarded as his by
right the crown from which the electors had excluded him
because of his autocratic ways.   He had even gone so far
as to possess himself of the imperial insignia, but had been
obliged to surrender them to Adolphus.   Now all the
enemies of the latter rallied to the Austrian's banner.
With an army of Rhenish knights Albert marched to Göllheim and flung down the gauntlet to his rival.   The two
flaunted the same imperial banner — a white cross on a red
ground.   Albert's men, armed with poniards, were told
to strike for the horses and not for the heavily armored
knights.   One exciting moment has made the battle
memorable: the two kings suddenly found themselves
face to face; Albert's blow struck his enemy full in the
bared face and the blood streamed down to the ground.

His horse fell under him, and the daggers of the Austrians put an end to his reign and to his life.

Albert was a stern, strong man — "hard as a diamond" one chronicler calls him. In one of his illnesses he had submitted to being held upside down by his physicians until the blood gushed forth from eyes, nose, and mouth, in consequence of which he was half blind. He was rigidly zealous in upholding the empire's rights, and he came, as we shall see, in another connection, into bitter war with the electors. On the whole, he was successful, but in the midst of his triumph occurred the horrible crime that gained for its perpetrator the name of John the Parricide. Albert's own nephew, a moody, discontented youth who claimed that a part of his inheritance had been withheld, formed a plot to lure the king to a lonely spot on the bank of the Reuss; here they fell upon him and stabbed him to the heart. The principal culprit fled to Italy, where, seven years later, the new king came suddenly upon him in a monastery and imprisoned him for life. *Character of Albert of Austria.*

Henry of Luxemburg, known as Henry VII., is described by a contemporary as forty years of age, half French by education, graceful of figure, not tall, but "just about tall enough," with prominent eyebrows, bright cheeks, and fair hair. He had a very high sense of his own importance and earned the name of a second Barbarossa. He spoke of himself as head of the world, and of his crown as the crown of crowns, and had the code of Justinian amended to read that every human creature must obey the Roman emperor. He went to Italy in all the pride of a heaven-ordained restorer of law and liberty: we have his own description of how in the long interregnum the communes had possessed themselves of all the imperial prerogatives; how the citizens, divided into factions, were warring to the *Personality of Henry VII.*

death with one another or driving the vanquished into
exile.  In every city the powerful Guelph nobles were
opposed by equally powerful Ghibellines.

Henry VII.
in Italy.

The coming of a new emperor, the first since Frederick II., was hailed with unmixed delight.  Even the Pope
in Avignon grew eloquent over the prospect; he calls
Henry the peace-bringer, the glorified of God, the cynosure
of all eyes, the gentle one who is to sit upon the throne of
majesty, and with his nod dispel all evil.  Another voice
we hear, too, — that of a banished Florentine, who thought
to see the day dawning after a night of perpetual woe.
Full of joyous excitement, Dante wrote a circular letter
to the princes and cities of Italy: justice, he tells them,
weak as heliotrope without the sun, will now revive again;
the strong lion of Judah has pricked up his ears; a second
Moses will snatch his people from the torments of the
Egyptians.  He is coming — he the bridegroom hasting to
the wedding, the compassionate Henry, glory of his people,
the godlike Cæsar and Augustus.

Dante's
disappoint-
ment.

Henry came, but he came as a partisan rather than as
the mild, compassionate one.  It is true he told exiles
who came to him at Turin that he was completely unpreju-
diced, but the new stadtholders he imposed on the communes were invariably Ghibellines; in Milan he declared
for the Visconti; in Cremona he threw down the golden
lion and imprisoned three hundred citizens.  Dante and
his party grew weary of waiting for the deliverer's appearance; there in Tuscany, the poet had declared, was the
sink of iniquity, there the heart of the hydra.  In a letter
to the emperor he still speaks of him as the Lamb that is
to take away the sins of the world, but cannot conceal that
many are asking, "Art thou he that shall come or must
we look for another?"

Henry died in Italy in August, 1313, among the reverberations of papal thunder. There were rumors of foul play. Into the cup of the Eucharist, which the emperor alone of laymen might enjoy, a priest was said to have infused poison concealed under his finger-nails. Men declared that the pious Kaiser had refused to take an emetic for fear of profaning the body of Christ. Death of Henry VII.

At each successive election the Hapsburgs had come forward as pretenders to the throne. Just as Albert had hoped to succeed Rudolph, so Frederick the Fair had hoped to succeed Albert; he had failed then, but now on the decease of Henry VII. he was able to play an important part. He was the least gifted of three brothers; but the youngest and most warlike, Leopold, was willing to draw sword in his behalf. Their rival now was Louis of Bavaria, who had drawn down on him, by his bravery at the fierce battle of Gammelsdorf, the eyes of all Germany. Louis had secured four out of the seven electoral votes, but the Hapsburgs maintained that an adherent of their own, Henry of Carinthia, as true king of Bohemia, should have replaced the actual king, John. There were two royal coronations: the one (that of Frederick) in the wrong place but by the right person; the other in the right place (Aix-la-Chapelle) but by the wrong person (the Archbishop of Mainz). Louis the Bavarian and Frederick the Fair.

There followed another of those long, wasting wars that Germany had known so well. The private resources of the Hapsburgs were greater, but Louis's followers more numerous. In physique, too, the Bavarian had the advantage; he was tall, slender, muscular, and fitted by nature to rule, says a chronicler, *as sometimes happens among the bees!* Men praised his eye like that of a stag, his elastic step, his healthy, bright coloring, his finely pencilled eyebrows, his hearty, merry nature. There was a trace of timorousness about him, indeed, for he daily took an antidote for fear of being poisoned.

For years the struggle went on between Frederick and
Louis in a desultory fashion; but at last, at Mühldorf on
the river Inn, the three Hapsburg brothers, aided by tribes
so wild that they fed on cats and dogs, came upon Louis
and King John of Bohemia, whose forces outnumbered
their own. It was the day of St. Wenceslaus, the Bohemian patron saint. Frederick was urged not to fight, but
declared that he had already made too many widows and
orphans to desist now. He headed his troops, and a
chronicler awards him the praise that "straight through
the fight there was no better knight than he." But Bavarian reserves won the day; fourteen hundred Austrian
nobles were taken prisoner, among them Frederick himself.
"I was never so glad to see you," Louis is said to have
remarked; "And I never so unwilling to see you," was
the rejoinder. Louis's later conduct toward Frederick was
influenced by each twist and turn of his quarrel with the
Pope: he released him after two years and a half of captivity, and afterward asked him to share his throne; a
document was signed at Munich in which he was formally
accepted as coregent. "In the church, in the street," it
ran, "and everywhere, we are to have similar honors; each
shall sign and call himself King of the Romans and Aug-
menter of the Empire; we shall speak of each other as
brothers and write to each other."

The events that conclude the reign of Louis are so inter-
twined with his relations to the electors and to the Papacy
that it now becomes necessary to retrace our steps for
more than half a century, and follow the developments that
led to such complications, taking up the events once more
reign by reign.

The electoral college, consisting of the three archbishops,
— Mainz, Cologne, and Treves, — of the king of Bohemia,
the Margrave of Brandenburg, the Duke of Saxony, and the

Count Palatine, first came into prominence at the election of Rudolph, though just on that occasion Bohemia's vote was usurped by Bavaria. From that time on, until the end of the empire, in 1806, these seven, and eventually nine men, played a part in German history scarcely second to that of the emperors; they claimed themselves to be the seven pillars on which the empire rested. They imposed what conditions they pleased upon their candidate, and forced him to sign an instrument called the *Wahlcapitulation*, which may well be translated an "election surrender." When the monarch began to grow restive and to walk in other paths, they often warred with, and occasionally deposed him. Their insatiable greed brought things to a most wretched pass; never in all history have there been worse scandals connected with elections than at the time of Rudolph's death. Adolphus of Nassau was called upon to reward his electors with incredible grants, — hand-ointment, a poet of the time calls it, — and was threatened with debtor's arrest and attachment of his private property until he should have paid. His final inability to keep these promises was one of the chief causes of their pronouncing the throne vacant and calling in Albert of Austria. Their act of accusation was full of the most bitter reproaches and the most partisan and unfounded charges, such as breaking into churches, slaying priests at the altar, and scattering the bread and wine of the Eucharist about the floor.

The rise of the electoral college.

If the electors had hoped to find Albert a more subservient tool than Adolphus, they soon found that they had reckoned without their host. In order to make sure of his election he did, it is true, make promises as ruinous as those of his predecessor; but no sooner was he on the throne than he took the offensive against those who had placed him there. Indeed, he seemed fairly to court the conflict, to such extremes had these men carried their pre-

Albert of Austria and the seven electors.

sumption and insolence; "In there I still have many kings," the Archbishop of Mainz is said to have remarked to the monarch himself, proudly tapping his own hunting-pouch. One of Albert's upholders wrote to the Pope that such rapacity made it fairly impossible for any king to rule with dignity; "Hence come wars and tumults, and there is nothing to look forward to but desolation and ruin for our land and danger for our souls."

The unlawful imposition of exorbitant tolls on Rhine shipping, at a point where there was no passing round by land, gave Albert his opportunity. This matter he declared had been settled by law and precedent in the reign of his father. In a war manifesto issued in May, 1301, he accused the electors of every kind of avarice.

Albert of Austria and Pope Boniface VIII.

The ally upon whom the archbishops would naturally most rely was Boniface VIII., Pope of Rome, and a lineal descendant, in a spiritual sense, of Gregory VII. At his jubilee, in the year 1300 A.D., the most successful demonstration over which the Papacy had ever presided, he is reported to have appeared in costly robes and to have declared, "I, I am the emperor!" He now summoned Albert to come to Rome within six weeks, assuming as a matter of course that his voice was final in the matter of elections to the German throne. Among the charges for which the king was to answer was the killing of Adolphus of Nassau; should he fail to cleanse himself, his subjects were to be freed from their allegiance.

The news of Albert's military successes, joined to the Pope's own critical situation with regard to France, soon caused him to change his tone. The king had brought the Count Palatine to his knees in a single expedition and held the Archbishop of Mainz besieged in Bingen; Boniface's conflict, moreover, with Philip IV. of France was fast nearing its ignominious and fatal conclusion. Loftier than ever, indeed, were his assumptions; "It is altogether necessary to salvation that every human being be subject to the Roman pontiff," was the ending of one of his decrees. But Albert he now formally acknowledged as rightful ruler, explaining his change of front on sufficiently remarkable grounds; the German people, he declared, were corrupt and diseased in every fibre of their being, and their ruler must be left free to heal their wounds with "soothing oil and sharp vinegar." The emperor has been placed above kings and kingdoms to the end that, sitting on the throne of justice, he should dispel all evil with his glance.

On the murder of Albert, King Philip of France tried hard to seat his own brother, Charles of Valois, upon the German throne, and to this end a French writer of renown had the audacity to propose that a papal decree should once for all do away with the whole electoral college. But the latter body was far from moribund, and returned to its policy of choosing a weak instrument of its will. Henry of Luxemburg, acceding to all their demands, had abandoned the field to them for the sake of pursuing his ambitious, but unsuccessful, policy in Italy. *Babylonian captivity of the Papacy.*

By this time the popes had altogether fallen from their high pedestal. Boniface VIII. had been bearded in his own palace at Anagni by the envoys of Philip the Fair, and grief and indignation had put an end to his life. Figuratively, if not literally, the iron glove of the Colonna had smitten him in the face. The Papacy had gone into its captivity at Avignon, to last, like that of the Jews by the Babylonians, for seventy years. When Henry VII. demanded the imperial coronation in Rome, it had to be performed by cardinals deputed for the purpose. St. Peter's was held by Robert of Anjou, king of Naples and son of the murderer of Conradin, who was the mainstay of the Guelph party; accordingly, after some fierce fighting, the ceremony was held in the church of the Lateran, and Henry revenged himself by swinging his sword toward all four quarters of the heavens in token that the whole world belonged to him.

Death of Henry VII. in Italy. Henry issued a manifesto against Robert, in which he charged him with growing fat on the spoils of the empire, kicking up the heels of rebellion, and spewing out the poison of injustice. He is declared to have forfeited his titles and dignities and is sentenced to death on the block. Robert replied with similar vituperations: Henry was a garrulous old woman, he said, who talked instead of fighting; he was following in the footsteps of those Fredericks, Manfreds, and Conradins who "had sown the bitter pest of sedition and hate" against the zealous upholders of the church.

Pope Clement's friendship for Henry had grown cold as ice the moment he found that there was a chance of his invading Naples. The memory of the Hohenstaufens rushed back upon him when he found the emperor allying himself with Frederick of Sicily, who, on the female side, was one of that "viper brood." The shades of the past seemed, indeed, to have risen when the Germans adopted as their ensign the head of Conradin. Clement sent to remind Henry of the oath of fealty taken at his coronation, but received answer that oath of fealty the emperor owed to no man, nor was he aware that his predecessors, the Roman emperors, had ever sworn such oath. Then came threats of instant excommunication against any one, "be he of priestly, imperial, or kingly rank," who should attack Robert of Naples or his lands. The attack was made, but this was the juncture at which Henry was seized at Buonconvento by the fever of which he died.

The struggle between Pope and emperor, the last but not the least bitter of a long series, broke out almost imme-

diately, but on other grounds.  John XXII., who ascended
the pontifical throne in 1316, at the age of seventy-two,
was tiny in stature, bald, lean, and of sallow countenance.
He went around with his little body bent forward and
muttering all sorts of things to himself; he spent his time
in hearing reports, in discovering new ways by which to
tax his clergy, and in issuing countless bulls and briefs.
Although needing little for his personal wants, he loved
to amass gold for its own sake; and the Florentine historian, Villani, whose brother was papal banker, is authority for the statement that, at John's death, his fortune
amounted to the enormous sum of twenty-five million
guldens.

Strange that a Pope who lived at Avignon almost as a
minion of the French king should have continued to hold
so lofty a conception of his own prerogative!  There is
no reason to doubt but that John shared the views of the
popular theologian, Augustino Trionfo, who dedicated to
him a writing in which he declares that secular laws have
no force, except in so far as the Pope confirms and approves
them, and that, should the welfare of the church demand
it, he can withdraw the power of choice from the electors
and set up an emperor of his own.

In the beginning John had held aloof from the dispute
between Louis of Bavaria and Frederick of Hapsburg concerning the possession of the German crown.  In the same
non-committal terms he had announced his own accession
to each of the rival kings; his hope seems to have been
that they would hold each other in check at home and
allow to him full sway in Italy.  Had not one of his predecessors, Clement V., formally declared that so long as the
imperial power was in abeyance the administration of the
imperial lands in Italy rested *ipso facto* in the papal hands?
John appointed Robert of Anjou, the old enemy of the

Germans, his vicar general, and Robert's subordinates
were sent all over northern Italy. Here they came in
contact with similar emissaries of Louis of Bavaria, and
it was on this matter of disputed jurisdiction that the
conflict broke forth.

John took the ground that the struggle of two kings for
the German, and consequently the imperial, throne constituted a state of affairs with regard to which the Pope
was, by the nature of the case, the arbiter. Louis should
have applied to him, he claimed, and have bowed to his
decision in the first place before exercising the royal functions. It was necessary for him, now, to lay down his
crown within three months under penalty of the church's
ban. In March, 1324, the Pope actually did resort to this
weapon, which had done the church such good service
against the Hohenstaufens. The times of Barbarossa
seemed, indeed, returning when Louis, having heard of
John's intention, issued furious manifestoes, declaring
that the election of a German king needed no confirmation from the Pope of Rome, and that the person chosen,
even without receiving the crown of the empire, might
exercise all imperial rights; that between rival claimants
not the papal fiat, but the sword alone, was to decide; that
this Pope was wallowing in crime and endeavoring to sub-
vert the empire; that he had openly said that the peace of
the church meant Germany's discord; that he would use all
his power, he had declared in the consistory of cardinals,
to crush that brazen serpent; that he was himself a heretic
for not believing in the doctrine of the poverty of Christ.

The Minor-
ites against
the Pope.

This last allusion was to a violent dispute that was
going on within the fold of the church, and that had split
the Franciscan friars into two hostile factions. Whereas
the rule of its founder prescribed absolute poverty, that
order had in reality, through gifts of pious persons and in

other ways, acquired great riches. In order to quiet rising scruples, the nominal ownership of this property had been vested in the Papacy, and the Franciscans retained simply the usufruct of their estates. The discussion was revived with great spirit in the time at which we have arrived, and it was debated at endless length whether or not Christ and His apostles had held possessions in common. The Minorite friars, without consulting the Pope, promulgated Christ's poverty as a dogma, to which John retaliated by pronouncing them heretics and making them take back their own property. They were thus forced over to the side of the Pope's political antagonists, and did Louis good service by gaining the ear of men of high position — princes, and even electors.

John for his part drew closer to the Hapsburgs, though not willing to commit himself to the extent of acknowledging Frederick the Fair as king. Yet this fear of closer union of his two chief antagonists seems to have greatly influenced the policy of Louis. We find him liberating his rival after two and a half years of arrest; we find him soon after not merely making a treaty of peace, but also arranging a marriage alliance between his own son and Frederick's daughter. Should the peace fail to be sanctioned, however, by the Pope and by Leopold of Austria, the Hapsburg was voluntarily to return to his prison.

Alliance of the Pope with the Hapsburgs.

As a matter of fact this sanction proved impossible to gain. John insisted on Frederick's breaking his oath to Louis — he would absolve him from it, he said — and roundly forbade him to return to captivity. Leopold in the meanwhile had had dealings with France, promising in return for the aid of Charles IV. to procure him the throne of the empire. These foreign complications explain in part Louis's treatment of Frederick; in part we have to reckon with the king's own fickleness and caprice.

Was it really merely to propitiate Leopold of Austria that Frederick was appointed successor to the throne, with right to exercise the royal prerogatives in case of the absence of Louis?

When the plan of the anomalous double rule was placed before the electors, they seem to have rejected it absolutely; but Louis soon afterward came out with a scheme still more radical, and offered to resign altogether if the Pope would confirm Frederick in his stead. The grounds for such a proposition are not altogether clear; but Louis seems to have known, for a certainty, beforehand, that the Pope would refuse to enter into the project.

Literary assailants of the Papacy.

The time had now come when the German king was less under the necessity of making concessions. The death of Leopold rendered Frederick less formidable; as a matter of fact, he plays no further rôle to the time of his death, in 1330. And against Pope John, Louis was now able to marshal the force of literary assailants that have made his reign so memorable. It is the dawn of a new age, the first sign of mediæval assumptions bowing their head beneath the crushing blows of a popular literature. In a manner unprecedentedly free the whole relation of church to state was beginning to be ventilated.

The *Defensor Pacis.*

Marsilius of Padua, the body physician of Louis, developed a new political system, differing in many respects from the teaching of the long-revered Aristotle, yet rational and thorough. His great book, the *Defensor Pacis*, in which he defines the position of the church within the state, contained the deadliest single assault ever aimed at the Papacy. No wonder Pope John dubbed its author and his assistants "monsters from the deeps of Satan and the sulphur-pools of hell!" Clement VI. maintained that he had extracted from the work no less than 240 heretical utterances.

Marsilius started with the assumption that the legislative power, in the final instance, rests with the people themselves; the head or ruler, who should be chosen for his merits, not for his parentage, simply carries out their will. Every citizen has rights to enjoy and duties to perform; a priest is in no wise exempt and in no way superior to others. Within the hierarchy itself the last resort is not the Pope, but a general council of the whole church; such a body and none other may rightfully impose the ban or interdict; all priests are equal among themselves, and equally subject to conciliar decrees. Did Peter ever assume authority over his fellow-apostles? Or, granted that he did, was there any real proof that the popes were his successors; could any one state positively that he had ever been in Rome? Why was the Gospel of St. Luke, why were the Acts of the Apostles, silent on the matter? As for heresy, it was not a crime, but possibly a disease to which the priest might minister. A man's opinions and convictions were his own; he was not to be punished for them unless they led him into acts contrary to the law.

The claim to jurisdiction over the affairs of the empire, continues the *Defensor Pacis*, and to the right of controlling elections, was laughable — nothing more; if the Pope could calmly set aside the results of their deliberations, any seven blear-eyed barbers could fill the offices of the electors. The Pope's assertion that he will not interfere with the rights of the latter, strikes Marsilius like the assurance upon the part of a man who knocks out another's eye, that no harm is intended; the claim that the head of the church must watch over elections to the headship of the empire, lest some heretic be chosen, is baseless when one considers that three out of the electoral college are high church dignitaries.

The success of the *Defensor Pacis* was phenomenal;

Imperial
coronation
of Louis the
Bavarian.

it spread all over Europe, and very old manuscripts of it have been found in Germany and England, as well as in Italy. When the Reformation came and the art of printing was pressed into its service, this writing was among the first to be published with great care and magnificence. Marsilius was, indeed, the direct precursor of Luther. The ideals of the *Defensor Pacis* seemed about to achieve their realization when, in 1328, Louis entered Rome and was proclaimed emperor, not by a Pope, but by the Roman people, who had assembled for the purpose on the Capitoline Hill. The two Italian bishops who anointed him were under the church's ban; the city itself was declared under the interdict, and orders given that that most precious of all relics, the handkerchief of St. Veronica, should be hidden away in the Pantheon from the desecrating gaze of heretics. The duty of actually placing the crown on the emperor's head was performed by a Colonna, in all probability the very one who is reputed to have flung his iron gauntlet into the face of Pope Boniface VIII.

Judgment
passed on
John XXII.

Louis's next step was to hold such judgment over John XXII. as Otto the Great had once held over John XII. News had meanwhile come that the Pope had declared a holy war against the emperor, and was offering to those who took part in it such absolution as was otherwise given only to crusaders. Collection boxes were to be placed in all the churches, that funds might be forthcoming for the enterprise. Louis, for his part, caused to be publicly read in the Square of St. Peter a list of the Pope's misdoings, — Marsilius had helped to draw it up, — his miserliness, his promulgation of heretical dogmas, his attacks on the rights of the empire. He is the mystical anti-Christ, the rider on the red horse who is mentioned in the Apocalypse. In absenting himself from Rome, in preaching the cross against innocent people, he is scorning the express commands of Christ.  He is declared deposed from the Papacy and is ordered to be handed over to the secular arm.  The election of a new Pope is promised, who shall take up his permanent residence in Rome, and not absent himself for more than a two days' journey without permission from the clergy and people.  An acceptable candidate was found in the person of Pietro Rainalducci, who took the name of Nicholas V.  For a short time the new emperor and he who was thus declared to be the spiritual head of Christendom basked together in a flood of glory, but the rays were the rays of the setting sun.  Not ten weeks later the failure to repulse Robert of Anjou, the defection of the Minorites, the demand of a subsidy from the Romans, had so lessened the reverence of the people that Pope and emperor alike had to flee the city for fear of being stoned.  After two years Nicholas repaired to Avignon, craved and obtained forgiveness of John XXII., and remained in honorable durance to the end of his life.

The later years of Louis the Bavarian's reign are as unedifying as those of the worst of Germany's rulers; his impetuosity, his vacillation, his utter want of true statesmanship, brought it about, to use the drastic figure of a contemporary, that "his good odor began to stink in the nostrils of the princes."  The most impracticable plans rushed through his head: he would restore the imperial prestige in Italy; by humbling himself to the ground, if need be, he would force the Pope to grant him absolution from the ban; no matter at what cost to others, he would increase his own family possessions.  Then came an astounding project, which undoubtedly originated in the councils of the Papacy and France, for abdicating wholly in favor of a cousin, Henry of Lower Bavaria, a prince who, by a secret compact, which may still be read, had agreed to give a large portion of his gains — the whole of

*Growing unpopularity of Louis.*

Burgundy and the bishopric of Cambray — to the French king should his efforts in his behalf meet with success.

The mere idea of this arrangement, of which, naturally, the half was not known, raised such an outcry that Louis was forced to deny all concern in the matter, to request that such "fables" be not believed, and to declare that nothing would induce him just then to lay down the responsibilities of his position.   Soon afterward we find him ready to make peace on the most unfavorable terms with Pope Benedict XII., successor of John XXII.   He will give up all communication with Marsilius of Padua and his like, he will openly condemn the *Defensor Pacis*, he will submit to a new imperial coronation at the hand of the Pope, thus acknowledging the invalidity of that pompous ceremony in Rome.   He will do any penance that may be imposed.

The meeting of the electors at Rense.

Benedict insisted that Louis should go one step deeper in his humiliation, and actually lay down his royal and imperial dignities until his title should have been more thoroughly investigated by the church; but this was too much for the emperor — too much even for the self-centred electors; and now we see a demonstration against the Papacy which marks an era in German history.   Indignation meetings were held at Rense and in Frankfort, and at the latter place, in 1338, a manifesto was drawn up by the electors, which vindicated in powerful language the rights of the empire.   That empire's head, so the writing declares, is head by election of the seven; his legislative power has descended to him directly through the Son of God; unto Cæsar must be rendered the things that are Cæsar's; there is absolutely no need of the approbation, authority, or consent of the apostolic see or of any person whatever; to doubt this assertion is high treason.

These were utterances such as many a better king than

Louis had never heard from his subjects.    They are to be explained in part by the fact that the emperor had for once made a popular move in espousing the cause of Edward III. of England against the king of France.    It was the beginning of the great struggle that was afterward to be known in history as the Hundred Years' War.    King Edward, who had promised large subsidies in return for two thousand men, came in person to Coblenz and placed himself at the feet of Louis, who sat on a throne in the crowded market-place in full imperial splendor.    Philip of Valois was declared deposed from the throne of France, and Edward was named imperial vicar for the German provinces on the lower Rhine.

Well might a contemporary call Louis of Bavaria the "foolish wise man, the dallying eager one, the lazy zealot." On a mere pretext and apparently only in the hope that the French king might speak a good word for him with the Pope, he broke the English treaty by stopping the supplies for the German contingents.    A storm of abusive pamphlets greeted the step.    A complication with regard to the Tyrol brought matters to a climax, and brought forward the House of Luxemburg as a rallying point for all the long pent-up discontent.    The Tyrol, through a marriage with its sole heiress, Margaret Maultasch, had come into the hands of John Henry, son of King John of Bohemia, and therefore grandson of the Emperor Henry VII. When, now, a party of the Tyrolese drove out John Henry after declaring that his marriage with Margaret had never been consummated, and offered her hand to Louis's son, Louis of Brandenburg, the emperor was foolish and grasping enough to accept the offer.    The discarded husband, the worst charge against whom was a bodily infirmity, was held up to the general derision of Europe, the pride of the Luxemburgers being cut to the quick by the shame

Opposition to Louis of Bavaria.

and injustice of the whole proceeding.   Fiery King John, who had all the more influence from the astounding number of political intrigues he had carried on in all parts of Europe, and his eldest son, Charles, who was now openly brought forward as a candidate for the throne of the empire, became the centre of a strong opposition.

Charles of
Luxemburg
as anti-
king.
The Pope, now Clement VI., who had inherited the hostility of his predecessors and who had a new, tangible grievance from the fact that the marriage of Margaret and Louis was bigamy according to canon law, roused himself to deal a last crushing blow.   Receiving the young Charles of Bohemia at Avignon, he agreed, in return for base concessions, to support him as candidate for the German throne.   Then he issued a new bull of deposition against Louis, which, taken all in all, is the best example extant of a withering papal curse.   With blindness, idiocy, and madness the Lord was to afflict the so-called emperor. Lightning was to strike him, flame to envelop him in this world and the next; the earth was to open and swallow him up.   Nor was he to be alone in his hideous sufferings, for his sons were to be homeless and share in his fate.

In summoning the electors to proceed to a new election, the Pope renewed once more the old threat of Gregory X., of himself imposing a king on the land.   At Rense, in July 11, 1346, the vote was cast, the three archbishops, the Duke of Saxony, and the king of Bohemia voting for Charles; the Palatinate and Brandenburg, being in Wittelsbach hands, were not represented.

It soon became evident that the German nation, as a whole, were not in sympathy with this revolutionary proceeding; a diet held at Spires declared roundly that they would never recognize this Luxemburg usurper; the cities of Cologne and Aix refused to admit him within their walls.   Charles and his father retired to Luxemburg, and when next we hear of them they are both in the heat of the world-famous battle of Crécy, on the side of their friend the French king. King John reached here the end of a checkered and adventurous career; by this time utterly blind, he was led into the battle by two knights, and fell desperately fighting. It is said that the English princes, doubtless in memory of his bravery, adopted from him the emblem of the three feathers and the motto "Ich dien." His son, too, was wounded, but was able to return to Luxemburg, and thence, but only in disguise, to Bohemia. He found adherents in the Tyrol, and was about to inaugurate a fierce struggle for the crown when the news came that the old emperor had died while bear-hunting, from a stroke of apoplexy.

# CHAPTER VII

## THE RULERS OF THE HOUSE OF LUXEMBURG

AUTHORITIES: Lindner covers this period as well as the preceding, as does also Prutz. We are fortunate in having a detailed biography of the Emperor Charles IV. by Werunsky, in which separate chapters are devoted to the persecution of the Jews, the Flagellants, and the Black Death. The Golden Bull is translated in full in Henderson's *Select Documents*. See also Lamprecht, *Deutsche Geschichte*, and Sach, *Das deutsche Leben*.

Personality of Charles IV. By the sudden death of Louis of Bavaria Charles IV. was left master of the situation. Here was a successor all ready to hand; he had been chosen with some show of legality; he belonged to one of the great houses from which the selection must necessarily have been made; his lands, including Bohemia, were nearly as extensive as those of the Hapsburgs themselves. Charles was too little known in Germany to be personally popular; he had spent the greater part of his time in Paris, where he had been educated after the manner of a French prince, and in Bohemia and Italy. He had shown bravery and received a wound on the field of battle, he was not backward in the joust or tourney, but his strongest talent was for settling matters by diplomacy. For this, from Petrarch down, he has been generally decried by all, — accused of lack of heroism and of having the soul of a petty merchant.

When the Germans came to know Charles better, they found that he had a habit of never looking one straight in the face; that, while listening to reports, he seemed to be bending all his energies to whittling wood; that he was

146

hypochondriacal, superstitious, and far too subservient to
the Papacy, through which, indeed, he had been elevated
to the throne.   He was simple in his dress and his personal
wants were few.   Ready and eager to administer justice, he
requested that complaints should be made directly to himself.   For Bohemia he caused to be drawn up an elaborate
code of laws — the *Majestas Carolina* — which his nobles,
however, refused to adopt.   He was zealous in his religious
observances—not from ulterior motives, but from a decided
bent in that direction.   On his frequent journeyings, the
most eager of relic hunters, he caused many a tomb to be
opened that he might kiss the holy remains ; the skulls and
bones of which he acquired possession were splendidly
housed and richly adorned with gems ; when not in use, his
new Bohemian crown habitually rested on the hallowed
pate of good St. Wenceslaus.   In memory of visions that
had once appeared to him he founded monasteries ; and in
his famous autobiography, which he carried down to the
time of his accession, he has much to say of mystic influences.

Not altogether unnaturally, this monarch's heart turned
more fondly to his own hereditary lands than to his German kingdom.   The Emperor Maximilian once spoke of
his predecessor as the arch-father of Bohemia and arch-
stepfather of the empire ; indeed, Charles is quoted as
having said himself that, could he have been sure of being
left in peace within his own dominions, he never would
have stretched out his hand for the German crown.   The
city of Prague was his idol, and he devoted much time
and money to beautifying it.   Here, as a lasting memorial
to his name, he founded the world-famous Carolina — the
great Prague University, the earliest of all such institutions in German-speaking lands and the destined scene of
the labors and sorrows of John Huss.

With the dukes of Bavaria, the sons of the former

*Hapsburg against Wittelsbach.*

emperor, it was only natural that Charles should remain in hostility. They refused to concur in their fate, and were able to procure the calling of an assembly at Lahnstein, at which four men, claiming to be electors, were present. Here the forms of a new election were gone through with, and, to the surprise of no one more than the person most concerned, the vote for head of the Holy Roman Empire fell on Edward III. of England. That Edward never for a moment seriously thought of accepting the proffered honor is shown by the gracious reception he accorded to Duke William of Julier, Charles's own special envoy.

The false Waldemar of Brandenburg.

The latter monarch, for his part, found a means of annoying the Wittelsbachs beyond measure by encouraging a rival claimant to the margravate of Brandenburg, to which office also was attached the electoral vote. Down to 1320 A.D., Brandenburg had been ruled by the descendants of Albert the Bear, a contemporary of Frederick Barbarossa; but in 1319 had died the spendthrift Waldemar, and in the following year, his son, the last scion of the line. Waldemar had been given a sumptuous funeral, pompous and impressive, as a last tribute to his extravagant tastes. After four years of contention between various claimants, Louis of Bavaria had pronounced Brandenburg a lapsed fief of the crown, and had bestowed it upon his own son. Now, after twenty-eight years, the story was diligently circulated that the old Margrave Waldemar was not dead at all; that, conscience-stricken at having offended the church by his marriage with too near a relative, he had determined on a crusade of expiation, and had caused the corpse of another, a wandering conjurer, to be laid in the tomb prepared for himself. Then, taking the pilgrim's staff, he had trudged to Palestine, had for years remained a captive in the hands of the infidels, and, at last escaping, had heard of the woes that had fallen upon the Mark under the Wittelsbach rule, and had determined for the sake of his people to return and resume his sceptre.

Few knew at the time what is well known now, that the real Waldemar had long since obtained a dispensation for his marriage from Pope Clement VI., so that conscientious scruples could scarcely have driven him to such renunciation and penance. In the story itself there was nothing inherently improbable; Count Henry of Schwerin, long given up for dead, had returned after a similar captivity for a similar length of time. To romantic tales in connection with crusades there was no end. The people of the Mark, finally, were not likely to prove over-incredulous when it came to be a question of ridding themselves of a hated ruler. The Wittelsbachs' one idea of ruling had seemed to be to squeeze money out of the nobles and cities of this northern possession, and to spend it for the advantage of Bavaria and the Tyrol.

For the weak and the wavering the decision was made as easy as possible. The elector of Saxony and the counts of Anhalt vouched for the genuineness of this man's claim. According to common report, the Archbishop of Magdeburg had heard the whole story in the confessional, and given his word of honor that this was the real Waldemar. A signet ring played a prominent part in the matter of identification, while facts were repeated which could only have been known to the margrave and his intimates. The pretender must indeed have borne a strong likeness to the person he was counterfeiting, for men of all classes — priests, knights, and squires, declared that this was the prince they had known in their youth. *Acceptance of Waldemar by Charles IV.*

Charles IV. reaped more advantage than any one else from this conspiracy to oust the Wittelsbachs from Brandenburg, though there is not the slightest evidence to show that he was in any way directly concerned with the original imposture. A commission, made up apparently of fair-minded men, was appointed to look into the matter; on the strength of their report that persons who had seen and known the margrave were sure of his identity, Charles invested the false Waldemar with the Mark, having first, however, stipulated that his own share of the spoils should be the Lower Lausitz. The chief conspirators seem to have been Saxony, Anhalt, and Magdeburg, who hoped for the realization of claims of their own. The ceremony of investiture took place in a public assembly held on the heights of Heinersdorf near the road to Frankfort-on-the-Oder. The false Waldemar approached Charles's throne, which was erected on a richly decked platform, and took the oath of homage; the king then bestowed upon him the Mark and the electoral dignity, promising protection against all comers and exhorting the people to accept him as margrave. A number of cities had already handed in their allegiance.

Election of Gunther of Schwarz-burg as anti-king.

As a counter move to these doings in Brandenburg, the Wittelsbachs hastened once more to obtain the election of an anti-king — this time at Frankfort-on-the-Main. They could reckon on the votes of Mainz and of their own relative, the Count Palatine. The head of their house, that Louis who had been ousted from Brandenburg, they naturally considered as still an elector, while the requisite additional vote was gained by recognizing the Duke of Lauenburg as claimant to Saxony. By these four, Count Gunther of Schwarzburg, brave as a knight, but possessed neither of wealth nor of following, was invited to Frankfort, and, after some demurring, done homage to by the citizens. They proved, indeed, his only adherents. Charles IV. soon made one of his master-strokes of diplomacy by offering his own hand in marriage to the daughter of the

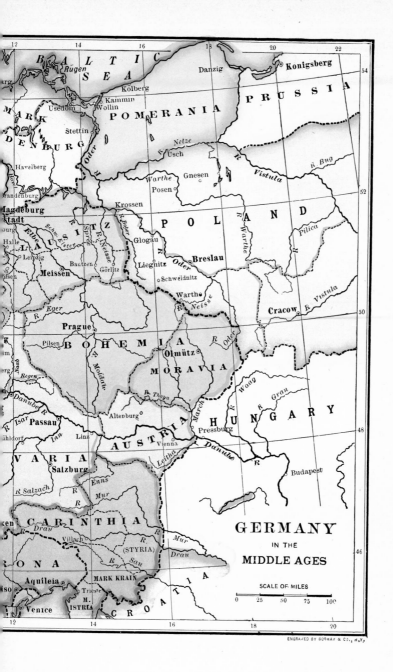

GERMANY
IN THE
MIDDLE AGES

SCALE OF MILES

0    25    50    75    100

ENGRAVED BY BORMAY & CO., N.Y.

Count Palatine, who, in consequence, weakly abandoned Gunther's cause. A short, fortunate campaign rendered the other Wittelsbachs more pliable; concessions did the rest. The dukes agreed to make peace; Charles to let fall the false Waldemar. Gunther had already been overtaken by what proved to be a mortal disease. Having agreed to abdicate, he was borne on a litter to Frankfort, where, before he died, he solemnly released the citizens from their oath.

The Brandenburg matter was not so easily settled; in 1350 A.D. Waldemar was declared an impostor by the Diet of Nuremberg, but not until five years later did he formally abandon his claims. By a treaty with the Wittelsbachs, by half compelling and half bribing, Charles procured the reversion of Brandenburg for his own family. We shall see how one of his sons finally conferred it on the line that has now held it for nearly five centuries. *Settlement of Brandenburg affair.*

If from the larger political events of the reign of Charles IV. we turn to the social developments and striking occurrences, we find this period more remarkable than any of its predecessors. An unheard-of calamity half depopulates Germany, and gives rise to superstitious excesses and wholesale persecution. On the other hand, in these days a document is drawn up, deliberated upon, sealed, and signed, which for the next 550 years is to be the criterion for imperial elections and for the rights and privileges of the electors. *The Black Death.*

Epidemics and even plagues were not infrequent in the Middle Ages, but the most deadly of all such visitations was the Black Death of 1348 – 49 A.D., the same great wave of destruction of which Boccaccio wrote, and which swept England as well as the Continent. Lasting for six or seven months, there were few German towns that escaped its ravages. The rate of mortality was incredibly high, and

Bremen alone, according to statistics drawn up at the time by the *Rath*, or city council, lost seven thousand of her citizens. The sickness was a loathsome one, where even in the most favorable cases the body of the patient was covered with great sores, and where death usually intervened on the third day.

The Flag-
ellants.

In the wake of this plague, and in many cases undoubtedly spreading the infection, came the Flagellants, or flying penitents, calling upon men to repent and to rend their hearts in the face of so evident a judgment of God.    There were scenes of indescribable excitement, and whole populations of towns would march out to meet the fanatics, who would approach in long procession, with flags flying, candles burning, and crosses borne on before, chanting the while the dreariest of hymns and dirges.   Bound by their vow not to stop more than one night in any one city, the Flagellants moved like fleeting spirits from place to place.   In the course of their religious exercises, which were publicly held in the streets, they roused themselves to frenzied pitches of enthusiasm, scourging themselves with flails bound with iron spikes which entered so deeply into the flesh that, as an eye-witness assures us, great strength was required to remove them.   It was easy for the Flagellants to gain recruits : we are told that in Strassburg alone they were joined by a thousand citizens, although their rule was by no means to accept every one who presented himself; husbands had to bring express permission from their wives before their cases would be considered at all.   Distinctive of the sect was their hatred of the clergy, and in so far they were precursors of the Reformation ; indeed, they openly attacked the dogmas of the church and denied to the priesthood its spiritual supremacy. Like all such associations or brotherhoods, the Flagellants degenerated in consequence of too much success.   Vagabonds joined them, in order to gain the nimbus of martyrdom and to be well cared for by generous admirers. But the clergy girded itself for the attack; the Pope banned and proscribed the whole organization as a danger to the state and an insult to the Divine Majesty. The civic authorities and the territorial lords took such stringent measures that before long the whole agitation had entirely subsided.

Not so the general spirit of alarm and unrest among the people. In so far as they had ceaselessly recommended the wholesale massacre of the Jews — who, they declared, had polluted the wells and caused the Black Death — the leaven of the Flagellants continued to work. No darker blot upon mediæval civilization can be found than the relentless persecution of one whole, defenceless part of the population by another, of Jews by Christians. The fanatical attacks upon the Jews had begun at the time of the crusades; until then they had been allowed to live quietly in the towns and to engage in trade like the rest of the inhabitants. In certain towns, like Spires, they had even been given special commercial privileges; they were allowed, too, to hold real estate, to have their own special burial place, to sell meat to Christians, and to have Christian servants. But with the crusades had come in the wild desire to avenge the blood of Christ on all who might be classed among His enemies. Countless stories were invented of sacrilege and murder committed by the Jews; the chronicles tell frequently of children sacrificed or of the bread of the Eucharist stolen and dishonored.

Fanatical attacks on the Jews.

The Hohenstaufen emperors interfered in favor of the Jews, but with the unfortunate result that their legal status came to be that of special dependants on imperial protection, for which protection they were compelled to pay a high tax; *Kammerknechte*, or slaves of the exchequer, was their official title. But one step further, and the theory was formulated that, whenever the specific time for which

Legal status of the Jews.

the protection was granted had elapsed, the emperor might do as he pleased with the belongings of this outcast race. Each new lease of protection meant a new heavy payment; Charles IV. went so far as to farm out these revenues to the cities, which then, in turn, extorted all they could from the luckless victims. Louis the Bavarian had already invented the shameful "golden sacrificial penny" which was retained by his successors. Every individual Jew or Jewess over the age of twelve, and owning more than twenty guldens, was to pay a tribute of one gulden, the collection of which was likewise eventually placed in the hands of revenue farmers. And added to the regular taxes were the still more galling special ones — a policy of oppression that was to reach its climax in the next century, when the Emperor Sigismund demanded that the Jews should pay the expenses of the Council of Constance!

**Insults heaped on Jews.** It is useless to dwell on the frequent slights and indignities that were put upon this people; no amount of details could open up a darker vista than the decrees of the Lateran Council of 1215 A.D. Jews are not to show themselves upon the streets from Maundy Thursday until Easter. Christians are never to eat with them under pain of excommunication. Jews are to dress in such a manner as to be easily distinguishable; they are to buy no fish in Lent lest the prices be increased for fasters.

**The Jews driven to usury.** Is it any wonder that the victims of such a policy became as despicable as even their tormenters could wish? Forbidden to hold office over Christians, forbidden to look on while honorable knights were disporting themselves in the tournament, forbidden even to carry on the commercial enterprises in which they had hitherto been leaders, they sank lower and lower in the social scale. Only one resource was left them, the loaning of money; for centuries the church had pronounced the taking of interest to be usury and had forbidden all Christians thus to soil their hands. Yet borrowing money was an essential part of economic and mercantile advance, and all classes of men, from the emperor down to the knights and students, were at all times heavily in debt to the Jews. Among the objects pawned as security we find state revenues and even church tithes. Efforts were made to restrict the rate of interest, but we find it rarely, if ever, below $21\frac{2}{3}$ per cent, and rising from that to $96\frac{2}{3}$. Strangers, indeed, might be cheated to any extent; a contemporary bond has been preserved that calls for 166 per cent.

If hatred and jealousy had existed before, we can imagine how those feelings increased as the Christians saw these usurers fattening on the sweat of Christian brows, the handsomest dwellings coming into their hands, honorable men absolutely at their mercy. It was all directly opposed to the spirit of the trade guilds, that stood for honest manufactures and for equal profits; and communistic and revolutionary thoughts were already rife in all directions. The legend revived with full force as to how Frederick Barbarossa was to awake from his slumbers in the Kyffhäuser Mountain, and bring salvation to the oppressed, how rich men were to marry poor maidens, and how the clergy were to be made to cover their tonsures, with filth if need be, and go to work as common laborers.

The Jewish massacres of the years 1348 to 1351 A.D. were, then, one phase in what would to-day be termed a socialistic uprising. And barbarous enough were the details of the movement. In Basel the guilds with floating banners marched to the Rathhaus, and wrung a promise from the councillors that they would murder the Jews, and forbid any of the sect to enter the town for the next two hundred years. All the Jews within reach were then locked up in a building on a little island in the

*Jewish massacres.*

Rhine; fire was set to the base of the structure and all the inmates perished. In Spires a regular funeral pyre was erected in the cemetery, and a crowd of victims driven into the flames. In fifty different towns similar scenes were enacted; in some cases the Jews were buried alive; more frequently they ignited their own houses and perished in the ruins rather than fall into the hands of their pursuers.

The crown and the massacres.

It shocks the sensibilities to see the attitude taken by the crown in the matter of all this persecution and violence. There was no attempt to punish the heathenish excesses; in fact, formal charters of amnesty were issued to various towns. The proof, indeed, seems indisputable that Charles IV., even before any uprising had taken place, promised the citizens of Frankfort the ownership of all property that might accrue, should there be a general massacre. After all was over, on the strength of the Jews having belonged to his own exchequer, he claimed all ownerless lands, and even took over the lists of uncollected debts due to the victims. Many of these debts he forgave, but the rest he gave to the cities in return for a fixed sum.

In the end king, princes, and people alike found they could not subsist without these same Jews; their high taxes were too important for the public treasury, no one could be found to replace them in the matter of making loans. Almost immediately the reaction came: a large number of the extant deeds and charters of Charles IV. consist of permissions issued to various nobles, to receive back and tax Jews. Nor did the condition of the latter improve with time; indeed, the regulations concerning the wearing of the "Jew token," or mark of their outcast condition, became more frequent and more severe. In Nuremberg they were obliged to wear a red cap, in Augsburg yellow circles on their clothes. Ever pointed at with the finger of scorn, it is only in the most recent times that they have been able to vindicate their racial abilities.

In the midst of pestilence and of the disturbances caused by the fanatic persecution of the Jews, Charles IV. had not altogether lost sight of the usual goal of German kings, the imperial crown. But whatever steps he took toward acquiring it were marked by his usual caution and clever reckoning. In the spring of 1350 there appeared before *Charles IV.* him a fugitive, but one who for many months had centred *and Rienzi.* upon himself the eyes of the world, and who to-day is far more widely known and remembered than Charles himself. Cola di Rienzi, driven from that Rome where, as tribune of the people, he had displayed so much power and magnificence, came to Prague with the story that a holy hermit had pronounced it the will of God that a divinely chosen saint, aided by the emperor-elect, should divest the clergy of all their influence. He, Rienzi, would lead Charles to Rome, where both might be sure of a hearty welcome.

But Rienzi had made his reckoning without his host. Louis of Bavaria, indeed, had been willing to accept the crown from the hands of the populace; not so this devoted son of the church. After several interviews Charles placed Rienzi under arrest; for a year and a half he kept him near him, and then allowed him to return to Rome by way of Avignon and in company of the papal legate, Cardinal Albornez. The Roman populace received their former demagogue with great rejoicings, but soon after, in October, 1354, stormed his dwelling on the Capitol, and drove him to his tragic death.

Before this, already, while Rienzi was still chafing in *Charles* captivity, a second demand had come to Charles to hasten *IV. and* to Rome and assume the crown. The poet Petrarch, as *Petrarch.* Dante in the case of Henry VII., sent a passionate appeal depicting the wretched condition of the city, and urging him to come and complete the work begun by his grandfather. Charles returned answer that the old Roman Empire was a thing of the past, and could never be resuscitated.

Just how far this attitude was due to a desire to emancipate himself from the sponsorship of a patriot like Petrarch will never be known. Certain it is that Charles was very far from despising the title of Emperor of the Romans; for in 1355, when he found that he could have it in an orthodox way and that Innocent VI. would send legates from Avignon to perform the ceremony, he prepared in earnest for the expedition. Indeed, in return for the glory of the one day in Rome, he consented to recognize all those old pretensions of the popes against which his predecessors had struggled so furiously; his agreement that, in his official capacity, he would not remain over night in the Eternal City, amounted to a renunciation of every claim to jurisdiction. An emperor of the old stamp would never have condescended to steal in, garbed as a pilgrim, that he might enjoy a few days of sight-seeing previous to his coronation. No wonder Petrarch exclaimed that a title thus achieved would prove an empty honor, and in a reproachful letter asked Charles what his father and grandfather would have said could they have met him on the crest of the Alps. Bravery, he declared, was no hereditary quality.

Italian expedition of Charles IV.

At sunrise of Easter Sunday, 1355, the king in purple robes of state prepared to make his entry into Rome. His queen at his side and followed by a brilliantly accoutred escort, he rode in at the gate of Crescentius, conferring knighthood right and left as the procession passed along. Descending from his horse, he mounted the steps of St. Peter's accompanied by prelates and notables. In the vestibule he was received by the Cardinal Bishop of Ostia, the Pope's representative, and by all the clergy of Rome.

Before them he swore the coronation oath, and renewed a number of special agreements; then followed the confirmation of all the possessions, rights, and privileges of the church, the consecration with the holy oil, the celebration of mass, and the placing of the crown on the heads of the new emperor and empress.   Mounted on white chargers which awaited them at the foot of the steps, and sheltered by a magnificent baldachin of silk and gold brocade, they then rode through the densely lined streets of Rome to the sound of the city bells and escorted by all the chief dignitaries.    Gold coins were scattered in profusion among the crowd.   There followed a feast in the Lateran palace, in the midst of which, just as the sun was setting, the emperor rose from table, mindful of his oath to leave the city.

Little glory did the whole course of this Italian expedition bring to Charles; the party-torn cities had looked to him as they once looked to Henry VII., but they were equally disappointed.   Everywhere his policy had been to avoid danger, to side with the strongest in the civic disputes, to temporize and to make treaties which he would not or could not keep.   He had been right from a practical point of view when he declared to Petrarch that the old Roman Empire was not capable of being revived; he for his part did not intend to try.   We soon find him abandoning Italy and deep in the internal affairs of Germany.   He called a Diet of the Empire to meet at Nuremberg with a view to settling various questions — the duties and privileges of the electoral college, the peace of the land, the Rhenish tolls, the general finances of the empire.

The outcome of this Diet was the elaborate document known, from its peculiar seal, as the Golden Bull of the Emperor Charles IV., which, after careful deliberations, was promulgated in the year 1356.   In point of importance it can be compared only to the Magna Charta of England,

*The Golden Bull.*

for its provisions were followed in part down to the end of
the Holy Roman Empire in 1806. Starting out with a
prayer to God, that the Emperor Charles may lead His
people through the pleasant glades of flowering forests
into the holy shades, where the heavenly waters will
quicken the seeds that were sown in the life, and where
the ripe crops will be "cleansed in supernal founts from
all of the thorns they have gathered," the Golden Bull
goes on to point out the evils of discord in a state, declaring that, had it not reigned between Helen and her husband, Troy would never have fallen, nor, but for the
quarrels of Pompey and Cæsar, would the Roman republic have come to an end. And now against the empire,
and, more specifically against its seven columns, the
electors, Envy is "spewing with the ancient poison." In
order, then, to eradicate all occasion of discord, the Bull
goes on to settle definitely certain cardinal matters: the
exact proceedings at elections, the functions of each of the
seven, the order of succession to an electorate, the indi-
visibility of the holdings, the amount of escort to be furnished by those princes through whose lands the electors
may pass on their way to Frankfort. One sees what
sovereigns these men have become; tolls, coinage, and
treasure-trove are to be absolutely theirs; from the judgments of their courts no one can appeal even to the emperor. A crime against their persons, and even a refusal
to provide them with the required escort, is to be punished
as high treason to the empire. Their electorates are to
be hereditary, and now for the first time the laws of reversion are firmly fixed — exactly in what manner, in default
of male progeny, they are to pass to collateral relatives.
Carefully and thoroughly the heirs apparent are to be
educated for their office; with minute precision the languages are enumerated which it will be necessary for them

to learn, and the exact age at which such instruction shall begin.

On the death of an emperor, or king, of the Romans, the Archbishop of Mainz was to summon the electors to Frankfort, but no one of the seven was to enter the city with more than two hundred mounted followers. While the election was going on no other persons, of whatever dignity, condition, or standing were to be allowed admittance, and the citizens were to see to it that the peace was kept and objectionable persons removed. Following the example of the Roman conclaves, the seven were to carry their deliberations to the bitter end; if thirty days should have passed without their having come to an agreement, their sumptuous fare was to be changed to bread and water.

Gladly would Charles have made use of the electoral college as an advisory body in the affairs of the empire. He inserted a clause providing for regular yearly meetings; it was not his fault, but that of the electors themselves, that this remained a dead letter. For the occasional functions in which they would be likely to take part,— imperial courts or assemblies,— the most rigid ceremonial was established; each elector was to have his permanent place in every procession, his regular seat, so much higher than that of an ordinary prince, at every feast. The four secular electors, being at the same time arch-officials of the empire, were on grand occasions to perform their functions, the marshal to ride his horse to the flanks into a heap of oats and distribute them to the first comer, the chamberlain to hold the silver ewers and the fine towel, the seneschal and the cup-bearer to bring dishes of food and a goblet of wine. Doubtless, in arranging such pageants, the effect on the popular mind was fully taken into consideration. When a newly chosen monarch and his seven electors

*Method of election.*

*Ceremonial.*

passed through the streets of Frankfort and took their seats
in the hall, with all its various platforms and tables, it must
have seemed to the onlooker as if all the majesty of the
empire were actually and visibly unfolding itself before his
gaze. The imperial insignia lent their splendor to such
occasions — the crowns of Aix and of Milan, the orb, the
staff, the sceptre, and the sword. The seat of the emperor
in the hall of assembly was always three feet higher than
that of any one else in the room ; on the level immediately
below him sat the empress by herself, lower still the seven
electors, and below them the generality of the princes.

The chief aim of the Golden Bull was to prevent double
or disputed elections ; it seemed as though there could be
no longer the slightest doubt just to whom the votes belonged and how they were to be cast. Yet in the next
half-century came every kind of schism and disagreement.

Charles IV.
and Greg-
ory XI.

If the various regulations of the Golden Bull were of
great importance, still more so was one striking omission.
There is no mention of the Pope, no acknowledgment that
his assent or coöperation was necessary, either in the matter of electing a king of the Romans or of raising him to
the imperial dignity. In spite of the fact that Louis of
Bavaria had been ready to grant almost every claim the
church put forward, the Papacy, in reality, was completely
losing its grip on Germany. When, in 1376, Charles determined to revive the old Hohenstaufen custom of having
his successor crowned in his own life-time, Pope Gregory XI
attempted to assert what he considered his time-honored
rights ; he made the peremptory condition that the emperor
and his son in person should come to Avignon and swear
the same submissive oath that Charles had sworn at his own
election in 1346. They were then to formally petition the
Pope to permit the electors to proceed to the election, and,
finally, to promise that at no time in future should a son be

elected during his father's lifetime without such express permission.

Charles's conduct during this whole affair was most characteristic, and quite of the kind that roused the ire of Petrarch in earlier days. He temporized with Gregory, and held him off until the preparations for the coronation were completed; to the very last he could, with a good conscience, stand up before the electors and tell them that the Pope's consent had neither been asked nor given. But the votes once fairly cast, he determined to stand as well as possible with the Papacy. He sent polite messages to Avignon; he even went so far, now that nothing could be lost, as to compose a writing dated back before the day of the election, in which he asked for the papal sanction. Indeed, a whole correspondence in falsely dated letters took place, the election always being alluded to as about to be held in the future. One is surprised at the lengths to which in his subserviency the emperor was willing to go. He asked for the Pope's "assent, grace, favor, consolation, and benevolence," and, when Gregory insisted on his adding the words "good pleasure," that also he did without scruple. In the midst of these hollow negotiations the Pope died, and soon afterward, in 1378, the great schism broke out in the church, laming its resources and effectually preventing either the Pope at Rome or the Pope at Avignon from interfering in the affairs of the empire.

Whatever one's verdict as to Charles IV.'s character, it must be acknowledged that almost all of his ventures met with success. He had regulated the footing of the crown with the electors; he had not only secured the imperial dignity for himself, but had practically made sure that it would be handed on to his eldest son; he had, finally, brought into his hands larger territorial possessions than

*Charles IV. and Brandenburg.*

any monarch since Henry VI. Starting with Luxemburg
in the west, and Bohemia and Silesia in the east, he had
made it one object of his life to form, as it were, a bridge
across Europe by purchasing numberless estates — the
"Bohemian Islands" they have well been called. In order
to provide for a great heritage in the future, he had
wedded his son, Sigismund, to the heiress of Poland and
Hungary. But his master stroke was the acquisition of
Brandenburg, of which we have already spoken. Discords
had broken out among the Wittelsbachs, and Charles took
the side of the Princes Louis and Otto against a third
brother, Stephen. The emperor had made the stipulation
that, in case both of his allies should die without heirs,
the electorate should pass to his own sons. Louis did die,
and without heirs, whereupon Otto refused to be bound
by that former compact, and Charles determined to go to
war. In the end the matter was peaceably settled; once
more untying his purse-strings Charles bought the right
of succession for some half-million of guldens. Here was
a dynastic appanage such as few of the earlier emperors
had ever enjoyed, but it profited little either to Charles or
to his house. On the emperor's death, in 1378, Brandenburg fell to the share of his second son, Sigismund, who,
bent on making good his claim to Hungary, and wofully
in debt, pawned it ten years later to his cousin, Iodocus
of Moravia, and finally, in 1415, bestowed it on Frederick
of Hohenzollern.

Charles
succeeded
by Wen-
ceslaus.

To Charles's eldest son, Wenceslaus, there passed the
rule over Bohemia and Silesia, as well as the throne of the
empire; but never did prince fail more signally to rise
to the height of his responsibilities. At the time of his
father's death he was only in his eighteenth year. As
he grew older dissipation claimed all his thoughts and
caused him to neglect the weightiest affairs of the empire.

Whatever business he transacted had to be done in the morning before he was entirely overcome with drink.   At decisive moments he was simply not to be found, and no one knew where to look for him.   He was once taken prisoner by his cousin, Iodocus of Moravia, and the Germans knew nothing about it for a considerable period of time.   The administration of Bohemia, and plans for family alliances, kept him from visiting Germany save at very rare intervals.   From 1387 to 1395 he never came at all.   Again and again the electors sent to remind him of his duties, and urged him, if need be, to appoint a regent, or to allow them to form a council or directory.   Their complaints became louder and louder, their accusations more and more violent; it was common talk that this wretched rule must end.   A league was formed among the electors, and joined by all but Brandenburg; conferences and assemblies were held, to which the princes and cities were invited to send delegates.   No attention was paid to a message from Wenceslaus forbidding important deliberations in the king's absence; instead he was warned that, if he did not mend his ways, the electors would consider themselves loosed from their oath of allegiance.   Nevertheless, because his brother Sigismund would not accompany him he remained in Prague, to quote a contemporary, "like a pig in his pen."

At last the crisis came.   In August, 1400, a majority of the electors came together at Lahnstein, whither they had called as witnesses a large assembly of nobles and people. Then sentence of deposition was read against Wenceslaus, on the ground that he was lazy and useless, and that, far from being fit to govern the Holy Empire, he had attempted to dismember it for his own advantage.   He had done nothing to end the great schism in the church, nor had he established peace and order in Germany; he was

*Deposition of Wenceslaus.*

guilty of murder of both laymen and churchmen; he had issued signed blanks to his favorites allowing them to enrich themselves with grants and privileges at the empire's cost.

The best-founded of the charges against Wenceslaus, that of dismembering the empire, was based on the fact that he had sold to Gian Galeazzo Visconti — that Milanese tyrant who had annexed Verona, Vicenza, Padua, and Siena, and was intriguing against Florence — the right to the titles of Duke of Milan and Duke of Lombardy, and permission to bear in his coat of arms the imperial eagle. The price paid had been a hundred thousand guldens; the princes had not been consulted or advised with in any way. On the whole the action of the electors in deposing this worthless king, though technically indefensible, must be considered patriotic and necessary; indeed, in all these trying times, bereft for decades at a time of a proper head, the electoral college showed strength and firmness. The lasting harm of the whole episode was that the first attempt in centuries to have the son elected in the father's lifetime, as in the days of the empire's greatest prosperity, had produced such miserable results.

Rupert of the Palatinate.

The choice of the electors fell now upon Count Rupert of the Palatinate — Rupert the mild, he was called; but a little ferocity would have stood him in better stead. Wenceslaus, indeed, proved but a feeble antagonist, uttering terrible threats which he never carried into execution. A descent upon Italy, however, undertaken by Rupert, harvested him such mockery as to ruin his chances of gaining the respect of the Germans. He, the head of secular Christendom, was defeated by plain Gian Galeazzo Visconti in the first insignificant encounter; his funds ran so low that he had to send his crown to Venice and have it pawned. At home Baden, Würtemberg, and eighteen cities formed the league of Marbach against him and forced him into galling concessions. The Council of Pisa, which had undertaken the reform of the church, laughed at his protest against its proceedings and declared for Wenceslaus.

The year of Rupert's death, 1410 A.D., saw the unique spectacle of three rival emperors over against three rival popes: the Council of Pisa, in setting up a new head of the church, failed, as we shall see, to secure the abdication of the two already in the field; in Germany Wenceslaus returned to the charge, while one party of the electors chose Iodocus of Moravia, another, Sigismund of Hungary, Charles IV.'s younger son. The death of Iodocus, by poison or otherwise, soon cleared the atmosphere, and Wenceslaus compromised with his brother for the consideration of an empty title. *Three emperors and three popes.*

The reign of Sigismund was another long record of disappointment and failure; the best that was in him came out, as we shall see, at the time of the Council of Constance, but even then his achievements were small and his treatment of Huss left a dark blot on his character. He was in the bloom of manhood in those days, brave and handsome. A contemporary has left a description of how, at the time of the great assembly, he one day rode in disguise into the lists, overthrew two antagonists in turn, and then, raising his helm, was greeted by the spectators with rapturous applause. We have descriptions of his kingly presence, his striking, slender, graceful figure, his rich coloring, curly hair, and long beard parted in the middle. He possessed the gift of oratory as few kings before or after, could be denunciatory or persuasive by turns, could unfold a wealth of imagery or draw on a vast store of wit. At least seven languages stood at his disposal, and if, occasionally, he sinned in his Latin quantities, he had more right than *Personality of Sigismund.*

most men to boast that he was *supra grammaticam* — superior to grammar.

But there were shadier sides to this pleasant character. Sigismund, as many people learned to their disadvantage, proved also superior to the ordinarily accepted moral considerations. His officials at home in Hungary had already made up their minds how much they could exact in chancery fees from these rich Germans; throughout his long reign this emperor had a habit of borrowing and not returning that drew down upon him general contempt. A Frenchman who knew him personally avers that men of all nationalities suffered equally at his hands, and that "this man who wants to set the universe on fire and who threatens even the antipodes" is in reality the meanest beggar, ready to accept the smallest favor. We hear of the strangest alternations at court between extreme luxury and extreme shabbiness; we are seriously told how the head of the empire would sometimes go about with patched shoes and with rents in his clothes that showed the skin. We hear, too, alas, of nights spent in carousal and of escapades shocking even to those easy-going times.

Neglect of duty.

Perhaps the most fatal for Germany of Sigismund's characteristics was a propensity to neglect even the most important business. Incredible as it may sound, it was four years after his election before he made his appearance at all in his new empire ; then, indeed, he attempted to reform some of the crying evils, but was soon disheartened by opposition. After a similar failure in 1429 A. D., he retired in a rage to Hungary, intimated to the Germans that if they wished him to hold a Diet they must come to him at Pressburg, and told the Estates, when they protested at his absence, that he had never, as a matter of fact, set much store by the German crown, and had only retained it at the request of the Pope; bread and wine sufficient for his wants he could find at home. Of the twenty years of his reign that followed on the Council of Constance but two and a half were spent in Germany.

How far the general administration of justice suffered from this absence may be imagined when one considers the fact that the supreme court of justice was attached to the king's person. Only the most desperate state of affairs could account for the success of a secret organization like that of the Westphalian peasant court, the Holy Veme. In other parts of the empire the jurisdiction of the territorial lords replaced that of the emperor; for the electorates, indeed, the clause of the Golden Bull *de non evocando* had expressly forbidden all kinds of appeals. The Holy Veme could never have achieved its great fame, both in and outside of Westphalia, had not its methods at first been admirable, its judgments swift and sure. It was a local survival of the old free courts of Carolingian times, where judgment was passed by *Schöffen*, or bailiffs, whose president, or *Freigraf*, was accountable only to the emperor. The Veme concerned itself exclusively with a certain class of crimes, those against "God, law, and honor," and only with cases where a hearing had been denied by other courts. Death by hanging was the usual penalty. It accepted appeals from all parts of Germany.

Sigismund eagerly seized upon the Veme as a means of upholding law and order; he himself became one of the *Wissende*, or initiated. Under him the institution may be said to have reached its most flourishing development; its members were counted by thousands, and many of them were nobles. The most striking peculiarity of the whole was the inviolable secrecy that was demanded and maintained. The *Wissende* formed a great brotherhood, with strict rules and observances, with an elaborate initiation, mystic signs

*The Holy Veme.*

*Procedure of the Veme.*

and tokens, and a special grip.   Strangely enough, a number of formulas for procedure and other acts of the organization have been preserved: the candidate for membership was obliged to swear "to hold and conceal the Holy Veme from wife and child, from father and mother, from sister and brother, from fire and wind, from everything upon which the sun shines or the rain falls, from everything between earth and heaven."   The penalty for betrayal was hanging "seven feet higher than a corrupted, outlawed, ill-doing thief."   The traitor was to be killed at once whenever and wherever found.

Tradition and romance have represented the courts of the Veme as much more terrible than they really were.   We know now that, for ordinary cases, the *Schöffen* came together publicly in the open air, and not, like the terrible Venetian council, behind closed doors, with mummery and masking.   Only on rare occasions, when the most serious matters were in hand, did they go into secret session.   Sentences of death were accompanied by impressive ceremonies, the uttering of a most terrible curse, the throwing out from the assembly of a twisted rope, the spewing from the mouth of every member.

**Decline of the Veme.** When the Veme grew bolder in its attacks, when it began to coerce whole cities and to make war against them, when it dared even to summon before its tribunal the Emperor Frederick III. and all his councillors, it was already well on toward its decline.   It degenerated as the Flagellants had done before it, and doubtless from the same causes.   Its judgments could be bought for pay, and towns regularly hired *Freistühle*, or chapters, to look out for their special interests.

**Death of Sigismund.** But by this time the Emperor Sigismund had long since passed away.   For all his indifference, he had possessed a certain pride in his rank; "See what a king of the Germans can do!" he is said to have exclaimed, as Frederick of Austria, the friend of Pope John XXIII., knelt before him at Constance to renounce all his worldly possessions. When now, at last, in 1437, he realized that death was upon him, he elected to meet his great enemy sitting upright on his throne.   As the cold chill began to pervade his body, he directed that a shroud should be cast over his rich vestments.   He had already given directions that his corpse should remain long upon view; men were to know beyond a doubt that the "lord of all the world" had passed away.

# CHAPTER VIII

## THE TEUTONIC ORDER AND THE HANSEATIC LEAGUE

LITERATURE : Lamprecht gives a good account of the rise and fall of the Hansa and a less good one of the Teutonic Order. See also Prutz. The best monographs on the Hansa are Schäfer, *Die Hansastädte und König Waldemar von Dänemark*, and especially Lindner, *Die deutsche Hanse*. For the Teutonic Order good literature is scarce. I have culled many facts from Voigt, *Geschichte der Marienburg*, and from articles in Sÿbel's *Zeitschrift*.

Independent development of parts of the empire.

THE absence of central predominance in Germany was productive of certain results that were not altogether evil. In the different states that had become almost independent — like Saxony, Brandenburg, and Bavaria — much was being done toward organizing a stable government ; indeed, in those very three the ruling families of the fifteenth century have remained the ruling families ever since. Moreover, room and opportunity were given for certain quite abnormal political formations, like the Swabian League, the Swiss Confederation, the curious theocracy of the Teutonic Order in Prussia, and the great commercial organization known as the Hansa. The needs of the emperors, too, fostered civic independence ; for, in return for pecuniary gifts, there were few privileges that the crown did not renounce. Last but not least, the tide of colonization flowed slowly but steadily on into the Slavic east, until the territory thus acquired more than equalled the rest of Germany. Much of this colonization, which had already made great progress under the Hohenstaufens, was peaceful in its nature ; the Germans, Dutch, and Flemings knew

172

infinitely more about agriculture than did the Slavs, and especially about reclaiming marshy or waste lands, and were simply called in by the native owners and became their tenants. But much of it also was due to fierce wars, undertaken usually in the name of religion and often supported by the funds of crusaders.

Of all civilizing and Germanizing agents none worked greater wonders than did the Teutonic Order in the swamps and wilds of Prussia. Unlike the Knights of St. John and the Templars, from whom they had borrowed their organization and dress, the Teutons, or "Servants of St. Mary of the German House," unfolded the greater and better part of their activity after leaving the Holy Land. Banished from Transylvania by King Andreas II. of Hungary, they had taken part in wars against the heathen Prussians, and, through the efforts of Herman von Salza, the friend of the Emperor Frederick II., had been regularly intrusted with the mission in those lands and endowed with the province of Culm. The knights had made the important condition that they should be responsible directly to the emperor and the Pope, and subject to no intermediate power.

The Teutonic Knights in Prussia.

The first object was to subjugate numerous wild tribes that were scattered over a vast area; in civilization they were centuries behind the Germans, still worshipping in sacred groves and tending a never dying flame. The discipline and determination of the Teutons were at this time magnificent; their vows of chastity, poverty, and obedience were well kept, the slightest infringement being visited by the dreadful "year-penance," by which for the space of a year the culprit was condemned to the life of a slave, allowed no chair, but the hard ground to sit upon, fed for the most part on bread and water, and once a week publicly scourged. At best the life was one of extreme hardship, for the cells in which the brothers dwelt were bare and unheated.

Subjugation of the Prussians.

By the year 1231 the knights had crossed the Vistula and founded the town of Thorn; soon the whole bank of the river as far north as Culm was in their possession; by 1237 A.D. they had reached its mouth and begun spreading along the Baltic; in 1251 Memel was founded, in 1254 the important town of Königsberg. The manner of proceeding was the same that had been practised in Palestine; armies of crusaders sent out by the popes were drilled and led to victory. So soon as a strong point was captured, a fortress was built and a garrison left behind, while the main army pressed ahead, each such little centre in turn enlarging its sphere of power. Some of the conquests were made by water; as early as 1233 the order possessed two ships, the *Pilger* and the *Friedeland* — the oldest German war vessels of which we know the names. The progress was often checked by bloody uprisings and attempts to massacre all Christians, and more than once the whole enterprise was on the verge of failure. But perseverance and enthusiasm at last won the day, and within little more than half a century from the time of their first coming, the rule of the knights was practically undisputed. Such Prussians as were left after all the cruel warfare settled down as a subject people. Colonists from Holland and elsewhere streamed into the land, and by the year 1410 there were ninety-three new cities and fourteen hundred villages.

Administration of the order's lands.

More marvellous even than this triumphal progress was the perfection of the administration that was imposed upon the whole land. Here was an ideal republic, untrammelled by the traditions of neighboring states, or by any of the fetters of feudalism. Where in history can such a proceeding be paralleled? Where elsewhere can we find an established hierarchy settling down, just as they were, upon a conquered land ? The organization of the old order simply expanded into the organization of the new state. The grand master became the head of the whole; the *tressler*, or treasurer, the minister of finance; the marshal, the minister of war. Each knight became commander of a small district, and was bound, as before, to give frequent account of himself to the heads of the order. According to the original statutes, the marshal was to purchase the horses and mules, the armor and weapons, the mantles, undergarments, and leather hose for all the brothers; this he continued to do even as minister of state. But in addition to this a great commerce grew up in the products of the newly acquired lands, which far exceeded the needs of the order. In the year 1263 A.D. Pope Urban IV. issued a bull permitting the knights to exchange or even sell commodities, provided always this were not done for the sake of gain, but merely to get rid of a normal surplus. As the resources increased, and the demand for grain, wax, and amber required larger and larger exports, the clause in Urban's bull became more and more onerous, until at last the brothers helped themselves, as many a mediæval saint and abbot had already done before them, by forging a new bull which omitted the objectionable passage. The revenues became considerable, for in addition to the commercial gains there were imposts and duties; old ledgers and exchequer accounts show that these alone amounted yearly to some five million marks of modern German money. Works of considerable magnitude, extending over many years and requiring the services of skilled engineers, were undertaken, and immense tracts of land reclaimed.

The building of the castle of Marienburg, on the delta of the Vistula, was of great importance for the future of the order, forming as it did a centre for all the different

The Marienburg.

commanderies.  Striking enough it was, with its lofty
walls and its great statue of the Virgin, twenty-six feet
high, which to this day looks out protectingly upon the
landscape.  Here, in September, 1309, the grand master
held his solemn entry, abandoning the beauties of Venice
for the rigors of the North.  Here, too, an active, bustling
life began to unfold itself, potentates and knights journeying thither, partly out of curiosity, partly to help in those
wars against the heathen Lithuanians which now became
the order's holiest object.  So much dreaded was this
enemy that, on the lands adjacent, belts of impenetrable
forest were left standing, and every avenue of approach
was fortified and guarded.  But the missionary zeal of
the Teutons was not to be daunted; Lithuanian captives
were very serviceable as drawers of water and hewers of
stone, and thousands of them were set to work on fortresses and city walls.

Winrich
von
Kniprode.

The golden age for the Teutonic Order fell in the time
of the Grand Master Winrich von Kniprode, who, from
1351 to 1382, wielded a firm sceptre; those were days
when agriculture and trade were flourishing at home and
armies were successful in the field.  Winrich had ceased
to depend on crusaders and mercenaries, and had raised a
force of native Prussians.  The brethren themselves were
particularly trained in all the arts pertaining to defence;
regular archery practice was introduced, wooden birds
being set up on poles as targets.  But more than all this,
Winrich made the Marienburg a centre for science and
learning.  "Many people of distinction," says a chronicler
of the time, "declared that in no other land had they
seen such wise, sensible, learned people, and so skilled in
the law."  Winrich had founded a Latin school which he
maintained at his own cost.  Altogether the knights had
reason to be thankful for having obeyed the supernatural

voice that is said to have spoken out at the election and turned the votes on this candidate.

Soon after Winrich's death we find the order famous for its gun foundry and also for its falcon training. These birds were sent all over Europe as tokens of regard from the grand masters, while orders for artillery came from great distances. Gunpowder, too, was manufactured in quantities, and the tressler's accounts show large sums expended on saltpetre.

All through the fourteenth century the order flourished and grew in strength, but the old singleness of aim, the old simplicity, was gradually vanishing. Step by step we can trace the descent to Avernus. The entertainments at the Marienburg become more magnificent; we hear of princes and knights from the ends of the world being received and feasted in royal style; we hear of banquets that lasted two days and two nights, of fiddlers and trumpeters, rope-dancers and conjurers, leaders of tame bears and stags. At the beginning of the fifteenth century we find the good Grand Master Conrad of Jungingen contending against this too great luxuriousness of his knights, against the number and price of their horses, their inability to practise self-denial. They, for their part, began to mock at his preachings and to write satiric verses on the wall, telling him that he had better become a monk or nun. The license became broader and broader; the court jester dubbed Grand Master Conrad "Madam Abbess," and on one occasion threw into a ditch the image of the Virgin Mary, because, as he said, she had not graced with her presence a certain frivolous assembly. *The order degenerates.*

By this time the expeditions into Lithuania had ceased, after having degenerated into the merest hunting parties arranged to give pleasure to some distinguished guest. The order kept its scouts or pathfinders to track the *Lithuanian heathen hunts.*

enemy like bloodhounds. Under their guidance the forest would be crossed and a descent made upon some quiet settlement; the men would be slain and the women and children dragged into captivity. Such raids always ended in feasting and self-glorification and in wholesale dubbing of knights. Yet shameful as was this border warfare against a weak, defenceless enemy, its sudden forced termination proved an insupportable blow to the Teutonic Order. So long as the Lithuanians remained heathen there was a pretext at least for the order's activity, an excuse for its continued existence and for the maintenance of its many and great privileges. But the rational occupation of the knights vanished forever when, in 1386 A.D., Prince Jagiello of Lithuania married the heiress of Poland, united the two countries under his own sceptre, and imposed Christianity as the state religion. The weak neighbors had become part of a strong nation, and the wars with Poland fill the greater part of the order's remaining history.

The battle of Tannenberg, against the Poles.

Conrad of Jungingen had done his best to stave off these conflicts, though constantly opposed by his thoughtless knights, who little dreamt what disaster and servitude would be the outcome. As long as he lived, indeed, Conrad managed to withstand these influences; but he could not provide for what might happen after his death. "Do not choose my brother," he said on his death-bed, " though he is a fearless, brave warrior and bold hero; for I fear his wild thirst for war will plunge the whole order into irreparable woe." But a time of panic came, the warning was forgotten, and when the army of the order marched out Ulrich of Jungingen was in command. The largest cannon ever yet seen in Germany had been forged for this war; but the battle fought on the Polish frontier, near the village of Tannenberg, in 1410 A.D., was the most disastrous the order had ever yet fought. Grand Master Ulrich himself fell in the fight; the contemporary estimate of the numbers of the slain is too enormous for belief. The Prussian lands lay open to the Polish hordes, and fortress after fortress surrendered, until at last the invading army came under the walls of the Marienburg itself. By taking this, King Vladislas, as his own chroniclers tell us, hoped to put an end to the whole Teutonic Order.

But this time the Virgin Mary showed herself the best of patron saints, for there sprang into the breach one of the bravest knights of whom the order ever boasted. Hastening from the field of Tannenberg, Count Henry of Plauen had ridden into the castle ahead of the Poles, and had taken command. Determined to save what could still be saved he levelled all the surrounding buildings, offering the shelter of the Marienburg to all fugitives. So successful were his efforts that the Poles charged in vain from all sides; their shot recoiled against the heavy walls, but not without inflicting serious damage. Through the window of the Grand Master's hall crashed a great ball of stone, and lodged in the wall over the mantel, where it has remained embedded to this day.

Grand Master Henry of Plauen.

The force and cunning of the enemy alike failed of their effect, the frequent sorties of the garrison wrought havoc and dismay; starvation and sickness of man and beast did the rest. One by one the Polish contingents melted away, and after two months the siege was raised. Amid loud rejoicings Henry of Plauen was elected grand master, but his rule was destined to be short. The order was terribly impoverished, yet money was needed for everything, for repairs, for the payment of mercenaries, for the ransom of prisoners. As the iron hand of taxation descended upon them many of the knights became bitter and dissatisfied; a conspiracy was even formed to take the life of this stern taskmaster, although no one could ever have said that he in any way spared himself. In the end his enemies succeeded in having him called to account by a conclave of the chapter. Declared deposed and banished to a lesser commandery, he was then accused of secret dealings with the Polish king and was placed in a strong prison. For years the rescuer of the Marienburg lived in a lonely castle on the seashore, reduced to abject misery. A letter of his is extant in which he begs a later grand master for mercy, or at least for sufficient food and drink.

**Poverty of the order.** The order was indeed by this time very far downward on its way to the condition in which Martin Luther found it, "a thing serviceable not to God and not to man." Poverty was the worst curse of the once wealthy brotherhood; indeed, future generations could not believe that so much treasure had simply vanished, and frequent excavations have been made to find where it was buried. The granaries were nearly empty, and all appeals to the princes of Europe proved in vain. There came a time when a grand master had to literally beg for "a jewel, a relic, or anything at all that is decent and honorable" with which to requite the Danish king for a load of herring. In spite of small fluctuations of improvement, the flourishing days were gone forever; the Veme Gericht began to encroach on the order's jurisdiction, and its only resource was to have the burgomaster and one of the councillors of the town of Marienburg initiated into the dreaded court.

**Ruin of the order.** Disputes with its Prussian subjects sealed the order's ruin. It became clear that its yoke, however light, had always been regarded as a foreign one; there had been little murmuring so long as the knights had been true to their mission, but they were looked upon now as mere dissolute idlers. There was defiant murmuring at the heavy grants that were asked for in order to pay the indemnities to Poland, and wild revolt when resort was had to trickery and violence. Two of the burgomasters of recalcitrant Danzig were lured into one of the order's castles and put to death. The result was a formal league of the Prussians, an appeal to the emperor's court, and a regular trial before Frederick III. When the latter declared the league unlawful, the last fatal step was taken: the insurgents called in the aid of the Poles, who eventually occupied every castle in the land. Never did a once flourishing state so completely compass its own destruction. The war lasted for thirteen years, and the country was devastated from end to end. Danzig, Thorn, Elbing, and finally the Marienburg itself fell into Polish hands; by the Treaty of Thorn in 1466 half the land was annexed absolutely; the other half became a vassal dependency, the first duty of each new grand master being to swear the oath of allegiance to the order's old enemy.

At one point and one only did the Teutonic Order come into very close touch with the rest of Germany, and that was in the development of its cities; those along the Baltic became particularly important, and formed one whole group or quarter of the Hanseatic League. Danzig was one of the busiest ports on the whole continent of Europe.

*From rural to civic life.*

The great change from rural to civic life took place in Germany in the thirteenth century; the question has been raised whether the revolution of ideas was not greater at that time than even in the fifteenth century, with its compass, its gunpowder, and its printing-press, or in the nineteenth, with its steam and railroads. As Schmoller has pointed out, the transition was certainly a startling one from peasant communities to towns of fifty thousand inhabitants, from rural huts to the Strassburg cathedral, from country bartering and payments in kind to the use of money and bills of exchange, from exclusively ecclesiastical culture to the reading and writing of the masses, from monastic workers to civic artisans.

Burgher *vs.* knight. Among the German cities, particularly in the south and west, some sixty of the most flourishing grew to be free or imperial, owing allegiance to no one but the head of the empire, and securing his protection and the management of their own affairs by the payment of fixed sums. Such were Nuremberg, Augsburg, and Ratisbon, Ulm, Strassburg, and Frankfort-on-the-Main. Here centred eventually all industry, all wealth, and all refinement; the decisive rôle in history passes over from the knight to the burgher. The former finds it hard to acquiesce in his fate, and with a grim sense of being wronged takes to robbery and plunder. The *Raubritter*, the man who depends on fist-right for a living, becomes as distinct a type as ever the knight-errant or professional jouster. From behind his strong walls he descends on the cattle of the farmer or the goods-train of the merchant, or carries off their persons and demands a large ransom, leaving them in damp vaults until occasionally their very legs rot off — indeed, to "rot a peasant" becomes a well-known proverb in the language. The knights themselves only saw the humorous side of the matter, and gloried in such names as "hedge-rider," "highwayman," "bush-clapper," "pocket-beater," and "snap-cock."

Unsanitary condition of the cities. The proportions of the cities were generous compared to their population; the walls often enclosed gardens, vineyards, and pastures, and even miniature forests. Many of the old laws concern themselves with the pigs that were kept by private families. Frankfort in 1387 decreed that sties might not be built in the public streets, while Ulm in 1410 required its swine to be locked up except between the hours of eleven and twelve. The want of cleanliness was universal, and to this cause is attributable much of the sickness that was prevalent. There was no paving, no drainage, until nearly the end of the Middle Ages. The foulest matter, including dead animals, was allowed to collect, and was only removed on grand occasions. When the Emperor Frederick III. entered Reutlingen, in 1485, horse and rider all but disappeared in the bottomless filth. The state of the roads was a valid excuse for not attending the sessions of cathedral chapters, and wooden overshoes were such a part of every man's daily equipment that in the pictures by the old masters even the saints are made to wear them.

Even had we no other means of knowledge, we could form our opinion of the cities of the fourteenth and fifteenth centuries from the churches, city halls, and private dwellings, the bridges, fountains, and stone Rolands that still exist. The high walls were flanked with numerous towers — Munich had a hundred, Frankfort nearly seventy — and pierced by handsome gates. Within those carefully guarded confines was passed a busy, joyous life that was not thought of elsewhere ; old feudal distinctions were battered down, and even runaway bondsmen became free if they could prove that they had breathed the air of a town for a full year. *Fine buildings.*

The rule of the civic authorities, indeed, was strict, and their right of interference with men's private affairs practically unlimited. Every article bought or sold was subject to their inspection, and bakers whose bread was not up to the mark were ducked under water. For certain cases of fraud the penalty was death ; for other offences men were flogged, publicly mutilated, or exposed to the general view in iron cages. Blasphemers were tweaked with red-hot tongs, forgers boiled in oil, with cold water now and then poured in to prolong the agony. *Vigilant administration of the cities.*

The city watched over its inhabitants to see that they were not too extravagant, that they did not live beyond their means; it provided that at weddings only so many guests might be invited — in Frankfort, in 1350 A.D., the number was fixed at twenty, while a hundred years later it was extended to fifty, exclusive of spinsters, foreigners, and servants. But also the cost of wedding presents was restricted, even totally forbidden at times in Rothenburg, Ulm, and Nuremberg. In the duchy of Würtemberg, in 1400, it was enacted that parents, brothers and sisters, and brothers-in-law and sisters-in-law might give whatever they pleased, but that, with regard to others, the limit for married couples should be seven shillings, and for widowers, three. In Frankfort, in 1489, we find a rich patrician obtaining the formal consent of the city council before making as large a present as he would have done had his wife been still

Dress regulations. alive. Still more common was the interference of the authorities in the matter of dress; one of the first symptoms of civic prosperity had been a love of display, and the natural bad taste of the people had led them into curious excesses. Not content with wearing garments which did not accord with each other, they took to dividing the colors on their cloaks, their hose, and their shoes. One leg would be pink, another green. On festal occasions men wore silks and satins embroidered with gold and silver and adorned with pearls and other jewels. The borders were hung with little bells, an ornament much in vogue. The city councillors saw to it especially that in this matter of dress no one class of the population infringed on the rights of another; servants and apprentices in Frankfort, in 1453, might not wear "colored shoes with points or beaks"; while in Ratisbon, in 1485, none but the authorities themselves might appear in silks, in satin, or in damask. The different garments a person might own were often enumerated, while women were stopped in the street on the charge of wearing longer trains than were legally allowed — matters with which not only the local laws, but even the imperial edicts, concern themselves.

Of all civic institutions none affected the life of the people more closely than the guilds, great organizations embracing all the artisans of a given trade, with a rigid division into masters, apprentices, and servants. The guilds enjoyed, not only a commercial monopoly, but a political power so great that the old native patricians who held all the places in the *Rath*, or council, were almost everywhere obliged to give away before them. "The labor leagues and associations," writes an old chronicler, "are formed to the end that the whole life of the members may be ordered according to Christian discipline and love, and the work itself be consecrated." Brotherly love and fidelity were required by the statutes; mutual support was assured, and the more unfortunate were assisted from the general treasury. "Who does not help to bury his deceased brother," runs one of the articles, "and does not pray for the salvation of his soul, has broken the word he plighted at his entry into the guild." *The guilds.*

In Lübeck in the middle of the fifteenth century there were seventy different guilds, in Cologne eighty, and in Hamburg more than a hundred. In Nuremberg the weavers had their own quarter; in Augsburg, in 1466, they could boast of no less than 743 members. No one might ply his craft who had not joined one of these leagues, for their power was absolute. The guild provided all raw material; it determined the rate of wages and the amount of production, and tested the finished work. It prescribed what agreements the master should make with his apprentice, and directed that he should stand to him in the place of a parent; "he shall lodge, feed, and care for him day *Purpose and province of the guild.*

and night, and shut him in with lock and key." He must see that the apprentice is honorably brought up and that he goes to church; should he be "wanting in the fear of God and in obedience, he shall punish him severely; that does the soul good; the body must suffer pain that the soul may prosper." If, through negligence of the master, on the other hand, the apprentice shall have failed to learn his trade, he shall be handed over to a more worthy instructor at the cost of the first one, who, in addition, must pay a fine.

All-embracing activity of the guilds.

To enter into the spirit of these most characteristic of mediæval organizations one must see them from all sides; work, religion, mysticism, and pure joviality all form part in their composition. Each guild had its patron saint, its private altar in the cathedral, or often its own chapel, where masses were said for the living and the dead. The members had their grip and their signs and their lodges in different towns, where by making themselves known they would be sure of free entertainment. The feeling of solidarity was very strong; the brothers were bound by their vows *in Lieb und in Leid*, in love and in sorrow; the authority exercised, too, was very real. Regular courts were held that could inflict pecuniary penalties, and the legislation went so far as to punish even a matrimonial *mésalliance*. The wife of a master, says a decree of 1459 A.D., must be of honest and lawful birth and of German origin. Just as it had its hospital, so the guild had its own prison. Its festivals, too, were of frequent occurrence and lasted for several days. When war broke out, and the great bell called the people to the city walls, the members marched out together and formed a separate division in the army.

In time, as intimated, bitter conflicts arose between these democratic organizations and the old predominant aristocratic elements, and they ended usually in the fall of the latter. These struggles took place all over Germany, but were not always bloody; it often happened that for a sum of money the guilds could obtain the privileges they coveted of representation on the *Rath*, and a voice in the disposal of the public funds. At times, however, actual war was waged with brutal ferocity; in Magdeburg, in 1302 A.D., ten guild aldermen were burnt at the stake. Conflicts with patricians.

All through the time of these internal troubles the cities were obliged to wage war against the knights and princes, and, occasionally, against the emperors. Their ever recurring demand was for an acknowledgment of their claim to be considered an estate of the empire, and to be given a vote equal to that of the ecclesiastical and secular princes. The latter, for their part, complained that the towns were attracting a number of their subjects, who nominally became citizens, — *Pfahlbürger* or "stockade citizens," they were called, — but in reality retained their old possessions. As a means of putting through their demands, many of the towns joined the Swabian League, but the victory of the princes at Doffingen, in 1388, gave the death-blow to the whole movement so far as South Germany was concerned.

The most legitimate and the most successful of all these civic leagues was one formed, not for political purposes, but for the better carrying on of commerce with foreign lands. The early trader who went beyond the confines of his own town had almost inconceivable difficulties with which to contend. He was fair prey for almost any one he might chance to meet. On land he was subject to highway robbery, and, worse still, to the barbarous custom that allowed the ruler of a district to appropriate any vehicle, with its contents, that came to grief within his boundaries. This claim extended to any article that might chance to have Dangers and trials of the guild merchants.

fallen off. Still worse was the condition of things at sea, for piracy was carried on, not merely by the offscourings of society, but by men of rank in organized bands. And the so-called strand law was fully as burdensome as the evil customs on land. Not only did a ship that was wrecked upon the shore, together with its cargo, fall to the owner of the coast, but the persons and belongings of all the crew were his to do with exactly as he pleased. They were his perquisite, as much a part of his revenue as treasure-trove or any other unexpected yieldings of his land. Even scows that temporarily ran aground were subject to the same rule, while in Höchstädt, in 1396 A.D., a claim was entered for a whole ship's cargo because of one single cask that had floated away.

That these evils were not sporadic is proved by the many local laws on the subject; the town of Lübeck, up to the year 1312, had already signed twenty-one strand-law treaties. The shores of the North Sea were particularly dreaded because of the constant changes being worked by the water in the friable banks; new islands rose up unexpectedly, and in 1277 a whole immense bay, known as the Dollart, was formed by the washing away of an intervening strip. And, to make these natural dangers still worse, it was not unusual for avaricious coast dwellers, by false lights and signals, to entice vessels on to the rocks, or to purposely refrain from offering help to those in distress. At best, lighthouses were rare, charts unknown, and compasses of very imperfect construction.

Necessity of coöperation.

There were other reasons, too, which rendered it natural, nay, imperative, that traders should unite for mutual protection. The owner of a single ship, if he stopped at a foreign port, was apt to be subjected to the most unjust and oppressive taxes. There would be thrown in his way impediments to further trade like the so-called staple law, which forbade his passing through a given town, — say to a larger and better market, — without first offering his goods to the local burghers. The home traders, who only admitted him at all because he brought products they could not obtain in any other way, were apt to receive him with envy and hatred.

Everything tended to consolidation. These merchants, for the most part, were God-fearing men. They needed common churches where they could register their vows at setting out, or return thanks for blessings received; they needed courts of justice to decide quarrels and legalize transactions, and to regulate weights and measures. It was necessary to have treaties with foreign countries to prevent the hurtful custom of reprisals, as well as to secure the property of men dying abroad for their rightful heirs at home. Out of all these various needs arose the great organization known as the Hanseatic League, the members of which could be either individuals or whole cities. It was a very gradual growth — a development, indeed, from earlier associations. For centuries a brisk trade had been kept up with England, and the city of Cologne, especially, had possessed important privileges in that country. The Osterlings, too, merchants from the cities along the Baltic, had been welcome visitors, their credit standing so high that the pound Osterling, or sterling, and Osterling silver, became the model unit of full weight.

Hansa was the common term used for a commercial union of cities, and many such unions had already been formed, the earliest of which we have record being one between Hamburg and Lübeck, in 1241. The crisis with Denmark, of which we shall speak later, brought about the general and more famous confederation. At no time, indeed, did the league in any way resemble a political

The first Hansas.

organization; it possessed no central fleet or army, no common treasury, seal, standard, or flag. Nor did it ever attempt to punish secession otherwise than by pronouncing the Hansa ban; a sort of ostracism for a long period which was only terrible if it happened to maim the trade of the city concerned. Individual citizens, indeed, who broke rules or treaties were subject to fines which might be so large as to utterly impoverish them, and even to arrest.

**Membership of the league.** The membership of the league varied from year to year, cities often being allowed to withdraw and afterward to return. Indeed, there existed certain smaller organizations within the large one, each with an important city at its head. We find three, and later four, divisions, known as quarters: the Wend quarter under Lübeck, the Saxon under Brunswick, the Cologne under Cologne and the Prussian-Livonian, which included the prosperous cities of the Teutonic Order, under Danzig.

**Extent of the league.** The Hanseatic League soon gained for itself a practical monopoly of all the commerce of the Baltic and of the North Sea, and numbered at its greatest some seventy-seven cities. It made treaties with all the more important commercial powers, and must be credited with the performance of a great civilizing task, abating many of the inconveniences, nay, horrors, that had hitherto hampered foreign trade, and opening up communication in every direction. Its vessels sailed out in fleets some thirty or forty strong and regularly accompanied by a man-of-war.

**Pirates.** The pirates, indeed, seemed rather to increase in boldness as the years went on; we hear of a considerable band of them who, from 1390 onward for nearly fifty years, were a terror to the European coasts from Reval to the Bay of Biscay. As late as 1491 we hear of a wicked escapade of a Duke of Holstein, who fitted out a ship and sailed in all directions, taking whatever booty came in his way. The

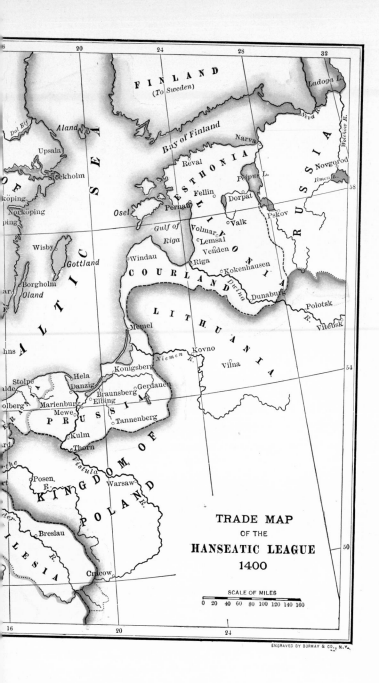

TRADE MAP

OF THE

HANSEATIC LEAGUE

1400

SCALE OF MILES

0  20  40  60  80  100 120 140 160

league kept regular police-boats in certain neighborhoods, and at times, when this did not suffice, sent out really warlike expeditions. The culprits once caught, their punishment was such as might well have deterred others from following their example. In 1401 the Hamburg fleet, one of the ships of which is known to have rejoiced in the name of the "gay-colored cow," took captive Hans Störtebeker and his crew after a sharp fight, and brought them to Hamburg to be executed. The story runs that Störtebeker offered to ransom himself with a gold chain, to be made from hidden treasure, which should reach around the city walls. This being refused, his last request was that so many of his companions might be pardoned as his body might run past after the head was cut off. He had reached the fifth, when the executioner, ill pleased at losing so many victims, threw an obstacle in his way that tripped him up.

Numerous indeed must have been the ships that plied in the name of the Hansa, even though we discard the estimate of an unusually sober modern historian, according to which from four to five hundred sail passed daily in and out of Danzig harbor. The vessels were often of considerable size — built broad and solid, and with high bows and sterns. The *Peter of Danzig*, in 1474, possessed a crew of four hundred men, and many others outrivalled her in this regard. These ships were never mere common carriers; their owners often sailed along with them, having purchased their cargo in one port with a view to selling it in another. The discipline on board was strict; some regulations that have come down to us for one special ship of the sixteenth century provide that there shall be no swearing by God's name, no mentioning of the devil. It was a serious offence to sleep through prayer-time or to play at dice or cards after sundown. The sailors were not to be hin-

*Number and style of ships.*

dered in the performance of their duty, and care was to be taken not to annoy the cook.

Products traded in. It is not uninteresting from the point of view of the civilization of the time to look at the sort of products the Hansa ships carried in their holds. In general these consisted of raw materials. Furs were in great demand, not merely for their serviceableness, but because, in a way, they were tokens of rank. To this day, we associate ermine with princely magnificence. Then, as now, the best skins came from Russia, with which there had long been a brisk trade. "Furs are as thick as manure there," — writes an old chronicler, Adam of Bremen, — "to our damnation, I fear, for by fair means or foul we try to get at a garment of martin skin as if it were our eternal salvation." Adam is sure that from all this comes the "deadly poison of sumptuousness and pride."

Some of the products then popular have since lost their importance; enormous quantities of wax went for seals to parchment deeds, and for candles to be used in churches. With Protestantism, too, amber rosaries, which once fairly glutted the market, have gone out of use. The trade in beer was very large, for it took the place of tea and coffee, and was consumed by rich and poor. We find fourteen casks a year set aside for the use of each of the nuns in one of the convents. The Hanseatic League paid great attention to correctness of measure, weight, and quality, and strange enough was the test which in some neighborhoods was applied to beer. It was smeared over a bench on which a man with leather breeches was made to seat himself; only in case, on rising, the bench adhered to him, would the specimen pass muster.

Trade with England. To England the Hansa ships carried woods for many purposes, but especially for the crossbows that did such excellent service against the French; furthermore, grain, of which it is calculated there were sent yearly six or seven hundred cargoes. The ships brought back woollen manufactures, silver, and tin from the mines of Cornwall. In London, as at Novgorod, Wisby, and on Schonen, the league had one of its famous permanent settlements — "courts" or "factories," as they were commonly called. The right to establish them was purchased from the various governments, and the high yearly taxes that the merchants paid made them welcome to those in authority, if not always to the native traders. To Edward III. these foreigners within his gates became almost indispensable. During the war with France they furnished immense loans, on one occasion redeeming the crown jewels, which had been placed in pawn. In return they obtained valuable privileges, as, for instance, the almost exclusive right to export English wool.

The "courts" consisted of enclosed spaces of considerable size in which were buildings of different kinds — warehouses, salesrooms, lodgings for the merchants, hospitals, breweries, and the like. The settlement, which was owned by the Hansa as a whole, in perpetuity, and was practically independent of the laws of the land in which it happened to lie, possessed its own docks, and usually its own churches. These latter, being solidly built, served occasionally as repositories for the more valuable goods. The Steelyard, as the court in London was called, was situated on the Thames, above London Bridge, and was strongly fortified — a necessary precaution against popular tumults, which more than once occurred. Contrary to the usual rule of the Hansa, the alderman or chief official of the Steelyard was always a London citizen. Occasionally, as we shall see, the Hansa merchants were altogether banished from England, and the Steelyard was taken from them, but they always regained it in time. Even when, in

*The courts or yards. The Steelyard.*

1666, the great fire of London swept away all of their
buildings, they clung to the land on which they had stood,
and hastily erected shops which, as their own trade was by
this time ruined and their league was reduced to the cities
of Hamburg, Bremen, and Lübeck, they rented to others.
In 1853 they sold their site for £72500 sterling, and
where their settlement once stood, one now alights from
the Cannon Street railway station.

Discipline<br>of the<br>" courts."     These Hanseatic courts, as far as their internal organization was concerned, present one of the most curious and
interesting phenomena of the later Middle Ages.   Monas-
ticism and practical commercialism seem here to have met
and agreed upon a compromise.   The religious element
is never wanting; in some of the courts clergymen were
regularly installed, while large expeditions carried their
own pastors.   All of the settlements were under aldermen
who, in some of the courts at least, had jurisdiction over
life and limb — power to execute murderers or to mutilate
those guilty of assault and battery.   Ordinary disobedience
was punished by expulsion.   The *esprit de corps* was carefully guarded ; there was at one period, at least, to be no
associating with the people of the country, although in
London we find the members of the Steelyard as a body
taking part in public functions and occupying places next
in rank and honor to the civic officials themselves.   During
his period of service the merchant might not marry, nor
might women enter the confines of the court.   We even
hear of vows of celibacy administered for as long a period
as ten years.

The members were divided into three classes: masters,
apprentices, and servants or " children," each class sitting
by itself at table.   The occupations of the day were prescribed with monastic regularity — so many hours for
work, so much time for pleasure.   At an early hour the

gates were closed, and all were obliged to betake themselves to bed. Heavy fines were placed on drunkenness, dice-playing, and immorality. In other ways more license was allowed; the entrance of new members into a court was accompanied by initiatory rites of incredible severity and cruelty; we hear of men half suffocated in noxious smoke and then thrown suddenly into ice-cold water. In vain the Hansa diets passed laws upon the subject.

Aside from the London Steelyard the principal Hanseatic courts were in Wisby, Novgorod, Bergen, and on Schonen; in Bruges and Antwerp the league had rights and privileges and even separate buildings, but no monopoly of trade as in other places. Indeed, the Germans met here with entirely different problems, with a rich set of merchants who lived in almost royal magnificence, with methods of trade better than their own, with cosmopolitan interests of every kind. These Flemish towns were the mediums through which the goods of the South were exchanged for the goods of the North; here Genoese and Florentines, Spaniards and Portuguese, met with the Germans on common ground. The latter learned to appreciate the artistic side of life, and we soon find their guild halls at home adorned with the rarest works of Flemish and German masters. Cologne had two Holbeins; Danzig, Hans Memling's *Last Judgment*, which the town still possesses. The latter picture, indeed, was one of the prizes secured by the good ship *Peter of Danzig*, which during the English War of the Roses went out with letters of marque and captured a Florentine galley on its way from Sluys to England, whence it had doubtless intended to carry the treasure to the rich gallery of the Medicis.

From 1568 onward the league possessed in Antwerp a rich palace of its own, with two great halls and a hundred

Various " courts."

Antwerp.

and fifty smaller apartments.   But the town lost its trade
during the terrible wars with the Spaniards, and in 1593
all the valuable books and documents of the Hansa were
removed to Cologne.   The remnants of the league clung
to their possessions in Antwerp, however, and in 1862 sold
the *domus Hansæ Teutonicæ* to the Belgian government
for a million francs.   In 1893 the venerable building was
totally destroyed by fire.

Wisby.

Interesting monuments of the Hansa are still to be seen
in Wisby, on the island of Gotland.   The city walls are still
standing, 11,200 feet in length.   They were flanked by forty-
eight towers, the great majority of which were from 60 to 70
feet high.   The town had always a reputation for immense
riches; the very hogs ate out of silver troughs, at least so
King Waldemar of Denmark told his soldiers when urging
them, in 1361 A.D., to descend upon the island.   According
to an old tradition, such fiery carbuncles were set in the
rosette-shaped ornaments on the church of St. Nicholas
that sailors at night steered their ships by their gleam.
St. Nicholas was but one of eighteen churches built by
the Hansa merchants; all of them now lie in ruins save
two, which are still used for their original purpose.

The fish-
eries of
Schonen.

A Hansa court of great interest, yet differing from all
others in character, was that on the peninsula of Schonen;
here the one object of trade was the herring, and the season
of activity was very short.   The fish ran in to spawn in
such quantities that the schools covered miles of area, yet
so closely were they pressed together that they could raise
a small boat out of the water.   Hither in late summer and
early autumn came men and women to the number of
twenty thousand, eager to engage in what, all in all, was
the Hansa's chief industry.   It is difficult to realize now,
when half of Europe no longer observes the church's fasts,
what those cheap, salted fish meant to the Roman Catholic

of the Middle Ages. For forty days they were his chief staple of diet, and doubtless the law forbidding Jews to purchase them during that time was salutary and necessary. A monopoly of the trade might otherwise have resulted.

Suddenly, in 1560 A.D., from no known cause, the supply of herrings off Schonen practically ceased; the useful little fish changed the habits of centuries and sought other shores. With them went the glory of Schonen, and the peninsula sank into utter insignificance.

The outwardly most flourishing period of the Hansa, the period when it played its part in the world as a great political power, falls in the second half of the fourteenth century. This is the time, indeed, of highest prosperity for all of the German cities; their architecture achieved triumphs which are still reckoned among the greatest of their kind; their master singers worthily took the place once held by the troubadours; learning had abandoned the monasteries for the public schools and for the universities, of which Heidelberg, founded in 1386, was the first to be established on German ground; the German language had superseded the Latin as the language of public affairs. These civic leagues, moreover, represented all that was left of German unity. What other powers than the Hansa could at this time have gone to war with Denmark, and achieved victories which actually gave them a voice in the disposal of the Danish crown? *Flourishing period.*

These victories followed on a long period of dejection and almost of discouragement. The rule of the Baltic, always the goal of their desires, seemed slipping away from the grasp of the allied cities; a Count of Holstein, Gerard the Great, sat on the Danish throne and showed himself a most redoubtable and inconvenient neighbor. He it was who first temporarily united Schleswig and Holstein under one rule. On the violent death of Gerard, *The Hansa aids Waldemar of Denmark.*

in 1340, it was but natural that the Hansa should help the exiled Waldemar, who had been brought up at the court of Brandenburg and always signed himself "true heir to the crown of Denmark," to regain his lost inheritance and throne. The attempt succeeded, though only by slow degrees; the Holstein counts, who had taken up their brother's cause, were finally banished from Denmark and restricted once more to their German principality.

War with Waldemar.

For all the gratitude that the new king showed, the cities might have spared their efforts. This slim youth, who goes in history by the name of Waldemar Atterdag, or Waldemar Some-other-day, had no intention of remaining the mere ward of foreigners; indeed, for twenty years the key-note of his policy was to purge his country of that same foreign influence. During that time he succeeded so well that, at the end of his reign, he could fairly call the greater part of Denmark his own, and was feared at home as well as abroad. Sweden and Norway, formidable only so long as they remained under one ruler, he managed to separate, causing a Duke of Mecklenburg to be made king over the former land. A severe blow to the Hansa was the reconquest of Schonen, which for thirty years had been in Swedish hands, and which, during that time, the German merchants had practically governed according to their will. To be sure, Waldemar at first seemed amenable enough to reason and ratified the Hansa's privileges, though only in return for a goodly sum of money. But when, soon afterward, Waldemar attacked the Swedish Wisby, a commercial centre of the league, and a strategic point of great importance; when, in July, 1361, he defeated a Gotland army before the city, and, disdaining to enter by the gates, marched his army through a breach in the wall to show that he was conqueror, it was felt that a vital question had been brought to issue. Four days later an embargo was laid on Danish trade by the Wendish and Prussian cities; a common tax, or pound-toll was levied, an agreement was made with other enemies of Denmark, with Sweden and Norway, and with the Counts of Holstein. Mercenaries were employed, nor did knights of renown hesitate to enter into the service of the cities.

None the less this first venture met with disaster and defeat. The fleets encountered each other off the coast of Schonen; of the Hanseatic ships, which numbered fifty-two, one-fourth were destroyed. The preparations had been hasty, there was nothing in reserve, and it only remained to be seen what could be gained by negotiation. Purposely Waldemar dragged along the matter for several years, and at last, in 1365, signed the Peace of Wordin-borg, which could not have been more unsatisfactory had it been concluded in the greatest haste. Everything was shifting, everything temporary. Nor did Waldemar seem inclined to observe even these unsatisfactory terms. Not six weeks had passed, when, according to his enemies at least, he had broken his agreements, restricting the commerce and interfering with the fisheries of the Hansa. " Tyrant " and " pirate " are the terms that were applied to him. *Peace of Wordin-borg.*

The cities, one and all, were now fully alive to the dangers that threatened them, fully aware that they must make a desperate struggle, if they were to keep their supremacy in the Baltic. Bitterly they had felt the disgrace of the recent impotent struggle. Lübeck had condemned its burgomaster, Hans Wittenborg, who had shown incapacity in leading the city's forces, to death in the market-place by the hand of the common executioner. *Renewal of the war.*

Very different was to be this expedition from the former one, for the cities were unfolding their whole power and might. In November, 1367, a firm defensive and offensive league was formed, and was joined by fifty-seven towns; those refusing their assistance were to be boycotted for ten years, their havens to be avoided by all loyal ships. The most memorable Diet in the whole history of the league took place in Cologne in that hall of the Rathhaus which has ever since, in honor of this one occasion, gone by the name of the Hansa Hall.

Expedition against Copen- hagen.

Never before had so firm a front been shown to an enemy, never had there been such general unity of aim. There was help from without, too, for Mecklenburg and Holstein on the one hand, and King Albert of Sweden on the other, joined in the war against the common foe. Even from Jutland itself twelve nobles joined the expedition. Waldemar was surrounded as by an iron ring. He could count only on Norway, of which the new king, Hakon, was his son-in-law.

The great fleet of the Hanseatic League sailed forth to a whole succession of victories. Waldemar did not even await its coming, but fled to the mainland to seek help from different foreign princes. He left, indeed, a competent council of state, and it is not improbable that he hoped for better terms for his land in the absence of his own hated personality. At all events, resistance seemed hopeless. Copenhagen was taken, twice plundered, and finally razed to the ground; its harbor was rendered impassable by ships sunk midway in the channel; the great fortress or castle was kept for a while as a base of operations, and then, after the capture of Helsingborg, dismantled. The coasts of Norway, too, were plundered, the royal residence at Bergen destroyed; the whole land lay at the mercy of the indignant cities, and their ships could now venture unmolested on all the high seas.

Peace of Stralsund.

It was with the war council, not with Waldemar, that the Peace of Stralsund was signed in 1370, the unfortunate king being obliged to ratify it in the following year. The most glorious treaty it was to which the cities had ever affixed their names; it marks the culminating point, the climax of their greatness. All their old valued privileges on the island of Schonen were renewed to them, and as a pledge of good faith, the fortresses on the island were placed in their keeping; a war indemnity was granted and pledges given for its payment. In Denmark itself the Hansa received concessions that amounted to a monopoly of trade. Most humiliating of all, however, was the clause that no successor to the Danish throne, either now or at Waldemar's death, might be chosen without the sanction and approval of the league.

But no sooner had the latter reached the culmination of its glory than there began for it a long period of decline. The causes were varied and numerous: chief among them were the civil dissensions arising from the usual struggle between aristocratic Raths and plebeian guilds; the fact that the former were here unusually successful only served to keep the old wounds open. Then, too, Denmark rallied from its fall; under Margaret, the Semiramis of the North, all Scandinavia became united, and under her successor, Eric, Dutch and English ships were allowed to pass through the "Sound" into the Baltic and enter into competition with the Hansa trade. In spite of the strongest opposition a mercantile bureau or exchange for English merchants was opened in Danzig. *Decline of the Hansa.*

Worst of all, violent dissensions, fomented by England, arose between the Westerlings and Osterlings — between Cologne and her satellites on the one hand, and the Baltic ports on the other. Her cold reception by the Osterlings had caused England to retaliate on the Westerlings and to curtail their trading privileges. A great crisis came in 1468 A.D. King Edward IV., claiming that English ships *Internal dissensions.*

had been plundered in the "Sound," seized upon the persons of all the German merchants in his lands.  Cologne, more seriously crippled than the other cities, made her own separate peace, but by doing so called down upon herself the whole wrath of the Osterlings.  She was formally placed under the Hansa ban, which meant expulsion from the league.  The remaining cities were still strong enough, and still had the courage and fire, to declare war against the whole mighty realm of England.  It was the last heroic struggle of a waning power.  A dauntless little fleet sailed against the English, and succeeded so well that the Peace of Utrecht, signed in 1474, ratified all the Hansa's privileges and accorded damages to the extent of ten thousand pounds.

Antiquated methods.

Cologne was taken back into the league after a long banishment, but the old solidarity of interests could never be restored; in the fourteen years from 1476 to 1490 A.D. but one general Diet of the cities was held.  To add to all this, by the end of the fifteenth century the Hansa's methods of commerce had grown antiquated.  The discovery of new lands and of new routes opened up far-reaching opportunities, of which, however, the German cities were the last to take advantage.  The tide of traffic receded and left them stranded, while the dominion even of the Baltic passed over to Sweden.  No longer dreaded either commercially or politically, the cities had to stand by inactive while their privileges were annulled by Gustavus Vasa and Queen Elizabeth in their respective kingdoms.  Lübeck and Danzig continued to enjoy some measure of prosperity until even to them the death-blow was struck by the Thirty Years' War.  An attempt of ten cities to renew the league in 1641 A.D. failed completely, and Danzig, which had exported a hundred thousand tons of grain in 1619, sent out in 1659 but little over five hundred.

# CHAPTER IX

## THE ERA OF THE CHURCH COUNCILS

LITERATURE : Lindner is good authority for German affairs at the time of the councils. See also Prutz. For the transactions of the councils themselves, no better accounts can be found than those of Creighton in his history of the Papacy during the Reformation.

MORE, even than the other nations of Europe,— because political weakness kept pace with religious disunion,— did Germany suffer from the discords and scandals that throughout the fourteenth and fifteenth centuries disgraced the Roman church.   For more than seventy years, the term of the so-called Babylonian captivity, the popes at Avignon intrigued constantly in the interests of France.   Then followed the great schism, during which one pope sat at Rome and another at Avignon, each drawing heavily on those lands which remained in his obedience, and too often spending the money for secular and political purposes.   It is known that the Avignon court made loans to the amount of more than three and a half million guldens to the French king.   The burden of taxation, thus doubled by the schism, grew fairly intolerable ; no church office or church benefice, no exemption or dispensation, no hope of future preferment, not even forgiveness of sins, could be gained without cash payment.   There seemed no limit to the number of ecclesiastical holdings that one man, were he sufficiently rich, could bring into his own hand.   We have the record of these transactions under the first Avignon Pope ; for the sixteen years of his pontificate, they fill no

*Extortionate demands of the Papacy.*

less than ninety-one volumes. The matter was open, notorious. Æneas Sylvius Piccolomini, who later himself became Pope as Pius II., declared frankly at the time of the Council of Constance, "Nothing does the court of Rome give without payment, inasmuch as the very laying on of hands, and the gifts of the Holy Ghost, are for sale." That simony, against which the Gregorian popes had fought so bitterly, was everywhere rampant; each slightest opportunity was exploited to the utmost. Boniface IX., — a better man than his predecessor, who had inflicted physical torture on his cardinals, — yet brooded, like a perfect vulture, over his clergy when they lay dying, ready to swoop down upon their belongings the moment life was extinct. Their benefices he disposed of several times over, selling to one candidate a promise of "preference," and to another one of "prepreference," whereby it might happen after all that a third party carried off the prize. Even the institution of the Jubilee, which was lucrative because of the offerings the pilgrims brought to Rome, was distorted more and more into a purely money-making scheme. Boniface VIII. had started it in the year 1300, intending that it should be held at the beginning of every century. But the temptation of presiding over such a remunerative function proved too great; succeeding popes quickly reduced the term to fifty, to thirty-three, and eventually to twenty-five years, while the full absolution, which was to reward the pious journey, could finally be bought for the sum that journey would have cost.

The great schism in the church. We have here in this general system of extortion one of the prime evils that was driving the church toward the great catastrophe of its history. It was Germany's place to enter in and administer a cure, a task which, under stronger rulers, she undoubtedly would have attempted. How many of her former emperors had descended upon

Rome to cleanse those Augean stables! By its very position, as well as by its traditions the empire was called upon to be the arbiter in the matter of the schism, for the reason that, unlike Italy and France, no pope was in its midst. It was to the emperor that men were looking with longing eyes; one of the avowed grounds for deposing Wenceslaus was his failure to restore the peace of Christendom.

On the death, in 1394 A.D., of the Avignon Pope, Clement VII., the university of Paris wrote to his cardinals that the golden opportunity had now come; it was as though the Holy Ghost were standing and knocking at the door. But fearful that their own power and prerogative might become extinguished if not used, they proceeded, nevertheless, to a new election, salving their consciences by agreeing to bind their candidate to resign the Papacy, should the interests of the church so demand. Benedict XIII., at the time of being chosen, declared that he would abdicate as readily as he would take off his hat; but even when Wenceslaus of Germany and Charles VI. of France combined together to depose both existing popes and elect a new one, he clung to his position with great tenacity. Boniface IX. died in Rome in 1404, and his successors, first Innocent VII., then Gregory XII., acted much as Benedict had done.

Gregory was known as a good, quiet old man at the time  The Council of his election, in 1406 ; but he was possessed of a host of  of Pisa. ambitious relatives, who descended on the Vatican like a swarm of bees; it was soon reckoned that the sums expended for sugar alone equalled what previous popes had paid for their food and clothing. And all attempts at settling the schism in personal interviews with Benedict XIII. failed utterly: to use the simile of a contemporary, one pope, like a land animal, refused to approach the shore ; the other, like a water animal, would not leave the sea. But such obstinacy gradually defeated its own ends; adherents and resources melted away from both, and Gregory XII. was reduced to such straits that he sold the papal states and even Rome itself to his ally, Ladislaus of Hungary, for a paltry twenty-five thousand florins. By the Council of Pisa, in 1409, both Gregory and Benedict were declared in contumacy and a new pope elected, who took the name of Alexander V. He, dying soon afterward, was succeeded by the pugnacious John XXIII., a man whose past had been open to the gravest reproach.

Three popes at once.

It has been necessary to dwell upon these matters in order to appreciate the highly dramatic yet wretchedly unfortunate condition of imperial-papal affairs. In one and the same year, 1410 A.D., three emperors — Wenceslaus, Sigismund, and Iodocus of Moravia — claimed the secular headship of the world; while three popes — Benedict, Gregory, and John — pulled and tore at the seamless coat of Christ. The Council of Pisa had acted too hastily; before deposing two and electing a third pope it should have made more sure of the general allegiance of Europe; now it had engendered new evils instead of doing away with the old ones. It is true, the sentence which was read at the door of the Pisan cathedral had been formulated by one hundred and twenty doctors of theology; it had been proclaimed by the magistrates with bells and trumpets, and signalled on from village to village. But Benedict merely retired to his rocky fortress of Peniscola, while Gregory called an opposition council at Cividale and declared the proceedings of Pisa void.

Calling of the Council of Constance.

Fortunately at Pisa it had been voted that a new council should soon be called, and this command John XXIII., as the council's pope, did not dare to disregard. In the struggle for the imperial crown, Sigismund, as we have seen, had come forth triumphant, and he, while acknowl-

edging John as pope, soon showed that he was determined
to bring about a radical reform.   John had first fixed upon
Rome as the place for holding his council; but, failing to
procure attendance, and beset by Gregory XII.'s patron,
Ladislaus of Hungary, he was fairly driven to join forces
with Sigismund and accede to his conditions.

The result was the holding on German ground of the
Council of Constance, the greatest assembly of its kind that
had come together in a thousand years.   A summons had
been sent to Gregory XII. and to Benedict XIII., as well
as to all the nations of Europe.   It was evident that the
whole matter of the schism was to be probed to the bottom,
and also that a man of such evil record as John XXIII.
had everything to fear.   " This is a trap for foxes," he is
said to have cried as he stood at the top of the pass and
looked down on the town of Constance.   A short time
before, his sleigh had broken down and he had invoked the
devil in no orthodox terms.

This council was in reality an international congress;
the sovereigns were represented by envoys, while princes
with splendid retinues took their places among the cardinals and bishops.   John had created fifty new bishops as a
sort of body-guard, but the council frustrated his schemes
by deciding to vote by nations and not by absolute majorities.

*John XXIII. promises to abdicate.*

The pomp with which Sigismund, accompanied by his
queen and a host of high-born personages, entered Constance on Christmas Day, 1414, must have shown John
XXIII. the insignificance of the rôle that was apportioned
to himself.   In the wake of the royal party came pleasure-
seekers, mountebanks, and musicians, until the number of
strangers in the little town, which ordinarily contained but
seven thousand inhabitants, rose to more than ten times
that number.   It was a giddy, adventurous throng, and it
is worthy of note that during the sessions of the council

there were some five hundred deaths from accidental drowning in the lake.

John XXIII. received a severe blow when the council decreed that the envoys of Gregory and of Benedict were to be received with respect and allowed to wear their cardinals' hats; a severer one still when his own cardinals joined in recommending that all three popes should be made to resign as a preliminary to further proceedings. Under dread of an inquiry into the whole sullied history of his own past life, he was at last brought to promise to abdicate if his rivals would do the same. *Te Deums*, tears, shouts of joy, and clanging of bells greeted the news of his decision. When, publicly in the cathedral, he had read the formula prescribed, Sigismund knelt before him and kissed his feet, in sign of gratitude. Ten days later the emperor accepted from him the consecrated golden rose, the highest mark of papal approval.

Flight of John XXIII. from Constance.

But all these outward signs of amity only masked a determination on John's part to escape at any and every cost; his absence from Constance, he thought, would invalidate all the proceedings of the council. He won over to his side Frederick, Duke of Austria, who had his own private and particular grievances against Sigismund. Frederick arranged a tournament outside of the city walls, in which he himself was to break a lance with the brother-in-law of the emperor; in the midst of the excited throng few noticed a man looking like a servant, in a gray cloak and slouched hat, mounted on a poor steed, with his bow dangling from the saddle. It was the fox escaping from his trap.

Although seven of John's cardinals left Constance the next day, although such disturbances arose that many really thought the council had come to an end, the Pope's flight on the whole did more good than harm to the cause of unity. It gave Sigismund an opportunity to assert himself more boldly than was his wont; he showed himself everywhere, and his speeches and proclamations did much to restore quiet. But beyond and above this there was brought fairly and squarely to an issue the question: Just what authority was wielded by a general council of the church, — did it or did it not stand above the elect of the cardinals, the acknowledged head of Christendom? The council answered this question in its own favor; it decreed that a synod lawfully assembled in the Holy Ghost held its power directly from Christ, and that all men, irrespective of rank, were bound to obey it in matters of faith, and to aid in extirpating schism. A terrible indictment was then brought against John, charging him with the commission of fifty-four crimes; he was a liar, a robber, a poisoner, and a pagan, and not the least of his offences had been an offer to sell to the Florentines the holy skull of John the Baptist. He was pronounced " unworthy, useless, and noxious," was declared deposed, arrested, and sent off to the castle of Heidelberg, where he was kept confined during the three years that the council still continued in session.

*Decree that councils are above popes.*

Meanwhile the council had long been busied about another matter that was arousing intense excitement, and that was to plunge Bohemia and parts of Germany into civil war, — the trial for heresy, namely, of John Huss. The latter represented in his own person the ideas not only of the famous university of Prague, which up to the secession of the German element in 1409 had been the largest in Europe, but also of the extreme patriotic Bohemian party. His love for his countrymen extended to their language, from which he strove to banish foreign expressions; the orthography that he introduced has ever since held its own. From the point of view of the church there is no doubt that he was a dangerous man — a

*John Huss.*

violent political agitator, a heroic reformer.  He preached doctrines that had been formally condemned — mainly those of the English reformer Wyclif — and he preached them with a flaming eloquence that carried all before it.  Not content with holding up to scorn the vices of the clergy, he struck at the whole pretension of the Papacy to absolve from sin through the granting of indulgences, John XXIII. having promised the rewards usually offered for a pilgrimage to Palestine to those who would undertake a crusade against the ever active Ladislaus of Hungary.

Huss and the Archbishop of Prague.

It was with the Archbishop of Prague, Sbynek, that Huss had first come in conflict.  Armed with a bull from Pope Alexander V., the archbishop had summoned the reformer to answer before his inquisitor for defamation of the clergy, upholding of Wyclif, and political intriguing; and had finally excommunicated him, and ordered that two hundred volumes of Wyclif's writings should be burned.  But Huss was supported by King Wenceslaus and a large portion of the population of Prague.  As Sbynek appeared at the door of the cathedral to make public the act of excommunication, he was driven back with contumely, and his revenues were seized until he should have paid back the price of the books he had burned.  Huss's affair had become a political matter and also played its part in the struggles of the rival popes.  When John XXIII. excommunicated him for opposing the sale of his indulgences, the students of the university, headed by Jerome of Prague, dragged through the streets a car on which stood one of their number dressed as a courtesan, with the Bull fastened around his neck.  The Bull was then formally consigned to the flames.  Three students, for calling out in church that the indulgences were a lie, were publicly executed by the magistrates.  Their comrades took possession of their bodies and buried them to the sound of the martyr's chant "*Isti sunt sancti*."  Thus was ushered in one of the bloodiest periods in Bohemia's history. Prague was declared under the interdict, and the papal excommunication was repeated against Huss, who, indeed, at the request of Wenceslaus, went into temporary exile. This did not prevent him from writing controversial treatises, or from keeping up a brisk correspondence with his followers. He had declared his intention of appealing from the Pope to Jesus Christ, the true head of the church.

The Emperor Sigismund, full of enthusiasm for his council and anxious to purge from the taint of heresy that kingdom of Bohemia which he hoped soon to inherit from his childless brother Wenceslaus, had urged Huss to go to Constance and submit to an inquiry into the whole question of his belief. Totally, as the event showed, did he misconceive the reformer's character and the strength of his convictions. Huss might have bearded a pope, he thought, but surely he would submit without murmuring to the decrees of a body representing the whole Christian church. He willingly furnished a safe-conduct to cover the journey to and from the council and the time of sojourn there. Huss expected to be able publicly to defend his doctrines, and hoped to sway and electrify his hearers as he had done to his Bohemian congregations.

*Huss goes to Constance at Sigismund's invitation.*

How different was the reality! Huss arrived at Constance before the advent of the emperor, and therefore before the flight of John XXIII. By order of the latter, who sought to make a scapegoat of him, he was placed under arrest, a short hearing having been given him before the cardinals, but not before the council at large. The charges against him were: teaching that laymen as well as priests should be granted the cup of the Eucharist, attacking transubstantiation, and insisting that the moral character of the priest affected the validity of the sacrament, and that the discipline and organization of the church ought to be reformed.

As a result of the hearing, Huss was soon thrown into a dark, damp dungeon, close, we are told, to the mouth of a sewer.

Sigismund, on his arrival, stormed and raged at the violation of his safe-conduct, and threatened to leave the city at once if the captive were not liberated. The council took the attitude that a heretic was outside the limits of even a king's protection, and formally declared that no promise was binding to the prejudice of the Catholic faith. It was impossible, wrote King Ferdinand of Aragon, to break faith with one who had already broken faith with God.

As for Sigismund, on learning more and more the perniciousness of Huss's doctrines, a real horror of such heresies seems to have grown up within him; there was no longer any question, even after John's flight, of allowing Huss to ventilate his teachings, but at each of the four hearings that were now held before the council he was treated as guilty and was urged to retract. At the second audience Sigismund publicly abandoned him. "If you persist in your errors," he said, "it is for the council to take its measures. I have said that I will not defend a heretic; nay, if any one remained obstinate in heresy, I would burn him with my own hands." Huss thanked him for his safe-conduct and went back to prison. Sigismund had become the reformer's worst persecutor; the evidence was more than sufficient, he declared, let this heretic be burned.

The final hearing, July 6, 1415, was marked by the bringing forward, without witnesses, of the monstrous charge that Huss had declared himself the fourth person of the Trinity, and by the blush that was distinctly seen to mantle Sigismund's face when Huss looked fixedly at him, and mentioned his own coming to Constance, trusting in the imperial safe-conduct. That very same day, with all the cruel symbolic acts that outraged orthodoxy could invent, the victim was degraded from the priesthood, expelled from the church, handed over to the secular arm, and, wearing a paper cap, — that was painted with fiends and adorned with the unchristian motto, "We commit your soul to the devil," — was led out to the stake, where he sang from the Liturgy till the flames swept up and choked him.

We have dwelt so long upon the story of Huss, partly because of his influence on the later reformation, partly because this funeral pyre was the signal for the fierce war that spread over into Germany, lasted for half a genera- tion, and left behind it ineffaceable memories of ruin and misery. The remaining history of the Council of Constance may be disposed of in a few words. Two days before the execution of Huss, Pope Gregory XII. had formally handed in his resignation and agreed to content himself with the title of Cardinal of Porto. Benedict XIII. remained obdurate, but agreed to have a conference with Ferdinand of Aragon and Sigismund. In order to fulfil this engagement, thus ending the schism, and then to pacify Christendom by making peace between France and England on the one hand and between Poland and the Teu- tonic order on the other, Sigismund peregrinated Europe for a year and a half. Everywhere his efforts wrought harm instead of good, except that Ferdinand of Aragon was induced to send a deputation of Spaniards to the council. Far from healing the discords of England and France, and making France forget Agincourt, Sigismund openly espoused the cause of England, and reappeared at Con- stance wearing the Order of the Garter; thus calling down upon himself the unbending hostility of the whole French contingent. By the alliance of the Latin nations the German-English project of reforming the church before choosing a new head was thoroughly frustrated, though the schism at last was brought to an end. Benedict

*End of the schism and frustration of reform.*

was formally summoned to appear at Constance, and, on his refusal, was sentenced to degradation and expulsion from the church. With incredible stubbornness he held out until his death in 1424, one of his last acts being to create four new cardinals, who promptly proceeded to inaugurate a new schism of their own, which troubled no one but themselves.

**Martin V.** The council had meantime proceeded to the new election, and the votes had fallen upon Odo Colonna, who took the name of Martin V. The folly of merely changing the men and not correcting the abuses now became apparent. So unhampered was Martin by restrictions, that on the very day after his accession he issued rules for the papal chancery which upheld the whole former iniquitous scale of taxation and extortion. Yet so happy were men to be free from the long weary sessions, that the general sentiment was one of rejoicing. Even Sigismund prostrated himself with fervor before Martin, kissing his feet and afterward holding his bridle. Then the emperor of the Western world prepared to leave the scene of his labors, but was prevented by his clamorous creditors. Calling them together, he persuaded them by his eloquence first to consent to take his gold and silver plate in pledge, and then to accept instead his fine linen and hangings, which he never took the trouble to redeem.

**Excitement over death of Huss.** Indescribable was the excitement which had ensued in Bohemia when the news of the death of Huss became known. The clergy, nobles, and cities sent a stirring protest to Constance against the " eternal, shameful wrong." To their last breath they agreed to uphold religious freedom. Stung to madness by the derision and taunts of the Catholics of Prague, a number of Hussites rushed into the Rathhaus, seized some seven of the councillors, dragged them to the windows, and hurled them to the crowd below, who, with the fury of wild beasts, tore them limb from limb. It was the irrevocable signal for a bloody revolution, and one of the first victims was the much-tried King Wenceslaus, who, in the midst of the tumult and excitement, died in a fit brought on by rage at what had happened. He passed away, to quote a contemporary, "with great clamor and with a roar as of a lion." The rôle he had played had contented no one, and his body had to be secretly buried in order to escape the wrath of the Hussites. To the other difficulties there was thus added the question of choosing a successor to the throne of Bohemia. Sigismund, the natural heir, had ruined his prospects by his treatment of Huss; it was all too evident that nothing would induce the people to recognize as king the man who had put to death their saint and hero. He tried to fight for his rights, but could not prevent the election of Withold, the Lithuanian prince.

This Hussite rebellion that fills the years between 1415 and 1433 A.D. was peculiar in its character; it was no mere act of revenge nor yet solely an outbreak of religious fanaticism; it was a revolt against the whole narrow spirit of the Middle Ages, much as the military tactics adopted were a protest against the old heavy armor, the unwieldiness of the forces and, in general, the worn-out methods, of mediæval knighthood. It was a national, anti-German uprising, and at the same time a peasants' war or communistic outburst. According to the proclamations, all class distinctions were to fall away, all goods to be held in common, all wrongs to be righted. For it had come at last—the year of retribution and the day of vengeance. *Character of the Hussite war.*

A grim, desolating war was thus started, and cruel and stern were the efforts made for its suppression. The Pope decreed that a crusade against the Hussites should be *Ziscka's methods of warfare.*

preached all over Europe, and, in 1421 at least, the German contingent were instructed to kill right and left, sparing none but children. In the eyes of the church, these utraquistic heretics who demanded the equality before God's altar of priests and laymen were a thousand times worse than the rankest infidels. One after the other, immense armies were sent against Prague, but only to recoil before a power that seemed invincible. The soul and inspirer of the movement was the one-eyed, and later wholly blind, leader, John Ziscka of Trocknaw, who has been called the Cromwell of Bohemian history. A man of great natural ability, he had gained experience on many battlefields, had fought with the Poles at Tannenberg, with the English at Agincourt, and with Sigismund in Hungary against the Turks. And he admirably understood the training, and disciplining of the enthusiastic crowds that flocked to his banner. Armed with their threshing flails, which they bound round with iron, his peasants were a match for heavy cavalry in any hand-to-hand conflict. A chief feature of their tactics was the use they made of the *Wagenburg*, a moving fortress of heavy wagons, which protected the soldiers as they marched, or which could at will be drawn up into a square or circle, roofed over with boards, and firmly held together by huge iron chains. From behind these refuges, which served as a perpetual vantage-ground, the cannoneers could take deliberate aim, and the cavalry and infantry could form anew after making their sallies. Occasionally, the camps would be formed in the shape of different letters of the alphabet, so that while an enemy would find himself in a mere labyrinth, those who were initiated could readily trace their way. When the lay of the land permitted, the wagons could be filled with heavy stones and rolled down upon the enemy. But the boldest of the manœuvres of these improvised war-chariots was to drive in a line into the midst of the enemy, then, separating right and left, to enclose a considerable number, who were thus cut off from the rest and could be hewn down at will.   Altogether Ziscka relied a great deal on feints and quick evolutions, which were a new experience for the heavily armed Germans.

As has been already intimated, the Hussite war was by no means confined to Bohemia; these brown, sinewy, wild-eyed fanatics made terrible inroads into Saxony, and indeed into nearly every part of the empire.   In 1430 they penetrated as far as Meissen, invaded Franconia, and threatened to besiege Nuremberg.   The spread of their socialistic ideas, too, filled Sigismund with alarm.   He tried his best, though in vain, to gain means for equipping a really powerful army by imposing a small tax on every inhabitant of the empire.   *Inroads into Germany.*

The battle of Tauss, fought in 1431, proved one of the bloodiest of the whole war.   The stateliest army that Sigismund had yet been able to raise went down, almost without a struggle, before the grim, determined Bohemians.   The whole empire was in an uproar, and the general feeling was one of shame and dread: these heretics were growing too presumptuous for endurance.   To the door of Martin V.'s own palace at Rome a protest was affixed, by one of their number, against the whole attitude of the church; a new council was necessary, it said, and every Christian who refused to strive for it was guilty of mortal sin, while a pope who put obstacles in the way must himself be condemned as a heretic.   *The battle of Tauss.*

The Council of Basel, which opened in this same year, was the result of all this agitation, although the settlement of the Bohemian troubles was not the only one of its objects: reformation of the church, the reconciliation of the schismatic Greek church, also a crusade against the Turks, were in-   *Opening of the Council of Basel.*

cluded in the programme. It was the bane of Christendom
that the Pope would not unreservedly concur in such worthy
objects. The narrow-minded and self-satisfied Eugenius
IV. had jealous fears regarding the council's activity, and
scarcely had it assembled before he declared it dissolved.
In vain Cardinal Cesarini urged upon him that the Bohemians had been formally and regularly summoned, and
that a shrinking from the conflict on the part of the church
would be as disgraceful as the flight of the German army
at Tauss. The position of Eugenius was much stronger
than that once occupied by John XXIII., for he was the one
legitimate and universally recognized head of the church;
nevertheless, he only called down upon himself a reissue of
the famous Constance decree affirming the absolute supremacy of a council.

Sigismund
and the
council.

The Emperor Sigismund was far from holding the commanding position at Basel that he had once held at
Constance. He felt, to use his own expression, like the
fifth wheel to a cart. More than ten years of unsuccessful
warfare had greatly damaged his prestige. Nor were his
motives as unselfish as of yore. He wished to pacify
Bohemia that he might himself rule it; he dreaded
to offend the Pope, with whom he was negotiating for the
imperial coronation at Rome. To him and to the Pope's
own straitened circumstances in Italy was due a temporary
truce between Eugenius and the council, during which the
coronation ceremonies were performed with great pomp.
The Pope went so far in his gratitude toward his imperial
supporter as to pay the expenses of the coronation banquet,
and thus rid Sigismund of the necessity of pawning more of
his belongings. So low were the latter's finances at this
time that on his arrival at Basel in October, 1433, he had to
send to the magistrates for a pair of shoes, on the plea that
his baggage had been detained. The emperor's advocacy

of the Pope had the effect of staving off severe measures that the council was debating against him, in the midst of which deliberations Eugenius, driven to bay by the attacks of his political enemies in Italy, sent in a full and free withdrawal of all his animadversions against the assembly.

At this juncture it was that envoys sent by the Hussites in answer to an invitation from the council arrived at Basel. As early as 1421 the demands of the Bohemians had been formulated into four articles, known as the "Four Articles of Prague," and accepted by the clergy, nobles, cities, and peasants. They called for freedom of preaching, for the communion under both kinds, for poverty of the clergy, and the repression of open sins. Here at Basel, after endless discussions on each point, after envoys of the council had twice travelled to Bohemia to negotiate on the spot, and a new embassy had been despatched from Prague, a compromise, remarkable for its fairness, was agreed upon. For the first time in its history the church treated on equal terms with heretics. Into its fold the Bohemians were now to be called back; but the so-called Prague Compactates, signed in 1436, allowed them communion with the use of the cup, the free preaching and reading of the gospel, and the right to draw the clergy before the secular tribunals. *The Bohemians and the council.*

It was the bane of the Hussite movement that from the first its promoters were divided into factions, between which, even before the signing of the compactates, a war of annihilation had broken out. There were on the one hand, the Calixtines or utraquists, and on the other, the more fierce and radical Taborites who had rallied around Ziscka, not to speak of minor sects and subdivisions. The terrible earnestness with which men clung to their special tenets is shown by the joy with which some fifty of the so-called adamites accepted the sentence pronounced by Ziscka that they should be burnt to death at the stake. "To-day we *Civil war in Bohemia.*

shall reign with Christ," they declared, as they entered the flames with a smile on their lips.   Yet Ziscka's party, which after the death of its adored leader took the name of the " Orphans," was less extreme than the fanatical Taborites. Over the question of what concessions to make to the council, bitter disputes had arisen which ended in civil war. The weapons that had done such good service against the outer world were now turned inward, and the battle of Lipan or Böhmisch Brod witnessed a bloody holocaust of the Taborites.   The exhausted land soon after made peace with Sigismund, and allowed him in 1436 to enter Prague as king; but he died in the following year.   At Basel,

Schism in
the Council
of Basel.

meanwhile, the reforms that should have rendered unnecessary the great struggles of the next century were far from making progress.   Incredible it seems that this great assembly, which lasted for eighteen long, weary years, should have found it possible to accomplish so little.   The secret lay in the renewed antagonism between the council and the Pope, and this, strangely enough, was fomented by the application of the Greeks for such a conference as might lead to an ending of the old schism of centuries.   It came to be a burning question whether the splendid embassy that was projected should appear before the council at Basel or before Eugenius IV. at Ferrara or Florence.   A number of severe decrees that cut every possible revenue from under the Pope's feet were directly owing to a desire to render it impossible for him to receive the Greeks with honor. One blow after another was dealt to his authority.   The annates, or first-fruits of benefices, were sweepingly abolished, as were also the dues for the pallium, the mark of the archiepiscopal dignity.   The number of cardinals was reduced, the methods of election changed, and popes were not to be recognized until they had sworn to observe the Basel decrees.

This council was growing democratic and revolutionary; it assumed the right itself to bestow the pallium, and to grant indulgences from sin. There was some truth in the accusation that the vote of a cook was as good as that of a legate or an archbishop. The undignified proceedings that went on in its sessions lost for it, gradually, the respect of Europe; there were scenes of outrageous violence between the rival parties, — thundering protests and hubbubs, we are told, as on a field of battle. Thoroughly wearied with the course events were taking, Eugenius called together a council of his own, first at Ferrara and then at Florence, and scored a great triumph by inducing the Greeks to attend. Thus a new kind of schism had broken out in the church. Of popes and antipopes the world had seen enough; new and strange, it was to have a council and an anti-council. The assembly at Basel summoned Eugenius before its tribunal, and declared him contumacious for not coming. He retaliated by pronouncing the council dissolved, or, rather, transferred to Ferrara. In January, 1438, he was suspended from office by the council, and in June, 1439, formally deposed. In his stead Amadeus of Savoy was made pope, and the ban hurled at all those who should refuse to obey him. Thus once more was the seamless coat of Christ rent in twain. To this point had things come after so many years of common deliberation.

To the new emperor of the Romans, Frederick III., who had followed Albert of Austria, Sigismund's short-lived successor, it was no hardship to have to pursue a waiting policy. For a time he advocated the closing of both councils and the summoning of a new one; but as the cause of Eugenius slowly gained the ascendant, it became evident that it was for Germany's advantage to do as France had already done, and, by means either of a concordat or a pragmatic sanction, to secure the benefit of such salutary decrees as

The Emperor Frederick III. and the schism at Basel.

the council had already passed, even while making peace
with that council's enemy.    Many of the oppressive exac-
tions of the Papacy would thus be done away with, and the
valuable principle upheld, that councils were above popes.
Such was the course advocated by a large party, to which
many princes of the empire belonged, and the mouthpieces
of which were John of Lysura and Gregory of Heimburg.
Unfortunately these two men, who were sent to Italy as
delegates in the matter, were far inferior to such antagonists as a Cardinal Cesarini or an Æneas Sylvius Piccolomini.    Gregory is mockingly described by Æneas himself
as totally lacking in self-command — as stalking around
Rome in the sweltering heat, with dishevelled hair and
disordered garments, cursing loudly against the Papacy.

Æneas
Sylvius.

Æneas, himself, on the contrary, was circumspect and
full of cunning, and not choice in the selection of his
means.    From serving many masters and sojourning in
many lands, he had become an adept in all diplomatic arts.
As secretary of Frederick III. and poet-laureate at his court,
he had learned thoroughly to know both the emperor's
character and the ways of looking at things at Vienna.
Æneas, at first, had been a warm adherent of the Council
of Basel and of its pope, Felix V.; but, ever on the watch
for his own advantage, he had found means of being reconciled to Eugenius IV., and had become his henchman.    To
this man is due the credit, if credit it be, of drawing over
Frederick III. to the cause of papal reaction.

Character
of Freder-
ick III.

The reign of Frederick III., which lasted for the unusually long space of fifty-three years, was, all in all, an
infliction upon the land.    There was, during all of that
time, no great public calamity, no important war; but, from
beginning to end, there was a certain stagnancy and want
of progress.    The House of Hapsburg was everything, the
empire nothing.    It was Frederick's unalterable conviction

that Austria was destined to rule the whole world. His favorite motto or device, which he even stamped on his clothing, consisted of the five vowels (a, e, i, o, u), signifying in German " alles Erdreich ist Oesterreich unterthan," or, in Latin, " Austriæ est imperare omni universo." In daily life Frederick must have been a most exasperating personage; conservative to the last degree, phlegmatic, seemingly possessed of no human passions whatever, whether good or bad, he had always a trite remark with which to settle every emergency. "Time avenges all things," he would say to his Portuguese wife, when she urged him to right some wrong; when told of confusion in the courts of justice, he would answer that such things were nowhere perfectly managed; and once, when grossly insulted to his face, he simply remarked that thunderbolts usually made for high towers.

Frederick had been brought up in the narrow atmosphere of the Styrian court, and was anything but princely in his tastes and habits. His favorite way of opening a door was to kick it, through which propensity he is said to have become lame. His mother, a Polish princess, was noted less for her intellect than for her intense piety, and for a physical strength that enabled her to crack nuts with her fingers, or to press nails into a wall. The emperor himself delighted in trivialities, and a memorandum book that he has left behind is full of feeble plays upon words and of household recipes, estimates, and inventories. An ardent collector of jewels, he would sit and play with them by the hour; he dabbled in astrology, astronomy, palmistry, and transfusion of metals. Especially fond of fruit, he is said to have fixed his residence near Vienna, simply because the pears were plentiful.

Under Frederick, the zenith of indifference on the part of the rulers toward the affairs of the empire was reached.

Again and again he summoned diets at which he himself failed to appear. Once, leaving Germany in disgust at the failure of his plans, he remained beyond its boundaries, or at all events away from its diets, for twenty-seven years. Even when, in 1453, Constantinople, the very bulwark of Christianity, fell into the hands of the Turks, he could not be roused to action. "He sat idly at home," writes one of his chroniclers, "planting his garden and catching birds."

The Concordat of Vienna.

One can readily understand how a weak character like this could be completely turned round the fingers of the wily Æneas Sylvius. Frederick was induced to play traitor to conciliar reform by an elaborate series of bribes conducing to his own private advantage and not to that of Germany at large. The benefits were assured to him in two treaties: the one with Eugenius in 1446; the other in the form of a concordat, two years later, with Nicholas V. By the first instrument he was granted the right to nominate the incumbents of six great Austrian bishoprics and the overseers or visitors of the Austrian monasteries. He could dispose at will of one hundred ecclesiastical benefices. Should he succeed in winning over the German nation to the papal side, he was to have the imperial crown, a hundred thousand guldens for his coronation expenses, and certain revenues from church lands.

The Concordat of Vienna, which did not even mention the Council of Basel or its decrees, consisted mainly of concessions to the Papacy, over and above those granted at Constance, and of petty favors conferred for his lifetime on the emperor. Nicholas V. was to grant him a magnificent coronation at Rome, and a tenth of the clerical revenues of the empire. Frederick and a hundred others whom he was at liberty to name were empowered to choose their own father confessors, and the emperor was to have the special privilege of carrying around an altar at which, even in places that were under the interdict, mass might be said at any time. At seasons when other people were obliged to fast, he and his guests might indulge in milk and eggs; he might impose certain moderate taxes upon the clergy of Austria in order to provide a dowry for his daughters; where it would be greatly to his advantage, he might employ the services in war of men who were not Christians.

It was a paltry price for which to betray one's country; a miserable ending to conciliar deliberations that had been going on for nearly a score of years.

It is interesting to glance for a moment at the attitude of the seven electors during all these happenings, for it must not be supposed that they, in general so much more active than the emperor, remained absolutely quiescent where it was a question of such important reforms. In the year after Sigismund's death, in 1438, they had taken a very decided stand. They had publicly announced in a formal document that they would pay no heed to measures passed either by the Pope or by the council, until such time as the unity of the church should have been restored. They had induced the short-reigned Albert of Hapsburg to join them in their policy of neutrality — a policy which was maintained for nine years, during the whole of which time the only ecclesiastical jurisdiction allowed in Germany was that of individual bishops. When in 1446 A.D., secure finally of Frederick III.'s assent and obedience, Pope Eugenius had taken the bold step of deposing as heretics and rebels the archbishops of Cologne and Treves, the whole electoral college had arisen in its might, had renewed the old agreement made at Rense in 1338, had demanded the reinstatement of the two deposed electors, and insisted that the reform decrees passed at Basel should be clinched and ratified. Eugenius was to acknowledge the supremacy of councils over popes, and a new assembly was speedily to be called.

Negotiations were still pending on these matters, and some slight concessions had already been made, when Eugenius died in 1447. But bribery and dissension had meanwhile done their work among the seven, who now receded from one position after another. The Margrave of Brandenburg, one of the most stubborn champions of church reform, and the last to withdraw his opposition to the papal-imperial alliance, finally did so on receiving permission to nominate for the three bishoprics in the Mark, and to turn the cathedral chapters of Havelberg and Brandenburg into secular institutions. As to the Archbishop of Mainz, Æneas Sylvius acknowledged to having spent two thousand florins in bribing his advisors.

Frustration of the reforms of Basel.

The result of the whole agitation was that Pope Nicholas V., successor of Eugenius, was able in April, 1449, to declare the Council of Basel at an end. Frederick III. had already withdrawn his safe-conduct from it, and forbidden the city of Basel any longer to harbor it within its walls. The remnants of the great assembly then removed to Lausanne, where, finally, its pope, Amadeus, came to an amicable understanding with his rival, renouncing the Papacy, but receiving the rank of cardinal, and being granted in all things the place of honor next to Nicholas himself.

Had Frederick III. acted a different part in this matter of the council, the whole course of German history would have been altered. The decrees that he failed to ratify had struck deep down into the roots of papal absolutism, had declared that bishoprics and abbacies were to be filled by free election, that the use of the interdict and the competency of the papal tribunals were to be restricted, that the annates, the pallium dues, and other burdensome taxes,

which were to cause such an outcry a few years later,
should be done away with altogether. Now, as things had
turned out, nothing whatever was gained. Even the principle insisted upon both at Constance and at Basel, that
councils were above popes, was annulled and obliterated by
Æneas Sylvius himself, who ascended the papal chair in
1458, and, in memory of pious Æneas, took the name of
Pius II. By his bull, *Execrabilis*, issued in January, 1460,
he pronounces it an " execrable abuse, unheard of in former
times," that any one should appeal to a future council. The
last trace of the conciliar movement was thus wiped out of
the ecclesiastical law, and all the old abuses allowed re-
entry — soon, indeed, to become so glaring that nothing
short of secession could remedy them.

# CHAPTER X

## GERMAN LIFE ON THE EVE OF THE REFORMATION

LITERATURE: Brant, *Ship of Fools*, and Erasmus, *Praise of Folly*, give brilliant satirical pictures of the times. Bezold, *Geschichte der deutschen Reformation*, devotes considerable space to the causes that led to the Reformation. See also Lamprecht, *Deutsche Geschichte*, and Sach, *Deutsches Leben*. Jansen's *Geschichte des deutschen Volkes*, written from a Roman Catholic standpoint and endeavoring to prove too much, is nevertheless an invaluable storehouse of facts for our period. It has been translated into English. For Maximilian, see Ulman, *Kaiser Maximilian*, and Huber, *Geschichte Oesterreichs*.

Condition of the empire.

FROM the middle of the fifteenth century on, Germany progresses rapidly towards a crisis that can only be compared, in its world-wide importance, with the crusades and the French Revolution. It becomes necessary, therefore, in order to have a fitting background for stirring national events, to picture in small compass the general condition of affairs: the weakness of the state, the peculiarities of the ruler, the material and intellectual, the social and religious, position of the people, and the spread and effect of new ideas.

The Holy Roman Empire, as it still was officially called, although it embraced little territory that was not German, had come to be scarcely more than a lofty conception. Its revenues were those of an ordinary well-to-do private individual; its hold on its outlying districts was so slight, that one hardly knows whether the land of the Teutonic Order belonged to it or not. We do know that the Hanseatic League could make war on foreign powers and close treaties

228

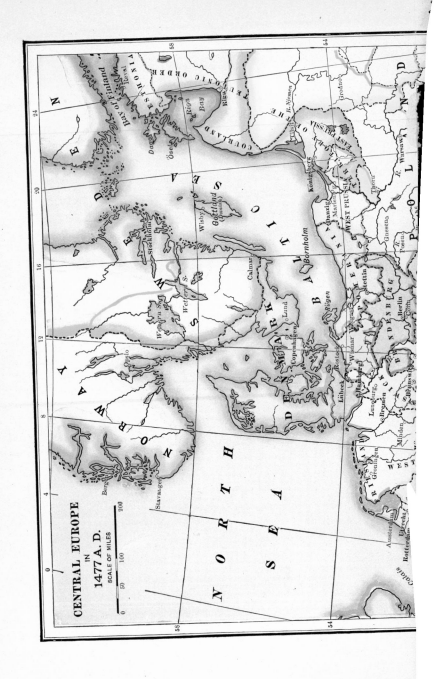

CENTRAL EUROPE
IN
1477 A.D.

SCALE OF MILES

NORTH SEA

NORWAY

SWEDEN

FINLAND

BALTIC SEA

DENMARK

BRANDENBURG

POLAND

TEUTONIC ORDER

ESTHONIA

COURLAND

EAST PRUSSIA

WEST PRUSSIA

MERCK

WESTPHALIA

FRIESLAND

Bergen

Stavanger

Oslo

Stockholm

Calmar

Gottland
(Swedish)

Wisby

Wetter's.

Wenern S.

Oesel

Dago

Riga

Reval

Revel

Bay of Finland

Riga Bay

Königsberg

Dantzig

Marienburg

Thorn

Gnesen

Posen

Warsaw

R. Warsaw

R. Niemen

Grodno

Bornholm

Rügen

Stettin

Berlin

Coln

Brunswick

Hamburg

Lübeck

Rostock

Wismar

Wargast

Copenhagen

Lund

Lüneburg

Bremen

Minden

Groningen

Amsterdam

Utrecht

Rotterdam

Calais

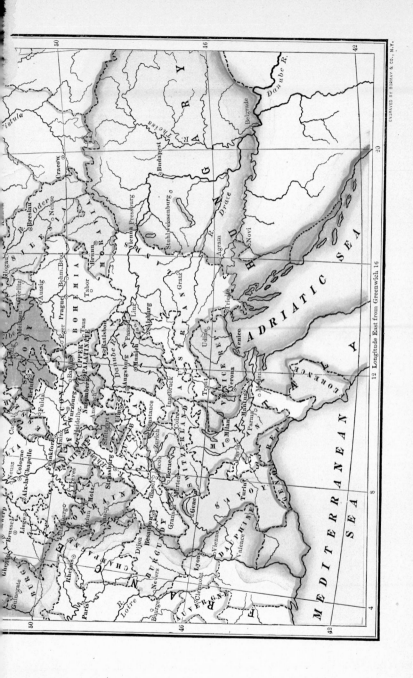

ADRIATIC SEA

MEDITERRANEAN SEA

Danube R.

Belgrade

H U N G A R Y

Tistula

Cracow

Oder

Breslau

Neisse

Glogau

SILESIA

Görlitz

Aussig

Budapest

Theiss

Novi

Agram

Drave R.

Stuhlweissenburg

Vienna

Pressburg

Brünn

MORAVIA

Prague

BOHEMIA

Böhm.Brod

Eger

Tabor

Taus

Graz

S T Y R I A

Triest

Trieste

Udine

Venice

Verona

Mantua

Parma

I T A L Y

Milan

MILAN REP.

Turin

SAVOY

Valence

DAUPHINY

Lyons

Vienne

AUVERGNE

Clermont

Burges

Nevers

Dijon

BURGUNDY

Besançon

Geneva

SWITZERLAND

Basel

Zurich

Constance

Ulm

Augsburg

Munich

Salzburg

Linz

Passau

UPPER PALATINATE

Ratisbon

Danube R.

Innsbruck

Coire

TYROL

VENICE VICEROY.

LORRAINE

12 Longitude East from Greenwich 16

Novi

FRANCONIA

Nuremberg

Würzburg

Bamberg

Heidelbg.

Stuttgart

Strasburg

Freiburg

Mulhausen

Gray

Granson

Morten

Berne

Jacob

Genoa

Trent

GENOESE REP.

Metz

Verdun

Thionville

Treves

Luxemburg

Frankfort

Mainz

Fulda

PALATINATE

LOWER LORRAINE

Cassel

HESSE

Erfurt

SAXONY

Leipsic

Merseburg

Elbe

F R A N C E

Paris

Loire R.

Rheims

Guingate

BURGUNDY

Ghent

Brussels

Liège

Aix-la-Chapelle

Cologne

Neuss

without consulting it at all; that Switzerland, rather than contribute to a common tax, went to war with Maximilian, the son and successor of Frederick III., defeated him in 1499, and wrested itself entirely free. Italy had been practically lost ever since Hohenstaufen times; but Maximilian still clung to his claims and spent much of his time in warring on Italian ground — first as ally of Spain, the Pope, and Venice to drive out the French king, Charles VIII.; then as ally of France, Spain, and England, to dismember Venice; then as enemy of the Pope, to dismember the papal states and perhaps ascend the chair of Peter himself; finally as ally of Venice, the Pope, and the Swiss, to dismember France. In all of these wars he was unsuccessful, and they cost him much treasure as well as the confidence, though not the love, of his subjects; but in another direction, from the point of view at least of the House of Hapsburg, he was more fortunate, thoroughly exemplifying the old adage, *Bella gerant alii ; tu felix Austria nube.*

While his father was still alive, he had wedded Mary of Burgundy, daughter of that Charles the Bold who, in his effort to form a middle state equal to France or Germany, had become involved in war with the Swiss, had been defeated in the great battles of Granson, Murten, and Nancy, and had fallen on the last-named field. The effort to secure his wife's inheritance led Maximilian into a war with France, in which he won the battle of Guinegate, and, by the Treaty of Arras in 1479, secured the Netherlands for his house. Later, he changed the history of Europe for better or for worse by affiancing his son Philip to the princess known as Joanna the Insane, daughter of Ferdinand and Isabella of Spain, and mother of the great uniter of kingdoms, the Emperor Charles V. *[The marriage alliances of Maximilian.]*

Even within the acknowledged confines of the empire the process of disintegration could not be prevented.

Sub-
divisions.

Saxony, in 1485, divided its territory between two branches of the House of Wettin — the Ernestine, or electoral line, and the Albertine, or ducal, with its capital city of Dresden. Their respective heads were the two princes whose abduction in their youth forms such a dramatic page in Saxon history. It mattered little that this subdivision was counter to the provisions of the Golden Bull, in disregarding which the Palatinate also had done its part.

Weakness
of the
administra-
tion.

If, on the whole, the political organization of the empire was weak, still more was this true of the internal administration. We have seen that the Emperor Frederick III. was present at no Diet for 27 years. The chief court of justice followed the monarch's person, and the course of justice was halting and slow. Quarrels between individuals were settled by private feud — too often by burning of house or barn. The system of recruiting the army was so cumbersome that without the troops of the Hapsburg dependencies Maximilian could have accomplished nothing, and, at the first suggestion of taxation, there were revolts in all directions. Some of these evils were remedied at the famous Diet of Worms of 1495, where an *ewige Landfrieden*, or perpetual peace of the land, was decreed for the whole empire, a *Kammergericht*, or standing court of justice, established; and also, much against Maximilian's will, a *Reichsregiment*, or virtual council of regency.

Personality
of Maxi-
milian.

As regards his personality, Maximilian, known as the "last of the knights," is one of the most attractive figures in German history — a really popular ruler. His deeds and doings were in every one's mouth, whether it was a matter of the latest eloquent speech, of a dangerous hunting adventure, of a daring deed in battle, or of some purely mythical happening, as when a stone is said to have fallen from heaven to give him special warning, or two stags and a pheasant to have done him homage. People had that enthusiastic love and sympathy for him that stopped at no extravagant utterance; since Christ, it was declared, no man's sufferings had equalled his. The dream of his life was to lead a crusade against the Turks, an object which he might have accomplished but for the enmity of France.

Yet there was another side to Maximilian's character that made his reign a failure; he was too little of a statesman, too violent, too unreliable. His contemporary, Machiavelli, speaks of him as in a state of constant excitement, both bodily and mentally; as often taking back in the evening what he had determined upon in the morning. He was all indignation, all petulance, all vehemence. Through his head chased too many different projects. He could not make up his mind at a given moment whether troops were to be sent to France, to Italy, or to the Netherlands. He could brook no opposition from his Diet, but would declare that he had no intention of being bound hand and foot and tied to a nail; or, again, that he would soon be driven to throw down the crown of the empire and snatch at the pieces. He even threatened to renounce his idea of taming the Turks, and to join with them against his other enemies. Some of his political plans are almost too wild for credence, as when he aimed to do away with the Papacy altogether and unite the two highest offices in Christendom in his own person; or when he took up the cause of the pretender, Perkin Warbeck, and allowed himself to be designated as eventual heir to the English throne. He was always combining, always making projects; yet the prospect of a good hunt would chase even the most important political plans from his head, and while in the midst of a campaign he would endanger his person and his cause for the sake of a chamois or a stag. A bad husbander of resources, he was always in debt; we

*Wild projects of Maximilian.*

have a notice of a payment to come to him from the banking house of Fugger, of which a thousand guldens are im-
peratively demanded in advance, " or his majesty will have
nothing to eat." Machiavelli declared he would never have
enough, " though the trees bore ducats instead of leaves."

Inventions
and reforms
of Maxi-
milian.

Nevertheless, in some respects, — chiefly in the fields of
military science and of humanistic learning, — Maximilian's
reign was of great benefit. Strangely enough, this " last of
the knights " did more than any other man to kill knighthood, for he it was who replaced the old, useless, heavy-
armed and undrilled cavalry by artillerymen and by
nimble foot-soldiers, organized on the plan of the Swiss
mercenaries, and known as the *Landsknechts*, or " country
knaves." The artillery itself he greatly improved, invent-
ing new kinds of cannon and transport wagons, and giving
pet names, such as *Weckauf*, or Wake-up, and *Purlepus*,
to individual guns. He rearranged his troops so that one
category seconded the other, the riflemen the cannoneers,
and the *Landsknechts* the riflemen.

The *Lands-
knechts.*

The *Landsknechts* made war their trade, not caring
greatly on which side they fought; the yellow gold
was their god, and they would desert the most renowned
leader were it not forthcoming; many a campaign was thus
frustrated. In time of peace noisy and swaggering, they
were a perfect infliction on the land; but once in the midst
of fighting they displayed magnificent courage, and their
bristling squares did even more than gunpowder to destroy
the remnants of chivalry.

The *Landsknechts* were for the most part burghers; but
many knights also joined the regiments, receiving double
pay and being allowed to fight in the front ranks. Uniforms
were as yet unknown, and the ordinary costume was as gay
and varied as the plumage of birds. If the " pious " *Landsknechts* sacked a town their first care was to masquerade

in all the rich attire they could lay their hands on.  The ordinary covering of their lower limbs was the so-called "*Pludderhose*," or bag-trouser, consisting of yards and yards of rich material drawn together at the waist and knees.  The *Landsknechts* were called pious because of their habit of kneeling in prayer or singing a hymn before a battle; on rising they brushed the dust from their doublets and threw earth behind them, in token that they were casting off everything common or vile.  Then, to the sound of drums and with lowered spears, they would rush to the attack.

In the reign of Maximilian, and greatly fostered by him, falls the height of the period known as the German Renaissance.  It came later than in Italy, had its home rather in the universities than at the petty courts, and had to contend with a scholasticism that was not worn out but distinctly aggressive.  The aim and object of the Renaissance may be designated as the search for the naked truth, — the truth brought forth from the concealment where authority had placed it, the truth in life itself, in literature, in philosophy, in art.  But one step farther and it merged into the search for truth in religion, where the movement known as the Reformation took up the work. *The German Renaissance.*

As in Italy, so in Germany, there was immense activity in studying languages, in unearthing old manuscripts, and in publishing the classics in the original texts.  John Reuchlin of Pforzheim even went back to the Hebrew, and published the first grammar and lexicon of that tongue.  Erasmus of Rotterdam edited numberless Latin authors.  He could not read Cicero's ethical writings without kissing them, and thought Cicero and Horace worthy of eternal salvation.  He tells us that he felt like praying: *Sancte Socrates, ora pro nobis*.  The study of Greek was fostered by the flight of Greeks from Constantinople, which fell into the hands of the Turks in 1453. Men like Ulrich von Hutten welcomed the new language in the most extravagant terms. "The spirits have awakened, it is a delight to live," Hutten wrote. But narrower minds felt aggrieved and injured. "A new rebellious language has been invented," cried a Dominican from the pulpit; "it is called Greek; in it has been written a book full of dangerous passages, the New Testament by name!"

The new-found enjoyment of life.

A distinguishing feature of the Renaissance was the enjoyment of life that it inculcated; the monastic theory of the vileness of the body was thrown aside, humanity and nature became the subjects of literature and of art, and the appeal to the senses was no longer a sin. One might even be amusing, might talk philosophy without technical terms, and sing the praises of wine and conviviality. We find the most learned men drinking in the fresh air of life, we meet them supping together, we hear them warning against too close an application to study and recommending a little joking and hilarity. "I have left you," writes Celtes, in an ode to the people of Ingolstadt, "because I cannot stand your bad beer; because no wine grows on high mountains, no hill rises above your city, no shady river flows by you except the huge Danube." He will go to the Rhine, where delicious wine grows, and where "merriment accompanies drinking."

Invention of printing.

Of immense importance in disseminating learning, as well as in fostering new ideas, was the invention of printing with movable type, for which the credit is to be given to John Gutenberg, who was active in Mainz in 1450, and whose productions are still preserved. Books of importance, hitherto existing in very few copies, could now be in the hands of every student. There was some truth in the mocking words of Conrad Celtes, that priests could no longer keep their holy science to themselves, and that heaven and hell must give up their secrets. The rapidity with which the art was taken up shows what a need was felt; there are known at the present day the names of some thousand printers who carried on business before the year 1500, and there still exist some thirty thousand books published before that date. Anthony Coburger of Nuremberg, in 1470, worked with twenty-four presses and one hundred apprentices. In connection with printing, wood engraving was brought to its highest perfection, and the works of Albrecht Dürer and others in this line have rarely been surpassed. The influence of woodcuts in moulding public opinion cannot be overestimated; it was greater, as regards the lower classes, than printing itself, and the productions ran the whole scale from inspired illustrations of sacred themes to the most scurrilous caricatures.

If we take the trouble to inquire into the relative popularity of the more important publications of the presses of the fifteenth century, we shall find that, while the interests of the students ran to classical learning and science, the burning questions with the masses were socialism and hierarchical reform. From the point of view of the printer, the Bible was already the most important book; up to the year 1500 no less than ninety-eight editions of the Latin Vulgata had appeared, some of them printed in a type that has never been surpassed for clearness, and with exquisite woodcuts. The *Imitation of Christ* was also widely read and went through many editions, while school-books and texts of classic authors found a wide circulation. Strangely enough, the most popular form of general literature of the day was the almanac or calendar: the belief in astrology was widespread, and it was taken for granted that the "knowing" could lift the veil of the future. Horoscopes and weather prophecies were taken

*Relative popularity of publications.*

with absolute seriousness; and the poor man searched eagerly to see under what constellation he had better be bled or what was the meaning of the new comet. Strange effects of light or massing of clouds portended blood, famine, pestilence, or drought.

Erasmus's
*Praise of
Folly*.

In the matter of inflaming the masses against the priests and the nobles, and in driving them on to the great outbreaks that were so soon to take place, the pamphlet, the satire, and the news-leaf played as prominent a part as did the spoken words of the political or religious agitator. Erasmus, in his *Praise of Folly*, which ran through twenty-seven editions, and for which Holbein the Younger supplied illustrations, attacked the evils of the church in the wittiest terms, though sparing that church's doctrines. He scourged the *fictæ scelerum condonationes*, or imaginary forgiveness of sins; the reckoning of time in purgatory by hours, days, months, years, and centuries; the running to this saint for toothache, to that one for the pains of childbirth; the ridiculous subjects that theologians were wont to discuss, — whether God if he wished could have taken on the form of a woman, an ass, a pumpkin, or the devil; how the pumpkin would have spoken and what miracles it would have performed. The monks come in for their share of blows; we are told how little piety they display, how they roar out their psalms with the bray of donkeys, how they appear before the throne of heaven and are refused admittance. Even the popes are not spared, but are accused of having persons of doubtful reputation at their court, and of leaving their work to Peter and Paul, while claiming for themselves the splendor and enjoyment.

Inflamma-
tory
writings.

Sebastian Brant in his *Ship of Fools* had written in a similar strain, as did dozens of lesser lights. Geiler von Kaisersberg says of the bishops, that their chief occupation is "to ride many horses, fill their money-bags,

eat good pullets, and run after the girls," while an unknown
writer declares of the nobles, that they no longer need
either senses or limbs since their letters are read for them,
their bread cut, and their clothes put on by others.   Woodcuts represented the peasants with pitchforks and threshing-
flails, and driving before them the Pope and the emperor.
Thousands of sheets were sent abroad representing Rome
as a hideous monster, the ship of St. Peter going to pieces
on a rock, the clergy being maltreated by the common man,
the peasant conducting the service before the altar, or the
priest guiding the plough.

For success in attaining a definite object, no satire can
compare with the *Letters of Obscure Men*, in the composition of which Ulrich von Hutten had a share.   The
greatest of the actual clashes between the old theology
and the new learning of the Renaissance had been the
conflict of the great Hebrew scholar, John Reuchlin, with
the Dominican monks of Cologne, whose mouthpiece was
Ortuin Gratius, a lecturer in the university, and who were
egged on by one Pfefferkorn, a renegade Jew.   The latter
had celebrated his conversion to Christianity by writing
venomous articles against his former brethren, and was so
successful in his propaganda that he obtained a decree
ordering that all Jewish books should be brought to the
town hall and carefully searched for insults against the
Christian religion.   As the greatest Hebrew scholar,
Reuchlin was invited by the Archbishop of Mainz, in the
name of the emperor, to report on a plan for burning all
Jewish books with the exception of the Old Testament.
In a formal writing the humanist gave his judgment in the
negative; the Jews, whose religion was allowed by law,
could not, he said, be reproached for explaining and defending their faith; only where there were direct attacks
on holy persons or institutions should the books be con-

*The
Letters of
Obscure
Men.*

demned — otherwise it would do Christians good to study them; indeed, he would warmly recommend that chairs of Hebrew be established in each university.

The Reuchlin feud.

The feud that was now carried on was of the bitterest description, Pfefferkorn even accusing Reuchlin of having been bribed by the Jews. Pamphlets rained thick and fast on either side. Hochstraten, the censor and inquisitor for the diocese, summoned Reuchlin to declare his horror of the Talmud and to prove his allegiance to the Christian faith. Gradually the old humanist lost his temper, and attacked Ortuin Gratius in particular with bitter insults — calling him a perverter, not a professor of good arts; a *versifex, metrifex, imo fex omnis sceleris et perfidiæ*. Hochstraten caused Reuchlin's chief pamphlet, the *Augenspiegel*, to be burnt as heretical, but in turn was made to do penance for his act by the Pope. A suit at law was begun at the papal court, but before it was decided Leo X., although a humanist himself, although he was having an edition of the Talmud printed for his own use, and had established a chair of Hebrew at Rome, pronounced against Reuchlin merely for the reason that he could not afford at that moment to break with the Dominicans.

Contents of the *Letters of Obscure Men*.

The *Epistolæ obscurorum Virorum* are a collection of 118 letters purporting to have been written, during the course of this struggle, by Dominicans themselves. Out of their own mouths they are to be made to condemn themselves, for their expressions, their manner of thinking, their pettinesses, are shown forth with such veiled ridicule that members of their own order were deceived. The letters are addressed to Ortuin Gratius, and present problems that are supposed to be troubling the "obscure" men. Is a person about to receive his degree at the university to be called *magister nostrandus* or *noster magistrandus*? Can you say a "member of ten universities," when a member can only form part of one body? If you eat a hatching egg on Friday, have you broken your fast? Will it not make the Jews too proud if everybody learns their language? Some derivations of words are discussed: magister is from *magis*, more, and *ter*, thrice, because a master should know three times as much as other people; or is it from *magis* and *terreo*, I frighten, seeing that he should inspire his pupils with fear? It crops out in the course of the correspondence that the monks have many weaknesses, that Ortuin himself is in love with a *bellula mulier*, who turns out to be none other than Pfefferkorn's wife. He defends himself by saying that friends should have all things in common. The satire grows more and more pungent and more and more comical, the language being turned and twisted in every way, rendering it impossible to translate. Its effect was to convulse the literary world, and to rouse its victims to fury.

But satire apart, the evils in church and state alike were crying to heaven for redress. The popes of the last half of the fifteenth century, whose deeds were soon to be trumpeted throughout Germany, were making for themselves a record for shamelessness that has never been surpassed. Their names have become a byword for hideous depths of crime. Paul II., successor of Pius II., was so inordinately vain that he would have preferred to call himself Formosus, and so fond of jewels that he would appropriate them if he could obtain them in no other way. Sixtus IV. was renowned for his worldliness and for his nepotism, and his nephew, Cardinal Riario, who gave Lucullan festivals, brought forward a plan for secularizing the Papacy and for making it hereditary. Innocent VIII. filled the Vatican with his sons and daughters, and became the jailer of the Turkish Djem, whose throne the latter's brother Bajazet had usurped. There was money to be

Evil character of the popes of the period.

earned, and, lest Bajazet might secretly poison Djem, his envoys to the Vatican were rubbed down, told to kiss the towel they had used, and also to lick the letters they presented. Innocent's death involved that of three young boys, whose blood the doctors were transfusing into his own veins. If a climax were possible, it was reached under Alexander Borgia. He did, indeed, refuse an offer of three hundred thousand florins for Djem's dead body, but sold him living to the king of France. Of the innumerable murders laid to his charge, two at least are conceded, even by his defenders, to rest on strong evidence. The last scene in his career was a supper at the house of a rich cardinal, where he and his son Cæsar partook by mistake of poison they had prepared for their host. Julius II. chose his name in memory of Julius Cæsar, and took the field in person ; while Leo X. openly expressed an intention of enjoying the Papacy while he had it, and is quoted as saying that the " fable of Christ " had been very lucrative. The triumphal arch erected in honor of his inauguration was adorned with heathen gods, and the inscription upon it ran that the reign of Minerva was about to follow on that of Venus and of Mars!

Character of the German clergy. If the German people as a whole troubled themselves little about the orgies that went on at Rome, there were plenty of examples at home of wicked and worldly priests and members of religious orders; — we hear of cardinals who went to masked balls and joined the dances ; of bishops making war and using the ban and interdict for their own personal advantage. Archbishop Gunther of Magdeburg read his first mass in the thirty-fifth year of his pontificate, while Robert of Strassburg never read one at all. The lower clergy paid blackmail to the higher for liberty to evade the law of celibacy, and, in turn, took their share of the profits of wine-shops and gambling resorts. The monks of Leubus refused to hold masses for the dead unless the abbot would give them daily a measure of beer as good as that which he drank himself; an abbot of Volkesrode, in 1484, restricted the usual quantity of wine so that his monks might at least be sober when entering the choir. We hear of cathedral chapters so aristocratic that candidates for membership had to show at least thirty-two noble ancestors; we hear of men who held as many as twenty-four ecclesiastical livings without occupying or performing the duties of any. The nunneries were too often mere temples of frivolity. "I never saw so many pretty women in one convent in my life," writes a Nuremburg citizen, in 1466, and tells as a matter of course of the pleasurable dances, the number of men-servants, and the pretty dresses.

What affected the Germans more than the personal character of the popes, or even of their own clergy, was the fact that much of their money found its way to Rome, which had become the great central trading house of Europe. A perfect army of notaries and copyists, of jurists and accountants, was employed, and church livings and indulgences for sin were dealt in like any other wares. A brisk trade was carried on in expectancies, or the right to succeed after the death of the first and even the second incumbent. Some bought them on speculation and re-sold them at a profit, and even laymen, like the bankers Fugger in Augsburg, are known to have been mixed up in transactions of the kind. Enraged at the extortionate prices paid at every turn, an envoy of the Teutonic Order, whose report we have, bursts forth indignantly, "We poor Germans continue to look on him [the Pope] as an earthly God; better if we could look on him as the earthly devil he really is!" The number of the taxes and the amounts required were appalling: bishops-elect had to pay thousands of guldens to be confirmed in their positions, thousands more for the pallium, the narrow neck-band that

*The mercenary spirit at Rome.*

was the badge of their office. The lower clergy had to pay the annates, which amounted regularly to half the income of the first year. Add to these the extra payments for special occasions, the gifts that had to be distributed right and left, and the continual levies for crusades which never came to pass.

The theory of the indulgences.
When Pope Leo X., the patron of Raphael and Michael Angelo, set his heart on rebuilding St. Peter's, and determined to raise the money by selling indulgences throughout the whole of Christendom, there was nothing in the measure itself to shock the public sentiment of the time. The institution dated back some three hundred years, and toward the end of the crusades it had been a common proceeding to remit the vows of pilgrimage for sums of money, which would procure the same absolution as the burdensome journey itself. Even at that time the scholastic philosophers had begun to teach that the church possessed, in the works of supererogation, or surplus good works of Christ, Mary, and the saints, an inexhaustible supply of wealth. Of this St. Peter held the keys, and from him the right of administration descended to the popes. The indulgences were drafts on these treasures, which were to be sold now at a fixed price. Why should not the church's possessions, it was argued, conduce to her own emolument, the more so as people were only too willing to commute their severer penitential duties for money payments? The Pope for a time seems really to have been considered as conferring a great boon on heavily laden sinners. It was, after all, but an application to religious offences of the method followed for centuries by the old Germanic law of labelling each crime with its appropriate fine.

It is true that remission of sins had been obtainable for centuries at a much less price than was now asked. Pope Boniface VIII. was once quoted as saying that if the

people only knew what absolutions were heaped up in
St. John Lateran they would sin a great deal more. By
merely looking at the handkerchief of St. Veronica one
could gain remission of sins for fourteen thousand years;
by listening to a mass in St. John's on Saturday one could
free one's mother from purgatory; one could do the same
by kneeling before a certain altar in St. Peter's, putting
one's finger in a hole in the stone, and saying five pater-
nosters. One Pope granted as many years "as it rains drops
of water in a single day."

All this would be incomprehensible should we fail to
recognize that this whole age, before science had unlocked
her mysteries, was one of the grossest and most widespread
superstition. No one, for instance, in all Christendom
seems to have doubted the existence of magic or supernatural powers. Pope Sixtus IV., in a bull of 1471, expressly
reserved for himself the manufacture of certain little figures representing lambs, which were efficacious against
witches, and the touching of which would insure against
fire, shipwreck, lightning, and hail-storms. The *Hexenham-
mer*, or *malleus maleficarum*, published in 1489, reduced the
hunting of witches to a system, and the most distinguished
men, even among the humanists, egged on the persecutors
and were present when the victims were burnt at the stake.
Men spoke seriously of giants with heads higher than the
roofs, who brought plague in their course; of dances of
death; of battles between spirits in the air. Alchemy, and
particularly the transmutation of metals, was experimented
in at various courts.

One phase of this belief in the supernatural, was that
constant running to saints for the cure of evils, which
called forth the ridicule of Erasmus. St. Anthony was
especially good for inflammation of the limbs; St. Erasmus
for stomach-ache; St. Martin for sick cattle; St. Gumprecht

Supersti-
tion of the
age.

for hydrophobia; St. Blasius for stiff neck. There were even fashions in saints, many having their day of glory only to be afterward neglected. At the very end of the fifteenth century there arose a new star of the first magnitude in the person of St. Anna, whose glory almost outshone that of her daughter, the Virgin Mary. Alexander VI., of poison fame, decreed that whoever should say an *Ave Maria* before her image, and acknowledge the immaculate conception, should have remission for 10,000 years from deadly and 20,000 from ordinary sins.

Collections of sacred relics.

In these dying days of a church universal all this was taken very seriously: because of a notorious swindle with regard to the Virgin Mary four monks were put to death in Berne in 1509. Pilgrimages to holy shrines seem to have been undertaken in greater numbers and with greater fervor than at any time since the crusades. Arrived at their destination, men would fall in ecstasy, stretch out their arms so as to form a cross, and adore the sacred object. At no other period do we hear of such zeal in making enormous collections of relics: Nicholas Muffel brought together enough to procure him remission for 246,400 days; he was eventually hanged by the city of Nuremberg for stealing public funds, a part of which had doubtless gone toward increasing his hoard. The collection of the Saxon elector, Frederick the Wise, could boast of more than 5000 numbers, consisting of the skulls, the bones, the hair of saints, the different objects with which Christ came in contact at the time of His passion, the skin of the face of St. Bartholomew, drops of the milk of Mary, bits of the rod of Aaron, of the burning bush, of the hay and straw on which the Christ child lay — enough in all to give absolution for half a million years. Yet even these did not equal the treasures of Archbishop Albert of Mainz, who possessed eight entire bodies and 9000 particles, not to speak of wine from the wedding of Cana, manna from the wilderness, a sample of the earth from which man was created, and a pair of nether garments once worn by Thomas Becket.

A peculiar feature of the period we are considering, was the formation of numerous brotherhoods for the heaping up of good works, which could be drawn on in time of need. Membership in the association of the 11,000 Virgins at Cologne could be gained by repeating 11,000 prayers. Regular ledgers were kept, and this particular brotherhood could show at one time a balance of 6000 masses, 3500 whole psalters, 200,000 tellings of rosaries, the same number of *Te Deums* and 10,000 times 63,000 Lord's Prayers and *Ave Marias*. When the Counts Palatine, in 1501, joined the Dominican order, they were assured by charter a share in all " masses, prayers, divine services, vigils, meditations, tears, sighs, penances, disciplines, fasts, abstinences, pilgrimages, studies, and other good works that are performed by the brothers and sisters."

All this was the straining of a bow that was soon to break.  While the timid were clinging blindly to the old church, and trying to prop themselves up with the good deeds of others, bolder men were already coming forward with sentiments that a few years earlier would have cost them their lives.  Church usages and even fundamental doctrines were being held up to ridicule.  Conrad Celtes declared that he wished to practise his devotions in the woods and fields, and not within musty church walls which echoed with the babble of priestlets.  He mocked at fasts and remission of sins, at hell and devils, and was not even sure of the existence of God or of the soul's immortality. In the *Letters of Obscure Men* the holy coat of Treves is called a lousy old doublet.  Reuchlin, in translating the Old Testament, departs from the authoritative renderings of St. Jerome ; " Although I venerate Jerome as an angel,"

Prayer brotherhoods.

Rise of scepticism.

he wrote, "I adore truth as a God!" We find other humanists comparing the Christian with the Mohammedan religion, the birth of Christ with that of Hercules, the Virgin Mary with the true Diana and Lucina who "brought for us the threefold giant into the world."

Condition of the German peasant.

The class in which hatred of the priesthood and of ecclesiastical authority in general took deepest root, was the great body of the peasants; but no less deep was their hatred of the noble. Indeed it is a question if the old Hussite ideas concerning personal liberty and community of goods had not much to do with their feeling against both. Nor can it be denied that there were many real and crying grievances, or that at the beginning of the revolt they acted with dignity and moderation.

Of the German peasants some few were completely free, some few were absolutely slaves, but between these two extremes lay the whole body of the rural population, bound by every gradation of servitude. The undoubted tendency, however, at the end of the fifteenth and beginning of the sixteenth centuries, was in a downward direction. Old liberties were taken away, new hardships imposed, while more and more disregard was shown for all the smaller distinctions. The blame for this state of affairs is to be thrown chiefly upon two great causes: the increase in luxury of the upper classes, consequent in part at least on the improved facility for intercourse with other nations; and, secondly, the introduction of the old Roman system of legal procedure into the law courts of Germany.

Luxury and gluttony.

That luxury, or in other words extravagance in dress and the tendency to excess in eating and drinking, was felt by the better minds of the day to be the canker-worm eating at the heart of the national prosperity, is shown by the frequency with which the matter was brought up, both in the imperial and in the local diets. At Nuremberg, in 1524, it was seriously proposed that, as the current modes of apparel were out of all proportion to the demands of rank and station, and as drunkenness and revelling were becoming far too common, there should, on the one hand, be stringent dress regulations, according to which he who procured the conviction of any one on a charge of wearing a forbidden article might be given the article in question; and, on the other, that crimes committed while in a state of intoxication should be much more seriously punished than ordinary offences. The committee to which this motion was referred reported the reform impracticable, unless it were to be made applicable first of all to the princes themselves. The city of Nuremberg had its own particular wagon to bring in the drunkards from the streets.

We have the memoirs of a tailor's apprentice, who tells how he was obliged to adorn the most ordinary garments of the nobles : "Like painters we had to embroider upon them clouds, stars, blue skies, lightning, hail, clasped hands — not to speak of dice, lilies, roses, trees, twigs, stems, crosses, eye-glasses, and countless other foolish things." "The lords and knights," says another contemporary, "think of nothing save of making their long hair curly and blond; they try to imitate women in clothing, voice, and gait, put on jewelry, and tear out the hairs of their beards." We know from other sources that men occasionally laced, wore long hair, bared their neck and shoulders, and displayed necklaces and bracelets. While their upper garments, of the richest and gayest materials, were ridiculously short, their legs would be encased in tight-fitting hose of the most startling colors and with the two sides differing completely. The length of the points on their shoes was often so great that an ordinance of Ratisbon, in 1485, restricts it to two inches.

Nor were women far behindhand in the matter of

*Extravagance in dress.*

extravagance; they wore strange head-dresses and immensely long trains of costly material. "There are a thousand different inventions as to costume," writes Geiler von Kaisersberg, "at one time wide sleeves as in monks' frocks, at another so narrow that one can scarcely get into them." A law of Ratisbon for the suppression of luxury sets as maximum for each woman eighteen dresses and eighteen cloaks or outer garments.

The grinding down of the peasant.

All this is not unimportant, for inability to keep pace with such expenditure completed the moral and material ruin of the knights; while the burden too often fell upon the poor peasants, whose labor was their masters' only source of income. The most hated impositions were the *Frohndienste*, or menial services, and the *Todfall*, or inheritance tax, that took from each property so often as it changed hands the best head of cattle or the best piece of raiment. Among the services required were some of the most trivial and galling character — to frighten off the wild beasts from the garden by continuous shouting, or to quiet the frogs in the pool while the master slept. Small was the chance for redress, for the introduction toward the end of the fifteenth century of a system of law that had originated in an imperial slave state furnished timely aid in this process of grinding and oppression. What did Roman law know of the old Germanic liberties, what sympathy did it have with the old custom by which the villagers enjoyed their woods and pastures in common? The code of Justinian had no words for the different relations between master and man; the term *servus*, or slave, was a convenient one under which to group all peasants. Many who had considered themselves mere tenants came to see that they had been bitterly mistaken. At the same time they were goaded to madness by numberless petty oppressions. Their children were required to do service in the master's household; they themselves were called upon for extra labor without payment; water was withdrawn from their mills, their fields were hunted over, and their crops ruined with no possibility of obtaining compensation. Their general condition at the beginning of the sixteenth century was one of extreme wretchedness; their farms were mortgaged at a high rate of interest, and it was a common thing to pledge the coming harvest in return for an immediate loan.

All the while just enough enlightenment was spreading among the masses to enable them to perceive the degradation of their position.     Exactly how many of them were able to profit directly by the art of printing, is a question that cannot be answered, but certain it is that long before the Reformation inflammatory pamphlets circulated widely among them.     Many editions were struck off between the years 1476 and 1497 of a curious writing, entitled *Emperor Sigismund's Reform*, which recommended an entirely new order of things, in which the "lowly were to be exalted, and the mighty cast down."     In the country, water, wood, and pasture were to be free; in the cities, monopolies and guilds were to cease.     The clergy were to be deprived of their estates and to live on a small yearly salary.     An even more dangerous form of literature was that furnished by the astrological pamphlets and woodcuts, which are said to have actually outnumbered the theological writings of the reformers.     With their silly prophecies they kept the people in a fever of excitement: for the year 1524 they had announced that all the signs had united in foretelling a general deluge, which was especially to drown the mighty.     Nor were there wanting direct appeals to the worst of human passions.     One such writing, issued anonymously, called for the annihilation of all lords, and pointed out that, of seventy-six Roman emperors, thirty-four, on

*[margin: Inflammatory writings.]*

account of their tyranny, had met with a violent death. The day of slaughter, it declared, was now at hand for the fattened herds which had so long pastured their lusting hearts on the poverty of the common man.

Peasant
revolts.

No wonder, in the face of such agitation, that various attempts at open revolt should have taken place from time to time. The conventional emblem of such an uprising had come to be the *Bundschuh*, or common laced boot of the peasant, as opposed to the buckskin of the knight; it was depicted on a banner or raised aloft on a pole. For years a certain Jost Fritz had been active in different parts of Franconia in rallying followers to his standard, and in trying to effect the downfall of all princes and prelates. He is said to have "spoken such honeyed words as to make all who heard him believe that from that time on they would be happy and rich." In Würtemberg, in 1514, it had been found necessary to put a bloody end to the activity of a league known as the Poor Conrad, and more than a dozen ringleaders had been seized and beheaded. So the *Bundschuh* had not been idle, and its very name struck a certain terror into the hearts of the upper classes.

Into religious and social agitation such as has been described fell the first manifestations of the Reformation; it was like sparks igniting gunpowder. In the rock on which Peter had built his church clefts were riven that never again could be bridged over.

# CHAPTER XI

## MARTIN LUTHER AND THE EMPEROR CHARLES V

LITERATURE : An English translation of Luther's three great addresses to the German people has been made by Wace and Buchheim. Beard's *Martin Luther* is excellent for the first four great years. Köstlin is exhaustive. Baumgarten's *Karl V.* is a monumental work. Freytag's *Dr. Luther* is a charming sketch. Bezold has written the best history of the whole German Reformation, more full, even, than the work of Ranke. Egelhaaf's *Reformation* has its own merits ; his smaller work, *Deutsche Geschichte im Zeitalter der Reformation,* is convenient and well written.

THE age being fully ripe for revolution, all that was needed was a leader fearless, overbearing it might be, but strong enough to win the respect of friend and foe alike. Such a one was the monk Martin Luther, a man who had fought such struggles with his own conscience that at times in the monastery at Erfurt he would fall on the ground and remain in a swoon for hours. To use his own language, he had "suffered such great and hellish pain as no tongue could tell and no pen describe"; he had reached a condition of such utter despair as to make him recoil before every image of Christ, seeing in it the devil in person. The strength of such a nature lay in its conservatism; it would take much to destroy its creeds and ideals, but the process once begun had to go on at any cost, even to the bitter end.

*Mental struggles of Martin Luther.*

An experience of great moment for the future had been a journey to Rome in the interest of his order, a journey which he made on foot, relying on the hospitality of monasteries. He had long been anxious to go, expecting to

*The journey to Rome.*

251

find there more holiness than in other places. He intended to make a grand confession of all the sins he had ever committed in his whole life. He once said himself, later, that he was in those days a "most mad papist, so drunken, so drowned in the papal dogmas" as to be willing to slay the Pope's detractors. The consecrated priest, so he thought, was to the ordinary Christian as the morning star to the flame of a candle. On reaching the city which was the home of his beloved saints, he fell on his knees with a "hail, holy Rome!" He ran round among the churches like a "mad saint"; he was sorry his father and mother were still alive, so simple a matter would it have been to release them from purgatory. He began to mount the *scala santa* on his knees with prayers and contrition; but there kept ringing in his ears the words "the just shall live by faith," and he desisted before he reached the top. His was indeed a rude awakening! He heard priests at the altar make blasphemous witticisms in Latin; he was himself once told when performing mass to hurry and send back her son to the mother of God!

Tetzel the indulgence-hawker.

The sale of papal indulgences in the neighborhood of Wittenberg brought about the crisis of Martin Luther's life. It was not the institution itself that aroused his wrath so much as the particular attendant circumstances. The Archbishop of Mainz, that same Albert of Brandenburg who possessed such a quantity of relics, had borrowed a large sum of money from the banking house of Fugger, to pay for his pallium; but was allowed to set aside for repayment of this debt a portion of the indulgence money collected in his diocese. That the sum might be as large as possible, the conduct of the affair was handed over to one Tetzel, a Dominican and a man of great experience. Tetzel had sold papal privileges for the benefit of the Teutonic knights, for a copper roof on the church at Görlitz, for a bridge across the Elbe at Torgau, and had also been agent for the so-called butter-charters, or permits to eat butter when otherwise forbidden. On the present occasion he offered various kinds of privileges, for which men were to pay on a sliding scale, according to their rank and wealth: plenary remission for the moment, the release of souls from purgatory, the right to choose a confessor, and to be absolved in the last agony. Accompanied by an agent of the Fuggers, who was provided with a duplicate key to the strong box, Tetzel, with a noisy train bearing banners and tapers, and holding the papal bull aloft on a golden or velvet cushion, would enter a city and march to the church to the clanging of bells. There in the nave would be erected a great crucifix displaying the crown of thorns and the nail holes, as well as the papal arms and standards; on particularly solemn occasions the red blood of the Crucified One was seen to run down the wood. In front of the cross was an iron-bound coffer; to one side a pulpit, to the other a table at which the actual business was transacted. It was a royal road to salvation that was here presented; for a paltry sum of money an instant escape was offered from all the weary pilgrimages, all the fastings, and all the abject creepings to the foot of the cross.

If Tetzel's methods were shocking to sensitive souls, it must be said in his defence that he preached exactly as he had been told to preach by the archbishop of the diocese. One of his well-known sayings, that as the money rattled in the box the soul flew out of purgatory, was later defended by a churchman of high standing as a justifiable spice for an indulgence sermon. Another that Luther mentions, to the effect that absolution could be bought even if one had offered violence to the mother of God, was formally denied by Tetzel. Luther was most directly

Defence of Tetzel.

affected by the permission to choose a confessor; for members of his own flock, on whom he had imposed penance, left him and sought remission elsewhere.

The ninety-five theses. In a hesitating way, not entirely denying their value, or the right of the Pope to issue them, Luther began to preach against the indulgences; finally, on the eve of All Saints' Day, 1517, he formulated his objections into ninety-five theses and nailed them on the door of the Wittenberg church. There was nothing defiant in his attitude; the same door had often done service as a university bulletin board, and the academic nature of the theses was shown by the fact that they were written in Latin. Luther took the ground that the church had never formulated its doctrines regarding indulgences, and that the matter was open to discussion. No one was more surprised than he at the sensation caused by his act. We are told that within four weeks his theses flew, as though borne by angels, sheer throughout Christendom.

Luther maintained that he was not attacking the Pope, but merely the excesses of the pardoners; that could Leo know the truth, he would let St. Peter's burn to ashes, rather than build it up with the skin and flesh and bones of his sheep; that Christians must seek Christ through pains, deaths, and hells, not by royal roads. "Away with all those prophets who say to the people of Christ, peace, peace, and there is no peace!" Yet he could not refrain from asking a few plain questions:—if Leo could release souls for money, why does he not empty purgatory, "for the sake of most holy charity"? or, seeing that he is richer than Crœsus, why not build St. Peter's himself?

Effect of theses. In the Roman camp the effect of the theses was tremendous. Archbishop Albert, though he rebuked Tetzel for "injuring the holy business," instituted a formal trial, and Luther was summoned to appear before the Pope, in

Rome, within sixty days. Orders were sent to arrest him, to bind him hand and foot, while ban and interdict were to be hurled at his defenders. The elector of Saxony, whose subject he was, was asked to hand over this child of iniquity. Tetzel, now Doctor of Theology, wrote counter theses, in which he answered Luther's appeal to the authority of the Bible with the naïve remark, that many of the Catholic truths were contained neither in the Scriptures nor in the church Fathers. Prierias, "Master of the Holy Palace," argued so ably, to his own mind, that Luther, he said, "must have an iron nose and a brazen face" if he refused to be convinced. Yet, in rough terms, his argument was simply that the Pope, as highest sovereign in the world, might do as he pleased in all things, and was to be thanked for not demanding, as a direct tax, the sums he deigned to accept in return for the indulgences.

Luther's own humility at this crisis was almost excessive; he begged that his theses be not accepted as an irrevocable expression of his opinions; he was doubtful on some points, ignorant on others, some he would even deny. In a letter to Albert he speaks of himself as the "dregs of humanity," of the archbishop as "at the height of sublimity." He says later that he felt "more like a corpse than a man"; he writes to Leo, asking him passionately for comfort and advice, "I cannot revoke, though I see the multitude inflamed against me!" He is only a plain, narrow, not finely educated man, in an age that might displace even a Cicero; "but necessity drives me on; the goose must cackle among the swans. At thy Holiness's feet I prostrate myself with all that I am and all that I possess. . . . In thy voice I will recognize the voice of Christ dwelling and speaking in thee. If I have deserved death, I am not unwilling to die."

Leo X. was no persecutor; his chief delight was the dis-

*Luther's humility.*

covery of a new manuscript or a new work of art; provided there were no interference with his own extravagances,
he was willing that all should be happy around him.   When
he first heard that Luther, an Augustinian, was in conflict
with a Dominican, he attached little importance to the matter.   "This Brother Martin is a clever fellow," he said,
"and it is only a case of jealous monks."   Yet all the same
Leo was dangerous because not master of his own actions,
and a journey to Rome would have exposed Luther to the
fate of a Savonarola or a Huss.   The reformer was not
minded to submit to useless peril before his work was half
begun; he even suggested, through his friend Spalatin,
that the Saxon elector refuse him a safe-conduct.   As a
result of correspondence between Frederick the Wise and
the Pope, permission was gained for the " son of iniquity "
to remain on German ground, but he was to appear at
Augsburg before the Cardinal de Vio, known as Cajetanus.

Luther and       A greater contrast than the two men who now con-
Cajetanus.   fronted each other could scarcely be imagined: the one
humble, yet alert and honestly seeking for truth; the
other haughty, magnificent, and overbearing, fast bound
in the chains of scholasticism ; — so ardent an admirer of
Aquinas, indeed, that he had changed his own name to
Thomas.   Hutten declared sarcastically that the cardinal
slept in his purple robes and drank out of goblets of gold;
that the wines of Germany fairly made him weep, and that
he considered it, therefore, a barbarous country.   A firm
upholder of papal infallibility, Cajetanus had been known
to intimate that the church only existed for the sake of the
Pope.   He had come now to Augsburg, where the Diet of
the Empire was in session, to preach a crusade against the
Turks; to make Bohemia conform to the mother church;
and to bring the red hat to the Archbishop of Mainz.

Arrived in the city after parting with friends who feared

greatly for his safety, Luther was visited by various persons who gave him sympathy if not encouragement. "Do you wish," said Serralonga, a good-natured Italian diplomatist, "to play at running the ring with the cardinal? Do you think that the elector will take up arms on your account?" — "I do not think it," was the reply, "nor is it my wish." — "And where will you be then?" — "Under the heavens."

At the first interview with Cajetanus, which was held in the presence of three of Luther's friends, of a papal legate and of this same Serralonga, the monk showed to the cardinal all the respect that was due from a subordinate to one so vastly above him in rank. He threw himself on the ground the whole length of his body, and only rose when bidden. The churchman had evidently thought that the mere magic of his presence was causing this heretic to quail; but Luther now asked him to point out in detail his particular errors. Cajetanus mentioned two, — the denial that the merits of the saints formed a treasure of the church, and the doctrine that faith was necessary to make the sacrament effectual. Papal bulls were brought out in favor of the church's position, and Luther found himself declaring that the papal bulls were of no account if contradicted by the plain sense of Scripture. The issue had been fairly joined, papal omnipotence had been denied, and the old conservative, stubborn theology stood over against the new spirit of criticism. Cajetanus kept repeating incessantly, "Recant and see thine error; thus the Pope wills it and not otherwise, whether thou like it or no." The interrogation was continued a second and a third day; Luther's request to have his teachings submitted to the great universities was denied, and the interviews grew more and more stormy. Upon Cajetanus imputing to one of the bulls a meaning which was manifestly false, Luther lost all

*The hearing at Augsburg.*

patience. "Do not let your Reverend Paternity think that the Germans are wholly ignorant of grammar," he cried in anger. "Go," said the cardinal, "and come back to me no more till you are willing to recant." He afterward said to Staupitz, "I will speak no more with this monster, for he has deep eyes and wonderful fancies in his head."

The flight from Augsburg.

The next that we hear of Luther, he is flying for his life from Augsburg, at night, through a postern gate, on a hard-trotting nag, and clad only in his monk's cowl, without trousers. He had heard that an attempt was to be made to hold him fast and deliver him up, and we know now that Cajetanus was actually provided with a papal brief designating Brother Martin as a stubborn heretic and ordering his arrest. Ban and interdict stood at the disposal of the cardinal; in whatever locality refuge might be offered to Luther no bell could be rung, no sacrament performed, no corpse even receive Christian burial. The fugitive had left behind him a letter for Cajetanus, in which he said that he had done everything as became an obedient son of the church. Notwithstanding the distance, his poverty, the infirmity of his health, he had come to Augsburg to be called to account. The legate had bid him begone unless he were willing to recant; now he could stay no longer. His last resource was to make an appeal, not only from the cardinal, but from the Pope himself, so long as the latter should continue to be misinformed concerning him. This appeal, which called for a fair and impartial hearing before learned and just men and in a safe place, was attached by a friendly notary to the door of the Augsburg cathedral soon after the escape. Luther carried with him one comfort in his flight: he had seen that there were other complaints against Rome than those which he himself had formulated; he had learned that his cause was in a fair way to become the cause of the country at large. The imperial diet at Augsburg had refused to contribute to the crusade on the express grounds of the evils inflicted by Rome on the German nation.

Nothing shows more clearly Luther's growing importance and influence in Germany, than the timid and cautious manner in which he was next approached. The case was intrusted now to a very different man from the haughty Cajetanus — to the papal chamberlain Miltitz, who was to begin the attack by bribing the elector Frederick with the golden rose. Miltitz, a German who had gone to Rome to seek his fortune, because he was hampered at home by being one of twenty-four children, was excellently fitted for his mission. He could rise to any occasion, could be serious and dignified, or could hold his own at the wildest drinking bout. The conduct of the present campaign was to be left to his discretion; he was to be affable or severe, to strike or conciliate as the case might demand. Should he need them, anathemas of various kinds were supplied against the "son of perdition, yea of Satan." "Miltitz has brought the rose," wrote a friend of Luther's, "and with it briefs by no means rosy."

*Miltitz and Luther.*

But when the legate found how widespread was the movement, and how warm the supporters of the reformer, he determined that severity would be of no avail, and called upon Tetzel, not Luther, to appear before his judgment seat. Tetzel refused; it was as much as his life was worth, he wrote, to leave Leipzig, "for Martin Luther, the Augustinian has so roused and moved the mighty against me, that I am nowhere safe." Miltitz went to Leipzig, interviewed the indulgence-hawker, heard all that he had to say, and then pronounced him a rogue. The poor Dominican, accused among other things of embezzling part of the money he had collected, was terribly hurt at the outcome of the interview, and never raised his head again.

*Miltitz and Tetzel.*

Six months later, hearing that he was on his death-bed, Luther had the generosity to write him a letter bidding him " be comforted ; that the affair had not been begun on his account, but that the child had quite a different father."

Luther was little affected by a hint of one of Miltitz's followers that a bishopric awaited him if he would only recant ; but the legate did persuade him to enter into a truce in the course of which the matter was to be referred to some erudite bishop ; in the meanwhile a conciliatory and submissive letter was to be despatched by the reformer to Rome.   Outwardly on the best of terms, the two men took their evening meal together, and at parting Miltitz gave the kiss of peace ; " The kiss of Judas," Luther called it later, and the legate's tears he described as " crocodile's tears."

John Eck.   The little period of rest did not last long.   Unaware of the agreement of Miltitz, other champions of the church were preparing to come forward, notably the great disputant of the age, the theologian John Eck.   As knights of old, seeking a joust, went round from court to court, so this literary gladiator of imposing presence and loud voice was ready for any fray.   It was said that it mattered little to him which side he espoused : he had once been employed by the banking house of Fugger to controvert the teachings of the church with regard to lending at interest.

Eck had written a commentary, called the *Obelisks*, upon eighteen of Luther's theses ; the latter had answered by *The Asterisks of Luther against the Obelisks of Eck*, and his erratic, flighty friend, Andrew Bodenstein, called Carlstadt, had written no less than four hundred and six theses attacking Eck and Tetzel.   Eck, who posed as a warm upholder of the old philosophy, and who was peculiarly annoyed at this time by the appearance of a satirical woodcut representing scholasticism in a coach and four driving rapidly to hell, while another coach surmounted by a crucifix was mounting heavenward, challenged Carlstadt to a public disputation at some university, and at the same time sent word to Luther, " You will see by the schedule of dispute that I have laid down propositions not so much against Bodenstein as against your writings."

Duke George of Saxony, liberal to a certain extent, though holding fast to the fundamental doctrines of the church, was pleased that his university should be honored by the presence of such great men, and offered his city of Leipzig, and even the hall of his own castle, as the scene of the dispute.   The greatest preparations were made for the event, and Luther, in the interim, plunged into studies in church history that were to yield him remarkable results. Gradually his horizon was broadening in all directions; he had already begun to have his doubts about the fundamental pretensions of the Papacy.   " I do not know," he wrote, " whether the Christian faith can bear having any other head of the universal church on earth than Christ himself; " and again, " I am looking through papal decrees for my disputation, and must whisper in your ear that I find it hard to decide whether the Pope is Antichrist or merely his apostle."   He was going to Leipzig " to strike out straight at the Roman snakes, at papal tyranny and deceit"; he was climbing a very different kind of *scala santa* from the one he had found in Rome!

Disputation of Leipzig.

The proceedings at Leipzig were opened with great form and ceremony, Leipzig students being detailed to walk with the Wittenberg masters in the grand procession, and Duke George himself attending the sessions.   The combat began by a discussion between Carlstadt and Eck on divine grace and free-will, — a discussion that unfortunately proved so wearisome as to send many of the hearers to sleep.   The professional disputant proved superior to his antagonist at every point, the more so as the latter desired and needed aid from books which he was not allowed to produce; nor was the dignity of the occasion enhanced by Carlstadt's willingness, when at a loss for words, to be helped by whispers and by notes from the lookers-on.

Luther a
Hussite.

But after a few days the real combat began, and Luther and Eck locked arms on the question of the divine right of the Papacy. The views that were now brought forward differed as totally as did the outward appearance and manner of the two antagonists. Eck, tall, solid, square, with the voice of a tragedian or of a town crier, insisted that, in the bishopric of Rome and in the power of the keys alike, the Pope was, and had always been, recognized to be the direct successor of St. Peter. Luther, at this time spare of frame, spent with care and study, though always with a cheerful countenance, pointed out that the church had flourished elsewhere before the see of Rome could possibly have been founded, that the proofs of Rome's precedence and antiquity were only the "very frigid" decrees of the pontiffs of the last four centuries, as opposed to the proven history of eleven hundred years. Had not the Greeks for centuries belonged to the Christian church and acknowledged nobody save their own patriarchs? Had the Council of Nicæa or the church fathers looked upon the Pope as head of Christendom?

But Eck had his quiver full of poisoned arrows, and he suddenly forced his antagonist into admissions that terrified his hearers, and evoked an oath from Duke George, which was heard in every corner of the hall. Eck answered the argument about the Greek church by saying calmly that the Greeks were heretics beyond reach of salvation, and showed triumphantly that among the errors for which John Huss had gone to the stake in Constance were the assertions that faith in the headship of the Roman church was not necessary to salvation, and that the church on earth needed no head at all. Luther was fairly caught in the toils of his adversaries; it was a part of the gospel of every Saxon to believe in Huss as the incarnation of sedition and heresy. Up to this time Luther himself had had the same feeling; he had once come upon a writing of the Bohemian preacher and had slammed the book to, and thrust it away as a thing of evil. Now, driven to bay, he was forced to acknowledge before friends and foes that many of these teachings were right Christian and evangelical, thus sealing his breach with Rome. He had asserted that a council of holy church could be in error; that the Council of Constance had been in error when it tried John Huss and condemned him to a cruel death: what need of further inquiries or disputations? " We are all Hussites without knowing it," he wrote to his friend Spalatin, the secretary of Frederick the Wise, " yea, St. Paul and St. Augustine were actual Hussites." He was amazed, he declared, that the pure evangelical truth should have been accursed for more than a century.

Meanwhile, of great importance for the future of the Reformation was the fact, that in January of this same year, 1519, the Emperor Maximilian had succumbed to an attack of illness, brought on, it is said, by rage at the attitude of the tavern-keepers of his own Tyrolese city of Innsbruck, who refused to harbor his retinue without better prospect of remuneration. It was June before the question as to who should succeed to the " Holy Roman Empire of the German Nation " was finally brought to a settlement. Within the limits of those five months falls one of the most active and exciting electoral campaigns ever waged in Germany. The rank and prestige of the different candidates, the sacrifices made by all parties to attain

The imperial election.

their ends, the interested concern of the chief European powers, the importance of the outcome for the rising tide of Protestantism, — everything combined to make this imperial election different from any that had gone before.

It is difficult to understand just why the imperial office should have been such an object of desire; neither Maximilian nor Frederick III. had seemed to greatly prize it; pecuniary benefit there was none. Yet in a way there was great respect for the time-honored institution; it was the fourth of the great monarchies mentioned in Daniel's vision, the one that was to endure until the end of time; a certain tacit precedence was accorded its head by all other European sovereigns. Moreover, the title was a convenient stepping-stone for men of large ambition — he who held it was, as a matter of course, considered the proper leader in a war against the Turks.

From the beginning of the sixteenth century, on through the next two hundred years, complications with the Ottoman Empire form the key-note to European politics. It is the reversal of the crusades — under the sign of the cimeter as many expeditions are hurled against Christian Europe as ever troubled the repose of Islam. The dream of Maximilian's life had been to lead a host against this enemy; ever since they took Constantinople, in 1453, they had harassed the borders of Hungary. Now, more than ever, there was need of stemming the swelling tide. No Adolphus of Nassau, chosen for his mediocrity, but a strong and resolute and warlike emperor was needed, with great resources at his command.

The early years of Charles V.

Although Maximilian, in fits of impecuniousness, had more than once bartered for the sale of his influence as regarded the succession, — notably with England and with Hungary, — he had, in his heart of hearts, always intended that the imperial mantle should fall upon the shoulders of his own grandson, the young King Charles of Spain. With Hungary, Bohemia, Naples, the Netherlands, Mexico, Peru, Jerusalem, and other realms, some real, some visionary, there would thus be united on one head no less than twenty-five crowns.

Naturally enough, a youth with such splendid prospects had been the object of solicitude in many directions. From the time when he was a year old, the question of his marriage had agitated all the courts of Europe; no less than ten times had he been affianced before wedding his Portuguese bride; for his guardians and councillors, chiefly leading statesmen in the Netherlands, like Chièvres and Adrian of Utrecht, had not scrupled to break one projected union after another, according to the weather-vane of policy. Nor had there been wanting other intrigues. The regent Margaret had been regularly paid by old Ferdinand of Aragon to keep the boy from appearing in Castile and attempting to gain popularity.

In such an attitude of calculation, with all natural family life rendered impossible by the insanity of his mother, who spent her time in brooding over the grave of her faithless husband, the boy had grown up cold, selfish, and taciturn. "He is as unapproachable as an idol," so an English ambassador described him when he had reached the age of seventeen. His development had been singularly slow; although before his tenth year he had shown a strong love for hunting, much to the delight of Maximilian, who was sure, now, he said, that the boy was a Hapsburg. A portrait of Charles, painted after he had already, at the age of sixteen, become king of Spain, shows the features of a much younger lad; nor had he up to this time succeeded in mastering either the Spanish or the German languages. His health often gave rise to anxiety; we hear of fainting fits, of something like epilepsy, of attacks so severe that recovery was doubtful. Was it consciousness of his own deficiencies, or was it the sense of a certain dormant power, that made him appear in a Spanish tourney with a snow-white shield on which was emblazoned the word *nondum,* or "not yet"? The regular motto that he later adopted was *plus ultra,* or "more beyond."

Maximilian's efforts to secure Charles's election.

By the time Charles, born with the century, was eighteen, Maximilian had determined to have him appointed "king of the Romans and future emperor" during his own lifetime. With this end in view, and supplied with funds from Spain, the emperor approached different members of the electoral college, and persuaded four out of the seven to promise him in writing that they would vote in favor of the plan. It was hoped that within a month the coronation might take place. The chief opposition came from the court of Rome, and one at least of Leo X.'s objections was entitled to consideration. How could there be chosen a new king of the Romans when Maximilian himself could boast of no other title, having never been crowned at Rome with the imperial crown? It is true he had commonly been called emperor, but that was by courtesy of the Pope! Never in the history of the empire had there been two kings of the Romans at the same time.

Leo's real cause for dread was lest a man who was already king of Naples should come to wear the imperial crown: it was the old fatal combination of Hohenstaufen times, the combination that made the Papacy feel as though its dominions were enclosed in a vice. "Do you know," Leo once said to the Venetian ambassador, who has recorded the remark, "how far it is from here to the borders of the Neapolitan territory?" — "Forty miles." "The Catholic king must not become king of the Romans." So bulls and decisions of former days were brought forward to support the contention, and it was evident that if a rival could be found for Charles, he would be sure of the Pope's favor.

Before his schemes had ripened into fulfilment, Maximilian was gathered to his fathers. In spite of the sums expended, in spite of the compacts made, the agreement as to the succession was pronounced null and void. It was a far different matter, said the electors, to choose a king of the Romans who might not be called upon to rule for many years, and to elect the actual head of the nation. The lists were thus thrown open and the great contest began. In answer to a letter of the young Spanish king announcing his hopes and expectations, Francis I. of France wrote back that he and Charles were "two friends who were suing for the favor of one and the same dame." Nor could a more redoubtable antagonist have well been found. Since the battle of Marignano, won over the Swiss in 1515, Francis had been known as a brave warrior and skilful general. Young, ambitious, unscrupulous, he was at the head of a strong, well-consolidated monarchy and with vast resources in his hands. Charles, on the other hand, lord though he was of many scattered lands, was already hard pressed for money; his Spanish cities, on the verge of revolution, turned a deaf ear to all his demands, while his old device *nondum* would as yet have fitly applied to his experience in war. *The rivalry of Charles and Francis I.*

Pope Leo espoused the cause of Francis as though it had been his own; his legates were instructed to instil into the mind of the French king that he was about to acquire the imperial dignity through the "favor and grace of his Holiness," for which favor and grace he was expected to make some substantial return. Nor was Leo's boast so utterly vain, — three of the seven electors were dignitaries of the church, and each was now promised advancement in rank in return for his vote. Treves and Cologne were to *Pope Leo and the German election.*

receive cardinals' hats, while the Archbishop of Mainz was to become perpetual legate of the Roman see for the whole of Germany. Had the Pope been actuated by the least regard for the larger interests of the church, he would, indeed, have thrown himself into the arms of Charles and moved heaven and earth to procure his election; for he, far better than his rival, was in a position to ward off the two great dangers that threatened Catholic Christendom. The rapacious Turks, who but recently had been ravaging the shores of the Mediterranean and had all but succeeded in capturing his Holiness himself, were actually quartered on the lands of the house of Hapsburg, and Charles's every personal interest would impel him to head an army that should drive them back. The bigoted character, on the other hand, and the early training of the grandson of Ferdinand and Isabella made it just as certain that he would wage war to the knife with the rising power of Lutheranism. It is true, with regard to both of these matters, Francis made great professions. His hand in the hand of the English ambassador, he swore on his honor that in the event of his election he would be in Constantinople within three years or die in the attempt. Already he had laid plans for restoring the empire of the East with the Pope's aid, and placing its crown on his own head. But all this was the mere selfish dream of ambition; Francis had no real reason for hating either Turks or German Lutherans, and the future was to show that, when it served his ends, he could condescend to an alliance with both.

Rival efforts.

The sums formerly squandered by Maximilian in the matter of Charles's election were the merest trifle in comparison with the outlays that now were needed. The French king had expressed his willingness to spend one-half of his yearly revenue for the attainment of his object; his agents travelled like princes, and eight hundred horses at one time were provided for the retinues of three of them. Their set plan was to dazzle by reports of their master's power, of his riches, of his great deeds. " As the sun out-shines the stars," they proclaimed, "so far does he surpass all other princes." The young king of Spain, with his finances already considerably involved, could not begin to compete with Francis in the single matter of bribing the electors, although it was computed afterward that he had spent in all nearly a million ducats.

The supporters of the Spanish aspirant were for a while in the depths of despair; the one and only escape from disastrous defeat seemed to be for Charles to renounce his pretensions in favor of his brother Ferdinand. The latter, although only sixteen years of age, had shown qualities that were likely to endear him to the German nation. He passed for clever and thoughtful; Pope Leo considered that he had *piu spirito* than Charles, while Erasmus wrote of him *in Ferdinando magna spes est*. But when the plan of withdrawing his own claim in favor of another member of his family was broached to the young king of Spain, it met with a downright refusal. The choice of Ferdinand, Charles declared, was not to be thought of for a moment, it meant loss and dishonor to himself, it meant the complete and perpetual ruin of the house of Hapsburg. Was he not the elder, had not his grandfather nominated him his successor, and the electors given their promise in his favor? It was absolutely necessary that he and no other should become emperor of the Romans, "for the good of the holy faith and the hurt and destruction of infidels."

In the rush and strain of the electoral contest a third and even a fourth candidate came to the fore. A hint from the Pope put it into the head of Cardinal Wolsey that there was a chance of success for the English king. An envoy was sent from England with directions to make

*Other candidates for the imperial throne.*

cautious proposals and see how they would be received; but unfortunately for the result of his mission, he was supplied with no funds for purposes of bribery. He was well treated on his arrival, but politely told that he had come too late. Far different was the candidacy of Frederick of Saxony, the patron of Martin Luther. This prince could easily have obtained the crown had he so desired; three of the electors, unable to unite on either Charles or Francis, were willing to compromise on him, while his own vote, which, according to the sentiment of the time, might well have been cast for himself, would have given him an absolute majority. But fear of responsibility and consciousness of the limited nature of his own resources caused this excellent prince to refuse the proffered honor.

Charles wins the election.

In the end the French king overreached himself by his very zeal. The autocratic electors came to the conclusion that a man so powerful as his envoys pictured Francis would not be at all to their liking; he had crushed all independence in France, he would, it was feared, do his utmost to be absolute in Germany. The emissaries from Spain had used far more tact and judgment; they had lauded the electors as the powerful allies whom their master needed and longed for in his approaching conflict with the Turks. A great tide of public sentiment set in in Charles's favor, and public sentiment was beginning to be a power with which it was absolutely necessary to reckon. Was not this a Hapsburg prince? Was he not the grandson of that brilliant Maximilian whom all had loved in spite of his faults? As for Francis, he was wholly of foreign blood; he was the natural ally, too, of the Pope, and even the hearts of good Catholics were filled at this time with anger on account of the abuses practised by the Roman court. The majority, indeed, would still have preferred Ferdinand, not only for his personal good qualities, but also because, unhampered by the possession of foreign crowns, he was likely to pass the greater part of his time in Germany. But this, as we have seen, was not to be; and at the final election, held at Frankfort, the vote in Charles's favor was unanimous. At the eleventh hour Pope Leo withdrew his opposition, and, in the face of the inevitable, tried to make friends with the Mammon of Unrighteousness.

The electors before finally committing themselves had seen fit to bind their new lord by making him sign a capitulation or electoral compromise in which he not only agreed to respect their own liberties and prerogatives, but promised to bring neither foreign soldiers nor foreign officials into the land, to hold all intercourse in the German or Latin languages, and to hold no courts of justice and summon no imperial subjects outside the boundaries of the empire. No one might be placed under the ban unless formal proceedings should have first taken place. In all the affairs which it covered the Golden Bull was to be carefully observed; vast monopolies like those in the hands of the banking-house of Fugger were to be restrained, and a halt was to be called to the aggressions of the court of Rome. *The electoral compromise.*

So undoubted a triumph as the election had been, the rejoicing in many quarters was forced and hollow. The new emperor himself was on the verge of bankruptcy; the discontent in the Spanish cities had blazed into open warfare. All the gold that Cortez could offer from the newly discovered mines of Mexico could furnish little relief, and at the different courts of Europe outward signs of good-will, such as public *Te Deums* and fulsome writings of congratulation, could not effectually conceal the most hostile intrigues. The Pope was arranging for a coalition of which the French king was to be the head; Francis was moving heaven and earth to secure the friendship of

England, and had already appointed that meeting near Calais which was to be known in history as the Field of the Cloth of Gold.

Charles's coronation.

In spite, however, of his poverty and his political cares, Charles's coronation at Aix was a magnificent pageant; the splendor of his apparel, the number of his mounted attendants, the skill with which he managed his splendid white steed, — all excited the utmost enthusiasm. In accordance with the tastes and desires of the person most concerned, the religious character of the ceremony was brought into special prominence. At the door of Charlemagne's cathedral the new emperor was met by the archbishops of Cologne, Treves, and Mainz, who gave him their blessing "as though he had been a bride." Before the high altar he prostrated himself in the form of the cross; he swore to uphold the Catholic faith, to protect the holy church with due subjection and fidelity, — vows which he never forgot and the maintenance of which became the ruling passion of his life.

Luther to the Christian nobility.

The most formidable antagonist the church had ever had was meanwhile keeping several printing-presses busy with ringing addresses to the German people, and with defences of his position. One to the "Christian Nobility" presented with the directness of a bombardment the most damning array of charges against the Papacy; "the time for silence is past, the time for speech has come," were the opening words, and one by one the walls of straw and paper set up around the church were undermined and demolished. It is not true that no one may judge a Pope, that he alone may interpret Scripture, he alone call a council. He is full of worldly pomp and pride, he is "carried by men like an idol," he is attended by three thousand secretaries — a "crowd of crawling vermin" — and rides out with from three to four thousand mule-riders. For his traffic in German benefices, for his "cheating and lying, robbing and stealing, debauchery and villany, and all kinds of contempt of God" he must needs have a special counting-house at Rome. All the grievances of the ages are mustered up: the Constantine Donation, the forged deeds of gift of Charlemagne, the claim to having founded the Holy Roman Empire, the question of investiture, the demand that the emperors should kiss the Pope's foot, should do him homage, should hold his bridle and stirrup, the spurning of the Hohenstaufens, and the assumption of temporal rule over Naples and Sicily.

In another writing, *On the Babylonian Captivity of the Church*, Luther attacked the fundamental doctrines of the church, and declared that four of the seven sacraments were of no binding force whatever. He thereby aroused a fiercer storm than by any possible attack on open and apparent abuses. Glapion, the father confessor of Charles V., who up to this point had been in favor of conciliation, declared that he felt now as though he had been scourged and pummelled from head to foot. Erasmus of Rotterdam, too, anxious as he was to reform certain abuses, turned coldly away and definitely declared for the old doctrines; while no less a person than Henry VIII. of England took up his royal pen against the bold iconoclast, and wielded it with such effect that he gained from the church the title of "Defender of the Faith." *The Babylonian Captivity.*

Luther's third great writing of this year, 1520, *On the Freedom of a Christian Man*, was not polemical in character, but rather gave a positive system of religion and showed the relation of faith and works. It was prefaced, however, by the letter he had once promised Miltitz to write to Leo X. This begins respectfully, though it warns the Pope against thinking he can do what he will in heaven, hell, and purgatory. The Roman court, on the other hand, *The Freedom of a Christian Man.*

is compared to Sodom, Gomorrah, and Babylon, and Leo is represented as sitting like a sheep among wolves, like Daniel with the lions, or Ezekiel with the scorpions. Luther is sorry for Leo; it is a pity he could not have been Pope in better days, and that he cannot now support life on a simple benefice or on his private income. But there is no help now for the pestilential state of affairs: "All is over with the papal see; God's unceasing wrath hath fallen upon it; it opposes general councils and will neither be instructed nor reformed; . . . the malady scoffs at the cure; neither horse nor chariot heeds the driver."

Papal bull of condemnation.

The *Babylonian Captivity* and the *Freedom of a Christian Man*, as well as the dedicatory letter to Leo X., were written with the knowledge that Rome had at last done her worst and issued a decisive bull of condemnation; the letter, indeed, was dated back so as not to seem a direct retaliation. This bull, *Exsurge Domine*, was to be the righteous retribution for the whole catalogue of the reformer's past misdeeds; in its composition all of his old enemies, Prierias, Cajetanus, and Eck, had a hand, and many a session was necessary to its completion. The former Leipzig disputant was intrusted with its publication in Germany. Beginning with an appeal to God, the saints, and the whole church, against the foxes, boars, and other wild beasts that are devastating the Lord's vineyard, the document goes on to vaunt the fatherly long-suffering of the Pope, — even now his heart is so oppressed that he can scarcely speak out, — and to declare that various errors condemned by church councils are being sown among the German nation by godless babblers incited by the devil. Forty-one passages are then quoted from Luther's writings and pronounced heretical, among them the denial that to burn heretics is in accordance with the Holy Spirit. The most prominent place is given to reflections upon the sanctity of the priesthood and upon the power assumed by the Pope. All of Luther's books, wherever found, are at once to be burnt; he himself and all his favorers, if they do not retract within sixty days, are to suffer the punishment of notorious, stubborn, and condemned heretics. Princes and potentates, all in short who do not help to carry out the sentence and eventually to bind and deliver over the chief offender, are freely threatened with ban and interdict.

Slowly the papal legates made their way northward with this dire instrument of destruction. Eck was given the privilege of inserting as many as twenty-four names of those who were to share in Luther's punishment; Carraciolo and Aleander were to appear at the Diet of the Empire, and rouse that body to a sense of its bounden duty. The reception accorded the bull differed greatly in different places: in some towns it was obeyed and the Lutheran books were committed to the flames; in others it met with scorn and derision. In Magdeburg it was affixed to the pillory; in Mainz, when the executioner from the scaffold asked the people whether he whose books were to be burned had been lawfully condemned, there was a universal shout that he had not been condemned at all; the ceremony was interrupted and Aleander almost stoned to death. At the very time when Luther was engaged on his *Babylonian Captivity of the Church*, it had appeared in Leipzig and been received with honor. "I hear," he says, in his peroration to that work, "that bulls and papal threats have again been published against me, in which I am urged to recant or be declared a heretic. If that be so, may this book form part of my future recantation." When the bull at last reached Wittenberg, his first thoughts turned to the emperor, the "noble young scion" who was just making his first appear-

The publication of the bull.

ance in Germany. "Oh, that Charles were a man," he cried, "and in Christ's cause would attack these Satans." But failing such help, he had long since made up his mind what steps to take in his own defence. He had written some months before, "I despise alike the favor and the fury of Rome; . . . let her condemn and burn my books; I, in my turn, unless I can find no fire, will condemn and publicly burn the whole pontifical law, that swamp of heresies."

The burning of the bull.

The moment for this demonstration had now come. It was announced to the students of Wittenberg that they were invited to the pious and religious spectacle of a judgment by fire. By the hour appointed a vast crowd had assembled in the square before the Elster gate, where a quantity of wood was heaped together and ignited. There was thrown into the flames not only a copy of the obnoxious bull, but a collection as well of the decretals and of the canon law. The fire was meant to symbolize the consignment to destruction and oblivion of the whole papal see. The students outdid their master in zeal for his cause; they sang dirges and *Te Deums* as the decretals vanished into smoke, and with a papal bull two yards long fluttering from a pole, they drove round the town and collected the books of Luther's enemies with which to feed the flames. Such a demonstration as this was of the kind that leads to revolution and bloodshed. "Hitherto," wrote Luther to Spalatin, "the matter has been mere play, now it becomes earnest." And again soon after, "The tumult rages gloriously; it seems to me as if it never can be calmed until the day of judgment!"

The Diet of Worms.

Up to this point the ways of Charles V. and of Martin Luther had not directly crossed, but the emperor's first general Diet, held in Worms in 1521, was to prove an epoch in the lives of both. Never before had an imperial

Diet been graced by the presence of so many distinguished princes; the city could scarcely harbor their splendid retinues. Young Philip of Hesse brought six hundred horses; while even before the sessions began, Elector Frederick the Wise had paid out some four thousand guldens in food for his followers. Games and pageants filled the intervals not occupied by serious business. The main question before the Diet, apart from the affair of Luther, was the reëstablishment of the council of regency, or *Reichsregiment*, which Maximilian had allowed to fall into abeyance. The matter resolved itself into a trial of strength between Charles and his princes, which ended in a compromise: there was to be a council, but with a *Stadtholder*, not a president, and the first *Stadtholder* was to be the emperor's brother Ferdinand. The council was to be permanent, but could only unfold its full powers in the absence of Charles from Germany. The import of all this for the Reformation was, that at the critical moment the emperor's actions were hampered by others, he could not proceed, as he would have proceeded in the Netherlands, and stamp out this heresy with fire and sword. Nor could he, without breaking his electoral compact, place Martin Luther, unheard, under the ban of the empire. He would gladly have done so; the papal legate, Aleander, who was constantly at his side, urged him to the step; but the princes had first to be consulted, and the princes decided to grant the reformer a hearing.

It was a strange position for Charles, who in this very same year defended the severity of the Spanish Inquisition against the Pope himself, to have to despatch a summons to the worst of heretics and to use the conventional form of address, " Honorable, beloved, and pious " ! Luther was asked to place himself under the charge of the messenger and to come to Worms and render an account of his

The summoning of Luther to Worms.

books and of his teachings. In the interval the Diet discussed the reform of the chamber court, and actually brought to pass a new military schedule or *Reichsmatrikel*, based on the "Roman month," or simplest levy of twelve thousand men with funds to support them for six weeks — the minimum term for an expedition to Rome. An artificial arrangement, but each prince knew henceforth what was his proportion of the general levy, and the whole number of Roman months could be indefinitely increased.

Charles's attitude toward Luther.
Luther's appearance at the Diet had been awaited with the greatest eagerness. Many believed that, could he be made to recant his errors of doctrine, he might prove a chosen instrument to correct the flagrant abuses in the church. Soon after the election of Charles V. the latter's ambassador in Rome had urged him to show favor to a certain Brother Martin, as the Pope was extraordinarily afraid of him and might through this fear be gained as an ally. Charles had been pleased with Luther's early writings; neither he nor his father confessor was blind to the need of reform. Glapion had even threatened him with divine punishment unless he should rid the church of scandal. But the heresies uttered at the Leipzig Disputation, the writing against the holy sacraments, and the burning of the papal bull were too much for the man whose one thought, as he wrote himself, was "the exaltation and the increase of our Holy Catholic faith." At this very Diet he angrily threw on the ground a letter from Luther appealing to him, as Athanasius had done to the emperors of old, and imploring that, true or false, his doctrines be not condemned unheard. The legate Aleander could write confidently to the Pope: "Cæsar has the best inclination of any man born this thousand years; . . . if he persevere as he has begun, he will carry everything according to our wishes."

Whatever the attitude of the emperor, Aleander could

not blind himself to the general sentiment at the Diet of Worms. For his own satisfaction he calls Luther thief, assassin, monster, Arius, and Mohammed, but he has to acknowledge that a legion of poor nobles as well as the " race of grammarians and poets of whom Germany is full " are all on the reformer's side. " All Germany," he writes, " is at present in commotion, nine out of ten cry ' Luther,' and the tenth, even if he cares nothing for what Luther says, cries ' Down with the court of Rome ! ' Every one shrieks and calls ' Council, council,' and will have it on German ground." At the very door of the hall of assembly the legate was treated to a humiliating poke in the ribs by a zealous Lutheran.

Public sentiment with regard to Luther.

The man who had caused all this commotion was now hurrying rapidly to Worms. Never for a moment had he thought of disregarding the summons ; well or ill, he would set out, he wrote to Spalatin, " for it is not permitted to me to doubt that if Cæsar call me I am called of the Lord." He hoped for Charles's own sake that the latter would not stain his hands with his, Luther's, blood ; no good had come to the Emperor Sigismund after the murder of Huss, seeing that his queen, Barbara, had eloped with another man, while he himself had died without offspring. When Spalatin warned him against trusting to the safe-conduct, Luther answered that he would go to Worms though the devils there were as thick as the tiles on the roofs. John Huss had been burned, but the truth had not been burned with him. The journey to Worms proved a veritable triumphal progress. The town of Wittenberg had placed a covered carriage at the reformer's disposal, and with him rode Amsdorf, a young Pomeranian noble, and a monk of his own order — two other friends, Schurf and Jonas, having gone on before. From every city crowds streamed out to see and welcome the man of the hour ; at Erfurt, the home

Luther's journey to Worms.

of humanism, he was met by a mounted deputation from
the university, with the rector, Eoban Hess, at its head;
the walls, the streets, and even the roofs of the houses
were thronged with excited people. He preached in the
Erfurt church, and Hess records that when he showed the
long-closed way to Heaven's blessings, the force of his
words melted the hearts of his hearers as snow melts
before the breath of spring.

Luther's
reception in
Worms.

Arrived in Worms, a crowd of some two thousand persons, men and women, accompanied Luther to his lodging
in the house of the Knights of St. John. One of Aleander's servants reported to his master that a priest had
taken the monk in his arms, "and having touched his coat
three times had gone away glorying as though he had
touched a relic of the greatest saint in the world." Each
day of his sojourn in Worms was marked by some such
incident. The young Landgrave of Hesse came to talk
with him in his lodging, and cried out, "Dear doctor, if
thou art in the right, so may our Lord God help thee."
"Blessed be the womb that bare thee!" cried a voice in
the street as he passed on his way. As he entered the
hall of assembly to face the grand ordeal of his life, the old
*Landsknecht* leader, Frundsberg, clapped him on the shoulder, — "Little monk, little monk, now goest thou thy way
to take such a stand as I and many a commander even
in our sharpest battles have never taken; art thou of good
intent and certain of thy affair, so go in God's name and
be comforted; God will not forsake thee."

The first
hearing.

On the afternoon of Luther's first hearing, the crowd in
the streets was so dense that the herald had to lead his
charge to the hall of audience, in the episcopal palace,
through gardens and by back ways. Within the building
was gathered one of the most august assemblies of electors,
princes, prelates, nobles, and delegates that had ever met

together in Germany. The reformer was told not to speak unless in answer to a question, and was then shown a heap of books which he was ordered to acknowledge and retract. To the surprise of all, the man whose message had rung like a clarion note through the length and breadth of the land seemed now, with the eyes of all upon him, actually to quail and tremble. In a low voice, in words that were hardly comprehensible, he declared that if he spoke without due consideration he might be overbold and run into grievous peril; would not his Imperial Majesty grant him more time for deliberation? The answer was that he well knew the grounds on which he had been summoned, and had had sufficient time for preparation; in the end, however, there was granted a delay of twenty-four hours.

The general impression among Luther's friends was one of disappointment; even the Saxon elector was not quite satisfied with his protégé. As for Charles, he could hardly believe that he had seen before him the author of such aggressive books; "That man would never make a heretic of me," was his final opinion. Aleander was jubilant, and even waxed witty at the expense of "the fool who had come into the assembly laughing, and had left it in a sadder frame of mind."

On the second day, with studied words and at some length, Luther gave his reasons for not denying his works so long as they could not be refuted from Holy Writ. His voice was steady now, and every trace of shyness had vanished. He asked for evidence against himself and for a fair trial, and then, suddenly striking a warning note, he turned to the young emperor and held him a fiery discourse, excusing his own boldness on the plea that it was a duty he owed to his country. He exhorted "this most excellent youth, Prince Charles, on whom after God many hopes are fixed," to walk in the fear of the Lord; not to

*The second hearing.*

make an evil beginning of his reign, and thus come to a shameful end, like the old kings of Egypt, of Babylon, and of Israel. Called to order and asked to give a plain yes or no to the questions that had been asked him, Luther answered in stirring words: "Since your most Serene Majesty and your lordships ask for a simple answer, I will give it 'neither horned nor toothed,' after this fashion: unless I shall be convinced by witness of Scripture or by plain reason (for I do not believe in the Pope or in councils alone, since it is agreed that they have often erred and contradicted themselves), I am overcome by the Scriptures which I have adduced and my conscience is caught in the word of God. I neither can nor will recant anything, for it is neither safe nor right to act against one's conscience. God help me. Amen." One of the contemporary reports, of which there are several, inserts before "God help me," the words, "Here I stand. I can no more."

By this time it was evening and the candles had already been lighted in the hall. Charles hastily dismissed the assembly. One who followed Luther reports that he seemed to feel an immense joy, and that on entering his inn he waved his arms and fairly shouted, "I am through! I am through!" He was through, indeed, though his worst dangers and perils had but just begun. Frederick the Wise said that night to Spalatin: "Well did Dr. Martin speak before the lord emperor and all the princes of the empire. He is far too daring."

Charles's dictum. If at this hearing Luther had impressed and astonished the members of the Diet, no less a surprise was in store for them the following day, when their emperor and head presented to them his written opinion on the case in point. It was the first public deliverance of this boy of twenty-one; yet so incisive was it, so imperious, so utterly characteristic of the bigoted Spanish tyrant, that many of the princes, as Aleander tells us in his report to the Pope, "turned paler than if they had died." He, the descendant of kings, archdukes, and dukes who had ever made it their care to defend the Catholic faith, was not going to be moved by this single monk, who, led astray by his own imaginings, was opposing the truths that had prevailed for a thousand years. "We have determined in this matter rather to stake all our kingdoms and dominions, our friends, our own body, blood, life, and soul." The very suspicion of heresy must be wiped away as an everlasting shame from the noble and most distinguished German nation. Luther is to be denied a further hearing; he is to be told to withdraw and his safe-conduct to be respected, but thenceforward he is to be proceeded against as an actual and convicted heretic.

In spite of the vehemence of this utterance, the princes demanded and obtained further hearings for the reformer, lest he should say that he had not been given a fair chance. These hearings were of a more private nature, two of them being before the Archbishop of Treves, who, if Aleander can here be believed, offered Luther a high church office if only he would recant at the eleventh hour. Charles was anxious to hasten the affair; he was alarmed at the various signs of sympathy and of revolt. A paper was found on the door of his own apartment with "Woe to the land whose king is a child": a placard on the town hall announced that four hundred knights had thrown down the gauntlet to the Romanists and intended to uphold Luther. The sign of the *Bundschuh* appeared on the wall, with a warning that the peasants "meant a great damage." The deliberations of the princes were hastened, and ended in the pronouncement that this man was incorrigible, that he must leave Worms, and that, after the twenty-one days reserved in his safe-conduct, he

Alarming demonstrations.

must be declared under the ban. To Aleander was intrusted the congenial task of drawing up the instrument of condemnation. Luther's own comment, addressed to the painter, Lucas Kranach, was that absolutely nothing had been accomplished by the hearing, and that it had not been fairly conducted. " Oh, we blind Germans," he wrote, " how childishly we act and how wretchedly we let the Romanists make fools and apes of us ! "

The edict of Worms. By the edict of Worms, which branded him as the evil one in human form, as the instigator of schism, murder, and arson, as the subverter of all laws, Luther was declared under the empire's ban ; no one might shelter or nourish him, but he was at once to be seized and handed over to the emperor. This decree was signed in irregular fashion by Charles and by a number of the princes, after the last session of the Diet and after the elector of Saxony and other possible favorers of Luther had already taken their departure. The petty subterfuge was adopted of dating the document back some three weeks, in order to give color to the introductory statement that it had been passed " by the unanimous advice and with the good will of all the estates." " Now you will be content with me," said Charles to Aleander, as he handed him the parchment with his seal and signature. " Surely, sire ;" was the answer, " but much more will be contented his Holiness, the Holy See, and all Christendom, and will thank God for giving them so holy and religious an emperor."

# CHAPTER XII

## FRIENDS AND ALLIES OF THE REFORMATION

LITERATURE : Spalatin's *Life of Frederick the Wise* is a contemporary account by that prince's secretary. For Hutten we have the excellent biography of Strauss, for Sickingen the equally good work of Ullman. See also Bezold, Egelhaaf, and Ranke, as before.

THE account given by Aleander of the religious ferment into which Germany had been thrown was by no means overdrawn; there was no class of the population that was not touched by the movement, and no form of expression in which men's feelings did not find vent. Between the years 1513 and 1523 the number of yearly publications rose from ninety to nine hundred, and by far the greater part of them were polemical. Luther's own individual writings up to the latter date numbered more than one hundred. Hans Sachs, the cobbler of Nuremberg, wrote a poem on the *Wittenberg Nightingale,* and announced that the false shimmer of the moon that had lured so many to the wilderness was now to be put to flight by the red love-light of the morning. Albrecht Dürer painted his famous Four Apostles with Peter standing behind "John whom Jesus loved." Lucas Kranach drew a series of twenty-six woodcuts of the church as it was, and the church as it should be, — on the one hand, the Pope with his triple diadem and with princes kissing his toe; on the other, Christ with the crown of thorns washing the feet of His disciples.

Not that all who railed at the abuses of the church were in favor of Martin Luther. Erasmus had come out in an

*Religious ferment.*

open attack upon some of his doctrines; Reuchlin repudiated him, and sent a weak letter of justification to the Catholic dukes of Bavaria. But even within the camp of Lutheranism there were fatal differences as to ways and means; what the scholar expected to gain by arguments and persuasion, the knight thought he could achieve more rapidly by force of arms, and the peasant by revolt and violence. Each of these elements was to try its turn singly in the course of this long struggle, with what success we shall see as our narrative proceeds.

The youth of Melanchthon.

The chief representative of the peaceful party, and Luther's most devoted personal friend, was a certain Philip Schwarzerd, of Bretten, son of an armorer who was so skilful in forging a suit of armor for Maximilian that the latter gave him as coat of arms a lion with one paw on a hammer, the other on an anvil. Young Philip had always had a strong religious bent, a keen sense of beauty, and an independent, critical spirit. The ceremonies of the old church, indeed, had so attracted him that he had erected an altar at which, in private, he imitated the forms of the mass; yet, even at this early age, he doubted a preacher who declared that the wooden shoes of the Franciscans had been cut from the original apple tree of paradise.

Reuchlin, who was Schwarzerd's granduncle, had taken the warmest interest in the training of the boy, selecting his tutors and his schools, and providing him with rare books. Out of love and gratitude Philip had induced some comrades to learn and perform one of the old humanist's own Latin comedies, which so delighted Reuchlin that he would not rest till he had changed the barbarous name of this learned youth into its Greek equivalent — Melanchthon. At every stage in his career the young scholar was looked upon as a prodigy; once at Heidelberg, when the professor was at a loss for a translation and won-

dered who could help him, there was a general cry of Melanchthon, Melanchthon, though the latter had not reached
the age of fifteen, and was denied his master's degree on
the ground of his childlike appearance.   Before he was
nineteen Erasmus was in raptures over him, and called
immortal God to witness the promise in this youth; whose
complete command of Greek and Latin, whose penetration,
and whose purity of diction, whose extraordinary memory
— in short, the "noble, even royal grace of whose gifts" —
made a profound impression on the first scholar in Europe.

Called at the age of twenty-one to preside over the
Greek studies in the university of Wittenberg, Melanchthon
by his very first discourse on improved methods of study
made a conquest of all his hearers.   Short of stature,
slender and weak-looking, with a bad habit of holding
one shoulder lower than the other, he had none of the
natural advantages on which orators are wont to depend.
He knitted his brows in an ugly manner, made awkward
and violent gesticulations, and occasionally stuttered.   But
on those who observed him closely, his beautiful eyes and
fine features did not fail of their effect, and all followed him
with breathless interest when in masterly sequence he
showed the evils in the prevalent methods, and went on to
unfold his plans for improvement.   A return to original
sources, the concernment with things themselves and not
with their shadows, the reading of Greek and Latin classics
in the tongues in which they were written, the study of theology from the Scriptures and not from bad text-books: —
these were his earnest injunctions.   "Who makes a beginning
has won half the battle — go bravely forward.   It may seem
difficult, but let not that deter you ; industry and zeal
conquer hardships.   I will help you to the extent of my
powers!"   "One marvels," a listener declares, "how in such
a little body there can be concealed so enormous a mountain

*Melanch-thon in Wittenberg.*

of cleverness and wisdom," and indeed the fame of the new
lecturer soon raised the number of students from the hundreds to the thousands !    Luther's relation to Melanchthon
was from the very first warm and confidential.  "Whoever "
he writes, "does not recognize and treasure our Philip
as just the right teacher, must be a perfect ass and eaten
up with self-esteem.    There is no one on earth, no one
on whom the sun shines, who has such gifts as Philip,"
and again : "He is a perfect Greek, learned to the core,
friendly and of cheery disposition.    He has a perfectly
crowded classroom, and has brought it about that especially all theologians — high, middle, and low — have
taken to Greek. . . .    His devotion and industry pass all
bounds."

Nor was Melanchthon behind hand in his appreciation of
the great pioneer of the reform movement.    He speaks of
him as the " God-inspired messenger of eternal wisdom and
justice," as the " blessed dispenser of the life-giving word,"
as the " faithful, never sleeping Shepherd who with the rod
of Moses casts down the superstitious priests and the foolish
hair-splitting sophists."   He accompanied Luther to Leipzig at the time of the disputation with Eck, and incurred
the latter's mortal enmity by occasionally prompting both
Carlstadt and Luther.    Eck declared that though Melanchthon might know Latin and Greek, it was not worth while
for any theologian to dispute with him, and thus called forth
the remark from Luther that he cared more for his Philip's
judgment than for a thousand dirty Ecks.    " I will not
praise Philip," he said on this occasion ; " he is a creature of
God, nothing more ; but in him I honor the word of God !
Perhaps I am Philip's forerunner, destined like Elias to
prepare the way."   The influence that Melanchthon was to
have on the future of the Reformation cannot be overestimated.   It is an old simile that makes him the coiner of

Luther
and Me-
lanchthon.

the gold which Luther brought to light; he it is who first reduced to a theological system the teachings of the new religion. Luther once excuses his own violence by the constant necessity of fighting against mobs and devils; he it is who must dig up the stumps and stones, level the thickets and hedges and break a path like the woodsman through the forest; "but Master Philip drives cleanly and quietly along, sows and waters to his heart's content according to the rich gifts that God has given him." When Melanchthon wrote his *Loci Communes,* or "common truths of religion," Luther ranked the book as second only, in point of excellence, to the Bible itself.

Melanchthon's great aim was to give a scientific form and scholarly basis to the theology of the Reformation. His was not a nature that would try to storm the fortresses of the Romanists, he sought rather by reasoning to show how antiquated and useless they were. His chief fault was a desire to please in all directions, and the future was to show how his efforts in the matter of conciliation were to weaken his party and to draw down upon him the disapproval, if not the contempt, of his own friends.

*Melanchthon as conciliator.*

In complete contrast to the life of this quiet scholar was that of another man who, for a short season, concentrated upon himself the gaze of all Germany as, rushing and storming on, he wildly endeavored to rouse his nation to that pitch where, once for all, it would irrevocably break with the tyranny of Rome. It is a singular part that which Ulrich von Hutten plays in the history of the Reformation. Knight of the pen as well as of the sword, he is, above all, the ardent patriot smarting and writhing under his country's wrongs. Independently of Luther, he had begun his attacks on indulgences and papal extortions. Long after the posting of the theses he had looked on the Wittenberg reformer as a mere squabbling monk, and more than once had been

*Hutten and Luther.*

known to pray that Eck and Luther might annihilate each other. "My desire is," he wrote, "that our enemies should live as much in discord as possible. . . . God grant that all who hinder the ripening of the new culture shall be destroyed!" However, the Leipzig disputation and the great writings that quickly followed it had awakened Hutten to glowing enthusiasm, and he had unreservedly placed himself on Luther's side. "Day and night," he wrote to him, "will I serve thee without wage; many a brave hero will I rouse up for thee. Thou shalt be the captain, thou the beginner and ender; all that is needed is thy command."

For a time the two names were constantly linked together; their portraits appeared side by side on the cover of one of Hutten's works; they were likened to Orestes and Pylades, and the litany was paraphrased into a prayer for their safety. Men watched with breathless interest to see how they would extricate themselves from the meshes cast round them by the agents and friends of Rome. But soon a cleft became apparent, their paths divided, and Hutten, having failed in his own great designs, died ruined, heart-broken, and in exile.

Hutten's early years. Hutten's family was of the old Franconian nobility. His immediate ancestors had been no better than their neighbors, and there were times when their castle of the Steckelberg was nothing less than a den of robbers and had to be raided as such by the emperor's commands. The young Ulrich's father, harsh and tyrannical, had destined his son for the church, had sent him to the monastery of Fulda to be trained for this vocation, and would hear of no argument in favor of any other career. In the very days when Luther, braving the wrath of his own father, was entering the Augustinian order at Erfurt, Hutten too cast off the parental yoke, burst these irksome monastic bonds, and fled from Fulda to worship the rising sun of humanism. To the full he experienced the hardships of the vagabond scholar's life, begged and worked his way from one university to another, endured shipwreck and plague, and ruined his health forever.

The knowledge of his peculiar powers came to him in a curious way and in the midst of his worst misfortunes. At Greifswald a certain Henning Lotz, professor of law and son of the burgomaster of the town, had received him into his house, had clothed and fed him, and supplied him with funds; then, for what reason we know not, a bitter quarrel had ensued, and the young scholar set out for Rostock without being able to reimburse his benefactor. The burgomaster and his son sent their retainers after him. He was seized and stripped of all he had, down to his own poetic compositions, and was forced half naked to continue on his way. Boiling with rage, he soon after wrote a satire on the two Lotzes, which revealed to the world of humanism its greatest master of invective.

Not many years had passed before the power of Hutten's pen was felt by the highest in the land: a poem addressed to the Emperor Maximilian exhorted him in stirring words to march against the Venetians who had obstructed his way to Rome; a number of epigrams were launched against that warlike pope who had taken the name and wished to emulate the deeds of the great Julius; a panegyric on Albert of Mainz gained for its author two hundred gold guldens and a position at the archbishop's court. There came a time when, in the presence of his whole court, Maximilian placed a laurel wreath on Hutten's head, proclaimed him orator and poet with all the advantages that officially pertained to those titles, and freed him from all jurisdiction save his own. The emperor hailed this scion of a noble knightly house as one whose writings were in every

one's hands and whom the most learned men in Germany
and Italy called their friend.

Hutten
against
Duke
Ulrich of
Würtem-
berg.
Nothing spurred on the genius of this man like some
injury to himself, to his family, or to his country. When
Duke Ulrich of Würtemberg, the most profligate and
reckless of the German princes, struck down with his own
hand a relative of Hutten's who had scorned the suggestion
of a dishonorable compact, the poet pursued him in a series
of orations that roused all Germany. Every chord was
struck that could move to pity and to indignation: the
advantages to which the murdered man was bidding farewell, the sorrows of disconsolate relatives, the iniquity of
the princely offender. Ever and anon a perfect volley of
abuse was let loose against this " blot on the Swabian name,"
this " Eternal shame of his people," no longer a prince, no
longer a German, no Christian, not even a man. Although
the Duke of Würtemberg had married the emperor's own
niece, Maximilian was forced to place him under the ban of
the empire. He soon forgave him, it is true; but Hutten's
day of vengeance came quickly enough, and he himself
was able to play a part in the overthrow of his enemy.
Duke Ulrich permitted himself in a moment of anger to
commit acts of terrible violence against the city of Reutlingen which belonged to the famous Swabian league. The
league raised an army and occupied his lands, and
Hutten accompanied the expedition, being allowed the
satisfaction of exhuming the remains of his relative and
transporting them to Franconia. Duke Ulrich went into
exile, his lands were handed over to the mercies of
Charles V. in return for payment to the league of the costs
of the war. It was thus the Würtemberg staghorns found
their way into the coat of arms of the house of Hapsburg.

In the Reformation, Hutten finally found a cause well
adapted to call out to the full his magnificent powers of

rhetoric. The dialogues that he now wrote contained utterances that never were, and never could be pardoned him: anathemas and excommunications, and the whole assemblage of papal weapons, were exposed to withering mockery; the abuses and the claims of the Roman court were scourged with a force and a realism beyond conception. The past, too, was made to give its relentless testimony: a writing of the time of the bitter quarrel between Henry IV. and the church was drawn forth from its long resting-place and given to print; a new edition was made, with a preface dedicated to the Pope, of the masterly writing in which Laurentius Valla exposed the utter falsity of the document known as the Donation of Constantine.

The writing in which Hutten may be said to have first thrown down the gauntlet to the Papacy is known as the Vadiscus, or Roman Trinity, in which, three at a time, the prevalent scandals and abuses are dragged to light. It is a terrible arraignment of the whole papal system, and here, as ever, Hutten's chief grievance is Rome's contempt for the credulity and generosity of the Germans. "Look there," he cries, "see the great central barnyard, where is heaped together the plunder of all lands. In the midst sits that insatiate weevil, which, with its followers, swallows unheard-of amounts. They have sucked our blood, they have gnawed our flesh, they are coming to our marrow; they will break and crush our every bone! Will the Germans never take to arms, will they never rush in with fire and sword? Those are plunderers of our fatherland, reeking with the blood and sweat of the German people; they are robbing us like hungry wolves, and we, forsooth, must continue to caress them, may not stab, or smite, or lay hands upon, or touch them! When will we finally grow wiser, and avenge our shame, which is the common shame of all!"

Every step in Luther's progress is followed by some new publication on the part of his literary champion, who now throws off the trammels even of humanism, and, disdaining the more elegant and scholarly Latin, writes directly for the people in the German tongue. A poem on the burning of Luther's works in some of the German towns, was followed by a republication of the papal bull, with ironical comments and glosses. We shall see presently how, at the Diet of Worms, each of the persons most concerned on the Catholic side felt the weight and the sting of this avenging pen.

Hutten's course, meteor-like as it actually was, would have been checked still earlier had it not been for the powerful protection of a man who was feared from end to end of Germany, and who now, for a brief moment, became intimately concerned with the fate of the Reformation. This was Franz von Sickingen, who was soon to perish in the double attempt to "open the gates for the gospel," and satisfy his own overweening ambition. Sickingen was a robber knight, but with certain noble traits, and with such a conception of his calling, that one wonders if he ought not rather to be put on the level of a belligerent prince. In carrying on feuds he seldom aimed lower than a duke, or a free city of the empire; and there are persons who insist to this day that his weapons were only drawn in favor of the oppressed, and of those to whom justice had been denied. Be that as it may, he was not above exacting enormous fines; and being an excellent manager, he greatly increased his family possessions. He was lord of many castles, the chief of which were the Ebernburg, near Kreuznach, and Landstuhl, near Kaiserslautern, which he furnished with splendid defences.

The feud which first brought Sickingen into prominence, was that against the town of Worms. With seven thousand men he laid waste its fields and vineyards, stopped its commerce, and cut off all communication with the outer world. Nothing daunted by the ban of the empire, which no one dared to carry out, he continued his hostilities until, after years had passed, his demands had all been granted. In the end, the ever needy Maximilian, instead of punishing the peace breaker, freed him from the ban, took him into his service, and sent him off to fight against Hutten's old enemy, Duke Ulrich of Würtemberg. His position as the emperor's commander did not hinder him from falling upon the young landgrave of Hesse, and wresting from him an agreement in favor of some neighboring knights, nor from compelling the magistrates of Frankfort to make him a large payment of money. At the time of Maximilian's death, his position at the head of an army made him such an important personage that his favor was regularly sued for by Spain and France alike. He declared for Charles V., who rewarded him with the title of imperial chamberlain, and even deigned to accept from him a loan of twenty thousand gulden.

Hutten and Sickingen first came together in the days just preceding the Würtemberg campaign; the poet visited the *condottiere*, probably in connection with that affair, and afterward sent him a translation for which Sickingen had expressed a wish. From that time on, through the three stirring years that followed, the two men were bound together by a friendship that knew no slackening. It was under Sickingen's standard that Hutten served in the bloodless campaign, even sleeping with him in the same tent. Himself without learning, Franz well knew how to appreciate it in others, while Hutten conceived a great admiration for his friend's natural abilities. In a letter to Erasmus he speaks of him as "a man such as Germany has long been without and who doubtless will bring the nation fame and glory." *Sickingen won for the Reformation.*

Far as theological matters had hitherto been removed from Sickingen's horizon, he was not without respect and feeling for religion. He had founded a nunnery near the Ebernburg, and Hutten was able to ridicule him roundly for a plan he had long cherished of "building the wooden-shoed Franciscans a new nest." Tolerant by nature, he had offered his support to Reuchlin when the latter's interminable difference with the Dominicans seemed to bring him once more in danger, and did him good service by declaring a formal feud against his tormenters. Hutten now talked to Franz of Luther, and little by little the knight became thoroughly interested in the man whom the Romanists so hated and pursued. He at last sent word to Wittenberg that, should Luther through his teachings come into difficulty and have no other resource, his castles were at his disposal. It was about this time that another knight, Sylvester von Schaumburg, offered to come to the reformer's aid with a hundred followers. Luther was pleased, if only for the moment, and he wrote to Spalatin, "Schaumburg and Sickingen have made me secure from the fear of men."

Hutten in danger from the Pope.

In the meantime Hutten's affairs had taken a new turn. The matter is somewhat obscure, but it seems clear that, about the time of Charles V.'s arrival in Germany, the poet had the definite prospect of a position at the court of the archduke Ferdinand and set out for Brussels, rejoicing profoundly that a new field for his activity had thus been opened. "Hutten goes to Ferdinand," writes Melanchthon, "to prepare a path for liberty with the aid of the great princes. What hopes may we not justly cherish!" On the eve of departure Hutten wrote to Luther, renewing his protestations of absolute and entire devotion, and urging him to fight for the common cause of liberty and to free the oppressed fatherland: "We have God on our side, if he be with us who can be against us? . . . To-day I start on my way to Ferdinand, to work for our cause as best I can." Hutten reached Brussels; but what happened to him there is clouded in obscurity, and the next that we hear he is hurrying back as a fugitive to the refuge offered by the castle of his knightly friend. The Pope meanwhile had awakened to a sense of this man's importance, and roundly rating the Archbishop of Mainz for having had him in his service, had sent word to a number of princes that Hutten must be seized and sent to Rome. Warnings of intended violence were sent him by his friends and caused him, in terror for his life, to write an appeal to the German nation. Was he, who had worked for the common good, to be torn with impunity from the land of his birth? Was he to be forced to leave altar and hearth, and to be dragged not even to a miserable life in exile, but to cruel tortures and to shameful death? "Help, help, my countrymen! Let not him who has undertaken to loose your chains himself lie in bondage!"

For many months, now, Hutten remained in hiding in the Ebernburg, still full of his plans of rousing the German nation to warlike endeavors. In the long winter evenings he began reading Luther's writings to his host, at first only in extracts and with copious explanations. That is an episode to be long remembered in German history as one of the famous conversions to a new cause. It was a slow process, but gradually the robber knight began to wonder and to comprehend, and soon the words carried entire conviction. He could not see, Sickingen declared, how any one could hope to overthrow such proofs, and soon it was the custom at every meal to have readings from Luther's or from Hutten's own works. The Ebernburg became, as Hutten expressed it, a "refuge for righteousness"; religious services were instituted under a regular

The Ebernburg.

chaplain, and numerous Lutheran leaders, among them
Aquila, Bucer, and Œcolampadius, found shelter under
these friendly walls.   Sickingen himself tried to convert
some of his great friends, and we have letters from him on
such subjects as communion in both kinds, the evils of celibacy, and the futility of adoring the saints.

Hutten's
estrange-
ment from
Luther.

Deeply did Hutten grieve at this time over the signs of
a growing coldness on the part of Martin Luther.   We hear
complaints from him that the great reformer seldom answers his letters;   that he does not send him his new writings.   The fact was, that a radical difference of opinion had
arisen between the two men.   If Martin Luther had ever
seriously thought of war,— and some of his violent utterances rather point to that conclusion,— on further consideration he had changed his mind.   " What Hutten desires
is known to thee," he wrote to Spalatin; "I, for my part,
am not willing that the gospel be fought for with violence
and bloodshed.   I have written to the man to that effect."
On the whole, if we take the verdict of history, Hutten was
right and Luther wrong; the future showed that wars and
revolutions could not be avoided.   The poet-knight had
the surer gaze; he knew what he was doing when he veered
round from the traditional standpoint of his class, and tried,
in one of his most thoughtful dialogues, to point out to the
burghers, whom his kind had so often wronged, the identity
of his and their interests.   More than a century of misery
and retrogression might have been spared to Germany had
the knights, cities, and peasants, as a unit, instead of each
separately, come forward at once in a fierce assertion of their
religious freedom.

Hutten and
the Diet of
Worms.

The culmination of Hutten's career came in the days of
the Diet of Worms.   Never did his chosen motto, the Cæsa-
rian *alea jacta est*, have a truer meaning; — and he lost
the throw.   He had plans for a great uprising, plans which

included the capture of the papal legates. The time had come, he declared, when Germany's rulers must show whether they were real men or whether they were dressed-up statues. From the Ebernburg, which was only a few miles from Worms, and whither secret messengers brought instant tidings of all important happenings, a perfect flood of small pamphlets was let loose upon those present at the Diet. The two legates, Aleander and Carracioli, came in for the chief share of abuse, and Hutten next turned the torrent of his eloquence against the assembled Catholic prelates. They were pronounced unworthy and immoral, unfit to be trusted with money or with woman's honor: "The measure is full. Away from the pure springs, ye filthy swine. Out from the sanctuary, ye cursed money-lenders, no longer touch the altars with oft-desecrated hands. . . . The measure is full. Can ye not see that the breeze of freedom is blowing; that men are wearied of the present state of things and would fain bring about a change?" It is his own vocation, Hutten declares, to "sting, spur, goad, and shove to freedom."

With unexampled audacity, Hutten, in a special writing, took the emperor himself to task. Has Charles nothing better to do than to please these priests, who can help him neither in the field nor in the council chamber? He can never gain Germany's favor unless he dismiss such men. He should sternly have repudiated Aleander's demands. "What has Germany done that with thee, not for thee, it should go to destruction? Lead us into danger; lead us against swords or through flames . . . but bid us not succumb like weak women." Then, in a sarcastic vein, "So great an emperor, king of so many peoples — yet so ready for servitude that he does not wait to be subjugated! . . . How will men speak of Charles, who has as many masters as there are around him cardinals' hats and bishops' mitres?"

Hutten accomplishes nothing.

All that Hutten had yet done was but child's play to challenges such as these. He who used such language must, it was universally thought, have an armed force at his back and be ready for revolution. When, on the contrary, nothing happened, reproaches came in from every side. "Men say of Hutten," wrote a friend, "that he barks but cannot bite." He was urged to rise and show what he could do, and above all not to let the papal legates withdraw with whole hides. He did indeed, if his own words can be trusted, lay an ambush for the latter which was unsuccessful.

In point of fact, Hutten had relied too much on Franz von Sickingen. There was no quarrel now; but the master of the Ebernburg, who was in the pay of Charles and had just accepted the command of fifteen thousand men against France, was not ready for the kind of uprising that his friend wanted, and was determined not to have his castle made the centre of such intrigues. He had even formed a plan of converting the emperor to Protestantism, or in some way, by an interchange of ideas, of healing the religious differences. Just before the Diet of Worms he had persuaded Glapion to come to the Ebernburg, and Luther was asked to stop and confer with him; but the reformer feared some trick, friendly or otherwise, to prevent his appearing at the Diet, and hurried on his way.

After the Diet of Worms, which had stirred him up to such violent denunciations, Hutten rapidly degenerated. Bereft of his strong protector, who had started on his French campaign, tortured by a dreadful disease, hiding in out-of-the-way places from real and imaginary enemies, he took to venting his spleen in discreditable feuds. We hear of an abbot robbed upon the highway and subjected to shameful indignity — a crime for which one of Hutten's servants atones with his life. Erasmus tells of two friars who lost their ears at the instigation of the embittered poet-knight. The revolutionary intrigues still went on, and Hutten is supposed to have been the author of a stirring appeal to the masses entitled the *Neu Karsthans*.

The fortunes of Sickingen, too, had undergone a change for the worse. The French expedition proved a failure, and the army was forced to disband. We know now that the fault rested, not with Sickingen but with a higher commander, yet at the time the knight's prestige was greatly impaired, and he suffered material losses. With his heart full of rancor, he fell back into his old ways and determined, by one brilliant feud, to restore the tarnished splendor of his name. Yet his own glory was not his only aim; he would help the whole order of knighthood to assert its dignity against the power of the princes and also carry out his cherished plan of blazing a way for the gospel; he would " honor God by fighting against the bishops and priests." A number of knights formally chose him as their leader at Landau, and he raised an army of seven thousand men with reënforcements in prospect. *Sickingen's last feud.*

Never had the adventurous man aimed higher than in this, his last undertaking; his mark was the Archbishop of Treves, an elector of the empire and a tower of strength for the Romanist party. Sickingen hoped that the archbishop's recent attitude in the French war would have rendered him unpopular, also that the great body of the Lutherans might be drawn into the struggle. But he reckoned without his host; the archbishop hastily fortified the town of Treves, while the count palatine and the landgrave of Hesse hurried to his rescue; and Sickingen, beating a retreat, took refuge behind the mighty walls of his castle of Landstuhl, where for a time he was unmolested though abandoned by all and declared an outlaw by the imperial council.

Sickingen's
end.

A few months later the enemy appeared in full force, demolished in a single day an outer tower with walls the thickness of twenty feet, and made a breach in the actual ramparts. Hurrying to the spot the grim commander was hurled back by a falling beam, and a bit of projecting wood tore a frightful wound in his side. He was carried to a deep, dark vault of the castle, where it was thought he would be safe from the cannon balls of his pursuers : such an unchristian shooting, he declared to an attendant, he had never heard in all his days. He was still of good courage, and by his commands Landstuhl was held until it was a mere heap of ruins which the enemy could easily storm. Then he surrendered, remarking to those near him that he would not be a prisoner for more than three days. His principal enemies, Treves, Hesse, and the count palatine, descended into his dark dungeon; the two latter seem to have addressed him kindly and gently, but the archbishop could not refrain from reproaches to which the dying man made a proud reply. He had now to do, he said, with a greater lord, and a few hours later he closed his eyes. The three princes knelt at his side and prayed God for the peace of his soul. Then hastily and unceremoniously he was buried at the foot of his castle.

Results of
Sickingen's
death.

Sickingen's death had far-reaching consequences. On the one hand, the Catholic faith escaped a great disaster; Pope Adrian rejoiced heartily and sent a special letter of congratulation to the Archbishop of Treves. On the other hand, the cause of the knights had received a fatal blow; the Swabian league united with the three avenging princes and razed to the ground some fifty three castles of those whom they considered favorers of Sickingen or thought to be dangerous in other ways. The day of glory for the free knights of the empire had passed away ; never again do they unite in any common undertaking. But some of them have retained their rank and their possessions almost down to our own day; and one of them, the Baron Stein, was destined to do alone for his country what hundreds of his like had failed in union to accomplish.

Among the indirect results of Sickingen's fall was the failure of the most earnest attempt at representative government made in many generations. The fate of the council of regency which had been revived at the Diet of Worms, and which had placed Sickingen in the ban, became so strangely linked with that of the robber knight that it would willingly have seen him defeat his enemies. Anxious to proceed against him by the ordinary means of justice, it had seen its authority defied by the three powerful princes who practically renounced their allegiance. Bitter disputes concerning the disposal of the captured property ensued, and the council completely lost its influence and its prestige.

Even before Landstuhl fell, Ulrich von Hutten, pursued by Sickingen's enemies as well as by his own, had left Germany. The king of France offered him an honorable post at his court; but he refused to serve his country's enemy, and sought rest and refuge in Basel. He had looked forward eagerly to meeting here with his learned friend Erasmus, and even cherished hopes of converting the noted humanist to the teachings of the Reformation. But a blow was in store for him which, in his wretched condition, doubtless hastened his death. Erasmus, not wishing to offend high patrons who were Hutten's enemies, afraid, too, as he later said himself, that he might be forced to take this demoralized knight into his own house, that he might catch his disease, that he might have to lend him money,—in short, in a nervous tremor for his own reputation,— sent word to his former friend not to compromise him by a visit unless he had matters of great importance to tell him; even

*Hutten and Erasmus.*

then, he said, he doubted extremely if Hutten would be able to bear the cold of his rooms; he, Erasmus, could never endure the heat of a stove!

The poor dying poet threw all the venom of his nature into one last invective against the former friend in whom he had placed such hopes; pusillanimity, envy of Luther, were cast up to his account, and above all, outrageous vanity. "One sees how it delights and tickles thee when great men greet thee and talk to thee on familiar terms!" The wonder of Europe, for his part, threw all self-restraint to the winds, and answered in terms that, for meanness and for downright cruelty, could hardly be surpassed. He named his writing the *Sponge;* it was to wipe out the little spatterings or aspersions with which Hutten had polluted him. He taunted him with his poverty, even with his sickness; and it was doubtless his doing that the poet was banished from Basel. He went so far as to write to Zwingli and to the city council of Zurich to beware of giving the fugitive an asylum, lest he should reward their good offices by some poisoned writing.

Hutten's death.

But Zwingli was not the man to be influenced by such advice. He nursed Hutten and was with him to the end, thus throwing a gleam of sunshine over the unutterable gloom of his last days. He had become absolutely indigent; even a collection of some two thousand letters written to himself by great men of all nations had in some way been lost. "He left behind him positively nothing of value," writes Zwingli, "no books, no household effects —nothing but a pen."

The personality of Frederick the Wise.

Among the friends and allies of the Reformation must be reckoned one who persevered in the observances of the Catholic religion to the day of his death, and who never spoke to Luther face to face, but who yet stood over him like a guardian angel, and more than once warded off harm.

A more attractive personality than that of Frederick the Wise of Saxony would be difficult to name in this whole age. He was so beloved by the old emperor Maximilian that if, at a diet, he stood too far away from him, there took place, to quote Spalatin, "such a waving, such a tugging of the hand, such an uproar altogether," as never before. His popularity would have gained him the imperial election, had he been willing to come forward as a candidate. His tastes ran altogether to the quiet pursuits of peace; he would suffer injustice rather than go to war; he forgave his enemies, spoiled his servants and retainers, and was never known, says Spalatin, "to utter a whole curse." Frederick had been on a pilgrimage to Jerusalem in his youth, had received the honor of knighthood, and had brought home the nucleus of his great collection of relics. He was punctilious, almost ostentatious, in the performance of his religious duties. Spalatin notes with regret that at a critical juncture in the affairs of the Reformation his master was attending mass as often as three times a day.

Frederick's attitude in the matter of Luther was more firm than might have been expected from so gentle a prince. He discussed the case with papal legates, he wrote letters about him to German princes, but always in the same strain: — The man had not been given a hearing before "just, learned, pious, and unsuspected judges"; his doctrine had "not been refuted by true and solid arguments and clear witness of Scripture." The elector feared that if Luther were "put down by the mere terror of the church's power, the inevitable result would be to excite in Germany the sharpest offence and horrible and deadly tumults." It is probable that this enlightened ruler had already accepted in his heart some of his protégé's teachings; probable even that he refrained from openly adopting them because of a plot, in which the legate Aleander was

*Frederick's attitude to Luther.*

concerned, to oust him from the electorate and confer it on the Albertine line. Luther himself well knew the dangers that threatened his lord on his own account. " I leave your territory," he wrote, after the hearing at Augsburg before Cajetanus ; " I will go whithersoever a merciful God may lead me, trusting myself in any event to His divine pleasure. For there is nothing I desire less than that any man, and your illustrious Lordship least of all, should on my account be led into any odium or peril." The reformer had already assembled his friends for a farewell meal, when a letter of Spalatin's changed his purpose.

**Luther carried to the Wartburg.**

After the decided attitude taken against Luther at the Diet of Worms, the partisanship of the elector became a more serious matter ; had he openly refused to allow the ban of the empire to be carried out, that ban might have been turned against himself. One way and one only led out of the difficulty : the reformer must disappear, must be put out of harm's way. A few days after the great scene in the Diet, on the road from Worms to Wittenberg, Luther's carriage was attacked by five wildly gesticulating horsemen. To the accompaniment of loud curses which were supposed to be characteristic of fierce bandits, the victim, who had been warned of what might take place, was seized and carried past Eisenach up the slope that leads to the glorious old castle of the Wartburg. Here he was kept under gentle compulsion for nearly a year, unable to venture out save in the disguise of " Squire George." To be true to that character, he tried to hunt ; but the sight of a hare he had killed made him think of himself and his followers pursued by the fury of the papists. Many hours of each day he occupied in writing, and here he began that translation of the Bible which was to exercise such a powerful influence on German literature. Translations there had been before, but none directly from the original tongues, and none in the terse, clear style that appealed so strongly to north and south, to uplanders and lowlanders, as to make them forget their differences of dialect, and accept this as their highest model of literary excellence.

At Worms and elsewhere, Luther's fate at first remained a mystery. Many feared the worst for him. "O God in heaven have mercy upon us," wrote Albrecht Dürer, "Luther is dead . . . would that with my own life I could purchase the life of this man, the most godly on earth in these days!" Who, he wondered, would now be able to reunite the holy church? Aleander came in for a great wave of popular indignation; he was thought to have connived at Luther's destruction, and he narrowly escaped being stoned to death.

But soon the reformer's intimate friends found cause for comfort; letters arrived for them dated "from my Patmos," "from the region of the birds," and they knew that their hero was in safety.

# CHAPTER XIII

## ANABAPTISM AND CIVIL WAR

LITERATURE : Bezold, Ranke, Egelhaaf, and Lamprecht give good accounts of the Peasants' War. See also Zimmermann, *Geschichte des Bauernkrieges*, and especially for the anabaptists in Münster, L. Keller, *Geschichte der Wiedertäufer und ihres Reichs zu Münster.*

**Deviations of doctrine.** A SUCCESSFUL attack having once been made on the authority of the established religion, numerous sects and individuals found courage to come forward with their own peculiar views, and many who had broken with the Pope soon found themselves in no less bitter hostility to Martin Luther. Their ideas seemed to the Wittenberg reformers no less poisonous than the doctrines of Roman Catholicism: there were those who presumed to deny the existence of the devil — a being so real to Luther that he is popularly supposed to have flung an inkstand at him; there were those who could not and would not believe that there is any original sin in new-born babes; others doubted the Trinity, and others still maintained that the body and blood of Christ could not be actually present during the administration of the Lord's Supper. Luther himself says, at the beginning of the year 1525, " There are absolutely as many sects and beliefs as there are persons; the very lowest or coarsest fellow, if he dream or imagine anything, gives it out as an inspiration of God, and wishes to be thought a prophet."

There was common ground on which many of these dissenters could meet, and thousands of them were soon

herding together under the general name of anabaptists. The
It is easy to account for the spread of a sect, the basis of literalism
which was rejection — rejection of all theological subtle- of the ana-
ties whatever and a clinging to the literal text of Scrip- baptists.
ture. The point which their enemies seized upon, the
necessity of rebaptism in later years, was with them an
external and minor matter, one phase in their endeavor to
shape their lives according to the simplicity and truth of
the apostolic age as described in the Scriptures. The
Bible said, "Believe and be baptized," which must apply
to adults, as babes could not believe. This aim, a literal
interpretation under all circumstances, was just enough
like Luther's own insistence on the actual wording of
Scriptural texts, as, for instance, in the matter of transubstantiation, to fairly infuriate the reformer. It was
the *reductio ad absurdum* of his own methods. If told to
preach from the housetops, the anabaptists would swarm
upon the roofs; in order to be as little children, they would
run about without clothes. There was once an exodus
from all the gates of St. Gall in obedience to the command, "Go ye out into all the world and preach the
gospel"; at Appenzell twelve hundred persons waited in
vain for the food their heavenly Father was to send them
if they "took no heed to what they should eat."

These extreme radicals of the reformation movement, The ana-
whom Luther accused of "devilish stubbornness," came baptists in
into conflict with all the institutions of daily life; they conflict
would not serve in the army, and, as their "yeas were to nary insti-
be yeas and their nays nays," they refused to bind them- tutions.
selves by any oath. What was still more unpardonable in
the eyes of the reformers, they seized on texts that struck
at such cardinal truths as eternal damnation, the existence
of the Trinity, and the divinity of Christ. There was no
possible length to which these deductions did not go:

Biblical phrases were adduced to show that there was a higher authority than even the Bible itself; the words "where two or three are gathered together in my name, there am I in the midst of them" were taken to mean that Christ held actual communication with the faithful; and, for many, dreams, visions, and inspirations gave the ultimate sanction to strange conduct, and led, as we shall see, to the wildest conceivable excesses. And with these religious theories went others of a socialistic nature — an aversion to secular authority and a strong desire to abolish property distinctions; crimes were committed on the plea that they were the will of God, and the magistrates of St. Gall were obliged to decree that divine inspiration was no valid defence in a court of law.

The Zwickau prophets.

Switzerland was the real home of the anabaptists, but the little Saxon town of Zwickau soon came to be a hotbed for such sentiments. Here Nicholas Storch, the weaver, Marcus Stübner, a former student of Wittenberg, and Thomas Münzer, a wandering preacher, became the leaders of a band of "prophets," who declared themselves inspired of God, and set to work to overturn the existing state of affairs. Münzer we shall meet with again in the midst of flame and battle; his one aim in life was to create a sensation, to which end he had been known to sound a false alarm of fire and to run madly about the streets as though pursued. In the programme of the Zwickau prophets there gradually developed a plan to annihilate the "godless," by whom were meant all who were not anabaptists, but more especially the priests and pastors; Münzer adopted the hammer as an emblem of his prowess in smiting. But the day of triumph for the agitators had not yet come; the magistrates of the town interfered, the ringleaders were banished, and some fifty anabaptists placed in prison.

Surrounded with a halo of martyrdom, the prophets turned their steps to Wittenberg, arriving there at the time when Luther was half guest and half prisoner in the castle of the Wartburg. Eloquent these men were, if nothing else, and they soon won followers in the citadel of their enemy; even Melanchthon was moved by their appearance and showed them kindness and hospitality, while in Carlstadt, Luther's old supporter in the Leipzig disputation, they found a man after their own hearts. Strongly attracted by the idea of a higher personal inspiration, Carlstadt conceived a contempt for all learning and for all social forms. He dismissed his class from the university, telling them that learning was a vain thing, and then, donning the garb of a peasant, went to carry beer for his inferiors, and to sit at the feet of the lowly and learn from them. Others there were who, to emphasize their contempt for conventions, walked into their neighbors' houses and sat with their legs cocked up on the benches or tables.

The dreams so rudely interrupted in Zwickau seemed likely to be realized in Wittenberg. The agitation against the clergy met with signal success; monks were induced to marry, and Carlstadt himself publicly plighted his troth. Communion in both forms was freely administered; students and burghers broke into those churches where Catholic rites were still retained, and, with knives which they had concealed in the folds of their gowns, drove the priests from the steps of the altar. War was declared on crucifixes and confessionals; better, cried Carlstadt, that they should be in hell or in a fiery furnace than in the houses of God. Were they not the graven images of which the Lord had spoken in the Decalogue? Nor was the confusion and uproar confined to the precincts of the city; in one neighboring village an ass was marched through the centre of the church, in another contempt was shown for most

The "prophets" in Wittenberg.

sacred religious rites by allowing an unconsecrated butcher to administer the Lord's Supper.

The elector of Saxony was not a man to put down by force even such excesses as these; he was the friend of the lower classes and had immense charity for their weaknesses and aberrations. And who could tell just in how far these teachings were to be condemned? The authorities of the university met together to discuss the matter, but showed such lamentable disagreements among themselves that their only common action was to discuss a resolution for the total abolishment of mass. In the midst of the general confusion the thoughts of all lovers of order turned to Martin Luther; now, if ever, was he absolutely needed by his flock. The magistrates of Wittenberg finally sent an informal, but urgent, request that he might come among them and quell the uproar — and Luther decided to come.

The return of Luther from the Wartburg.

It was in vain that Frederick the Wise warned his protégé not to leave his sure refuge, and expose himself to the dangers that lay in wait for a proscribed man. He declared that he, the elector, would be powerless to defend him, and that Duke George of Saxony, through a part of whose domains led Luther's path, would surely take him prisoner. To such representations as these the reformer answered in the firmest and manliest tone: he had done enough, he said, in consenting to be taken to the Wartburg eleven months before; the devil knew well that fear had not brought him there. As for Duke George, were he, Luther, needed in Leipzig as he was now needed in Wittenberg, he would ride there though it rained Duke Georges for nine consecutive days. As for protection, Frederick must know that he was under the care of One higher even than his electoral highness; that his electoral highness, in fact, might be more in need of protection than himself. The letter ends with an exhortation to turn and believe and see the glory of God.

So Luther returned to Wittenberg and ascended the pulpit of his old church, whence, day after day, with untiring energy, he poured forth warnings and exhortations with regard to the new spirit that had crept into his fold. Warmly he urged his hearers not to imitate the fierce intolerance of the Roman Catholics, who saw in every one who differed from them a blasphemer tearing at the seamless coat of Christ, a heretic worthy to be put to death. It was a hard task the reformer had set himself, for a mighty breach had been made in the edifice so carefully reared. "All my enemies," he declared, "and all devils, nearly as they have touched me, have not wounded me to the quick as I have now been wounded by our own adherents. I must confess that the smoke bites deep into my eyes and stings and smarts almost to my very heart."

The line of argument adopted by Luther was that many of the abuses so recently attacked were *adiaphora* or indifferent things that might continue without hurt; crucifixes, it is true, might have led some men to make fools of themselves, but so, for that matter, had wine and women. Should the latter, too, be swept away? What was needed most was Christian charity; even where innovations were requisite they were not to be attained by violence and blasphemy, but by quiet coöperation with those in authority.

Luther restores order in Wittenberg.

While thus inveighing against force, Luther pointed to his own example: he had done nothing but to speak, preach, and write, yet that, "even while I slumbered or drank Wittenberg beer with my Philip (Melanchthon) or with Amsdorf, has done more to weaken the Papacy than was ever accomplished by prince or emperor!" And, indeed, so conservative up to this time had Luther been that, save when employing his disguise of knight, he still retained his monastic dress.

In the end such language and such an example could not fail of their effect, and quiet was restored in Wittenberg. Priests in their robes were once more allowed to perform their ministrations at the altars, and whoever desired the communion in both forms was obliged to take it in a separate place and at a special time. In recognition of his services, the magistracy of the town donated to Luther a present of wine and furnished him with cloth for a new frock. Carlstadt, for the moment at least, made his submission, and Stübner and his fellow-prophets from Zwickau left the city. For the second time they had failed in their plan of moulding men of common clay into fit denizens of an earthly Zion; but they did not give up the attempt, though few of them were to live to see the realization of their dazzling dream.

Religious agitation partly responsible for Peasants' War.

The next that we hear of the Wittenberg agitators they are playing a smaller part on an infinitely larger stage. Within two years of Luther's return from the Wartburg the whole of southern and central Germany was given over to scenes of violence that have never since been equalled in the civilized world, save at the time of the French Revolution. The Peasants' War, beyond a doubt, would have taken place without the efforts of the anabaptists; but their communistic ideas, falling on ground that was already thoroughly prepared, bore abundant fruit, and their unceasing activity in spreading those ideas would have entitled men like Carlstadt and Münzer to the doubtful glory of having been leaders in the disastrous movement, even had they not been prominent as actual combatants.

Nor is it possible to say that Luther's own teachings had nothing to do with causing the uprising; it is true that, as he said, he had only "spoken, written, and taught," but with him language was a weapon equal to many hundred peasants' flails. He had urged the people to wash their hands in the blood of "these popes, these cardinals, and all the rabble of this Roman Sodom"; his usual epithets for Roman Catholic bishops had been "wolves," "murderers," "tyrants," "apostles of anti-Christ," "thieves," and "usurers." The princes were "the greatest fools or the greatest rogues on earth"; "God deliver us from them," he once said, "and give us other rulers;" and he several times preached on the text, "He shall put down the mighty from their seats." The emperor was a "maggot-bag," who presumed to think himself the true protector of the Christian faith; the monasteries were dens of murderers and *ought to be reduced to ashes*. Whatever Luther's intentions in delivering such utterances, they were nothing more nor less than an invitation to iconoclasm, and as such they were understood by the peasants; Luther's name was foremost among those on whom they pinned their faith.

The actual incentive to the Peasants' War was the petty oppression of the Count of Lutphen, whose domains were down on the Swiss border near the Lake of Constance. The count drove his subjects to desperation by requiring them to abandon their fields in harvest time, in order to perform such trivial service as to catch fleas in the castle beds, to gather snail shells, on which the countess might wind her yarn, and to hush the croaking of the frogs in the neighboring pond. The movement, once begun, gathered force like a rushing flame. Superstitious fears helped to spread the excitement, for the astrologers had foretold for this very year, under the sign of the fish, a terrible revolution, in which the mighty were to fall and the lowly to be exalted. A leader was found in Hans Müller of Bulgenbach, of whom a chronicler tells us that he had a

Outbreak of Peasants' War.

ready wit joined to a singular power of oratory; that he was "good-looking, the right size for a man, and had previously taken part in the French war." At the head of his little army, and waving a black, red, and white banner, he rode into the town of Waldshut and formed a league with the citizens for mutual safety and protection. The next step was the founding of the "Christian Brotherhood in the Black Forest," which acknowledged no master save the emperor, and vowed destruction to castles and monasteries. Each member paid a small subscription, and a vigorous propaganda was begun. Clad in a red cloak and a red cap with plumes, Hans Müller made a dignified progress from place to place. He was preceded by a herald, who pronounced the "worldly ban," a form of ostracism, with threats of vengeance, on all who would not join the brotherhood. There followed him a wagon decorated with boughs and with ribbons, on which was erected a great standard, as a token of the liberation of the people. In some sections a stake was driven into the ground before the house of any one who refused to join the revolt, by which sign all should know him for a public enemy.

The movement once fairly under way, other bands and other leaders started up, and the numbers of the insurgents were swelled by contingents from the Swiss cantons. Jost Fritz, now an old greybeard, appeared in Hegau and declared that he would not and could not die until the *Bundschuh* had proved triumphant. Thomas Münzer, the Zwickau prophet, made a flying visit to South Germany, and is said to have furnished Hans Müller with many of his ideas. He returned to Thuringia, where he raised and equipped an army.

Duke Ulrich of Würtemberg, the old enemy of Ulrich von Hutten, thought that now the time had come for him to regain the duchy from which, six years before, he had been so ignominiously driven. He had curried favor with the peasants around his new home on the Lake of Constance by turning Lutheran, and he now gained their substantial help by promising, should he ever regain his power, to tax his rich subjects "till the blood burst from their eyes." He went so far in his affability toward his new allies as to sign letters with "Peasant Utz" (diminutive for Ulrich). The French king provided gold for this bold *coup* against the House of Hapsburg, into whose possession, it will be remembered, Würtemberg had come. With a band of Swiss mercenaries for the nucleus of his army, Ulrich came as an invader into his own lands, and settled down before the walls of his capital of Stuttgart. But the battle of Pavia, which, as we shall see later, ended so disastrously for the king of France, dashed all the hopes of the Würtemberg duke. The French subsidies ceased, the Swiss mercenaries were called home, and Ulrich himself, having taken to flight, was glad enough to find refuge at last in his Swabian castle of Hohentwiel.

Considering that within a short time the peasant revolt had spread over Swabia, Würtemberg, Franconia, and Thuringia, it is surprising to find what moderation was at first exercised on the part of the insurgents. Almost the only forces in the field against them were those of the Swabian League, an organization to which belonged a number of princes and cities, but which needed time to raise and equip its army. With this end in view it began to temporize and enter into fruitless negotiations. Ten months had passed since the beginning of the revolt before it dawned on the simple peasants that nothing could be gained by further parleying; that the lords, indeed, were determined to make no concessions unless they asked them barefoot and on bended knee.

Duke Ulrich invades Würtemberg.

The "twelve articles" of the peasants.

In the meantime, in various parliaments held in the free city of Memmingen, the peasants had drawn up a regular formulation of their demands in the so-called "twelve articles," which were adopted, with local changes, in all parts of Germany. They seem mild and harmless in view of the awful ferocity of the attempt to carry them through. First and foremost is freedom of choice and election, in each community, of a spiritual pastor, who shall preach the pure faith; then relief in the matter of tithes, the abolition of serfdom, the free enjoyment in common of water, woods, and pasture, a truce to the cruel death tax that took from widows and children the best portion of their inheritance. The ultimate sanction for their demands the peasants drew from the words of Scripture, and countless Biblical texts were inserted in the document; names were mentioned of those competent to expound the true meaning of the holy words, and among them were Luther, Melanchthon, and Zwingli.

The sack of monasteries and castles. At last, on March 30, 1525, the long pent-up fury of the masses burst with all its violence, and an assembly at Memmingen voted nothing less than death to all nobles and destruction to all monasteries. There resulted a carnival of violence, in the course of which numerous castles were destroyed and numerous religious houses devastated; in which the wine stored up in the cloister vaults flowed in torrents, and indescribable scenes of drunkenness added to the general disorder. The holy vessels of the church were used at riotous banquets; priests' robes and knights' plumes figured at ghastly masquerades. A horrible levity took the place of that grim seriousness which alone could have achieved a favorable result. Although three hundred thousand men were in arms, no attempt was made to regularly train and discipline them, no *Landsknechts* appointed to teach them the new tactics. The league, it is true, could oppose scarcely more than one-tenth of that number, but these were commanded by men like Philip of Hesse and the dukes of Bavaria and Brunswick, while reënforcements were rapidly mustering.

One and one only of the princes of distinction, Frederick the Wise of Saxony, seems to have felt sympathy for the rebels, and he at this moment lay dying — only the faint mutterings of the great revolt penetrated to his darkened chamber. He turned to his household servants at the last and confessed to them that the people had cause for discontent, seeing that the masters imposed upon them all sorts of hardships and useless things. On the very verge of the grave he came out in his true light; with trembling fingers he seized the cup and broke the bread, for the first time in his life taking the holy communion under the Lutheran form. Luther himself, with whom he had steadily refused to have personal relations, was hastily sent for, but arrived too late. The electorship fell to his son and soon after to his grandson, who was to prove a warm and heroic, though not fortunate, advocate of the Reformation's cause.

Death of Frederick the Wise.

Many were the different phases that the Peasants' War assumed, according to locality, to the particular form of the grievances, and to the personal peculiarities of the leaders. In general the Swabians would have been contented with the simple righting of their wrongs, while the Franconians unfolded a plan for the reorganization of the empire that should do away with all intermediate powers between the masses and the emperor. They established a parliament and chancery at Heilbronn, in Würtemberg, and debated the plan of establishing a standing army and dismissing the rest of the peasants to their homes. That in Thuringia the movement was more fanatical than elsewhere was due to the influence of the anabaptist, Thomas Münzer. In the town of Mülhausen he vituperated Luther

Thomas Münzer in Thuringia.

and preached his own kingdom of God on earth, while choruses of youths and maidens chanted the promises of Jehovah to the sons of Judah. The goods of the clergy and the lands of religious houses were declared confiscate, and Münzer ensconced himself in a comfortable dwelling that had belonged to the Knights of St. John. After gaining for himself a prominent place in the government of the city, he set to work to raise an army and to procure weapons, openly preaching the annihilation of the godless, and especially of monks and priests. "How merrily," he cried, "will God strike among the old pots with His rod of iron!" With pen as well as tongue he scourged the nobles and inflamed the masses; "You miserable maggot-bag," he wrote to the Catholic Count of Mansfeld, "who made you prince over that people whom God redeemed with His precious blood?" and he signed himself "Thomas Münzer with the sword of Gideon." To the Mansfeld miners he wrote to have no mercy even though Esau should give them smooth words: "Be ye not moved by the misery of the godless; upon your swords the blood must not grow cold. Strike a cling-clang on Nimrod's anvil!" The immediate response to such exhortations was the sack of some fifty monasteries and castles.

Horrors in Würtemberg.

Probably no single episode of the war aroused such a bitter desire for vengeance against the peasants as the events which took place at Weinsberg in Würtemberg. The peasants of the Odenwald, led by George Metzler, the tavern keeper of Ballenberg, had surrounded the town, in which was a small Austrian garrison commanded by Count Louis of Helfenstein. As so often happened in this war, the body of citizens sided with the peasants, and the count and his followers, many of whom were noblemen, fell into the hands of the insurgents. With the deliberate purpose of striking terror into the neighborhood, it was decided to make the prisoners run the gauntlet between two lines of spears. The poor countess, a natural daughter of the Emperor Maximilian, was obliged to stand by while, with hideous mockery, her husband, together with several nobles, was led to his doom. His former piper, Melchior Nonnenmacher, declaring that now he would play him the right kind of a dance, preceded him down the terrible avenue, wearing a hat with a waving plume which he had snatched from his master's head. Another of the ringleaders, Jacquelin Rohrbach, dressed in the count's damask doublet, stepped boldly before the countess as she clung to her infant son, who had been wounded in the confusion. She herself was afterward placed in a common manure cart and driven off to Heilbronn. Such scenes as this, it must be acknowledged, were rare in the history of the war. Valuable property was destroyed, nearly one thousand castles and monasteries were laid in ashes, and no heed was paid to the priceless treasures of the libraries and art collections. We hear on one occasion of the peasants wading knee-deep in the torn manuscripts of a monastery. But, on the whole, life seems not often to have been wantonly sacrificed. Nevertheless, enough had been done to rouse to furious opposition, not only the princes and lords of Germany, but also the very man on whose moral support the peasants had most counted, and who might, could he have adopted a different tone, have guided the movement into gentler courses.

The attitude of Martin Luther, himself a peasant's son, to the great movement which his own teachings had undoubtedly helped to further, can scarcely be defended or condoned with any show of fairness. The most that can be said in his favor is that he was, in a way, true to himself. He saw in the war the logical outcome of the doctrines of Münzer and Carlstadt; his whole theory, based

*Martin Luther's view of peasants.*

on texts of the Bible as to the humble place in society that the serf should hold was undermined and outraged. The man who could look at men and maid-servants as mere possessions "to be sold at will like other animals," or who could call God to witness that the "ass must have blows and the rabble must be ruled by force," must indeed have trembled at seeing Germany actually on the point of succumbing to the power of the masses. Nor was he alone in such feelings; the gentle Melanchthon quotes Scripture *ad libitum* to prove that it is a presumption and an act of sedition on the part of the peasants not to wish to be serfs. Did not St. Paul say, "Let each man abide in that calling wherein he was called"? "They are so obstinate, so bloodthirsty, the Germans, that they ought to have their liberties still more curtailed: for Solomon says the horse needs a bit, the ass a bridle, the fool's back a rod; and Ecclesiasticus xxxiii: 'Fodder, a wand, and burdens are for the ass; and bread, correction, and work for a servant.'"

Violence of Luther against the peasants.

In the beginning, as might have been expected from him, Luther had tried to mediate. He had written an "exhortation to peace," in which he addresses first the lords and then the peasants. The former, and more especially the "blind bishops and mad priests and monks," with their fleecing and extortion, their pride and love of display, are charged with having caused the whole disorder; the peasants, on the other hand, grievous as are many of the wrongs that they have suffered, are not to be excused for rebellion and rioting. But after the perpetration of some of the excesses already chronicled, Luther flung himself into the struggle, on the side of the lords, with a violence that knew no bounds. His next writing bore the title "Against the murderous and rapacious hordes of the peasants," who are called "brands of hell" and "limbs of Satan." Every man who can is urged to "strike

them down, throttle and stab them in secret or in public."
They are like mad dogs, who must be killed in self-
defence; they have deserved death in body and soul, and
a "prince can now deserve mercy better by shedding blood,
than others by prayer."

These are not words written in a moment of excitement
and repented of at leisure. Luther was as sure that God
was speaking through him as when he stood under the
flare of the candles in that august assembly at Worms.
Nor were the consequences of such language hidden from
his view. "All that God has done through me is now
forgotten," he wrote a few days later; "lords, priests,
peasants, and all others are now against me, and threaten
me with death." And Melanchthon exclaims, "We see
how the rabble hates us." Years afterward Luther wrote
as follows: "All their blood is on my head, for I bade
that they be struck down; but I put it all on to our Lord
God, who commanded me thus to speak!"

It was, indeed, to quote a Protestant writer of our own
day,[1] "a sad rôle for the greatest son of the then Germany
to serve as the herald and path-breaker of a reaction that
can find no equal for inhumanity." The intolerance of
this man against all who thought differently from himself
is shown here in its ugliest possible aspect, and his undaunted courage and indisputable greatness of intellect
should not blind the impartial observer to this other side
of his character. His own words are his most terrible
accusers; "I am very angry," he wrote in 1529, "at the
peasants, who cannot see how well off they are, sitting in
peace through the help and protection of the princes.
You impudent, coarse asses, can you not understand this?
May thunder strike you dead!"

Meanwhile the princes and lords were very far indeed

[1] Bezold.

from needing such inflammatory remarks to lead them on;
in the very days when Luther's most violent writing appeared the hammer of fate had already fallen in Franconia,
and had crushed the sword of Gideon. Bitterly the peasants had now to atone for not allowing themselves to be
regularly drilled. By the middle of that month of May,
1525, of which the beginning had seen the absolute
supremacy of the peasants in whole provinces of Germany, the dukes of Saxony and Brunswick and the Landgrave of Hesse had come up with a small but disciplined
army, and had met with the forces of Thomas ·Münzer
near the town of Frankenhausen. On the day of the
engagement Münzer did all that he could to animate his
followers and inflame them to great deeds. While, drawn
up on a hillside and surrounded by an improvised fortress
of wagons, they awaited the enemy, he held them a fiery
discourse. His appearance gave emphasis to his words;
clad in long robes and with flowing beard, he pointed to a
rainbow in the heavens and declared, in prophetic tones,
that God by this same token would surely help his people.
The peasants raised their voices in the hymn of "Come,
Holy Spirit, heavenly Dove," and advanced to the attack,
but a moment later they were all in mad flight. According to the Landgrave of Hesse's own report of the battle,
three-fourths of them were mercilessly cut down, while
three hundred prisoners were afterward beheaded. Münzer
himself was able to escape for the moment, but was soon
found and put to the torture. As the thumb-screws slowly
tightened on him, Duke George of Saxony is said to have
called out, "That hurts, Thomas, but still more have you
hurt those poor souls whom you led into such misery and
caused to be cut down." "They would not have it otherwise," was Münzer's reply; but his defiant spirit soon
left him, and before he died he revoked his heresies,

making his confession and taking the Eucharist in the regular Catholic form. The town of Mülhausen, where he had been so active, was forced to make bitter atonement for its wrong-doings. Its inhabitants appeared in camp, with bare heads and bare feet, bearing the keys of the city. A yearly tribute was imposed, the goods of the clergy were restored, and, in order to take away the last chance of renewed resistance, the walls, towers, and fortifications were levelled with the ground.

Once the current had begun to turn, the peasants learned how feeble were the ties by which they had bound to themselves many a supposed ally among the cities and among the nobles. Heilbronn, where their parliament had already begun to assemble, declared against them, while the famous Götz von Berlichingen — who had taken command of the Odenwald forces, ostensibly to check violence, but in reality from love of war and a desire to strike a blow at the Swabian League — stole away like a thief in the night, and his little army of eight thousand men disbanded without a blow. In all, some seven battles were fought, but the majority of these were the merest massacres. At Zabern, in Alsace, where seventeen or eighteen thousand were cut down after they had surrendered, the ditch where the corpses were buried is called to this day the *Ketzergrube* or heretic ditch. Another encounter, near Königshofen, was likened by a contemporary to a wild boar hunt; while of a third battle, near Ingolstadt, one of the participants relates in his autobiography, "Such a slaying and strangling there was, and with no attempt at resistance, as when a pack of wolves falls upon a flock of geese or a herd of sheep."

One hundred thousand peasants are estimated to have fallen before the swords of the victors; but more terrible even than the fortunes of war was the vengeance that was

*Subjugation of the peasants.*

*Vengeance on the peasants.*

afterward taken upon the survivors. The Margrave of Ansbach caused the eyes to be bored out of sixty persons, while of many others the fingers were cut off. The Swabian League gave orders for wholesale executions, and the official list, which a year later was laid before its federal council, numbered ten thousand victims. In the duchy of Saxony a formal report of the privy councillors declared that the peasants showed too little dread of ordinary death, and pronounced it a matter of imperative necessity to proceed against them with fire. Special tortures were meted out to those who had participated in the scene at Weinsberg, in which the Count of Helfenstein had been forced to play such a ghastly part; Melchior Nonnenmacher, the piper, and that Jacquelein Rohrbach who had insulted the unfortunate countess, were fastened by chains to trees and slowly roasted to death. Galling in the extreme were some of the punishments inflicted on those who had been less guilty; men were forced to shave half of their beards or to wear women's veils, so that every one might recognize them; others were forbidden to enter taverns or to go beyond certain fixed bounds. Some fifty thousand, who had fled, lost all their goods, while the Swabian League offered immunity to those who should strike them down.

Never did any great movement have a more utterly hopeless ending. The condition of the survivors became worse even than it had been before. The peasants in their fervor had torn up all agreements concerning tithes, rents, and services; in the most favorable cases, now, these were replaced by more burdensome ones, while many of the lords refused to be bound by any writing. A spirit of dumb submission settled down upon the masses; their condition became utterly wretched even in districts where they had not rebelled. No wonder that their faith in the newly revealed God was rudely shaken, and that Luther from this time forward had to look elsewhere for friends and supporters.

Of the anabaptists we hear little in the next few years, yet their tireless propaganda continued, and paved the way for the most extraordinary episode in the history of any country. The death of Thomas Münzer and of many others, in 1525, had been the beginning rather than the end of the movement. It was in that year that, when driven out of Nuremberg, Hans Denk, one of the chief apostles of the sect, began his ministrations. Two years later the anabaptists had grown so formidable to Protestants and Catholics alike, that in every part of Germany fearful punishments were decreed against them. The Swabian League sent out four thousand knights to hunt for delinquents, and to slay them without mercy; at Ensisheim, in Lower Austria, some six hundred, in Tyrol and Gorz, one thousand, were put to death in accordance with the Archduke Ferdinand's orders. In Vienna, Balthasar Hubmaier, once a Lutheran preacher of renown, was burnt at the stake, while his wife was drowned in the waters of the Danube. Duke William of Bavaria gave the merciless command that anabaptists who recanted should be beheaded, and those who did not should be burned. A Diet of the empire, in 1529, decreed death without form of trial to all members of the sect!

In spite of all this persecution, or possibly because of it, the anabaptists were able, after various failures in other places, to carry out their ideal of a separate community, of a "kingdom of God on earth," in the Westphalian town of Münster. Here Bernard Rothmann, a young, handsome, and eloquent preacher, had begun, in 1531, to thunder away at Catholic usages quite in the spirit of Luther, and had succeeded in winning for the Reformation the merchant guilds and the city magistrates.

*Persecution of the anabaptists.*

*Bernard Rothmann in Münster.*

When the bishop of the diocese, Franz von Waldeck, seeing his authority disregarded, tried to beleaguer and starve out the town, the citizens rose in a body and took prisoner the members of the cathedral chapter, as well as a number of knights. His resources at an end, the bishop was forced to make a treaty of peace and give over six churches to the Lutheran form of worship.

The victory of ana-baptism in Münster.

But Münster lay in a district where anabaptist doctrines were rapidly gaining ground, and better soil for extravagant theories could nowhere have been found than in this home of the mystics, of Lollardry and of Hussitism. Rothmann himself and his faithful adherent, Cnipperdolling, were drawn first under the influence of Zwinglianism and then of the more dangerous sect, and joined hands with noted anabaptists of the neighboring Netherlands, with John Matthias, the baker of Haarlem, with John Bockellson, the tailor of Leyden. The city councillors were horrified at the words that now fell from Rothmann's lips; they enjoined silence, they declared him deposed from his pastorate, they even drove him from the city, but his friends escorted him back through another gate. It came to violent encounters between the two parties, to a regular battle in the market-place, in which artillery played a part on both sides. "God" and "Christ" were the opposing battle cries. The anabaptists conquered, the magistrates were overthrown, and in the new appointment of offices Cnipperdolling became burgomaster, while John Matthias was recognized as head prophet of the whole sect. John of Leyden, a man of attractive personality and really remarkable abilities, married the daughter of Cnipperdolling, and thus secured an influential voice in the management of affairs.

When it became known among the brotherhood at large that here in Münster the old dream of a separate kingdom was at last to come true, a double process of purging and renewal went on; the more moderate minded persons being obliged to leave the town, while into it flowed a steady stream of those who had been exiled from other places or were otherwise ready for change and adventure.   The most pressing invitations had been issued on all sides; letters are still extant written by persons within the town and painting in most glowing colors the advantage of coming to Münster.   The last judgment was declared to be at hand; here in the new kingdom alone could salvation be found.   Books and pamphlets of the most inflammatory nature were spread far and wide throughout Westphalia. Expulsion of the "godless" from Münster.

At last came a day, it was the 27th of February, 1534, when the anabaptists in Münster felt strong enough to complete the process of purifying their city and ridding it finally of all the "godless."   John Matthias had voted to strike them dead, but the more moderate counsels of Cnipperdolling prevailed, and it was decided that those who would consent to receive the second baptism might remain, while the rest were to be driven into exile.   On the day appointed preachers were stationed in the market-place with buckets of water; those who would not accept their ministrations were mercilessly driven out, although a fierce snowstorm was raging at the time.   No regard was paid to sickness, weakness, or old age.   The newly baptized were then called together, and, after humbling themselves in the dust, were given a warning and placed under supervision.

Now at last the anabaptists were able to proceed to the realization of all their dreams.   The municipal council was disbanded, and an assembly of twelve elders, with the Bible as their law book, took its place.   The head of the community was John Matthias, who terrorized his subjects and suppressed a revolt with a hand of iron.   Community The realization of the anabaptists' dream.

of goods was established; willingly or unwillingly, the people were obliged to deliver up their valuables, which were taken in charge by deacons. In accord with the Scriptural command, "Be ye fruitful and multiply," polygamy was declared not only lawful, but necessary; and the women, who greatly preponderated, were divided among the men. In order that "everything that is ex-alted" might "be humbled," church towers were cut down, while on other pretences Christian names were abolished and all distinction between the Sabbath and ordinary days declared at an end.

War with the Bishop of Münster.

The events going on in Münster soon attracted the attention of all Germany. Bishop Franz von Waldeck raised an army and settled down to besiege the town; but his forces were not strong, there were constant defections to the enemy, and such infringements of discipline that the bishop was obliged to order the erection of "gallows, wheels, and other barriers to wickedness" for the coercion of his own men. Various princes, Protestants as well as Catholics, had offered to help him, but misunderstandings arose which greatly delayed these reënforcements.

The garrison of Münster, for their part, fought with the utmost daring and desperation: there were many among them who had served as *Landsknechts* in the imperial armies. Once the city was all but taken; the moat was filled up with sunken wagons and with bales of straw, banner-bearers had mounted to the top of the walls and were waving to their fellows to come on. But the defence was as heroic as the attack; men stood with clubs and beat back the invaders, women and boys poured quicklime and burning pitch upon them; others were allowed to enter the city that they might the better be overthrown.

There is no doubt that behind all the extravagances of the anabaptists there was an immense strength of convic-

tion. John Matthias suddenly left a meal, declaring that
a vision called him to meet the enemy. With only forty
men he marched out to inevitable death. He was succeeded in office by John of Leyden, more cruel, more
unyielding, and more fanatical than himself. More than
once he struck men down with his own hand for disobedience to his commands.

On the strength of a vision announced by one Dusentschur of Warendorf, the new prophet took the name and
rank of king, with the title of "John the Just, on the
throne of David." He began to claim the rule, not only
over Münster, but over the world at large, and caused a
second crown to be made in token of his increased dignity.
He established his throne in the market-place, surrounded
himself with a body-guard, and dressed in splendid garments. The widow of John Matthias became his queen,
and together they administered the sacrament to the
"brothers and sisters" in the Lord. He despatched
twenty-eight apostles to announce to the world the coming of the "King of Sion"; and it is a significant fact
that nearly all went to certain death without a murmur.

*John of Leyden.*

For a whole year this anomalous community at Münster,
although forced to rely entirely on its own resources, continued to hold the enemy at bay. An expedition with
thirty ships had, indeed, been despatched by the faithful
of Amsterdam, but it was intercepted and overcome. A
certain Hille Feiken, burning to emulate Judith, had
gone forth from the beleaguered city meaning to bring back
the bishop's head; she met instead with torture and death.
The heroism with which the garrison endured starvation
and every other hardship was in keeping with the usual
fortitude displayed by the adherents of this strange sect.
The town fell at last, but not until a diet of the whole
empire had met to take action in the matter, and decreed

*Overthrow of the "kingdom of God on earth."*

that each estate should provide the equivalent of a " Roman month." By treachery one of the chief gates was won, then lost, then won again; a desperate struggle was kept up to the last, no mercy nor quarter being shown on either side. Rothmann was cut down by the blow of an axe; the king, queen, and Cnipperdolling were taken prisoners. John of Leyden acknowledged that as a rebel he had deserved death, but insisted to the last on the truth of his religious system. He was tortured on the spot where he had once erected his proud throne; his tongue was torn out, and an eye-witness tells us that red-hot pincers were applied to "all fleshy and veinous parts of his body." The same punishment was meted out to Cnipperdolling and to Krechting, another faithful follower. The bones of these three were then placed, as a perpetual warning, in the famous iron cages that still hang from the tower of St. Lambert's church in Münster. The anabaptists chose a new king, who remained concealed in Utrecht, where he was discovered and burned in 1546. About this same time Menno Simons began to exert his great influence on the sect, causing it to relinquish its most pernicious doctrines.

# CHAPTER XIV

## THE EMPEROR'S WARS AND THE PROTESTANT PARTY IN GERMANY

LITERATURE: See the lives of Luther by Köstlin, Lenz, Kolde, and Ledderhose, all excellent. Baumgarten's *Karl V.* extends to 1540. See also Bezold, Ranke, Egelhaaf, and Lamprecht.

THE ultimate success of the Reformation is largely due to the fact that Martin Luther was no political agitator. Had he seized the proffered leadership of the peasants, he would have estranged the upper classes; had his teachings threatened the thrones instead of the pulpits of the princes, the latter would not have been willing to remain so blind to his whereabouts as after the Diet of Worms. Yet if Luther's movements were unhampered by political considerations, such was not the case with Charles the Fifth. The latter had declared, it is true, that he would give his body, blood, life, and soul to extinguishing this heresy; but in point of fact he was forced by external circumstances to adopt a most tortuous policy, now sternly repressing, now actually making advances to the new party. This incarnation of bigotry, this true descendant of Ferdinand and Isabella, was once carried so far by irritation at papal intrigues as to declare that Martin Luther might after all prove a useful man.

*Charles V. hampered by political considerations.*

If we look closely into the matter, we shall find that there was another object to which Charles was equally determined to devote his entire being, — that was the restoration of imperial preponderance in Italy. In the way stood the claims and pretensions of Francis I., the French king, and until this rival should be removed from his path the emperor could pay little heed to German affairs. These wars with the French were to fill the best part of his life; not for nine years after the Diet of Worms was he again to set foot on German soil; not for a quarter of a century was he to be in a situation to oppose the progress of the Reformation by force of arms. It is true there were other tasks to perform in the meantime, such as the holding in check of recalcitrant Spaniards and the leading of expeditions against Turkish pirates; but none of these enemies could compare in pertinacity to the old rival for the imperial throne.

The wars for the possession of Milan.

In Milan the French had maintained a garrison since the battle of Marignano in 1515, which had brought about the expulsion of the dukes of Sforza. But the recovery of this territory had occupied Charles's thoughts ever since his accession, and to that end, on the very day on which he issued the Edict of Worms against Martin Luther, he had also signed a treaty of alliance with Leo X. There is reason indeed to think that his severity to the reformer was partly out of complaisance to the Pope. Into the details of the campaigns, fought as they were with mercenaries and on Italian soil, it is not our province here to enter. The utter hollowness and corruption of the French administration is shown by the fact that the sums needed by Lautrec, the stadtholder of Milan, and despatched to him by Francis, were intercepted by the queen mother and appropriated to her own private uses. It is interesting to note that Swiss mercenaries fought on both sides, and that those in the pay of Lautrec, for quailing before the idea of shooting their own countrymen, were punished by their home government.

Charles captured Milan, Pavia, and Lodi; but at the news of the victories Leo X. died of joy. The loss of this ally and the recall of his Swiss troops crippled the emperor for a moment, but the victory of Bicocca made all good again. Pious old Frundsberg, the same who had bidden Luther Godspeed at the door of the assembly hall at Worms, bent the knee as he saw the French coming, then, with a "forward in the name of God!" plunged into the thick of battle.

For a time the scene shifts to France, against which country, in alliance with England, Charles made a futile invasion; he was aided by Bourbon, the former constable of France, who had turned traitor to Francis; and when in 1524 the latter sent Bonnivet to attempt the recovery of Milan, Bourbon led the opposing army.

Bourbon had, indeed, gone over heart and soul to his new master; on the eve of heading an expedition into southern France in this same year, he wrote to Charles: "Your affairs will prosper, sire. Should we fight and win our hoped-for battle against the king of France, you will be the greatest man that ever lived, and can dictate laws to the whole world." But the promised battle was not won. A few not unimportant towns in Provence fell into the renegade's hands, who fought *con amore* for the conquest of his own territories. But the protracted siege of Marseilles, and the feeling that they were needed in Italy, proved too much for the patience of his soldiers. The news of their retreat gave courage to Francis, and he determined to risk all on a personal expedition for the recovery of Milan. On the sleeves of his body-guard was embroidered the motto, "Once more and for the last time." So rapid was his march, that he crossed the river Tessino, farther up the stream, on the very day that the army which had been invading France traversed it near Pavia; as he entered Milan by one gate, Pescara passed out by the other. To Pavia with its garrison of imperialists, Francis now

*Expedition of Francis I. into Italy.*

laid siege.  He hoped for an easy victory; he had reason to
believe that there were traitors within the enemy's camp.
But all his efforts recoiled against the high spirit of the
Germans and Italians; even aristocratic ladies took part in
the throwing up of earthworks for defence.  Every moment
was of importance; for Bourbon, Pescara, and Lannoy, the
viceroy of Naples, were eagerly recruiting in different quarters.  Of natural objects in the way, the river Tessino proved
the most serious; in vain Francis tried the adventurous ex-
periment of turning aside the waters into another channel.
Violent autumn rains made the undertaking impossible.
The days rolled on; imperial reënforcements arrived and
concentrated at Lodi.  The French were between two fires.

The capture of Francis I.

Francis sought the strongest position he could find,
which happened to be the park where stands the beautiful
Certosa di Pavia.  Pescara's soldiers tore a breach in the
park wall.  A hand-to-hand conflict followed, in which the
French king took part with desperate courage.  He was
still confident of victory: "To-day," he said to one of his
suite, "I shall be able to call myself lord of Milan."  But
his Swiss mercenaries trembled as the Spanish musketeers,
advancing with glowing fuses, their mouths full of bullets,
sent volley after volley at regular intervals.  They held
their ground reluctantly, until they saw the Duke d'Alençon
take to flight, when many of them followed suit.  At this
moment the long-penned-up garrison of Pavia made its
appearance on the scene.  Although Francis saw that all
was lost, he still fought on.  Before leaving France he had
promised the lady he loved best — not his wife; she lay at
the moment at the point of death — never to turn his
back to the enemy; through all his fighting he wore her
token upon his sleeve.  But when at last his horse was
stabbed under him and fell to the ground, he consented
to yield up his sword.  The richest prize that a monarch

could desire fell to the lot of Charles the Fifth. An envoy of the Duke of Mantua was present when the splendid news was brought to Madrid, and relates what occurred: "Your Majesty has won the victory," said the messenger, "the French army is annihilated, the king himself was taken, and is in your Majesty's power." Slowly the emperor repeated the words, as if scarcely comprehending; then silently retired to his bedchamber and knelt down before a crucifix.

"To-day," wrote one of Charles's generals from the scene of battle, "is the feast of the apostle, St. Matthew; on this day, twenty-five years ago, your Majesty is said to have been born. God be praised and thanked for his mercy twenty-five thousand times. From this day on, your Majesty is in a condition to dictate laws at will to Christians and Turks." It seemed, indeed, as though all his enemies, Lutherans included, would have to bow before the all-powerful emperor; but it was Charles's misfortune never to reap a full harvest from his various victories. He was apt to misuse his triumphs; in the present case he pulled the bow so tightly that the string broke. He ignored the fact that the French nation might be willing to abandon their king, and that even the queen mother herself would rather have seen her son a prisoner all his days, than submit to such humiliations. Charles began by demanding terms of peace from his captive which would have ruined France. All of Burgundy was to be given up to the emperor, all of Provence was to go to Bourbon, and a number of small claims of imperial adherents were to be gratified from other parts of France. Had Charles restricted his demands to Italy, had he merely demanded a ransom, however large, the results of the battle of Pavia might have been more lasting. As it was, the French king, after passing miserable months in captivity in Spain; after

*Captivity of Francis.*

being brought to death's door by the climate, by vexation, and by the studied neglect of Charles; after having made a fruitless attempt at flight, which brought upon him further severities; after having actually caused to be drawn up the deed of his own abdication: agreed to sign a treaty which he never meant to keep. Italy, Burgundy, — the Netherland border-districts were formally renounced; the king was to marry the emperor's widowed sister, while his two sons were to remain as hostages in Charles's hand.

**The treaty of Madrid.** Such was the famous treaty of Madrid of 1526 A.D. When the day came for signing it, an altar was erected in the prison chamber of the king, an archbishop celebrated mass, and the captive, who was thus to regain his liberty, swore on the gospel to keep his promises. Nor was this all. The emperor's representative, Lannoy, asked the king on the honor of a knight if he meant to fulfil his agreement, and Francis bared his head, laid his hand in the hand of Lannoy, and promised as a nobleman to return to his captivity if within six weeks the terms of the peace should not be carried out. Yet on the very day before this solemn asseveration, Francis had formally declared to his suite that the emperor's demands were exorbitant, that he regarded these promises he was about to make as null and void, and that nothing should force him to sacrifice the rights of the crown of France. The miserable farce of exchanging the king for his sons was gone through: ships set out from the French and Spanish coasts and met at the Bidassoa, the transfer taking place on a pontoon that was anchored in the middle of the stream. The king embraced his sons and took his place in their bark. On

**The league of Cognac against Charles V.** reaching Bayonne, he could not wait to land, but sprang through the water and mounted his horse, with a shout of, "Now I am King, I am still King!"

Francis might not have dared to break his word had he

not been sure of the moral support of England and of the Papacy. Henry VIII., as fickle in his alliances as in his love affairs, was willing to desert Charles when he found that the latter could not procure him the crown of France. Wolsey, the great cardinal, who wanted to be pope, had also lost faith in an emperor who gave him only fair words. Clement VII., the Medici who sat upon the throne of Peter, was a time-server of the worst kind. It is said of him that he always took the side of him who had *slightly* the advantage. An ascendency, such as that gained by Charles at the battle of Pavia, frightened him and caused him to veer back to his first predilection. His one idea now was to drive the emperor and his German landsknechts from the soil of Italy; he found sympathizers in Venice, Milan, and Florence. In order to make matters easier for Francis, he freed him by apostolic authority from the fetters of his promises to Charles.

For Clement VII. no treachery was too base. He connived with the Milanese chancellor, Morone, in an attempt to bribe the imperial commander, Pescara; the glittering bait was the crown of Naples. But Pescara, while apparently taking the matter under serious consideration, kept the emperor informed of the progress of the intrigue.

The league that was now entered into at Cognac between the Pope, the king of France, and the representatives of Florence, Venice, and Milan, is known in history as the "most holy league," because of the part played in it by the head of the Roman church. Its outspoken object was to rid Italy of all strangers and to recover the persons of the sons of Francis I. It has well been described as a union of all Western Europe against the consequences of the battle of Pavia. With England ready to join his enemies at any moment, with his pecuniary resources, which from the day of his accession had never been satisfactory, now in a really desperate condition, Charles's whole plight was pitiable in the extreme. Blow upon blow continued to fall upon him. His mainstay, Pescara, was taken ill and died; petty revolts took place in different parts of Italy against the German troops, who, unpaid and starving, had been forced to make cruel requisitions on the lands around them.

**No time to attend to Luther.**

We have reached a point where we are able to pause and inquire more closely how these political happenings and the results of the war in Italy reacted on the fate of the Lutheran party. It was fortunate for the new sect that the two men who had the strongest interest in combating it — the most holy Pope and the most Christian emperor — had found a common concern in questions of a different character. Already early in 1525 Clement, pressed with the necessity of declaring for or against France, had written to the emperor's envoy, "There is no time now to discuss this matter of Luther"; a few weeks later Charles had uttered his astonishing remark as to the possible usefulness of the reformer. We can now see why it was that the Edict of Worms, pronounced with such emphasis in 1521, had remained to all intents and purposes a dead letter. It was never formally revoked; nine years later, because of it, Luther was not allowed to be present at the diet that heard the first regular profession of the Protestant faith; but, on the other hand, reiterated efforts at different diets to have it rigidly enforced had been of no avail.

**The governing council.**

When Charles V. left Germany in 1521, the conduct of affairs had fallen into the hands of that governing council which had been created or rather resuscitated at the time of the great diet. The establishment of this council was the most liberal measure that had ever been tried in the history of the Holy Roman Empire. Its members were made up of delegates chosen by the electors and the circles, as well as by the emperor. At the first session of the new body, which took place simultaneously with the meeting of a general diet at Nuremberg, really excellent plans for taxation, and for the establishment of a common customs tariff for all Germany, were brought forward. But the council never succeeded in putting through a single salutary measure; it never was able even to raise money enough to pay for its own expenses. It aroused the enmity of the free cities by wishing to tax them too highly; of the Landgrave of Hesse, the Count Palatine, and the Archbishop of Mainz, by not proceeding as they wished in the matter of Franz von Sickingen; of many other Catholic princes by its lenity toward the Reformation. After a checkered existence of ten years, it died a natural death in 1531, at the time of the election of Charles's brother Ferdinand as king of the Romans.

One reason why the council had not in the beginning been more severe against Luther is to be found in the fact that one of its influential members was the elector Frederick the Wise. Another ground for its inaction was because it feared a popular outbreak should it use too great severity against Luther. Besides, Luther's conduct in putting down the revolt at Wittenberg, and in showing up abuses which the then Pope, Adrian, Leo's short-reigned successor, frankly admitted to have existed at Rome, had won for him considerable sympathy. It was in vain that Duke George of Saxony, Luther's fiercest enemy among the princes, tried to insist on the carrying out of the edict, sparing no effort to this end. The duke sent to the diet the violent writing composed by Luther against King Henry VIII. of England as a proof of the manner in which this heretic treated the allies of the emperor. The papal legate Campeggi did finally succeed in wresting from a diet the

*No enforcement of the Edict of Worms.*

acknowledgment that it was bound to carry out the edict. But the restraining clause, "so far as possible," robbed the concession of all its force.

Confused beginnings of Lutheranism.

Thus practically left to itself, Lutheranism made rapid progress, and struck deep, strong roots. When the legate Campeggi came to Germany in 1524, he found it a changed land from that which he had known a few years before. At his entry into Augsburg, when he raised his hand to give the church's customary blessing, he was so derided that on going to Nuremberg he thought best to leave his cardinal's hat behind him, to give no blessing, and to make no sign of the cross. Among the thousands who flocked before his very eyes to take the twofold communion were members of the governing council itself. When he began his plea in the diet for carrying out the edict, some of the members grew angry and others fell to laughing. Yet there is no denying the fact that in many ways the condition of things was deplorable: the old order of things had been destroyed, and the result was temporary anarchy. At the time when he nailed his theses to the door of the Wittenberg church, Luther had no programme ready for the unanticipated revolution; he had thought out no form of ecclesiastical government; had arranged no liturgy; had made no plans for distributing the spoils from the Catholic bishoprics and monasteries.

Luther's organizing activity.

Yet manfully in the years that ensued did Luther take up the burden thus cast on him, frequently changing his views, but gaining experience as he proceeded, and learning to control the whole vast field of reform. No man ever more completely accepted the consequences of his own acts. He wrote catechisms to unify the faith, liturgies for the use of preachers, forms of prayer for every occasion; he introduced the custom of congregational singing, wrote hymns that are known and loved to this day, and, indeed, composed the first serviceable hymn-book in German. Eras-

mus had drawn attention to the fact that the love of pure
literature was altogether vanishing; that men bought nothing at all save the writings for or against the new doctrines.
Luther, too, grieved at the decline of secular learning, and
wrote a stirring exhortation "to the burgomasters and
councillors of all German cities" to found schools for the
study of languages. He recommended the establishment
of libraries which should contain not merely sacred books,
but works on oratory, poetry, and the liberal arts, "be their
authors heathen or Christian." At his instigation, doubtless, Melanchthon composed a Latin grammar, which continued in use in Germany until the beginning of the
eighteenth century.

When the monasteries began to throw open their doors, *Luther's*
and helpless nuns returned to the world with no knowledge *marriage.*
of life and without means of support, Luther made it his
especial care to find shelter for them and to arrange the
difficult matter of their future subsistence. One especially,
a person of high station named Catherine von Bora, gave
him considerable trouble; he found a husband for her, but
the man broke his word and left her in the lurch. To the
scandal of his friends and the jubilation of his enemies, he
decided to make her his own wife. He himself has admitted frankly that love had little to do with the match, but
his Käthe, as he called her, proved a solace and a comfort.

The outbreak of the peasant war had greatly altered *The princes*
Luther's views and policy. His first idea had been to have *as supreme*
the main authority in religious matters reside with the *bishops.*
different congregations themselves. In his great address to
the Christian nobility he had laid stress on the common priesthood of all believers, and he had been particularly averse
to state interference of any kind. But a closer experience
showed that neither the peasants nor the lesser nobility
could be trusted with the choice of pastors, still less with the

administration of the rich revenues sequestered from
Catholic monasteries.  Partly, therefore, at Luther's instigation and partly by the natural trend of events, the
political rulers of reformed districts became the spiritual
heads, the *summi episcopi* or "supreme bishops."  As a rule
they devoted the income of the lands that had formerly
belonged to the church to maintaining poorhouses, hospitals,
and educational institutions.  Visiting boards were established in the different states, with a view to procuring
uniformity in the religious services, and to seeing that
preachers did their duty.

At the head of the princes who took up the cause of the
Reformation stood John, the new elector of Saxony, and
Philip, landgrave of Hesse.  By their efforts was formed the
Torgau or Gotha League, which was joined by Luneburg,
Mecklenburg, Anhalt, and others, and the object of which
was to form a compact party at the next diet of the empire.  When that diet came together in 1526, the world
saw for the first time the spectacle of princes of the Holy
Roman Empire flouting the usages of the holy Roman
church; the Lutheran preacher of Philip of Hesse held
public services, while on one of the regular fast days the
landgrave caused an ox to be roasted whole in front of his
lodging.  As a device on his coat of arms he had placed
the words, *verbum Dei manet in aeterno*.

The con-
ciliatory
Diet of
Spires.

The progress of this Diet of Spires showed plainly the
intimate connection between the foreign wars of Charles V.
and the fate of the new religious party.  To the astonishment of all who knew the emperor's actual straits, Charles's
commissioners at first came out with a stern demand that
the Edict of Worms be immediately enforced; it seemed a
strange moment, when voluntary contributions of men and
money were most needed, to press an almost obsolete claim,
sure to be repellent to a number of the princes and still

more so to the cities, which were counted upon to furnish the main pecuniary supplies. But it soon developed that the envoys had received their instructions before the breach of the treaty of Madrid, and before the forming of the holy league of Cognac. It was out of the question that now, while practically at war with the Pope, Charles should make great sacrifices to uphold the authority of the Roman See over his own German subjects. It was a time for compromise and for concentration of all national interests, and the Catholics at the diet came to the conclusion that some concessions must be made. By unanimous vote, therefore, an embassy was despatched to the emperor to acquaint him with the impossibility of carrying out the edict, and to ask him to call a general German council for the settlement of religious affairs. Until it could convene, there was to be a truce to hostilities; and one of those ambiguous formulas was invented, of which the Reformation was to furnish still other specimens, and which either party might interpret as it pleased. Each estate of the empire was to shape its conduct with regard to carrying out the Worms edict, "according as it might hope and trust to be held answerable before God and his imperial Majesty." If this meant anything, it meant that the Lutheran princes, without fear of interruption, might conduct the religious affairs of their lands as pleased themselves. But they did not take into account how completely the emperor's attitude would change so soon as the fortunes of war might turn; they could not know that the archduke Ferdinand wrote to his brother that matters with regard to the "accursed Lutheran sect" were going too badly for words; that Charles must hasten home or all would be completely lost.

But Charles at the moment was in Spain, celebrating his nuptials with Isabella of Portugal, and the moment he could move Italy claimed his serious attention, his affairs Charles's straits.

there continuing for some time in a desperate condition. The Milanese were in open revolt, the allied forces of the Pope and the French king had captured Lodi and Cremona. At the same time the Turkish sultan, taking advantage of the discord between the heads of Christendom, was threatening Hungary, the latest acquisition of the house of Hapsburg. Thus attacked on all sides, and with England threatening in the background, the emperor had written to his brother Ferdinand at all hazards to raise an army, which should come down to Italy and coöperate with Bourbon, who was still holding Milan as best he could. Ostensibly, the new forces were to be directed against the Turks: "What Turks are meant, every one will know."

Frundsberg raises an army.

Unable himself to leave Hungary, Ferdinand gave the commission to George von Frundsberg, the brilliant leader of landsknechts; — how completely religious matters had been, for the moment, thrust into the background, may be judged from the fact that Frundsberg was known to be at heart a Lutheran. But what of that? No other commander of the age could instil such devotion into his troops. When, at Pavia, he had called upon his landsknechts to help free his captive son, they had declared with one voice that he was their father and they would follow him to the very death.

The chief difficulty at present was to raise the necessary funds. Ferdinand gave full powers to his representatives to mortgage lands, cities, or castles. Frundsberg himself sold his own estates, and even pawned the jewels of his wife. He was filled with bitter hate against the Papacy. Its methods had been made clear to him in his last Italian campaign. His private secretary, too, James Ziegler, had lived long at the Roman court, and was eventually to write a life of Clement VII. that shows to the full the contempt and scorn felt for the Pope by honest Germans.

In great haste, and by a narrow, dangerous, and almost unknown path, Frundsberg crossed the Alps on what was to be his last undertaking. A body-guard of landsknechts protected the aged commander and lent him the support of their spears at all troublesome places. His intention had been to join the rest of the imperial forces in Milan, but the enemy blocked the road; Bourbon, however, with half of his forces, cut his way through to Frundsberg's camp. The mercenaries by this time were clamorous for their pay, loud, too, in their denunciations of the Pope, on whom the blame of the whole war was laid. The notion had been formed, and received with enthusiasm, of marching on Rome and extorting a subsidy from Clement, when news came that the latter had made peace with the emperor through Lannoy, the stadtholder of Naples. The result was a mutiny of the Spanish and German soldiers, who saw no hope of obtaining their pay. Bourbon fled for his life to Frundsberg's tent; his own quarters were plundered, and his richest garments were later found in a neighboring ditch. Frundsberg himself, ordering the drums to beat and a circle to be formed, would have held a discourse to the mutineers; but to his bitter mortification his own landsknechts levelled their spears against his breast, and the old hero of twenty battles fell in a convulsion to the ground and never recovered from the shock.

*Frundsberg and Bourbon in Italy.*

But the episode had, at least, the one good result of calming the passions of the soldiers, and, under Bourbon's leadership, they continued on their way to Rome, which they reached without further incident. Here they found that, although Clement had in truth closed a treaty with Lannoy, the terms had not proved acceptable to the emperor, and it had not been ratified. Disregarding the command of the Pope to begone under pain of hanging, they laid siege to the city, and though unprovided with cannon or

*Steps that led to the sack of Rome.*

battering rams, they managed to scale the walls by the aid of ladders formed from the trellises of neighboring vineyards. A great misfortune overtook them in the death of Bourbon, who fell at the first onslaught ; Benvenuto Cellini, the inimitable worker in metals, claims to have fired the shot that killed him. Bourbon lived long enough to see his troops in possession of the city, and his body was buried, it is said, in the Sistine chapel.

Such were the steps that led to the horrible and ever memorable sack of Rome of the year 1527, an event that had great consequences for the power of Charles V. and for the fate of the Reformation. The Pope was preparing to say mass in St. Peter's when he was attacked by the Germans, and two hundred of his body-guard were hewn down before his eyes ; he himself had barely time to escape through a secret door — in such haste, says an eye-witness, that he "sweated as though soused in water." But the sheltering walls of St. Angelo once gained, he remained obdurate to the demands for a subsidy.

The sack of Rome.

Outside in the streets there began meanwhile the wildest carnival that Rome had seen since the days of the Goths and Vandals. With Bourbon's death the last lawful restraint had been removed, and the soldiers rioted and plundered with inexpressible greed and wantonness. Catholics and Lutherans joined hands in one great outburst of iconoclasm; the skulls of martyrs and saints were kicked about the streets; horses were stabled in the chapels of St. Peter's, and their beds were made of bulls and indulgences ; an effigy of Luther was paraded about clad in the Pope's own garments; a priest was ordered to administer the sacrament to a dumb beast and was killed for refusing.

For ten days the starved adventurers from the north revelled in the richest city of the world. All the horrors of the Spanish inquisition were practised on those who were

suspected of concealing their valuable property. Clement
VII. held out in St. Angelo for more than a month: on his
head fell the blame and the retribution for much of what
had taken place. "I have been in Italy twenty-eight years,"
wrote the emperor's envoy in Genoa, "and have noted that
of all the wars and misfortunes during this time the popes
alone have been guilty." Charles is exhorted, now that
he is lord of the whole earth, to eliminate the cause of so
much evil. It became a question whether such a worn-out
institution as the Papacy should continue to exist at all,
and the young Gattinara wrote seriously to Charles for information on this point. The Pope was, at last, forced to
surrender, with twelve of his cardinals. Schärtlin, the
landsknecht captain, described the entry of his own troops
into St. Angelo with all the terseness of a modern telegra-
pher, "Great grief among them and much weeping: we
all became rich."

The march on Rome and the subsequent acts of violence
had taken place without the command and without the
knowledge of Charles the Fifth. His attitude in the matter
is curious and interesting. He professed to be horrified at
all that had happened, and caused prayers and masses to be
held for the deliverance of the Pope. Yet far from giving
orders for Clement's release, he prepared to make capital
out of the Pope's misfortunes. He first planned to carry his
Holiness off to Spain, but desisted for fear that the prisoner
might be rescued under way. He then demanded possession
of all the important strategic points in the papal states,
intending to leave to Clement nothing but his spiritual
power.

*Charles V. and the sack of Rome.*

But the exigencies of the European situation at last
forced Charles to be less severe than he had originally intended. The crushing blow was averted from the head of
the Pope, as it had been the year before from the Lutheran

party. Charles learned to his dismay that France and
England, alarmed at the course of recent events, were
drawing closer together. Henry VIII. declared that this
matter of the Holy See, this infliction of the greatest
injury the Papacy had ever suffered, was the common concern of all princes. In August, 1527, Cardinal Wolsey, in
the name of his master, brought to Francis England's renunciation of her claim of centuries to the French crown.
France in requital offered to pay England a yearly sum of
money, regularly and unremittingly, " until the end of the
term which Divine Providence has set for the human race."
The peace of Amiens was drawn up on these lines, and
France, aided by English gold, was free to concentrate her
forces upon Italy. Various towns in northern Italy were
taken, Genoa joined her fleet to the French forces, and
Lautrec marched off to the south to strike a decisive blow
against the kingdom of Naples. Henry VIII. meanwhile
put the seal on his enmity to Charles by attempting to
divorce Catherine of Aragon, the emperor's own aunt and
the trusted representative of Charles's policy in England.

The
peace of
Barcelona.

In the great struggle for supremacy that seemed approaching, Charles could hope for no assistance from his
brother. Ferdinand, so often his stanch supporter, was
now engaged in the struggle that was to confirm the house
of Hapsburg in the possession of the crowns of Bohemia and Hungary. In his early youth, Ferdinand had
contracted a marriage with the daughter of Vladislav of
Hungary. Her brother, the last king, who was childless,
was killed by the Turks at Mohacs in 1526. A party of
the Hungarians attempted to put up John Zapolya as their
own king, and a civil war resulted, in which Ferdinand
with difficulty held his own.

With France and England actively opposing him; conscious of the fact that his treatment of the Pope was

awakening marked displeasure in Spain; eager, too, to employ for the defence of Naples the troops stationed in Rome, Charles determined to grant to Clement better terms than the latter could possibly have expected. He gave him back his liberty and the main part of his possessions, only requiring him to pay an indemnity, to remain neutral, and, it is said, to refuse his consent to the divorce of Henry VIII. The negotiations culminated two years later in the peace of Barcelona, whereby Charles was to have Naples, Clement was to be securely reëstablished in the papal states, and Florence to be given back to the Medicis. The two heads of Christendom became once more the closest friends, — an evil token for the cause of Lutheranism, — and in February, 1530, the last coronation of an emperor by a pope took place in the cathedral of Bologna.

Meanwhile in Europe at large the heavily charged atmosphere had cleared itself. One by one the restraints fell away that had hitherto forced Charles V. to deal so charily with his Lutheran subjects. Cardinal Wolsey's fall was followed by a change of policy which drew England away from the French alliance; while upon France there fell at this time a series of heavy misfortunes. The fondest hopes had been placed upon the expedition against Naples, in which Lautrec was assisted by a Genoese fleet; but Andrea Doria for some petty reason became offended with Francis and recalled his ships. Then the plague broke out in Lautrec's army, the ranks were decimated, and the commander himself was among the victims. And at the same time, within the confines of the French monarchy, the continued warfare was engendering famine and riot.

The "ladies' peace."

Charles V. also, unable to arouse much interest in Germany for these Italian wars, had well-nigh exhausted his resources, and welcomed any chance for a favorable peace. He had already thought out one way of settling his difficulties, and that was to summon the king of France to fight a duel. After all, the questions at issue were largely of a personal nature; the mutual jealousy between the two rulers had been the cause of most of the bloodshed. Charles sent a message to the French king that was sure to provoke a challenge; he was told in return that he lied in his throat and had better prepare for single combat. But matters were not allowed to come to such extremities. After the last French army in Italy had been defeated, Louise, the queen mother of France, and Margaret of Austria, the aunt of Charles, were able to bring about that peace of Cambray which is known in history as "the ladies' peace." The negotiations were conducted entirely by the two women themselves, who inhabited adjoining houses at Cambray, and had a door cut through to better insure privacy of communication. The basis of the new treaty was the peace of Madrid; but great concessions were made to Francis, who gave a large ransom for his sons, and renounced his Italian possessions, being allowed to retain Burgundy until the emperor should have made good his claim by legal procedure.

**Charles free to act against the Lutherans.** The conclusion of the treaties of Cambray and of Barcelona had paved the way for what was to be the crowning work of Charles's policy, — the suppression of the hated heretics in Germany. With the repulse of a Turkish invasion the last obstacle was removed. The infidels had besieged Vienna, but had been gloriously beaten back; not only the arms of the Germans, but also the cold of the northern winter had, to quote the words of a Mohammedan chronicler, "saddened the mood of Islam's warlike champions."

Meanwhile, events had been happening in northern Germany which rendered the solution of the religious

difficulties, in a Catholic sense, more and more problemati-
cal. Deeper and deeper the Reformation had been striking
its roots; the time-honored institution of the Teutonic
Order had been abolished in 1525, save for a few scattered
chapters, and on its ruins had risen a secular duchy, which,
although a fief of Catholic Poland, had formally accepted
the new teachings. In Bavaria, the Lutherans were already
clothed with the nimbus of persecution, and between the
years 1527 and 1529 a not inconsiderable number of martyrs
had gone to the stake. In Brandenburg, the elector had
given his own consort a term within which to recant her
heretical opinions, and had seriously thought of putting her
to death for having caused the new form of communion to
be celebrated in her apartment. The electress had fled
to Saxony, where she had been entertained at court, but
where she had also spent three months under the humble
roof of Martin Luther and his wife.

Among the Lutheran princes there had already been
signs of a willingness to fight to the death. Philip of
Hesse had held a notable interview with Otto von Pack,
chancellor of the savagely orthodox Duke George of
Saxony. Pack had agreed, in return for a sum of money,
to furnish conclusive evidence of the existence of a great
league for the instant and violent suppression of all religious innovations, and had laid before the landgrave what
seemed to be an authentic copy of the hostile agreement.
It was sealed with the seal of the Saxon chancery, as well
as with the private signet of Duke George, which bore the
well-known crown of rue and the two lions. It declared
that Mainz, Saxony, Brandenburg, and Bavaria, as well
as the archduke Ferdinand and a number of bishops,
had united for the purpose of dispossessing all princess who
should continue to favor Martin Luther. Philip of Hesse
hastily raised an army of eighteen thousand men and

2 A

invited Charles V.'s enemy, the king of France, and Ferdinand's rival in Hungary, John Zapolya, to join his standards. He issued a war manifesto, calling the Catholic princes servants of the devil, and extorted money from the Archbishop of Mainz. To Luther and to his patron, Elector John of Saxony, belongs the credit of having averted a horrible catastrophe. An investigation was begun, the document was published, and was found to be an arrant forgery. Pack was arrested, and atoned for his villany with his life; but the rancor kindled in Catholic hearts by Philip's attitude did not abate.

The Diet of Spires of 1529.

Meanwhile the future course of Charles V. became of more and more moment to the people; the emperor would soon be coming to Germany, his sentiments were not in doubt, and certain advance measures foreboded little good. The citizens of Augsburg were told that, because of their changes in ritual, they no longer enjoyed the emperor's favor; the councillors of Strassburg were threatened with loss of their fiefs for not opposing the abolition of mass. A diet had been called to meet at Spires in 1529, and it was generally understood that it would mainly concern itself with religious affairs. When this memorable assembly met, the favorers of the Reformation found themselves in the presence of an overwhelming Catholic majority; every single adherent of the old church who had a right to sit in the diet was present in person or was represented by delegates. Those who were known to have Lutheran sympathies were not treated with the ordinary forms of politeness. No one visited the Elector of Saxony, who, for his part, made a point of publicly running counter to the old ecclesiastical usages. The emperor had sent his brother Ferdinand and several commissioners, and, at the instigation of these envoys, a most radical measure was proposed, discussed, and carried. This was nothing less than the repeal of that article passed in the diet of 1526, which had been interpreted as granting to the different estates the liberty of choosing their form of faith until such time as a general council should definitely settle the matter.

In the form in which the vote of repeal was passed, the Lutherans were not boldly ordered to return to the lap of the old church; but the new measure, if rigidly enforced, would inevitably have brought about this end. No one was to interfere with a bishop's jurisdiction, no one to hinder the performance of mass. Such toleration would, at that time, have meant the crushing out of the new religious party.

On the 19th of April, 1529, when the protocol embodying the hateful clause was drawn up, the Lutheran princes asked for a moment's delay and withdrew for consultation to an adjoining room. Archduke Ferdinand, acting in the emperor's name, refused to await their return, and, declaring the motion for repeal passed, withdrew from the building. Greatly angered on their return, the princes, in the presence of those of the assembly who still remained, read the famous protest that has ever since given its name to their whole party. It was not couched in vague or general terms; its authors took the firm attitude that this diet of 1529 had no legal right, without the consent of all parties concerned, to undo such an arrangement as had been entered into three years before. For their own parts, in matters that pertained to the honor of God and to the salvation of individuals, they proposed to continue to conduct themselves according as they should be answerable before God and their emperor. They requested that this their declaration be appended to the protocol, and placed with it among the archives. On Ferdinand's refusing this, the document was read in the presence of a notary and then made public. It bore the signatures of six princes, at the head of

*The Protestants.*

whom were Hesse and electoral Saxony, and of fourteen cities.

The die had been cast, the declaration of independence made. Henceforward there were to be the two parties, the Protestants and Catholics, and no efforts of rulers or governments were to be able to heal the breach. And the process of disintegration was to go still deeper; for within the Protestant party itself new disagreements and ultimately new secessions were to take place.

The very year that witnessed the great protest at Spires saw also the disputation at Marburg, and the thrusting away, on the part of Luther, of the hand offered by the Swiss reformers; it was a foretaste of the still more relentless struggle between the orthodox Lutherans and the Calvinists — a struggle that was to result in the loss of many districts for the Reformation.

Independently of Luther, Ulrich Zwingli, the Swiss patriot, had in 1516 begun his preachings. Called to Zurich three years later by a city council which was thoroughly in sympathy with his advanced views, he had begun a crusade against all the enemies of Swiss progress. He saw in the hiring out of citizens as mercenary troops the evil that was most harming his country; but his attempt at reform in this direction brought Zurich and its ally Berne into a war with the other cantons, in the course of which the reformer himself was to perish on the field of battle. In all his sentiments, as well as in the outward circumstances under which he labored, Zwingli differed widely from Luther: Luther was a born peasant, Zwingli a nobleman; Zwingli was a disciple of Erasmus, Luther, as far as humanism was concerned, was merely "a goose cackling among the swans"; Zwingli from the first had at his beck and call a body of magistrates ready to banish, imprison, or slay those refusing to accept the new doctrines. Zurich became a veritable theocracy, where the inhabitants were shadowed in their homes lest they should relapse into Romanist usages.

There was something political, something socialistic, something warlike about the Swiss Reformation that never could appeal to Luther; but the greatest difference between himself and Zwingli lay in the field of doctrine. The theories of the two men regarding sin and salvation were diametrically opposed, and on one point at least the difference was one that could never be reconciled. Luther believed in the actual presence of the body of Christ at every true celebration of the Eucharist: the Swiss Reformer, on the contrary, considered it a debasement of the Most High, who was in heaven at the right hand of God, to think that at the bidding of men He must so often descend to earth. To the one theologian the words of Scripture, "this is my body," meant "this is a token or reminder of my body," while the other never could and never did abandon the literal meaning of the phrase; as Luther afterward expressed it, in order to remove every chance of misconception, the actual body of Christ was "bitten with the teeth" at every proper celebration of the solemn rite. *Differences between Luther and Zwingli.*

The darling wish of Philip of Hesse had been to reconcile the differences within the fold, and to form an alliance with the Zwinglian towns of South Germany, and for that purpose he had arranged a formal disputation that was to take place in his own town of Marburg. Luther joined in the disputation most unwillingly; he seems to have feared for his personal liberty, and sought and obtained a formal safe-conduct before crossing the Landgrave's frontier. Luther's mood was intolerant to the last degree; he was determined to crush and not to conciliate; he had come, he declared, not to change his beliefs, but to bear witness to them. He had laid down for himself the unbending alternative, "The one side or the other, they or we, must be servants of *The disputation of Marburg.*

Satan." As he sat facing Zwingli, he wrote in chalk on the table before him, " this is my body," and maintained to the end that these were words which he " truly could not disregard." After various efforts to effect a settlement, the meeting broke up ; the attempt had only served to foster rancor and bitterness on both sides. Philip of Hesse declared the schism to be " madness and raving," and indeed, for the time being, it utterly prevented Protestantism from becoming a decisive factor in the history of the empire. The spirit of passive acquiescence, the unwillingness of Luther to believe for a moment in the fallibility of his own judgment, had gained the victory over the progressive anti-imperial policy of the landgrave and the Swiss. As for Luther's personal feeling toward the Zwinglians, he regarded them exactly as he did the anabaptists. In his new system only two sacraments, baptism and the Lord's supper, had been retained : Thomas Münzer and his like had attacked the one, this new antagonist was endeavoring to undermine the other. No papal anathema could have been stronger than the terms of his condemnation of the Swiss : We cannot, he said, look on them as members in Christ ; " they may claim our charity, nothing more."

Charles obliged to conciliate.
Surely at this time there was every need of a united effort ; Charles V. was returning to Germany, and the Protestants had good reason to fear his coming. They knew that he was very angry ; he had treated the envoys who announced to him the protest made at the Diet of Spires like so many convicts. The papal legate, Campeggi, was urging him to proceed with fire and sword, and, if need be, to introduce the Spanish inquisition ; his new father confessor, Loyasa, advised conciliating the heretics of high rank by flattery and bribes, but applying to those of lower degree the " true balsam for their wounds." If Charles did not at once proceed with the utmost severity, it was not from

lack of the will to do so, but because of new constellations in his political firmament, and because of the knowledge that he could not trust too much to the good conduct of France and of the Pope. The emperor favored the project, which now took form, of having his brother Ferdinand chosen king of the Romans; the elector of Saxony had grounds for denying the legality of the whole endeavor, and it eventually became necessary to propitiate him by kinder treatment of the Protestants. Loyasa's very practical advice to Charles was to make the heretics serve his own purposes, "even though toward God they are worse than devils." "If they will be dogs," he wrote, "let them have their way. Do thou, then, close thine eyes since thou hast not the power to give them their merited punishment." So the emperor sent a friendly summons to the Protestant princes, for a diet to be held at Augsburg, promising to give due consideration to every man's opinions. The invitation was received with joy; it was felt that to some extent this assembly would take the place of that general council for which men had been clamoring for so many years, and many of the estates brought with them skilled theologians and disputants.

The emperor was received with honor at Augsburg, where he displayed great magnificence; a single garment that he wore is said to have cost some two hundred thousand guldens. But it was evident, from the beginning, how frail were the hopes of achieving anything like lasting agreement. On the feast of Corpus Christi, Charles took part in the procession with bared head and with a burning taper in his hand. He had invited the Protestant princes to join him, but they deliberately stayed away. He forbade their preachers to hold public services in Augsburg, and in this they had to obey; for even by the decree of 1526 Charles had a right to say what form of religion should prevail during his presence in one of his own imperial cities.

Charles V. at Augsburg.

The Protestants had been invited to draw up a confession of faith which they were to be given an opportunity to publicly read. Melanchthon had undertaken the task, and with infinite labor had composed what was to be the accepted creed of his party for many generations. It described all the accepted doctrines with great exactness, drawing the line, not only against Catholicism, but also against the Zwinglians and the anabaptists. One single paragraph, that which defined that "in the communion the true body and blood of Christ are actually present under the form of bread and wine," was later to be slightly changed by Melanchthon's own hand, and to give rise to a long and unhallowed strife. In its original wording it served as a conclusive rebuff to the South German cities which had adopted the doctrine of the symbolic nature of the Lord's Supper. Four of them, accordingly, — Strassburg, Constance, Lindau, and Memmingen, — drew up their own "apology," which goes by the name of the Tetrapolitana.

Melanchthon's "confession" was read as agreed, but the emperor had appointed a chapel so small that only some two hundred persons could be present. However, a reader was chosen with voice so stentorian that those below in the courtyard could catch every word. The reading lasted some two hours: Charles was present, but his ignorance of German prevented his following what was said. A Latin copy was given him for his own perusal.

The confession was most conciliatory in tone, Melanchthon's one object being apparently to secure at any cost a reunion with the church of Rome. The document carefully avoided all offensive questions; papal infallibility, the sacredness of the priesthood, the proper number of sacraments, were not brought under discussion at all. Some matters that needed reform were mentioned at the end. In the negotiations, too, that followed the reading, Melanch-

thon showed himself so servile, so ready to make concessions, that he lost the respect of both parties.  The Catholics concluded that he would do anything for a bribe; the
Protestants lamented his lack of firmness.  He would even
at one time have gone so far as to allow the restoration of
private mass.  Luther, who, still under the ban, was not
allowed to come to the diet, but who, from a neighboring
fortress, had followed its proceedings with bated breath,
grew weary of the whole discussion, and wrote to urge its
discontinuance.  A reconciliation between himself and the
Pope he declared to be as feasible as a union between
Christ and Belial.

The Catholics, for their part, had drawn up a confutation
of the arguments used by the Protestants.  Their writing
displayed no logic and showed little merit of any kind;
abuse took the place of discussion and proof.  Not one
concession was made, and all the old teachings of the
Papacy with regard to the sacraments, to transubstantiation, to celibacy of priests, were maintained with the utmost
tenacity.  Yet to the bitter disappointment of the Protestants, Charles simply adopted the confutation and forbade
further discussion.  When some of the princes tried to
leave, they found the doors guarded, although to the
emperor's great anger Philip of Hesse managed to escape.
When the protocol of the diet was drawn up, it merely
stated that the Protestants had been proved in the wrong,
and must make their submission within a term of six
months; should they fail to comply with this demand, the
emperor "would do his duty."  As to the hostility of
Charles's attitude, there was no longer room for doubt.
He intended, as he had told the Pope, to "avenge the
shame inflicted on the Lord Christ."  Luther had already
written to a friend: "If war must come of it, then let it
come; we have prayed and done enough."  After the diet

The con-
futation of
the con-
fession.

had closed he wrote to Elector John and congratulated him on having escaped from that "hell at Augsburg." In a published "warning to his beloved Germans" he promised not to resume the attitude he had adopted during the Peasants' War, and not to brand as seditious men those who should take arms against these "murderous and blood-thirsty papists."

# CHAPTER XV

## CHARLES V AT WAR WITH THE PROTESTANT PRINCES

LITERATURE : As for previous chapter.

IT must have been extremely difficult for Charles V. to determine just what sort of measures to inaugurate against the Protestants. He could not well cause a crusade to be preached against them, as the Emperor Sigismund had done against the Hussites; while a declaration of war against any individual prince would have simply meant adding one more to a long list of dangerous enemies, with many of whom religion was only a side issue. Charles finally took the most rational course open to him, and appealed to the Chamber Court, that body of judges which had been established in 1521, and which was reorganized in the very year of drawing up the Confession of Augsburg. One suit at law after another was now brought, for the recovery of church lands that had come into possession of the Protestants through the change of faith of their holders. *Charles V. appeals to the Chamber Court.*

It was mainly for the purpose of resisting the decrees of this court, which was overwhelmingly Roman Catholic in its sympathies, that a number of princes and civic delegates came together in the Hessian town of Smalkald, in 1531, and laid the foundation of a Protestant league. The first signers were the elector of Saxony, the fiery landgrave of Hesse, the dukes of Anhalt and Luneburg, and the counts of Mansfeld. As the months went on more than a dozen cities handed in their allegiance, among them several of those South German towns which, on account of their *Formation of the Smalkald League.*

Zwinglian sympathies, had been debarred from a share in the Augsburg Confession. But recent events had made Luther more ready to make friends; he had come to the conclusion that " the world, the flesh, and the devil, the Papacy and the Turks combined," had not injured the cause of the gospel so much as this schism. He was ready now to waive at least one disputed question, whether godless men partook of the actual flesh of the Saviour when they ate the consecrated bread. Melanchthon, on the one side, and Martin Bucer, on the other, drew up a formula with regard to the Eucharist, on which both parties, in Germany at least, declared that they could agree: Christ's body was "actually present," but as "food for the soul." The Swiss Zwinglians, indeed, filled with bitterness at the outcome of the Marburg disputation, refused to reopen the subject: unaided they fought out their own fight, and succumbed to superior numbers on the field of Cappel.

Agreements of the Smalkald League.

The formation of the League of Smalkald was a very decided step in the direction of armed resistance. The league was for six years, and provided that, if any member should be attacked, either by arms or in the courts, the rest should render him assistance. A rigid line was drawn against the anabaptists, and the severe punishments decreed against them by the government were expressly affirmed. A much-discussed question, and one that was finally decided most unfortunately for the cause, was that concerning the headship of the league. For the first time the fatal import of a certain jealousy between the elector of Saxony and Philip of Hesse became apparent. The young landgrave, warlike and fond of bold combinations, would have been the natural head of the new organization and the leader of its forces. This, Saxony could never brook, and the unnatural subterfuge was resorted to of dividing the presidency of the organization as well as the com-

mand of the armies: Philip and John were to wield the
chief power in turn for six months at a time, while the
military headship was to be exercised by the one or
the other, according as the tide of war should flow near to
his domains.

What made the Smalkald League especially dangerous
to Charles V. was the fact that a rallying point was
thus given for all his enemies, Protestant and Catholic,
domestic and foreign.   The powerful dukes of Bavaria,
rigid Catholics though they were, did not hesitate to make
a formal alliance with Hesse and Saxony in order to oppose
the choice of Archduke Ferdinand as king of the Romans.
Another avowed object of this union was to reinstate Duke
Ulrich of Würtemberg, who had been obliged in 1519 to
relinquish his lands to the Hapsburgs.   To add to Charles's
perplexities the Sultan of Turkey was preparing to invade
Germany with an army like that of Xerxes.   He refused
to address Charles as emperor, — that title, he declared,
belonged to the ruler of Constantinople, — but wrote to
him merely as "king of Spain."

*Enemies of Charles V.*

This danger from the Turks soon assumed such alarming
proportions that all other conflicts were dwarfed for the
moment, and Catholics and Protestants alike eagerly
sought a basis for reconciliation.   Even the Pope was
roused to a sense of the perils that threatened Christendom,
and interfered, as no Pope had yet done, to straighten out
the religious affairs of Germany.   He laid the Augsburg
Confession before Roman theologians, who gave their verdict that some clauses were actually Catholic, others capable of a Catholic interpretation, and that, as to others still,
a compromise was possible.   He was willing, if need be,
to grant communion in both kinds and the marriage of
priests.   Charles V., however, finally determined to make
no specific concessions, but rather to declare a general truce.

*The religious peace of Nuremberg.*

Of such nature was the so-called first religious peace, signed at Nuremberg in July, 1532. Until the meeting of that *fata morgana*, a general council, there was to be a cessation to all hostile measures, including the suits at law in the Chamber Court. Only actual members of the Smalkald League were to be included in the peace, Charles refusing to consider the possibility of new accessions to the cause.

The
Turkish
war.

All barriers being thus removed, Catholics and Protestants prepared with a will to march out against the Turks. A stately army of eighty thousand men was speedily brought together, but the greater part of it never saw active service; a slight skirmish near Vienna with Suleiman's light cavalry was the extent of the fighting that fell to its lot. Once more the " warlike champions of Islam " had had their mood saddened; a garrison of seven hundred men in the little Hungarian town of Güns had withstood their attack for three weeks. The Turks had withdrawn at the very moment when they might have triumphed, frightened, it is said, by the yells of the inhabitants.

No less incomprehensible than the retreat of the Turks was Charles V.'s neglect in not pursuing them: sharp-tongued Schärtlin was probably right when he compared the emperor's usual method of making war with the slow progress of a ruminating ox from field to field. King Ferdinand declared the unmolested retreat of this enemy to be the most painful experience of his life. But Charles thought otherwise. Leaving his army, he hurried off to Italy to talk with Clement VII. about the general council. He naturally found the Pope averse to the idea; one of the first effects of such a council as the emperor wished would have been to curtail the papal prerogatives, and of this Clement VII. was fully aware.

After the Peace of Nuremberg and the retreat of Suleiman, the Protestants entered on an era of prosperity.

They soon felt strong enough to repudiate the Chamber Court, which, under one pretext or another, had continued its objectionable suits at law. Before the period for which their league was formed had run out, they renewed it for another ten years. Elector John of Saxony had died in the year of the Nuremberg Peace, but his son and successor, John Frederick, proved an equally zealous upholder of the Reformation. As for Philip of Hesse, he was at last able to indulge his warlike propensities, and, as champion of Ulrich of Würtemberg, to bring that long-banished prince back to his own. The armed opposition of Ferdinand's viceregent in the duchy was of no avail; the great mass of the people were tired of the Hapsburg rule, and the revolution was accomplished with little difficulty, and in a short time. Charles V. just then was away, taking part in his first really successful campaign — chasing Chaireddin Barbarossa and his Turkish corsairs from their newly founded settlement at Tunis. Ferdinand, isolated in his brother's absence, and fearing a popular uprising which might have cost him not merely Würtemberg, but also his crown as king of the Romans, signed the Treaty of Kadan (June, 1534), the terms of which included Ulrich's reinstatement, although the duchy was to revert to the Hapsburgs should there ever fail to be male heirs.[1]

Ferdinand had fought hard to obtain a promise, that Würtemberg should retain the shallow Catholicism he had succeeded in imposing upon the land. In this he failed, and the duchy became a new stronghold for the Protestant teachings, drawing in its wake, too, the neighboring principalities of Baden, Hanau, Falkenstein, and Fürstenberg. It even joined the Smalkald League in

> *The recovery of Würtemberg.*

---

[1] This latter clause was formally abrogated at the Treaty of Pressburg in 1805.

common with Pomerania, Anhalt, and four free cities. When an imperial envoy protested that violence was being done to the Peace of Nuremberg, he was answered that the first to break that peace had been the imperial Chamber Court.

Gains for the Protestant cause.

In every way the Protestant princes were rising in importance. We find Ferdinand inviting them to his court and treating them with marked respect. The king of France, although sternly repressing religious freedom in his own lands, sought the alliance of the league, as did also Henry VIII., once official defender of the Catholic faith, now "Supreme Head" of the English church. Pope Paul III., too, successor of Clement VII., sent his legate, Vergerio, to try and win back the lost adherents of the church, and to soften their hearts to the idea of having the looked-for council held on Italian instead of on German ground. Vergerio went so far as to invite Martin Luther to table, on which occasion, in order to do proper honor to the rank of his host, the former monk donned a fine garment with satin sleeves, bright jewels, and fur trimmings. He felt uncomfortable in his finery, but did not lose the opportunity of talking to the legate in very plain language. He soon after drew up the Smalkald Articles, which were to be the programme of the Protestants should they appear before a council. Here, more than ever, does he emphasize the utter hopelessness of a reconciliation with the Papacy.

The death of Duke George of Saxony, who, from the time when he had uttered his curse at the Disputation of Leipzig, had been a steadfast enemy of the Reformation, immeasurably strengthened the Protestant cause. George had taken every precaution to keep his duchy from falling into the hands of his brother Henry, even deeding in his will the whole land to the emperor. But all in vain.

There was no power that could change the lawful order of succession firmly established by the Golden Bull. Henry succeeded quietly in 1539, and Luther was soon preaching from the chief pulpit in Leipzig. In this same year, too, Joachim II., elector of Brandenburg, having inherited the faith of his fugitive mother, publicly took the utraquistic communion. Two more powerful states were thus won, and North Germany assumed the exclusively Protestant form that it bears to this day.

No doubt the spread of the Reformation might have been greatly checked, had Charles been able to remain in Germany; but now as ever he was forced to pay regard to other interests, and to fight for the possession of his outlying territories. No sooner had he ended his Tunis campaign, fought under the heat of a tropical sun, than the death of his ward, Sforza, reopened the dispute with the French king as to the succession in Milan. To the astonishment and scandal of Europe, Francis went so far as to ally himself with Mohammedans, and in 1536 Turkish and French ships joined in a descent on the coast of Italy. All France was just then in a state of bitterness and wrath against the emperor, believing that he had hired an Italian to murder their dauphin, who had died under suspicious circumstances; the Parliament of Paris declared him guilty of felony and rebellion, and withdrew his Burgundian fiefs. After a campaign in France, in which the French devastated their own fertile plains of Provence so as to cut off the enemy's supplies, an unsatisfactory truce was patched up by the Pope. Threatened as he was with a renewal of the war, in dread of a new invasion on the part of the Turks, and having found a new enemy in the person of Duke William of Cleves-Julier, whose possessions extended like a wedge into the Netherlands, and who was on the verge of changing his faith, Charles could not think of resuming

*Charles hampered by new enemies.*

2 B

hostilities with the Protestants.  On the contrary, he now made sincere efforts to bring about a peaceful settlement of the religious differences.  Disputations were instituted to which the Pope, too, sent delegates.  At Ratisbon, in 1541, great concessions were offered, but this very assembly brought more clearly than ever to light the fundamental antagonism of the two creeds.  The Protestants could not and would not yield; they stood as yet upon a vantage ground from which neither storm nor siege nor gentle wiles could dislodge them; it remained to be seen if the task could be accomplished by internal dissensions and jealousies.

**Religious scruples of Philip of Hesse.**

An incident relating to the private life of Landgrave Philip of Hesse proved in the end the cause of the downfall of the league armies.  When the commander-in-chief goes over to the enemy, no matter what reservations he may chance to make, all hope of ultimate victory may safely be abandoned.

Philip's morals were not much worse than those of his contemporaries.  But in his case dissoluteness was tempered by an excessive tenderness of conscience.  It troubled him greatly that the class of evil-doers to which he belonged was included among those shut out by St. Paul's words from the enjoyment of the kingdom of heaven; only once in a period of several years had he, one of the official heads of the Protestant party, ventured to partake of the Holy Communion.  He was anxious to reform, but in the way stood his antipathy to his wife, Christine of Saxony, who, to use his own words, he found "unfriendly, ugly, and ill-odored," which was probably a calumny; at all events, Christine proved most faithful to him in his worst adversities.

It had come to Philip's notice that nowhere in the Bible, neither in the Old nor in the New Testament, is bigamy de-

clared a sin; no prophet had ever chidden a king or prince Bigamous
for the number of his wives; St. Paul had not included marriage of
bigamists among those debarred from entering the king- Philip of
Hesse.
dom of heaven.    Moreover, the Wittenberg theologians
themselves, in the case of Henry VIII. of England, had
declared the taking of two wives to be preferable to divorce,
on the express ground that it was not prohibited by divine
law.    Moved by these considerations, the landgrave determined to marry Margarete von der Sale, with whom he
had already been all too intimate.    The lady's mother gave
her consent, but only on condition that the wedding should
take place in the presence of noted theologians, and of an
envoy of the Saxon elector.    Luther and Melanchthon, when
approached by Philip, were placed in a position of great per-
plexity : fatal as it would have been to alienate the powerful
landgrave from their cause, they were powerless to argue
with him on his own ground since Scripture gave no solution of the difficulty.    They recognized what confusion
was likely to ensue were bigamy to be generally allowed
in the Christian church, yet were finally brought to acknowledge that Philip's was a case for a special dispensation, and to give their consent to the wedding with
Margarete.    Lest evil should come of it, they insisted that
the whole matter be kept a profound secret, and that in
the eyes of the world the new wife should be nothing but
a concubine.    On these terms the strange wedding, to which
even Christine was brought by specious arguments and by
various guarantees to give her sanction, took place in due
form at Rothenburg-on-the-Fulda.    Among those present
were Bucer, Melanchthon, and a councillor of John Frederick, the Saxon elector.    The ceremony was performed by
Philip's court preacher, Melander, who is himself said to
have been the husband of three wives.    In the marriage
instrument it was expressly stated that the landgrave took

this step for the purpose of saving his body and soul. A few days later Philip wrote to Luther that "with a joyous conscience" he had again gone to Communion. He thanked the reformer for his kindly offices and sent him a cask of wine.

Evil results of Philip's marriage.

This marriage was, taken all in all, one of the most unhallowed incidents in the history of the Reformation. Where so many persons were concerned the facts could not be concealed, even though Luther, unswerving as he was in other matters pertaining to the truth, counselled a downright denial of everything. He urged that the "private yes remain a public no," compared this secret to a secret of the confessional, and said openly in a conference with Philip's councillors at Eisenach, "What is the harm of a good plump lie for the sake of the Christian church?" Well might the gentle Melanchthon fall ill from having this ill-odored matter thus dragged to the light. And the consequences of the marriage, and especially of its disclosure, were worse than even he could easily have foreseen. The Elector John Frederick refused to uphold Philip before the world, and stung him by his reproaches into fierce counter accusations. The landgrave, finally, at odds with his own party and fearing the severe punishment for bigamy which the law allowed, and which the emperor would otherwise have gladly inflicted, accepted Charles's overtures and became his friend and ally. All this at a time when swift and united action on the part of the Protestants was their only hope, — with France pressing for an alliance against the emperor, and Cleves-Julier only waiting for an invitation to join the Smalkald League! Philip promised to prevent, and did prevent, all overtures to France, England, or Cleves; he declared, indeed, that in case Charles directly attacked the league he should still consider him his enemy. The future was to show what he could do and what he could suffer for the cause he now abandoned; but the fact remains that he was a traitor, — he kept secret his relations to Charles, — and that he seriously injured the prospects of the league.

The elector of Saxony was unable, in spite of all his efforts, to organize the proper sort of union or to make proper preparations for common defence. Charles proceeded, without let or hindrance, to lead an army against William of Cleves, whom he utterly vanquished, depriving him of two provinces, Zutphen and Guelders, and forcing him to put down Protestantism throughout his domains. This Cleves expedition harmed the league in more ways than one, for it opened the emperor's eyes to the disunion and want of preparation of his enemies. For the moment, indeed, a new war with France forced him into further concessions, but the time was not distant when he was to profit by his knowledge. The Peace of Crespy (September 15, 1544) promised to be more lasting than any other of these French treaties. By its terms Francis was to renounce his Burgundian and Italian claims and not to join the Protestants; the Duke of Orleans, his son, was to marry a daughter either of Charles or of Ferdinand, in the one case her dowry to be the Netherlands, in the other Milan. In the following year a long truce was entered into with the Turks, who were meditating an attack on Persia. All was now quiet on the borders of the empire; the field was clear, and Charles could make final preparations for hunting down his prey. He felt now that his honor was at stake, that with the German Protestants so active he could no longer maintain himself in Flanders, Spain, or Italy. As his minister, Granvella remarked, it was time to show signs of life; and Charles himself wrote that, dead or alive, he wished to remain emperor in Germany. Luther's death, September 18, 1546, coincided with the fading of the lucky

Charles rids himself of his enemies.

star that had so long watched over the Protestants. Clouds
of every kind were gathering round them. The great
Catholic council, proclaimed as the fulfilment of the promise given so long before, met at Trent in 1545; but the
very wording of the summons was such that no friend of
Luther could think of responding. The Papacy had
begun to fortify itself by the aid of the Jesuits and the
Inquisition. The success of Calvin in France and Geneva
had roused the church to greater efforts than ever before.
"Hardly is it possible," wrote an Italian, "to be a Christian and to die in bed." It is true, the numbers of the
German Protestants were increased at this time by the
accession of the Palatinate, but that made Charles only
the more eager for war. Four out of the seven electors
were now in the ranks of his enemies, and endless opposition was foreboded in the diets.

Maurice
of Saxony
goes over to
Charles.

It was unfortunate for the Protestants that their period
of prosperity had lasted so long; Charles's policy of pro-
crastination had for once proved eminently successful. It
had lulled the league into a false security; it had worn
off the first great enthusiasm, and had given opportunity
for a new generation of princes to grow up who were
lukewarm in the cause. The emperor was quick to see
his opportunity, and, on one pretext or another, but especially by playing upon their greed and avarice, he drew
over to his own side the two Hohenzollern princes,
Albrecht Alcibiades of Culmbach and Hans of Küstrin,
and also Maurice, the son and successor of Henry, Duke
of Saxony. This latter prince, who was to play such a
part in the future of the Reformation, was a man in whom
splendid qualities were mixed with much weakness and
pettiness of character. He was selfish to the core, so
prone to excess in drinking as to excite comment and
blame even in that lax age, and so jealous of John Fred-

erick's power that the latter's acquisition of the bishopric of Magdeburg, on which Maurice had cast longing eyes, finally caused an irreconcilable quarrel. This drove Maurice into the emperor's arms; the immediate reward of his neutrality was to be the possession of Magdeburg and Halberstadt. But in a personal interview Charles intrusted to him, in addition, the duty of carrying out the imperial ban against the elector of Saxony, with the right to keep what lands he might conquer. He was not to be called upon in any way to oppress or injure the cause of Protestantism; in fact, Charles did his utmost to represent this war as having nothing to do with matters of faith. "These deserters will know well enough that it concerns their religion," he wrote to his sister, "but it will none the less be advantageous to assign to it another cause." So he seized on a quarrel which had occurred between the Smalkaldians and the Duke of Brunswick; declared that the former had broken the peace, and caused the eagles of the empire to be carried at the head of his troops, to show that the struggle concerned the welfare of the whole land. At the same time, in the interests of the Catholic religion, he gained the alliance of Pope Paul III.; who proclaimed a year of jubilee, agreed to send an army of 12,500 men to be used against "Protestants and Smalkaldians and every other kind of German heretic," and turned over to the imperial treasury one-half of the year's revenues of the church of Spain.

A prime condition for a successful campaign is that advantage be taken of the enemy's straits, and that no hesitation be shown when the chance offers of striking a decisive blow. If ever a war was lost through the blundering of leaders and advisers, it was this of the Smalkald League. The pacifically minded Protestant princes, who were thus thrown into a struggle for life and death, had had

*Shortcomings of the Protestant leaders.*

little experience with real war. The terrible Duke of Alva, whom Charles appointed general-in-chief of his forces, far outmatched them, one and all, in coolness and patience as well as in skill. Poor John Frederick of Saxony, with his burden of superfluous flesh and his slowness of decision and quickness of temper, was fitted for anything rather than a military command. Philip of Hesse had once written to his chancellor, " You know the elector; if he has not been asked to have a hand in a matter he is apt to throw chairs and benches into the mess so as to spoil it all." John Frederick proved now a very millstone around the landgrave's neck, while whatever harm was left undone was fully achieved and consummated by a timid and short-sighted war council that directed operations from Ulm.

Failure to capture Charles V.    Charles V. was at this time at Ratisbon with a mere handful of men; the forces that he awaited were to come from the four quarters of Europe, — from Italy, the Netherlands, from Spain, and from Austria. The Protestants, on the other hand, had almost immediately a large army in the field. Ulrich of Würtemberg commanded 10,000 infantry and 700 horse; the imperial cities of South Germany, which in addition controlled the powder-mills and cannon foundries, placed in the field 12,000 men; Saxony and Hesse could be counted on for 21,000 more. Charles himself, in his own accounts, designates the failure of the Smalkaldians to attack him in Ratisbon as one of their fatal mistakes. Their general, Schärtlin von Burtenbach, was sent, instead, to try and intercept the papal troops; he was hampered by contradictory orders and was soon called home by the panic-stricken war council, which feared for the safety of Ulm. Even then, had Ratisbon been chosen as the rallying point for all the Protestant forces, the small imperial army might have been surrounded and captured; but the different contingents united instead at Wörth, and Charles escaped to Ingolstadt, which was far more capable of defence. This town was at last bombarded on four consecutive days, but in a thoroughly unskilful manner, nine-tenths of the shots failing to take effect. The emperor moved quietly about without fear for his personal safety, and is said to have remarked sneeringly, " The Hessian shoots like a friend, not like an enemy." After exhausting their ammunition, the Protestants withdrew. From this time on Charles himself took the initiative, and Count Buren, with reën-forcements to the number of 22,000, managed to join him without molestation. By Alva's advice the imperialists avoided pitched battles, while the Protestants made marches and counter marches without fixed plan.

The two armies at last found themselves face to face a little to the north of Ulm. The power of resistance of the league was fast wavering ; the South German cities had already expressed their unwillingness to make further pe-cuniary sacrifices, beginning, as they did, to realize what it meant to lose their trade with Spain and Portugal. At this juncture the long-prepared blow fell on the electorate of Saxony. Maurice, with an army of his own subjects, aided by Ferdinand and his Bohemians, had invaded John Fred-erick's territories. The electoral dignity was formally trans-ferred by the emperor from the old Ernestine house, which for so long had been his enemy, to the Albertine or Dresden branch of the Wettin family. This gave the *coup de grâce* to the Smalkald League. John Frederick hastened home to fight for his hereditary rights, though intending to re-turn in the following spring. Philip of Hesse, too, fore-seeing an attack on his own lands, and hopeless as to the general outlook, withdrew in turn with all his forces.

One by one the towns and minor princes then made their submission, which the emperor accepted in the

Maurice invades electoral Saxony.

Subjection
of the
Protestant
princes.
haughtiest spirit.   The envoys of Ulm were received
in the little town of Hall, and in obedience to Charles's
command, fell on their faces before him.   "In Philip
Buschler's back room," writes a simple chronicler, "he
let them lie a quarter of an hour before he granted them
his pardon."   The terms of surrender for the members of
the league were hard, though not crushing: large fines were
imposed, and the money that their own side had failed to
secure, now found its way into the coffers of the emperor.

The latter intended to taste to the full the sweets of
victory, and remitted none of the tokens of subjection that
he thought his due.   Before this worn-out man, whose hair
had grown gray in the struggle, whose face was ashen
pale, and whose limbs refused him their obedience, envoys
and princes were forced to kneel in a long line, and sue for
mercy.

John
Frederick
in Saxony.
The last act of the Smalkald War remained to be played
in Saxony.   Here John Frederick showed himself in a
new and more favorable light.   All hesitation was gone
for the moment, and he won the hearts, not only of his
subjects, but of many of his enemies, by his energy and
tact.   The Bohemians who came from Prague refused to
fight longer against a prince who partook of the body and
blood of Christ with the same ceremonies as themselves.
Maurice's own subjects came to the conclusion that, while
on general principles the emperor's commands were to be
obeyed, the latter had no right to say to his subjects,
"Thou shalt call on dead saints," or "Thou shalt not
believe in forgiveness of sins."   John Frederick not merely
recovered his own lands, but also occupied Magdeburg and
Halle, and carried the war into the heart of the enemy's
country by besieging Leipzig.

But already Charles, the Duke of Alva, and Maurice
were on the march.   No amount of personal courage could

atone for the elector's real incapacity in military matters.
He made no preparations for intrenching himself or for
meeting the advancing force: he believed an idle tale according to which the emperor was dead and the Spaniards
were marching behind his corpse.  One misty Sunday
at Mühlberg, after he had quietly listened to the usual
sermon and then taken his morning meal, he suddenly
found himself involved in the great disaster of his life.
The sun broke through the fog and showed him the imperial army, five times the size of his own, on the opposite
bank of the Elbe.  His one thought was to reach the
fortress of Torgau in his rear, although, according to the
simplest rules of war, he should have left a detachment of
his soldiers to dispute the passage of the river, until night
could cover his retreat.  He hoped instead to outdistance
his pursuers in a fair chase.  But some of the Spaniards
swam the stream, seized his own boats, and hastily formed
a bridge, while others found a ford by which seven horsemen abreast could pass over at a time.  Charles V. crossed
by this latter way.  He was arrayed that day in the armor
in which Titian afterward painted him.  Don Luis d'Avila,
grand master of the Knights of Alcantara, was with him
at the time, and describes him on his brown Spanish
courser, with " dark red, golden-fringed saddle-cloth, and
a broad red gold-edged sash over his burnished breast-
plate; on his head a German helmet, in his hand a short
spear."

As twilight was coming on the vanguard of the imperial
army overtook the Saxons.  The latter made no attempt
at serious resistance; the infantry, trampled upon by their
own horsemen, took to mad flight, and even such artillery
as was ready to hand was not employed.  Every man
looked to his own safety, and John Frederick, less agile
than the rest, was taken prisoner and handed over to the

The capture
of John
Frederick.

Duke of Alva. Blood poured down his face from the sabre-cut of a Hungarian hussar. Charles met him in this plight. "Most gracious lord and master," the elector began; but the emperor cut him short with, "Am I *now* your imperial master?" John Frederick hastily replaced the hat that he had doffed. "I am in your power; do with me as you will." Even the Spaniards and Italians were impressed by his dignity in the midst of ruin. Charles caused a court-martial to be held over his captive, who was at once condemned to death; but no one, least of all the unfortunate elector himself, thought it likely that the emperor would venture to carry out the sentence. In point of fact, after the surrender of Wittenberg, the last Saxon position of importance, Charles began to show John Frederick some consideration, feeling perhaps that he might need a counterpoise against the pride and presumption of Maurice. The prisoner was treated with some regard to his princely rank, and on the occasion of a visit which the emperor allowed him to pay to his wife, Spanish noblemen held the baldachin which protected him from the sun's rays. Charles himself went so far as to go to Wittenberg to pay his respects to the Saxon electress. It is on this occasion that the younger Granvella is said to have urged the emperor to have Luther's bones cast out of their grave. But Charles answered, "I war with the living, not with the dead."

By the terms of an agreement known as the "Wittenberg Capitulation," John Frederick renounced the electoral dignity and relinquished the greater part of all his lands, reserving for his sons only the districts west of the Saale, including Weimar, Jena, Eisenach, and Gotha. The demand had been made, that in religious matters he should submit to the emperor or to the Council of Trent, but this John Frederick stubbornly refused. Though he might never regain that liberty for which his wife Sybilla had so urgently pleaded on bended knee, he would hold fast to the Protestant faith as laid down in the Augsburg Confession. He had to agree, under watch and ward, to remain at the emperor's court.

The fate of Philip of Hesse was even harder than that of the elector; these princes were atoning bitterly for their long attitude of passive opposition. Charles demanded nothing short of unconditional surrender; he had every reason to mistrust the landgrave and meant to secure his person. He did concede to Joachim of Brandenburg and to Maurice of Saxony, who had undertaken the office of mediators, that Philip's imprisonment should not be perpetual. Maurice was Philip's son-in-law, and seems to have felt that, out of regard for himself, Charles would exact only nominal submission. Philip shared this impression, and came to the appointed place of meeting at Halle in an unduly hopeful frame of mind. His cheerful smile angered Charles V.; "All right, I will teach you to laugh," he said threateningly as the landgrave knelt before him. Philip was decoyed to a dinner at the quarters of the Duke of Alva, where Joachim and Maurice were also present. In spite of all that the latter could say and do, the landgrave was forced to remain a prisoner when the feast was over. Charles spared him no humiliations; he was kept in close confinement under the most irksome surveillance — even by night he was not left alone, and at every change of guard the heavy steps and clanking arms disturbed his rest. An attempt at flight drew down upon him further severities; the man who had been the head of a league of princes, as well as the hope of the Protestant party, was actually threatened with torture.

The arrest of Philip of Hesse.

Charles V. stood at the zenith of his power; the year which was marked by the victory of Mühlberg witnessed

Charles V. triumphant in all directions.

also the closing of a long truce with the Turks, as well as the death of two monarchs, Francis I. and Henry VIII., who had given the emperor much trouble. Two German electorates, Saxony and Cologne, had just been filled according to his wish; to a third, the Palatinate, the Catholic Duke of Bavaria laid claim, — Charles needed but to speak the word, and the Protestant incumbent could be driven from his lands. The emperor's breast swelled with the pride of success; he had risen in his own estimation as well as in that of the world. At the "armored Diet" of Augsburg, so called, perhaps, because of the imperial guard of ten thousand Spanish soldiers, he had but to dictate his terms. It was noticed that when he dismissed the princes, he omitted his usual custom of accompanying them to the head of the stairs.

The Diet in question arranged more than one matter to Charles's liking. The rich province of the Netherlands was recognized as a Hapsburg possession and as practically independent of the empire. Money was granted for various purposes; while, with unheard-of foresight, a fund or treasure was levied to be used in case of emergency. Last, but not least, all promised, through their mouthpiece, the elector of Mainz, to conform to the so-called "interim," — an elaborate *modus vivendi*, or provisional settlement, of religious matters — which was to remain in force until all questions at issue should be definitely settled by the long-looked for council.

The "interim."

The "interim" had been drawn up, with ostensible fairness, by a commission consisting of Catholics and Protestants alike; but prominent among the latter were men who were renegades to their cause. John Agricola, court preacher to the elector of Brandenburg, had long been at enmity with the Wittenberg faction. He was inordinately vain, and boasted of having by his own efforts reformed

the Pope and converted the emperor. He had held a
service of praise and thanksgiving in honor of the outcome of the battle of Mühlberg. He rejoiced, he said, that
the sons of the fallen elector, at whose court there had
been such immoderate feasting, should now have to eat
out of tin dishes and drink out of tin cups.

It may be imagined to what sort of a document a man
like this would set his hand. The "interim" has been
well described as a "strait-jacket for German Protestantism." Communion in both kinds and the marriage of
priests were allowed, and a few differences of doctrine condoned; but this was all. The people who for a quarter of
a century had enjoyed religious freedom, were to be driven
back under the care of Catholic bishops, while all the
hated observances — the seven sacraments, the daily mass,
the stated feasts, the adoration of saints — were to be revived. Yet only one of the Protestant princes, the com-
paratively insignificant Hans of Küstrin, had the courage
to set his face resolutely against the introduction of the
measure into his lands. Joachim of Brandenburg seems
to have forged an interim of his own, and passed it off
upon his subjects as the real one; Maurice of Saxony made
an equally weak attempt to soften the imperial measures,
and employed Melanchthon to draw up what is known as
the Interim of Leipzig.

It is incomprehensible that a man once so fine, so loyal,   Melanch-
and so brave as the Wittenberg theologian, could work in   thon's
the interests of a time-server like Maurice; and perfectly   disloyalty.
gratuitous seem the insults which he saw fit at this juncture to heap on his dead friend and companion, Luther.
He declared to a councillor of his new master that he would
not oppose Maurice, whatever measures the latter might see
fit to introduce; he would be silent and bear the inevitable. He had suffered, he said, an "almost impossible ser-

vitude" under the violence of Luther. He denied having helped to form a separate or schismatic church, and pointed out how much, in his youth, he had loved the Catholic ceremonies. It was the case of Peter denying his Lord: when the letter was read to Charles V. in Augsburg, he exclaimed, "You have him fast; see that you keep him!"

**John Frederick in captivity.** Very different from the attitude of Melanchthon was that of the imprisoned Elector, John Frederick. When ordered to accept the "interim," or suffer the consequences, he replied, that to subscribe to doctrines which ran counter to the word of God, would be to commit the one unpardonable sin against the Holy Ghost. He bowed his head meekly under the storm of the emperor's wrath. When all his Lutheran books were taken away from him he said with a smile " *Omnia mea mecum porto*," " I carry with me all my belongings." That which he retained in his memory no one could seize. His attendants were ordered to give him no meat on fast days; his preacher was driven from him. No friendly intercourse would have been his whatever, had it not been for the faithfulness of the painter, Lucas Cranach, who would willingly have shared his captivity, and who constantly visited him.

**Failure of the "interim."** If, in spite of the pusillanimity of the princes and the dubious attitude of Melanchthon, the "interim" of Charles V. never really gained acceptance, the reason lay, on the one hand, in the attitude of the Pope, — who for political reasons, as he frankly acknowledged, and mad with rage at the murder of his son, Ferrante Gonzaga, for which he held Charles responsible, refused his dispensation for even the slight concessions that had been made to the Protestants, — but primarily in the stand taken by the common people. A new force, public opinion, had come to the front, and had developed mightily in the course of a single generation. The masses greeted the "devilish interim" with scorn and derision: after twenty years of pregnancy, wrote a journalist of the time, the emperor has given birth to a horrible monster — a three-headed dragon with a snake's tail, a scorpion's sting, and the foot of an eagle or a frog. The " Judas," Maurice, and Agricola and Melanchthon as well, came in for perfect storms of abuse, while the Virgin Mary was made to utter a fervid prayer for the downfall of the house of Ahab and the death of its royal head. The emissaries of " Pharaoh " or of " Herod," as the emperor was variously called, were glad enough as they passed through the land to hide their eagles in order to escape with their lives. Never had Charles V.'s inability to make a rational use of his triumphs and successes been more clearly marked than now. His insistence on the acceptance of the interim, his severity to John Frederick and the Hessian landgrave, and the tyrannical manner in which he trod with his Spanish heel on the susceptibilities of all his German subjects, brought about the catastrophe that marks the last act in the long drama of his reign. The crisis came when the emperor tried to secure the ultimate succession to the throne of the empire to his son, Philip. One dreads to think what might have been the fate of Germany had the husband of " Bloody Mary," the future grim lord of Spain and the Netherlands, actually achieved the imperial crown. Unfortunately for Philip, however, he had as rival candidate the knightly and popular Maximilian, King Ferdinand's son. Even those German princes who had but lately supported Charles, had now had more than enough of his foreign and oppressive ways. Already complaints had been made, that the presence of Spanish troops in Germany was contrary to law and to the solemn promise made by the emperor in his electoral compromise. Charles's stern reply had provoked the remark from a Brandenburg envoy that the Germans

Revolt of the younger princes.

2 c

were being treated as actual slaves. Early in 1552 a revolt broke out, headed by Maurice of Saxony and by several of the younger princes of the Hohenzollern family, among them that Albert Alcibiades of Culmbach-Baireuth whom a councillor of Ferdinand not unjustly called a "monstrous, senseless wild beast."

Maurice's grounds of complaint.

Maurice's two private grounds of complaint were, first, that, in spite of his constant intervention, his father-in-law, Philip, had been kept in captivity for five long years, with no immediate prospect of being set at liberty; second, that the reward for his own services to the emperor had not come up to his anticipations. He had contemplated completely crushing the family of his cousin by taking away all trace of sovereignty, and granting the sons of the former elector a mere annuity; but to this Charles had objected, requiring lands and offices for the young men. Moreover, Charles had reserved for himself the disposal of Magdeburg and Halberstadt, the very bishoprics which had first caused the quarrel between the two branches of the Saxon house. Magdeburg, indeed, had held out against the emperor himself; it had stubbornly refused to follow the "interim," and Maurice had been empowered to raise an army and carry out the imperial ban. It was this that gave him his opportunity against Charles. Magdeburg submitted in November, 1551; but the real terms were not the ones that were made public. Many of the garrison enrolled themselves under Maurice's own banner instead of under that of the emperor, raising the numbers in the rebel army to a total of thirty thousand.

Charles in great straits.

In danger of being penned up in Innsbruck by Maurice's army, the emperor made the attempt to escape to the Netherlands in a closed carriage, which ostensibly contained a "lady going to Wildbad." Finding the way beset, he was obliged to return, but later succeeded in crossing the

Brenner to Villach.  The Saxon soldiers entered Innsbruck
to find that their bird had flown.  No particular deeds of
violence are recorded against them, save that they seized
the effects of the Spaniards, strutted round in their rich
garments, and amused themselves immoderately by addressing each other as " Don."

All the old phantoms of his past were now rising up to
terrify the sick and weary emperor, and to punish him for
all his pride.  King Henry II. of France issued a pompous
manifesto in which he dubbed himself " vindicator of the
liberties of Germany and avenger of the captive princes."
The cover of the document bore the device of the old
Roman freedmen — a hat between two swords; the murderers of Cæsar had adopted it to show the purity of their
designs.  Henry had signed an alliance at Chambord with
the rebel princes of Germany at the price, everlastingly
disgraceful to the latter, of a surrender of the towns of
Metz, Toul, and Verdun.  The French king was to hold
them as " vicar of the Holy Empire," but Toul and Verdun
were never disgorged ; Metz only in our own day.  At the
same time the Turks declared their truce with the empire
at an end, and the Pope recommenced those Italian intrigues which had for their purpose the aggrandizement of
his own relatives.

But Charles had, at last, learned how to yield to The Treaty
the inevitable.  Before leaving Innsbruck he had of Passau.
sent his forgiveness to the former Saxon elector, setting
him free, but requesting that he remain in his vicinity,
to negotiate concerning the carrying out of the ban that
the emperor now intended to hurl at Maurice.  Three
days after the latter's entry into Innsbruck a truce was
declared, and Ferdinand went as his brother's representative to a meeting of the princes held in Passau.  The chief
demands here formulated were : the liberation of the land-

grave; the restoration of a "free empire of the German nation," within the limits prescribed by the Golden Bull; security against Spanish influence; and, finally, a perpetual peace between Protestants and Catholics.   On the subject of this latter clause all real agreement was found to be impossible; Charles would not and could not accept it as it stood.   He insisted that the peace should be merely temporary, to last until a Diet should take the matter in hand.   He had not yet given up the hope of bringing the Protestants back to the fold; he considered that when he should do so, it would be time for him to retire forever from public life.

But even the temporary peace, as finally agreed upon at Passau, was a great gain for the cause of the gospel.   For the first time an equal protection was to be granted to the adherents of the two faiths; neither party was to use violence against the other, and the "interim" was to be tacitly let fall.   Assurance was given that the other reforms would be taken in hand at the coming Diet.   The chief sufferer by the peace was John Frederick of Saxony. There was no longer any talk of dislodging Maurice, and although the former elector was allowed to return to Saxony, he was obliged to promise to keep the peace.   He assumed the title of "elector born," and was received like a martyr and a saint.   The magistrates, the clergy, the citizens, and the common people in "their armor or their best clothes" came out to meet him and to do him honor.

The release of Philip of Hesse.

Similar ovations awaited Philip of Hesse, whose case had come to be considered typical of imperial oppression and severity by nearly the whole nation.   The poor landgrave, indeed, bowed and broken, was no longer in a condition to enjoy such scenes.   He had been through the bitterest experiences of his life, and had even fallen so low as to offer by his own example to induce his subjects to accept the mass, if Charles would sign his release. His wronged wife, Christine, had repeatedly begged pardon for him on her knees in the presence of the emperor and his court. She had died before her prayer was answered, and the efforts of his friends had only served to increase the weight of Philip's misfortunes. We still have a letter of the emperor, written shortly after the attempt at flight, in which instructions are given for terrifying the captive into a confession: "Some one must whisper in the ear of the captain of the guard, without, however, directly threatening the landgrave with the rack." Through a course of such treatment as this, the former head of the Protestant party had become a changed man; his fire and energy were gone; he had taken to the study of the church fathers, and such a spirit of resignation had come over him, that, when parting with his jailer, he forced a fee upon him.

The Diet that was to settle the differences between the emperor and his princes, and between the Catholics and Protestants, was long delayed through the refusal of Margrave Albrecht Alcibiades of Culmbach-Baireuth to abide by the terms of the Passau Treaty. These terms were too lukewarm for him. He wished more decided results for the Protestant cause ; but above all no regard was paid to certain agreements which he himself had wrested at the point of the sword from a number of cities and bishoprics. While Maurice was marching on Innsbruck, Albrecht had been devastating Würzburg and Bamberg and other places in Franconia, and had calculated thus to increase his private fortune by about nine hundred thousand guldens. *The revolt of Albert Alcibiades.*

There are curious facts about this revolt of "the monstrous, senseless wild beast." Albrecht began as the ally of the French; he made Worms and Spires and Treves and

Mainz, which he took in quick succession, do homage to Henry II. He wished to show the king, he said, that faith and fidelity were still to be found among the Germans. Yet, in a very short time he went over to Charles V., closed with him a most iniquitous alliance by which the Würzburg and Bamberg bishops were abandoned to their fate, and led an expedition against the French, in the course of which he captured the Duke of Aumale. Charles himself engaged in a fruitless siege of Metz, his last military undertaking. He refrained from interfering while Albrecht fought his way through Würzburg territory, laying in ashes three hundred castles and villages. He kept singularly in the background, too, when Ferdinand and Maurice, having met together in Eger, entered the lists for law and order. Perhaps, after all, this was to be the solution of his own difficulties — a war of the princes among themselves which should drive them at last to appeal to him as their arbiter.

**Death of Maurice.** Maurice and Albrecht, the former friends, met face to face at Sievershausen; in the moment of triumph Maurice fell, pierced by a bullet through the neck. He was, strange to say, mourned as a hero by the German nation, yet at the end of his checkered career he was only thirty-two years old! Albrecht still maintained himself; many Protestants in high positions, such as Maurice's own brother and successor, Augustus, still looked to him as the hope of their cause. But at last the bold condottiere, who had so long laughed the nation to scorn, met with his deserts. The ban of the empire was hurled at him by the Chamber Court, the Circles prepared to aid in carrying it out. He fled the country and soon died.

**Abdication of Charles V.** This anomalous war had delayed, by nearly three years, the Diet that was to settle the religious differences. Charles V. had meanwhile wedded his son Philip to Queen Mary of England, and felt confident that in one direction, at least, no quarter would be shown to heretics. One by one he now divested himself of all his rights and jurisdictions; Philip received first the Italian possessions, with the title of king of Naples, then the throne of the Netherlands, and lastly the crown of Spain.

In the summer of 1554 Ferdinand was empowered to carry on the negotiations for peace with the German princes and cities, — in his own name as king of the Romans, not simply as representative of the emperor. The latter expressly declared that, for himself, conscientious scruples would prevent him now, as formerly, from making a lasting peace with the Protestants. This man, whose long reign had caused such warrings and upheavals to Germany, was at least consistent. True to the vow made at the Diet of Worms after the great hearing of Martin Luther, he had devoted his body, blood, life, and soul to wiping out this heresy. He had failed; he was ready to withdraw from the world and prepare for death. He vanished behind the walls of the Spanish monastery of St. Just, but even here the bane of his life pursued him — here in his immediate neighborhood the poisonous teachings of the Reformation took root.

Ferdinand, meanwhile, had opened that Diet of Augsburg, the rulings of which were to remain authoritative throughout the next two generations. It was here agreed that a peace should be established which might be "constant, enduring, unconditional, and forever and ever valid." Yet solidly as these men tried to rear their edifice, ponderous as were the chains by which they strove to bind posterity, the result was merely a series of faint-hearted half-measures by which, indeed, the final war of the two religions was to be staved off for sixty years, but which, in the end, were to bring upon Germany a scourge and a

The Diet of Augsburg.

visitation, longer and more deadly than has been suffered by any other nation of modern times.

The "reservatum ecclesiasticum."
So far as the Augsburg Peace had to do with the past, it was possible to come to a speedy agreement. The Protestants were allowed to continue in possession of all lands that, through change of faith in the holders, had come into their hands previously to the Treaty of Passau. But the far more difficult question, as to the future of the Reformation, still remained to be settled. Should the Protestants be allowed to continue taking away lands from the Catholics, and so, indirectly, from the empire? Some of the ecclesiastical holdings were regular principalities, owing allegiance to no one but the emperor. Might an archbishop of Cologne, for instance, by turning Protestant, keep his see, his vast possessions, and his electoral vote? Might he marry and support his family on his revenues, and, perhaps, hand them down to his descendants? The Papacy and the empire had once carried on a most desperate struggle on the matter of who should invest the bishops and abbots; the question was even more serious now. The loss of an election in any single bishopric, the conversion to Protestantism of an actual incumbent, meant the total loss of all claim to the holding.

These ecclesiastical principalities were, to quote a brilliant writer, the worst attributes of the empire's holiness. Wedged in among Protestant states, dependent politically on none of their immediate neighbors, but rather on a Pope who resided in Rome or an emperor who spent his time in Spain and Italy, they only served to perpetuate disunity in Germany, and to carry on every sort of foreign propaganda. Yet as the only possible way out of a hopeless situation, after a bitter conflict and after a deadlock in the Diet, the Protestants consented to a fatal compromise upon the subject. They allowed Ferdinand to promulgate a decree, known as the *reservatum ecclesiasticum*, or church's reservation, which declared that prelates who changed their faith should abandon their fiefs and dignities. It is true the Protestants declared at the time that they did not intend to be bound by the new measure, nor were they forced to give any guarantee or pledge in the matter. At the same time they insisted, but in turn without pledge from the Catholics, that in such "reserved" ecclesiastical holdings Protestant subjects should have free exercise of their religion. Ferdinand issued a "declaration" acceding to this demand, but in later years his party repudiated the work of their head.

A further unhallowed clause in this most disappointing peace document struck a blow at civic autonomy by requiring that, in the free imperial cities, religious affairs should remain in *statu quo*, and neither party attempt to drive out the other. In a different age such a provision would have been considered tolerant and wise; but in the present instance the fact remains that political ruin resulted for the cities. They were discriminated against in favor of the lords. The prerogative of determining the form of faith was taken away from them; no matter how hostile the one or the other party might be to all the aims and objects of the magistrates, the latter were forced by a higher power to quietly endure; they might not ostracize or expel their enemies. *Parity of religions in the towns.*

So much for the shortcomings of the famous Augsburg Peace. The great achievement of the treaty was the establishment of the principle *cujus regio, ejus religio;* each potentate might establish the form of faith that was to prevail within his own domains. Full religious liberty to the individual this clause did not give, but every worshipper who did not choose to conform might move unmolested, with all his belongings, to more congenial territory. *"Cujus regio, ejus religio."*

This then was the ending of the great revolt that had begun with the posting of Luther's theses. The chief loser had been the "Holy" Empire, which had renounced the claim to be the guardian of the universal faith; the gainers were the secular princes, no longer secular indeed, for now, as *summi episcopi*, or chief bishops, they had their people more than ever under their control.

# CHAPTER XVI

## THE ROMAN CATHOLIC REACTION

LITERATURE : Droysen, *Geschichte der Gegenreformation*, is the most readable of the accounts of this time ; Ritter, *Deutsche Geschichte*, 1555-1648, the most recent and complete. Ranke treats of the period in his book, *Zur deutschen Geschichte vom Religionsfrieden bis zum 30 jährigen Krieg*, also in his *Die römischen Päpste*. The best life of Ignatius Loyola is that by Gothein.

DURING the sixty years that followed the abdication of Charles V. and the signing of the religious Peace of Augsburg we look in vain for brilliant campaigns, for constitutional changes, for subtle diplomatic victories, for any episodes, in short, of more than local importance ; yet in view of the struggle with which it ended the period is one of great interest. The fluctuations in the mutual attitude of the two great religious parties ; the increase in the power of the one and the decrease in the power of the other ; the causes, finally, that led to their terrible locking of arms—form a guiding thread through what would otherwise be nothing but a dreary maze. The personalities of the emperors, of Ferdinand, of Maximilian II., of Rudolph II., and of Matthias need only concern us incidentally, and according as they affected the trend of religious affairs.

For twenty years following the Peace of Augsburg, the cause of the Protestants was very distinctly in the ascendent ; indeed, the Treaty of 1555 is considered by many to have saved the tottering cause of Catholicism from complete disaster and ruin. It is true that, of the seven elec-

*Protestants and Catholics after the peace.*

tors, four, — the emperor himself, as king of Bohemia, and the three Rhenish archbishops, — still adhered to the old church; but even here there were signs of a possible change. The young heir to the throne, Maximilian II., is known to have encouraged Protestant preachers in secret and to have lent a sympathetic ear to the new doctrines; while Cologne, easy of access to foreign influences, was, as we shall see, more than once in danger of abandoning the old faith.

In the whole of North Germany only three secular princes, Cleves, Grubenhagen, and Brunswick - Wolfenbüttel, remained on the Catholic side; while of the so-called imperial cities only one, Aix, could be counted on with absolute certainty. In the south, too, although the two largest states were in the strong hands of orthodox Wittelsbachs and bigoted Hapsburgs, it proved impossible to keep out the Lutheran teachings. There came a time when the local diets of Bavaria as well as of Hungary, Bohemia, and the five Austrian dependencies, sought and obtained the right to receive the communion in both forms at the hands of married priests. And worse for the church than these out-and-out defections, was the demoralization that spread and festered in its midst. Even after matters had begun to mend and a board of visitors was sent to inspect the ecclesiastical foundations, they reported that in thirty-six Austrian monasteries there dwelt, in addition to the normal quota of 182 monks, 135 women and more than 200 children.

This was indeed the heyday of Protestantism; never before or since has it been so near to becoming the universal creed of Germany. Not only was there present prosperity, but all the hopes of the future seemed about to be realized. The youth of the land no longer sought their instruction in Catholic institutions; the universities of Vienna, Ingolstadt, and Cologne were forced at times to close their theological faculties for lack of students and professors, whereas Witttenberg and Jena, Marburg and Heidelberg, were thronged by eager multitudes.

One would think that at least in the bishoprics the old faith would have been strongly guarded, but such was not the case. All the smaller sees in North Germany, with the exception of Hildesheim, were now annexed without difficulty by the neighboring princes, who exerted such influence on the canons, with whom lay the right of election, that in almost every case Protestant "administrators" were chosen in place of Catholic bishops. These canons, or chapter monks, were for the most part younger sons of princes and counts; only by a miracle could they have escaped infection from the doctrines that now pervaded the upper classes.

In one quarter alone were the efforts to keep out the Reformation in part successful. The three ecclesiastical electorates of Mainz, Treves, and Cologne formed a nucleus in the west for the surrounding districts, and kept a watchful eye on a whole circle of bishoprics, such as Worms and Spires and the Westphalian sees of Münster, Osnabrück, and Paderborn. It was evident that in these regions, which were of strategic importance as well, because of their nearness to the Netherlands and France, the struggle, when it came, was bound to be fierce. Would Catholics or Protestants win the day? *The West-phalian bishoprics.*

Pending this struggle, however, developments were going on within the inmost fold of each of the rival parties, which made the issue much more doubtful than it would have been in the first few years after the signing of the Augsburg Peace. Forces were at work which tended inevitably to disintegrate the Protestant organization and to strengthen and unify the Catholics.

Whatever the merits of John Calvin as a reformer, there is not the slightest doubt but that the introduction of his

Calvinism
as an ele-
ment of
discord.

teachings into Germany wasted the energies and ruined the political prospects of the adherents of the Reformation. There had been none of this during Luther's lifetime; whatever intercourse the aging Wittenberg reformer had held with the young lawyer of Picardy had been of a friendly nature. Calvin considered Luther a great and good man, though, strange as such an attitude may seem in the stern tyrant of Geneva, he saw reason to regret the great German's intolerance. So slight were the differences of doctrine between the two men that one marvels at the importance they later attained; on the matters of justification by faith and the authority of the Scriptures they were completely united, while, with regard to the real presence, Calvin was far from adopting the extreme attitude of Zwingli. For him Christ was actually present, but in a spiritual, not in a bodily form. It is true he considered belief in predestination the most important thing in the world, and callously drove people into exile for presuming to doubt it; but Luther, too, held this doctrine, although making it much less prominent.

Calvin's
*Institutes*.

Calvin first came to the fore in connection with the persecutions which Francis I. of France, at the very time when he was in league with the Protestants of Germany, inflicted on the adherents of the same faith at home. In order to appease the Germans, it was given out that the victims who had gone to the stake belonged to the universally hated sect of the anbaptists. It was to refute this idea that Calvin wrote his most famous work, the *Institutes of Religion*, which he sent with a long dedication to the king. The latter, he declared, could not possibly know the real character of the faith he was attempting to crush; far from being an innovation, it was as old as the church fathers; and he went on to give a complete statement of all the Protestant tenets. The book of this mere boy soon obtained great celebrity, going through many different editions. It is a curious fact that at the end of his life he had not altered a single view that might fairly be considered of the least importance. As much could not be said for Luther, while as to Melanchthon, his was the constancy of a weather-vane.

Calvinism would have been less dangerous for Germany had there not been connected with it a certain bareness and severity in outward observances that at once stamped its followers for what they were. Luther had been genial and human, had enjoyed the pleasures of life, and appreciated the beauties of nature and of art. The Genevan reformer, on the contrary, was stern and majestic, thinking always of God's justice and of His wrath. Although the scene of his activity was one of the loveliest spots on earth, there is never a word in its praise in his many letters. His mind was on the terrors of death and hell. By the sin of Adam all men had incurred damnation; for the glory of His righteousness God intended in all, save a few arbitrary instances, to see that the sentence was carried out. The houses in which Calvinists worshipped reflected this inward severity; altars and organs and pictures were banished from sight. Attractive surroundings were not required for a religion whose founder could cause a child to be beheaded because it struck and cursed its mother, and a woman to be scourged for singing a secular song to a psalm tune. During the term of Calvin's absolute power in Geneva, the usual punishments had been burning and strangling and tearing of the flesh with pincers. Teachings of Calvin, after marvellous successes in France and the Netherlands, found German converts in the Rhine Palatinate; not so much among the people, as among the learned doctors who taught theology in the halls of Heidelberg University. The point of chief im-

The Calvinism of the Elector Palatine.

portance, however, was the winning over of the Elector Frederick III., a man of very decided character, and the most sympathetic figure in all this period of German history. He protested, indeed, against being called a Calvinist, rejecting some of the more extreme dogmas, and maintaining that he went no further than the Augsburg Confession sanctioned and allowed.

Melanch-
thon's two
versions of
the Augs-
burg Con-
fession.

The ultimate blame for the ensuing complications rests on the head of the gentle Melanchthon. Since drawing up the first text of the Confession, in 1530, that timid theologian had changed his views on many points, and had, consciously or unconsciously, approached nearer to the standpoint of Calvin in the controversies regarding freedom of the will, the necessity of good works, and, most fatal question of all, the real presence. In a second version of the Augsburg Creed, issued in 1540, he had changed the wording of the all-important Article 10, so as to give it a broader and more comprehensive form. The change was a slight one[1] and seems, in the ensuing years, to have escaped the notice of every one save the wary Palatine elector, who saw that the amended form would leave room for the introduction of his favorite doctrine as to the spiritual presence of Christ in the Eucharist. Already doctrines preached by Melanchthon had been bitterly opposed by one Flaccius, called Illyricus, who enjoyed the protection of the dethroned Saxon line. Melanchthon's patron was the Elector Augustus, the coarse, stubborn, and unintelligent successor of Maurice.

In 1561, a year after Melanchthon's death, a number of princes came together at Naumburg to pass measures

---

[1] The original rendering was, " Quod corpus et sanguis Christi vere adsint et distribuantur vescentibus in cœna Domini." The revised version ran, " Quod cum pane et vino vere exhibeantur corpus et sanguis Christi vescentibus in cœna Domini."

which should heal all party strife, and once more to swear a common allegiance to the Confession of Augsburg. It was then that the matter of the two versions began to assume overwhelming importance. Frederick III. of the Palatinate, knowing well what he was asking, urged that the second edition be the one to receive the recognition of all. Carefully he refrained from mentioning the real grounds on which he based his request, simply declaring that the earlier wording had dealt too gently with transubstantiation. Every prospect of success attended his plan of gaining over the Naumburg assembly. The man who, more than all others, posed as the guardian of orthodoxy, the Elector Augustus of Saxony, had long given the preference to the second version, considering it as merely a more careful elaboration of the Lutheran teachings. But, before the final vote of adherence was cast, the theologians who were present had managed to put on their guard their respective lords. A majority of the latter signed the version of 1530, but, in order to spare the Saxon elector, appended a preface, in which they insisted on the real identity of the two renderings. Here was a triumph for Frederick III.! If the versions were identical, there was room for his interpretation of Article 10, and he published now the famous Heidelberg catechism, which has since come to be accepted by the Calvinists, or "reformed," in all lands of the earth. When the matter at last was fairly ventilated, the rest of the princes who had been at Naumburg cursed their own ignorance and made every effort to change the obnoxious "preface"; but to this the Palatine elector, as one of the original signers, refused his consent. Thus the assembly at Naumburg, far from healing the Protestant dissensions, had led to a new breach. Frederick III. came to be looked upon as a black sheep within the fold.

Nor was this to remain a simple question of religious

opinion, for a most vital issue was involved. The Augsburg agreement of 1555 had applied only to upholders of the "Confession"; could Calvinists be held to belong to this category? The Emperor Ferdinand had declared in the negative; what the attitude of his son and successor, Maximilian, would be was a matter for much speculation. Maximilian had played a deep and double game, often expressing his sympathy for the Protestants. At his accession he took the communion in both forms, but not until he had first obtained a secret dispensation from the Pope. We know now that political schemes outweighed all religious considerations. He aimed at the throne of Spain for his descendants, if not for himself, and hoped to achieve it by a series of family alliances, for which papal dispensations might well be needed. The only direct heir of Philip II. was the feeble Don Carlos, and him Maximilian intended to succeed. To favor the Protestants would have meant to lose the good will of the Spanish king, as well as of the Pope of Rome.

During the negotiations preliminary to his first Diet, Maximilian had asked the three ecclesiastical electors what course to pursue against Frederick of the Palatinate. They advised him to ask the Protestant princes formally whether they still considered the elector as holding to the Augsburg Confession. The princes, for their own part, had already sent the Saxon elector to demand of Frederick a profession of faith. The latter showed at this juncture much firmness and decision. He pointed out the dangers of a schism; the theological differences might be discussed at another time, for the present concord was necessary against emperor and Diet combined. None the less the princes were won for the publication of an imperial decree, accusing Frederick of breaking the Augsburg Peace, and ordering him to abolish his Calvinistic innovations. He was then summoned before the emperor, and the decree was read to him in the presence of a number of princes. He was wounded to the quick at the desertion of his colleagues, and declared himself the victim of rank injustice. His defence of himself, from a different standpoint, calls strongly to mind the great oration of Luther at the Diet of Worms. He began by complaining that sentence had been passed on him without even such trial as might be claimed by the worst criminal. With regard to the religious charge, he would have their highnesses know, that in matters pertaining to the salvation of souls, he could bow to no master save God alone. Had he erred in any way, he was willing to be confuted from Holy Writ: if his imperial Majesty would like to try, a Bible was easy to procure. "Should this my most humble confidence play me false, should stern measures be taken against me on account of this, my Christian and honorable declaration, I shall console myself herewith: my Lord and Master Jesus Christ has given to me and to all his faithful followers a sure promise, that all that I lose for the sake of His name or of His honor shall be repaid to me in the other world a hundred-fold. I commend myself most humbly to the mercy of thy imperial Majesty."

As a result of the fearless attitude of Frederick, the first great attack against Protestant unity proved a signal failure. Maximilian had expected for a moment to have things all his own way. He had anticipated a declaration from the princes, not only casting off the Palatine elector, but sweepingly condemning all Calvinists and "reformed." Under the influence of the elector's eloquence an answer was returned to him that frustrated all his hopes. It was acknowledged that differences existed with regard to the communion doctrine, but these would be settled at a future meeting of theologians; there was no ground as yet for excluding Frederick from the privileges of the Augsburg

The bigoted Elector Augustus of Saxony.

Peace. The Protestants themselves, and no one else, were to judge who belonged to their confession. The decree against the Elector was not valid; it had been signed by but a few of the princes and had only been intended as an admonition. As to the general condemnation of Calvinists, it was flatly refused.

There the matter might have rested, had it not been for the jealousy and ill-feeling of Augustus of Saxony against the Palatine elector. Far worse for the Protestant cause than any harm ever inflicted by his brother Maurice, was the constant frustration, on his part, of beneficent and necessary measures. Everything tended to nourish his hatred of Frederick: the latter's "apostasy," as he called it, his constant opposition to the emperor, his efforts to force concessions by refusing help against the Turks. Augustus himself was so placed that he had everything to hope from the friendship of Maximilian. Having annexed all bishoprics within reach, he wished no further changes to be made, and frowned harshly on Frederick's great endeavor to make the Turkish assessments, as well as the recognition of Maximilian's son Rudolph, dependent on the abolition of the hated "church's reservation." Not to fight the Turks meant to risk his own boundaries. For the Palatinate, on the contrary, the Turks had no terrors, and as to church lands, there were golden opportunities for further annexations. Then, too, generous and warm-hearted as he was, Frederick would like to have helped, and did help, the Calvinists of France and of the Netherlands. He sent his son with a small army to fight with Condé and furnished subsidies to William of Orange, besides intercepting Spanish supplies on their way down the Rhine to the Duke of Alva. As for the Saxon elector, though urged not only by the Palatinate, but also by Würtemberg, Hesse, and Baden to join in a general Protestant union, which was to include the

Huguenots, he declared, with a sneer at Frederick, that he would have nothing to do with Calvinists, and actually went so far as to offer the emperor a part of his troops to be used against the Dutch by Philip II. Verily, a meaner rôle than that played by Saxony in all the great crises of German history, from the Reformation to the War of 1866, would be difficult to invent or imagine.

When, indeed, Alva's administration in the Netherlands became the worst reign of terror the world has ever seen; when the inhabitants of cities were condemned as a unit to death, and the highest nobles in the land were sent to execution; Augustus scented danger for himself, and became more friendly to Frederick, joining in a request to the emperor to endeavor to obtain the withdrawal of the Spanish troops. To the joy of the French and the Dutch, a marriage was even arranged between Frederick's son and the daughter of Augustus. As to Maximilian, he did for a moment, in consequence of the representations of the electors, rise to the height of sending his brother as an advocate of peace to Spain. But the moment was critical; Don Carlos had just died, and, even before the answer came, Maximilian sent another envoy to express his approval of whatever course the Spanish king might choose to pursue.

*Maximilian the friend of Spain.*

When, in October of the same year, Philip lost his French wife, the emperor, with indecent haste, sent to offer him the hand of his daughter. He hoped to arrange two other unions between Philip's daughters and his own sons.

Such being Maximilian's attitude, nothing remained for the electors and princes but to enter the war on their own account or to remain disinterested spectators. The Palatinate advocated the first of these alternatives, Augustus of Saxony, the second. The friendly relations between

*Elector Augustus and the crypto-Calvinists.*

these two men, which had culminated in their alliance by marriage, was of short duration. A renewal of dogmatic differences — this time between two parties in Saxony itself — aroused to a white heat the mistrust and hatred of Calvinism which Augustus had always cherished. His was a narrow and bigoted mind, and so sluggish as to be peculiarly open to deception.

The elector prided himself on his strictly Lutheran orthodoxy; but at his own universities of Wittenberg and Leipzig there existed a party which adhered to Melanchthon's later views. They were variously called: Philippists from Melanchthon's own name, synergists because they differed from Luther on the question of good works, and crypto-, or secret, Calvinists. They dissimulated and cloaked their doctrines, hoping in time to win over the elector, and, with his aid, finally to prevail. They laid regular siege to him; their agents filled his palace; his physician, Caspar Peucer, his privy councillor, Craco, his court-preacher, Schütz, were all in the plot, constantly seeking to insinuate their ideas and to undermine his faith, yet all the while assuring him of their loyalty to Luther's teachings.

But another court faction, headed by the electress, developed a keen scent for heresy, and so worried Augustus that he called upon his theologians to give a "good Lutheran proof" of their views. They drew up the "Dresden Consensus" which delighted the elector, who banished 111 persons for refusing to affix their signatures. But the play was growing dangerous; news came that at the Calvinist university of Heidelberg the "Consensus" had been joyfully adopted. Again the theologians were called to account, but once more, by involving themselves in a web of lies, they managed to disarm suspicion.

The whole plan to Calvinize the Lutheran citadel was

at last laid bare by the interception of a letter; house visitations then furnished a number of irrefragable proofs. In some of the documents were disrespectful allusions to the elector's dulness of perception, while others contained warnings against the cleverness of "Mother Anna," Augustus's wife. The duped tyrant raged and stormed, and wreaked such vengeance on the "fat, jaundiced rogue, Dr. Craco, the patron and instigator of all the rest," that, after being put to torture on the rack, he died almost immediately. Another person concerned was kept in life-long captivity.

Flushed with the pride of victory at having routed this band of heretics, the elector caused a coin to be struck off, in which none other than he himself is represented as holding a scale where Christ on one side, waving the banner "omnipotence," weighs down four theologians with "reason" for their device. The gaping Dresdeners were treated to a display of fireworks, and were shown in flaming outlines their own valiant lord, as Hercules, slaying the Hydra of Calvinism! As a test of orthodoxy new articles were drawn up, which were supposed to combine the whole essence of the true teachings of Luther, of Melanchthon, and of the Augsburg Confession. When the Wittenberg professors refused to sign them, they were arrested and sent into exile.

With Frederick III. Augustus's ways had long since parted; he now openly repudiated him as a companion in the Augsburg Confession. Political and other causes served to widen the breach. William of Orange, who had married the Saxon elector's niece, now cast her off on the just ground of adultery, and, as fate would have it, took for his new wife Charlotte of Bourbon, the ward of Frederick and an inmate of his palace.

What the disunion of Saxony and the Palatinate meant

*The breach between Saxony and the Palatinate.*

for the Protestant cause, was soon to become apparent. Augustus drew closer to the emperor, visited him at Vienna, and received him at Dresden,— on which latter occasion the Saxon courtiers went so far in their servility as to attend mass with their imperial guest.  Two golden opportunities arose in 1576 for forcing Maximilian to confirm the Protestant privileges — the emperor expressed on the one hand a keen desire to have his son Rudolph chosen king of the Romans, and, on the other, sent an urgent appeal for aid against the Turks, whose Sultan he had irritated by scheming for the crown of Poland.  Frederick III. had drawn up a list of reforms of inestimable importance to his party; there is not the least doubt but that their acceptance could have been enforced.  But Saxony willed otherwise.  Thanks to Augustus, without a single counter concession, the splendor-loving but moody, arbitrary, and intensely bigoted Rudolph II. was chosen king, while, as to the reforms, and particularly in the matter of the confirmation of Ferdinand's "declaration," the elector had instructed his envoys first to support, and then to vote against, the measures of his own colleagues.  He believed "that the Turkish aid should be granted to the emperor even though the latter should wish to revoke the whole religious peace."

In their respective hours of triumph and discouragement Maximilian and Frederick died.  The latter's elder son, to whom fell the larger share of the Palatinate, bent his chief energies to the restoration of Lutheranism; five hundred preachers and professors and four hundred students were banished from the land.  But the little principality of Pfalz-Lautern, which fell to the younger son, John Casimir, grew to be the refuge and the centre for liberal Protestantism.  The "gymnasium illustre" at Neustadt became what Heidelberg had once been, and John Casimir kept in touch with all the powers of Europe in which the "reformed" religion had taken root.

That this distinction between "reformed" and "Lutheran" Efforts of has perpetuated itself down to our own day was essentially the achievement of Augustus of Saxony. Policy had induced him to betray his party in favor of the emperor; hatred of Calvinism now led him to start a project for revising Luther's doctrines, and reducing all Protestant Germany to a single iron norm of faith. In February, 1576, he had called a meeting of his theologians at Schloss Lichtenberg on the Elbe, and had induced them to condemn Melanchthon's *corpus doctrinæ* and the later edition of the Augsburg Confession. They had advised him at parting to "borrow" and establish at Wittenberg a certain Dr. James Andreæ, chancellor of Tübingen, who had recommended himself in Saxony through a writing on the "ten doubtful points which have arisen among . . . followers of the Augsburg Confession." On the arrival of the great authority a meeting was held at Torgau, and a new *corpus doctrinæ* compiled, which included the Bible, the three creeds, the original Augsburg Confession, and its apology, as well as Luther's Smalkald Articles and his two catechisms. Among the notes and explanations, Andreæ managed to smuggle in a new favorite doctrine of his own, on the "ubiquity" of Christ's body; and to this he clung, although in the whirl of infinite wrangling and opposition the "Torgau Compilation" had to give place to the "Bergen book" which was the basis for the final "Concordia."

This "Bergen book," which not only condemned but "damned" all Zwinglians, Calvinists, and Melanchthonites, was now imposed on all Saxon subjects almost at the point of the sword. Andreæ was intrusted with the task of gaining signatures; and, if we may judge by a previous experience, in which he called his opponents "hogs,"

Efforts of
Augustus
to establish
a norm of
orthodoxy.

" fools," " dogs," and " asses," his methods were not such
as to make him popular.[1]

In spite of the most violent opposition in various quarters, Augustus gained his object of imposing his " Concordia " on the greater part of Germany.  By the year 1580
eighty-six estates, headed by the three Protestant electors,
had introduced it into their lands.  Eight thousand theologians had affixed their signatures.

The
" harmony
of creeds."

The schism with the Calvinists was now irrevocable.  The
glorious hope which John Casimir of Pfalz-Lautern had so
long cherished, of uniting the German church with that of
the other countries of Europe, was forever frustrated.  Of
his own accord, John Casimir now called upon the European sovereigns to send envoys to a meeting at Frankfort.
Poland and Hungary, as well as England, France, and the
Netherlands, responded with alacrity, while Switzerland and
Bohemia expressed their sympathy with the plan of founding a union.  The final result of Pfalz-Lautern's efforts
was the *Harmony of Creeds of the Orthodox and Reformed
Churches*, which was published in 1581.  It condemned nobody, left room for individual differences, and yet served as
a strong bond; but none the less hopeless was the general
outlook.  Some German princes, like the Landgrave of Hesse,
refused to be bound by either formulation; while the adherents of the Concordia withdrew into themselves and closed
their eyes to the dangers which threatened to overwhelm all
opponents alike of the Catholic Church.  The latter institution had begun by this time to glory in this name of
" Catholic."  It saw in the dissensions of its enemies its

---

[1] A parody of the Lord's Prayer is extant which, as an expression of
contemporary scorn, may well be inserted here : " Almighty James who
art in the heaven of devils, dishonored be thy accursed name ; thy ubiqui-
tous kingdom be destroyed ; thy devilish will be done neither here nor at
Wittenberg nor at Leipzig. . . . Lead us not into thy accursed formulation,
but deliver us from thy sacrilegious book ! "

own opportunity of becoming universal. Inch by inch it had been gaining ground, while the Protestants had been wasting their energies in fruitless quarrels. The very Reformation which had robbed it of half its adherents had intensified its energies and awakened its dormant forces. In its recent defeats the Roman church had never really acquiesced. A private report drawn up in 1566, at the Pope's request, and concerning the validity of the Augsburg Peace, had declared that that instrument determined what actually was, not what ought to be, the case. " Properly interpreted, it remains in force only until the Catholics shall have increased in power and shall have roused themselves to the point of redemanding all their rights."

The two great levers that raised Catholicism from its slough of despond after the great blow struck by the Reformation, were the counter reform decrees passed by the Council of Trent, and the activity in carrying them out of the " Company of Jesus," or Order of Jesuits. *The early sessions of the Council of Trent.*

The great council which opened in the southernmost town of Germany in the year 1545, and dragged its slow length along, like that earlier assembly of Basel, for eighteen years, was ostensibly called in fulfilment of a demand reiterated by the Protestants themselves for nearly a generation. The mere idea of it had been a constant bugbear to the church, and fine observers have noted that every time the subject was seriously broached, the price of ecclesiastical benefices went down in the market. As the result of pressure brought to bear upon him in various ways, Pope Pius IV. had agreed to call the assembly together, and to have it held on German ground; but there his forced complacency ended. The wording of the summons sent to the Protestants precluded every chance of acceptance on their parts; they were invited before a judgment seat, not

to a place of disputation.   Nor was the German nation
fairly represented even by its Catholic bishops.   Fearing
for the safety of their sees should they be so long absent,
the vast majority of them remained at home.   The council,
therefore, was mainly composed of Spanish and Italian prelates, subservient tools of the Pope, — who was allowed to
summon whom he pleased, and did not hesitate, when it
served his purpose, to nominate and consecrate men who
would be likely to support his cause.   " Daily," wrote the
emperor's envoy at the time of the third session, " daily we
watch the arrival of worn-out old men and of bishops in
their first youth, whose knowledge reaches only just so far
that they invariably see in reform a grave detriment to the
papal dignity."

It was very evident from the beginning that the Catholics lacked not only the power, but even the wish, to conciliate; they began with an uncompromising enunciation of
their own dogmas, and a positive condemnation of those of
the Protestants.   The tradition of the church was declared
equal in authority to the words of the Bible; binding force
was attributed to the acts of former popes and councils.   In
one of the later sessions Pope Paul III. was even allowed
to proclaim the necessity of his own consent to the validity
of any future decree, while justification by faith — a doctrine that was the very mainstay of Protestantism — was
expressly declared heretical.

The Emperor Charles V. showed no interest in the council, politically at odds as he was with various popes.   His
brother Ferdinand, in whose favor, in 1555, he practically
resigned the imperial power, contented himself for a long
time with mild suggestions, which showed a misplaced reluctance to wound the feelings of Pius IV.   He was a just, conscientious prince, and had shown much tact in dealing with
the Protestants, although a man of more force would have

avoided the wretched slurring over, the temporary make-shifts, that were to lead so directly to the Thirty Years' War. Ferdinand would gladly have seen certain privileges accorded: the use of the cup for the laity at the celebration of the Holy Communion, the marriage of priests, a modification of the excessive fasting.   He wished such change in the church laws as would prevent the wholesale excommunications that had so often fallen on his Austrian subjects; he believed in the principle that councils were above popes. He would like to have seen this particular council take into its own hands the reform of the head and members of the ecclesiastical hierarchy.

Ferdinand came gradually to be thoroughly disgusted at the small results brought forth by deliberations extending over so many years.   After the sweeping condemnations of the first two sessions, he tried to have the third held elsewhere than at Trent, in order that it might be considered an entirely new council, unbound by the trammels of the past. In this he failed, but he found a way to exert more influence on the course of events, and with this end in view moved his court to Innsbruck, so as to be near the scene of action.   In common with France and Spain, he brought forward a new set of demands, to which the council was forced to listen.   It is true the Pope made a bold move, which, for a time, disconcerted his opponents.   He carried the war straight into the enemy's country, by threatening to bring forward a motion for freeing the whole clergy from the duty of paying secular taxes or appearing in state courts.   Ferdinand knew that this was no mere idle menace, and showed himself more conciliatory.   The end of the matter was a compromise, in which some of the emperor's demands were tacitly withdrawn.

*The reforms of the third session.*

But even the reforms that remained, and were now put through, were of world-wide importance for the future of

the church.   The whole ecclesiastical system was purged
and rectified; all the different bonds of order and discipline
were drawn more tightly, and at the same time that the
church became more narrow and conservative, it grew
purer, more holy, and much more powerful.   The authority of the Pope, which had at one time been threatened by
a proposed doctrine concerning the divine origin of the
episcopacy, was immeasurably strengthened.   It was distinctly decreed that he was to be looked upon as the vicar
of God on earth, and supreme ruler of all bishops.   His
word was to be above the dictum of councils.   To him was
to belong not only the sole right of interpreting the Scripture, but also, until the convening of another such assembly as the present, of interpreting the decrees of Trent.
The next general council, when it did finally meet in the
year 1870, ably supplemented the work of its predecessor
by declaring the Pope infallible.

As for the bishops, they were to be chosen henceforward
from men carefully trained in ecclesiastical seminaries;
their sees were no longer to be mere sinecures, but each
incumbent was actually to remain in residence.   Only by
special papal dispensation could plurality of holdings be
allowed.   On entering office, the bishops were to swear an
oath of allegiance to the Pope.   In common with all Catholic preachers and teachers throughout Christendom, they
were solemnly to promise obedience to the Trent decrees.
The duties of the clergy were clearly defined, and provisions were made for a system of visitation not dissimilar to
that which had proved successful among the Protestants.
Steps were taken toward the education of the masses, and
the strictest censorship was decreed with respect to every
kind of printed production, whether old or new.

Such was the programme for the counter reformation in
the Roman Catholic church.   All dallying with Protes-

tantism was forever at an end.  As dead branches are lopped
off from a tree, so, by the decrees of the council, these heretics had been separated from the true communion of saints.
No hope of reconciliation, no danger of further infection
from noxious doctrines.  The purified church could now
proceed to fix its own usages and to live its own life.

The task of the Jesuits.

The decrees of Trent once passed, it remained to see that
they were carried out in all the lands of the civilized world.
This was the mission, this the chosen task of that body of
devoted men who, already while the council was holding
its earlier sessions, had been gathering round the remarkable Spaniard, Ignatius Loyola.   The wonderful influence
exerted by the Jesuits, the tenacious hold that they obtained
in all quarters of the globe, is a direct result of the com-
pleteness and adaptability of the order's organization and
of the spirit breathed into it by the genius of its originator.
As compared with the old Franciscans and Dominicans, the
" Company of Jesus " possessed the advantage of having a
limited task and perfectly defined goals; it was therefore
able to array its forces so that every unit filled its place.
No drones were to be allowed in this busy hive; men might
enter other orders for the laudable purpose of saving their
own souls, but, according to Loyola's distinct assertion,
this was not sufficient reason for becoming a Jesuit.   If
the Dominicans were the watch-dogs of the Lord, the followers of Ignatius were to be his sleuth-hounds; they were
to chase and hunt down their fellow-men, and drive them,
willing or unwilling, into the fold.

In his own person Loyola had descended the whole scale
of life's experiences.  As a proud young Spanish knight,
with no thought but for his own honor and pleasure, he
had been injured while defending Pamplona against the
French in 1521.   A bone had been badly broken, and,
when the fracture healed, the youth found, to his dismay,

The early training of Ignatius Loyola.

that one leg was so much shorter than the other as to pre-
clude the possibility of riding a horse.  Twice, in the vain
hope that it would heal differently, the joint was torn
asunder and reset; for weeks the knight lay on a bed of intolerable anguish.  He called for romances of chivalry to
while away the hours, but nothing happened to be at hand
save lives of Christ and of the saints.  These he took up with
great indifference, but they soon chained him fast and filled
his whole vivid imagination.  Immediately on regaining his
strength, he determined to mount a humble mule and ride
to Monserrat, the holy mount of Aragon.  Here he hung
his weapons on an altar sacred to the Virgin Mary, and
kept a stern vigil in the church.  Then, giving his rich
garments to a beggar and donning a hermit's gown, he took
up his abode in the Dominican monastery at Manresa.

What the cell at Erfurt had been to Martin Luther, that
at Manresa was to Loyola: seven hours a day he prayed
regularly, three times each night he rose and scourged himself.  His spiritual struggles brought him to the verge of
suicide; once he started wildly for the window, intending
to make an end of his mental agony.  Luther had been
recalled from despair by the representation of his friend
Staupitz, but Loyola was forced to fight out his battle alone
and unaided.  He conquered in the end by the aid of his
clear intelligence, and came to the final conclusion that
scruples and doubts were works of the devil.  He began
to see visions of blessedness, and feel that Christ allowed
him to come into direct communication with himself.

The
spiritual
exercises.

Here at Manresa, Ignatius invented the famous spiritual
exercises which eventually became a necessary part of the
training of every Jesuit priest.  Never was scheme more
carefully thought out or better adapted to its ends; it filled
the needs of the age for definite discipline and for an actual
series of steps by which to rise from the prevailing sloth

and torpor. If we read the exercises to-day, they seem to us a mere dry catechism; but they dawned on the sixteenth century as something almost inspired. Loyola himself describes them as a sort of athletics, a running and walking for the soul. They were a military drill, always to be gone through with under the eye of some strict master; they were a training of the imagination on scenes from Scripture, and they necessitated a constant interrogation of the individual's conscience. By various mechanical contrivances, such as jotting down, adding up, and telling over the different sins committed, by the most ingenious devices for concentrating the attention, the pupil was finally brought into a sort of hypnotized state, in which everything that had to do with the spiritual life seemed real and tangible. He was dragged through the horrors of hell, made to smell the actual smell of the brimstone, and taste its bitterness, feel the scorching flames of the fire, and hear the awful howls of the lost souls. Then came a flight to heaven, a dazzling view of Christ, a thorough partaking of his sufferings, and, finally, a full realization of the joys of resurrection. The immediate object of the exercises was, by running the whole gamut of the emotions, to evoke a strong, dispassionate frame of mind that would fit one for the blind performance of any duty. At every crisis, before every approaching struggle, they were to be gone through with anew; and always, during their progress, it was a prime necessity that the eye of the preceptor should fathom every secret thought.

In one important respect Ignatius Loyola felt that his own training was still incomplete. He coveted intellectual power, yet had never had the advantages of even a passable education. He had now reached the age of thirty-three, but, nothing daunted, he went to a school at Barcelona and sat on the bench with the smallest boys. From here he

*The founding of the Jesuit order.*

passed to Alcala, and thence to the University of Paris, where he studied industriously for seven years. His desire to proselytize brought him twice into conflict with the inquisition, and once he was sentenced to be whipped as a corrupter of youth. After completing his course at Paris he went on a pilgrimage to Jerusalem, and afterwards appeared in Rome, where he became prominent as a social reformer, founding refuges and associations, and procuring legislation against particularly glaring abuses. His order was established in 1540, and entered into life under the most glowing auspices, the Pope conferring upon it certain powers of which the chair of Peter had never before been known to divest itself.

Well indeed might Paul III. encourage this new creation; in addition to the regular vows of poverty, chastity, and obedience was one of absolute and unconditional fidelity to papal commands. The name "Company of Jesus" was taken in the sense of a company or troop of soldiers; the Pope, its commander-in-chief, might make use of his forces for whatever purposes he pleased; and implicit subordination to superiors was insisted upon as in no other army the world had yet seen. The workman in the garden of the Lord was to rest with but one foot on the ground; the other was always to be raised to continue the journey. This was the watchword, this the key-note of Loyola's system. In the constitution of the order, in the hundreds of separate instructions that he issued, always he harps on the same theme. A member of the order must be like the staff which an old man holds in his hand, ready to serve him when and how he pleases; he must be like a ball of soft wax, that can be twisted and moulded into any form; like a little crucifix, that can be held at will head up or head down. He must obey *perinde ac si cadaver esset*, exactly as though he were a lifeless corpse, to be pushed or turned without resistance in any direction whatever. There were absolutely no lengths to which Loyola would not go when insisting on his principle; the tendency to private judgment was to be completely and permanently eradicated. If a superior command even mortal sin in the name of the Lord Christ, it is straightway to be committed; "if the church defines as black something that seems white to our eyes, we are at once to declare it black."

The necessity of inculcating such ideas as these in early youth, if they were to prevail at all, led the Jesuits to establish seminaries for the training of future members; in connection with them were schools, which might be attended by outsiders. The devotion of the teachers, their skilful methods of instruction, and, above all, the fact that these institutions were free, ended by making them very popular; so much so that ordinary schoolmasters felt injured and jealous, and a band of them once regularly stormed the Collegium Romanum, or great central institution at Rome. Parents, too, were often alarmed lest their sons should be forced to join the order, until the Jesuits themselves at last made it a rule that no one of their scholars might become a priest without permission from his family. Except for the system of espionage and the encouragement of taletelling, the spirit that pervaded these institutions was distinctly liberal; extremes of every kind were discouraged, and Loyola himself, on visiting one of them, ordered that some boys who had taken of their own accord to fasting should be dragged from their beds and forced to eat. We hear of a hungry scholar confessing that he had stolen some figs, whereupon he was presented with a whole basketful.

The priests of the order were chosen by a process of rigid selection. Great importance was attached to the ability to do their best in public; for silent worth there was little

*The training of the Jesuit priests.*

recognition. When, finally, they went out into the world on the mission for which they had been especially trained, they were given books of instructions which regulated their conduct down to the smallest particular. Even the expression of countenance — what we still call the Jesuit expression — was formally prescribed: the eyes cast down, the brows smooth, the lips not too firmly set, the whole air mildly gay, not sad. The new emissary was to accommodate himself, as far as possible, to the people of the place to which he went, and at once learn their language, and join in their pursuits. The brothers who were sent to Munich were especially told that they must try and acquire a taste for beer. Among the cardinal virtues to be cherished by all members were dispassionateness in general, and the ability to accept insults. Invective was not to be used in public discourses, nor were dogmas, which might arouse opposition, to be discussed. From the very beginning there was inculcated a certain wiliness and deception; Satan was to be fought with his own tools. He did not set to work by urging men at once to do what they perfectly well knew was wicked; even so the Jesuits were to humor their flocks, to listen to their side of the question, and only gradually to correct their faults. In fact, it was laid down as a maxim that the other party was always to be allowed to begin a conversation; the Jesuit was to listen, then slowly gather up the threads, and finally remain master of the field. But the fathers were not to trust too much to their own judgment; they were to travel, when possible, in pairs, not only to spy upon each other, but also in order that, if occasion demanded, responsibility could easily be shifted.

Such were the men, mere wheels of a machine, mere puppets of a policy, to whose tender mercies one country after another, and riven Germany especially, was now handed over; such were the future father confessors of emperors and kings, such the teachers of the rising generation. That Protestantism was the prime evil to be attacked was not only evident, but was candidly acknowledged; that war, cruel and wasting, was sure to come of their efforts, was not sufficient reason to swerve these men from the path of duty.

# CHAPTER XVII

## THE BEGINNING OF THE THIRTY YEARS' WAR

LITERATURE : One of the best accounts of the Thirty Years' War is to be found in Huber, *Geschichte Oesterreichs.* Gindeley is also good authority, and his shorter work is very readable. Gardiner's *Thirty Years' War* is an excellent short account. Ritter has not yet completed his work. Winter's book (in the Oncken Series) is a makeshift, and will doubtless make way for a monumental work of Droysen.

**Active campaign of the Roman Catholic church.**

AT that Diet of 1576, in which Augustus of Saxony succeeded in thwarting the plans of his own party, an official of the emperor's chancery cried out, " In ten years we shall hear no more of Lutherans ! "  And, indeed, so audacious a campaign had already been begun that the prophecy was not unlikely to come true.  Bavaria had been completely invaded by Jesuits ; the Elector Albert was their stanch friend, while his younger son, Ernest, who was destined for the priesthood, had been given into their keeping. All Bavarian officials were now forced to vow allegiance to the Roman Catholic church, and Jesuits were despatched to see that they took and kept their oath.  Protestant burghers were banished in crowds, and non-conforming peasants were hounded down and imprisoned.  Lists were drawn up of forbidden books ; the classics were banished from the schools and supplanted by the church fathers, while even the elector's own library was ransacked and purged.

**Struggle for the Western bishoprics.**

By this time the German nation was hurrying rapidly on its course toward war and anarchy.  Never was a drama worked up to its crisis in more consistent, more relentless, progression.  Stronghold after stronghold was falling ; at

422

every imperial Diet the opposition was increasing, and a deadlock becoming more and more imminent.   Desperate struggles were engaged in for individual prizes, but the losers were always the Protestants.   Duke William of Cleves was on the point of joining the latter when he was snatched as a brand from the burning by Spanish and Jesuit influence.   The chief efforts of the Catholic church were directed to these lands on the Western boundary — to the rich duchy of Cleves-Julier, to wavering Cologne, to the bishoprics of Westphalia.   Here the Protestants were largely in the majority, but with Spain, with Bavaria, and with the Jesuits, their recovery was looked upon as a matter of the utmost importance, on account of their proximity to the Netherlands.   The methods of the inquisition would be severely hampered should the intended victims be surrounded with friends, and that is why Philip II. placed his troops and his gold at the disposal of the Jesuits.

Everything depended on bringing the doubtful ecclesiastical principalities into the hands of men whose power and whose orthodoxy should alike be undoubted.   But among the greater Catholic princes there was only one, Ernest of Bavaria, who had chosen the church for his career.   On his devoted head, accordingly, by papal dispensation, it was determined to heap as many mitres as could be wrested from Protestant control.   With a train of Jesuits at his back, and with plenty of armed forces in reserve, he rapidly progressed from one dignity to another; actual incumbents were deposed by the Pope, and in the new elections that followed strong pressure was brought to bear on the different cathedral chapters.   Already Bishop of Bavarian Frisingen, Ernest was made coadjutor, and then, in 1573, Bishop, of Hildesheim.   One of his first acts was to encourage the Abbot of Fulda to banish all Protes-

*Ernest of Bavaria.*

tants from his lands. Burial in the parish church was refused their dead, their sick were catechised before they were received into the hospitals, while the delivery of coal and wood to the lower classes was made dependent on a profession of orthodoxy. It was in vain that the burghers drew up a protest, in which they complain of the Jesuits, that "they rest neither day nor night, but continue to plot against all the old civic liberties," that their one idea is "so to weed and thresh out a whole population that it may at last be glad to betake itself under their Baalitic yoke — which God forbid!"

The example of Fulda was followed in the Eichsfeld, a territory dependent upon Mainz. When the citizens of Düderstädt refused to deliver up their church to the archbishop and his two Jesuit henchmen, a blow was struck at their chief industry, the brewing of Düderstädt beer. For Ernest of Bavaria, indeed, there came a series of apparent defeats in Cologne, in Paderborn, and in Münster; but he knew well that if he bided his time all would be well: in these very days the Protestant dissensions had reached their height. And his defeat in Cologne had been in favor of a man who passed for a zealous Catholic, and whose appointment Pope Gregory XIII. did not hesitate to confirm.

Gebhard Truchsess of Cologne.

This matter of the choice of an incumbent for the archiepiscopal see of Cologne, was one on which there hinged immense consequences; the archbishop would be, not merely an elector of the empire, but he would be that one elector whose vote must decide whether the next candidate for the throne should be Catholic or Protestant. Gebhard Truchsess von Waldburg, the new incumbent of Cologne, entered upon the duties of his office with great zeal. In the lax days of his predecessors it had not been customary for these ecclesiastical princes to have a separate consecration as priest, but on this, for himself, Gebhard insisted.   He promised obedience to the Trent decrees, took the side of Spain in the fruitless peace negotiations with the Netherlands, and, in various ways, rendered valuable assistance to the Jesuits.   But whether it was that this powerful prelate had always been Protestant at heart, or that his faith had first been undermined by the influence of some neighboring nobles, he soon determined to leave the church and to marry the Countess of Mansfeld.   On Christmas Day, 1582, he publicly announced his conversion: " God has saved me from the darkness of the Papacy, and brought me to a true recognition of His holy word."   To the Pope he wrote that through his own investigations he had convinced himself of the corruption of the Roman Church, and no longer felt bound by the oaths he had taken.

Gebhard's first thought had been to retire to private life, but his Protestant friends saw here an opportunity for settling forever a momentous question.   Nearly thirty years before, at the peace Diet of Augsburg, Ferdinand had promulgated the " ecclesiastical reservation "; in all the time that ensued, although the spirit of that decree had been broken a hundred times, and numberless church foundations had come into Protestant hands, its letter had remained intact.   Protestants had been elected to Catholic bishoprics by the cathedral chapters, but no unmediatized Catholic prelate, no ecclesiastical prince of the empire, had attempted to go over to Protestantism and still retain the possessions he had held as a Catholic.   Just this was the issue now involved; the crucial test had at last come. *Importance of the Cologne matter.*

Knowing well that his object could never be gained by peaceful means, Gebhard hastily levied troops and garrisoned his strongholds, choosing Bonn for his centre of operations.   Everything depended for him on the attitude of the Protestant princes.   Would they rise and shake

themselves free from the slough of their own petty interests?   Could their hearts once more be warmed to a general enthusiasm for their party?   John Casimir, of the
Palatinate, the Calvinist, was Gebhard's warmest friend.
Would that old pillar of orthodoxy, Elector Augustus of
Saxony, ever consent to be involved with him in any common undertaking?

Defection
of Saxony
from the
Protestant
cause.

The archbishop for his part did his best to conciliate both
parties; so far did he go in his assurances to each that
John Casimir's envoy had grave doubts if "such tergiver-
sation would please our Lord God."   And at first he met
with success.   In outward accord the Protestant princes
sent a writing to the emperor in which they denied the
validity of the "reservation."   The electors of Saxony,
of Brandenburg, and of the Palatinate, then sent envoys to
a meeting at Erfurt.   But here, contrary to all expectations,
and in spite of a threatening letter that he himself had
despatched to the Emperor Rudolph, Augustus resumed his
old rôle of obstructor and general marplot.   Through the
mouth of his envoys he pronounced Gebhard in the wrong,
and, contradicting his own former assertions, insisted that
the "reservation" should continue to be binding.   Brandenburg upheld him, inaugurating the slack policy in religious matters, that was to cloud the glories of its ruling
house during the whole of the next half-century.

The weakness and apathy of the Protestants had reached
their climax.   What wonder that Pope Gregory XIII., the
indefatigable founder of Jesuit colleges, thought the occasion favorable for regaining a hold on German national
affairs!   He hurled the ban at Gebhard, deprived him of
all his dignities, pronounced the see of Cologne vacant,
and demanded a new election.   It daunted him little that
the man who was now to be dismissed without hearing
or trial was one of the seven electors.   Gregory was sure

of the support of Rudolph II., and, indeed, the emperor at once sent envoys to Cologne and ordered the cathedral chapter to choose a new head. Even the heart of Augustus of Saxony was stirred at this action of the Pope; in common with his Protestant coelectors he sent a protest to Rudolph, but to fight for the rights of his outraged party he had no mind. He now, on the contrary, completed the long list of his disloyal acts by permitting the elevation to the vacant see of the most dangerous enemy the Protestants had ever had — Ernest of Bavaria. In the next year, in common with Brandenburg, he formally recognized the pupil of the Jesuits as a member of the College of Electors.

Gebhard and his one ally, John Casimir, held out but for a short time; Spanish troops and Bavarian subsidies made their antagonists far too formidable. The Protestant general, John Casimir, was a poor commander, harsh, proud, and unjust, and only valiant over his cups. He had declared in his war manifesto that he was taking the field "for the protection of the true religion of the Augsburg Confession, and for the liberation of the German nation from the invading tyranny of the Roman Pope"; but when it came to action he showed himself dilatory and undecided. His troops, which he could no longer hold together, at last disbanded, at the bidding of the emperor, while Gebhard himself, a little later, was driven from Bonn and took refuge in the Netherlands.

Great and memorable was the victory the Catholics had won; they had kept their ecclesiastical reservation as well as their majority in the College of Electors; once more the voice of the Pope had been obeyed in Germany. And the fate of Cologne decided that of Münster, where, as in Liège also, Ernest was soon elected bishop. All over Westphalia the Jesuits held high carnival, founding schools and

Great victory of the Jesuits.

seminaries, and building churches. The giant proportions
of their buildings, their broad, flaunting style of architecture, show their firm belief that this their church militant
would soon become a universal church triumphant. They
had openly begun to attack the Augsburg Peace : in matters of faith, they declared, the church could alone decide ;
the Council of Trent *had* decided, and all who opposed
its decrees were heretics. When, in reply to such claims,
Protestant writers spoke of " bloodthirsty plots " and
" wicked practices," some of the Jesuits candidly avowed
" that they had, indeed, made it their goal to destroy Protestantism root and branch."

The
Protestants
continue
to lose
ground.

Everything tended to force the two parties into fierce
and irrevocable opposition ; the religious ties had been the
first to break, one by one there followed the snapping of
all political bonds. In the Diets, which voted by colleges,
the Protestants had enjoyed a majority among the princes
which gave them great influence ; in the Chamber Court,
or general court of the empire, they had been fairly represented. Both these advantages were gradually lost. The
Catholics challenged the votes of the Protestant administrators, or heads of the secularized bishoprics, on the ground
that the latter had not been confirmed in their holdings by
the emperor and the Pope. With regard to this matter it
must be said that more than once, in order not to inter-
rupt important transactions, individual administrators had
waived their rights in the Diet, on the understanding, however, that their action should form no precedent. More
than once, on the other hand, scenes of confusion had taken
place. When, at the Diet of 1594, the chancellor of Magdeburg, Meckbach, tried to take his place in the midst of the
princes, the Archbishop of Salzburg bade him retire, and,
in his excitement, even seized him by the cloak. When
Meckbach refused to move, all the Catholics present rose

and left the hall, and the negotiations of the Diet came to a standstill. As to the Chamber Court the manœuvre was resorted to of simply not summoning Protestant supervisors. In case of appeal the more important cases had to be brought before another tribunal, the *Reichshofrath*, composed of Catholics and completely subservient to the emperor's will.

So bitter was the opposition in every field that the Protestants rejected a great and really salutary measure, for the mere reason that it was conceived and inaugurated by Pope Gregory XIII., who thought to impose it upon all Christendom by simply issuing a bull. To the measure itself, the reform of the calendar, there was little to object. It is true the new calendar was not perfect enough for scientific purposes, and the old one was correct enough for ordinary use ; but the main ground of refusal lay in the fact that the Protestants would not accept a decree about which they had not been consulted, and which was promulgated by a pope whom they did not recognize.

For sixteen hundred years, since the time of Julius Cæsar, the Western world had made use of a system of reckoning by which the ordinary year, the time occupied by the earth in moving round the sun, occupied exactly 365 days and 6 hours. In reality the fraction should have been slightly smaller. The error had long been recognized, when Gregory XIII., in the year of the Cologne war, ordered the introduction of the calendar that still bears his name. By this time the ordinary year was ten days behind the astronomical, and, which was Gregory's chief concern, the festivals of the saints no longer fell on the days originally appointed by the church. In order to correct the past he decreed, that, for 1582, ten days should be omitted, the fifth of October of the old style becoming the fifteenth of the new ; in order to avoid future error,

The reform of the calendar.

three times in every four centuries one of the years that
would naturally assume an extra day was to return to its
normal length.[1]

The further cleft that was made by the introduction of
the Gregorian calendar into Germany was very real and
very serious.  Catholics and Protestants were no longer
to have their sacred days or their feast days in common ; at
work and at worship they were to be divided.  Employers
were to be constantly at odds with their laborers, forcing
them to work when they wished to rest, and to be idle when
they might well have been engaged in labor.  The public
feeling found vent in bitter irony.  " None the less," says a
writing of 1584, " will the bear remain in his hole until
the old Candlemas," while another pamphlet suggests that
the Pope might well be anxious to have the saints' days
in accord with the days of their martyrdom, for the reason
that, if a suppliant should come on the wrong date, his
particular patron might have gone a-walking.

Thus the Protestants adhered to the old style while the
Catholics adopted the new, and the differences between
them, only partially obliterated in 1700 A.D., were not
finally settled until nearly the beginning of the nineteenth
century.

The Donau-
wörth
episode.

Meanwhile, actual clashes had been growing more and
more frequent; a schismatic election in Strassburg had led
to a secession of the Protestants from the imperial Diet
of 1598 ; disturbances in Aix-la-Chapelle had ended in
the city being purged of heretics by Spanish troops ; a
dispute with regard to four monasteries in South Germany caused, finally, the complete obstruction of the
ordinary course of justice, the Protestants refusing to be
bound by decisions either of the imperial Chamber Court
or of the *Reichshofrath*, the emperor's privy council.  But

---

[1] The year 1900 is an example of one of these frustrated leap years.

nothing that had as yet occurred caused equal excitement with the happenings in the little town of Wörth, on the Danube, between the years 1602 and 1608.

Wörth was one of those free cities of the empire in which, by the terms of the Peace of 1555, Protestants and Catholics should have agreed to live peaceably side by side. But here, as in many other towns, Protestantism had so completely gained the ascendency that the adherents of the old church numbered less than thirty persons, including a congregation of Benedictine monks. The latter rented their monastery from the city, and had long lived quietly and without ostentation, forbidden by the magistrates to perform ceremonies or engage in processions within the city limits; if a Catholic citizen died, only one priest and two monks might be present at the burial; no display was to be made of crucifixes, no incense might be used, and flags, if carried at all, were to be closely furled.

But the Jesuits had long had their eye on this monastery of the Holy Cross, and by the year 1602 all of its sixteen members were pupils from the order's university at Dillingen, while a worthy head was found in the person of a certain pugnacious Abbot Leonhard. Gradually the old ceremonies were revived, burials were more and more pompously celebrated, processions were held on every occasion. In Holy Week of the year 1605 the magistrates interfered, and ordered the monks to lower their banners while within the city limits; the abbot refused, and only yielded to actual force. But the matter did not stop here. On the ground that the religious peace was being violated, Leonhard appealed to the Bishop of Augsburg, who in turn brought the case before the emperor's privy council. Without even investigating the matter, this tribunal took the side of the Catholics, and peremptorily ordered the magistrates to refrain from further interference with the

*The Jesuits in Wörth.*

monks.  Whereupon the abbot instituted a more noisy ceremony than before, on which occasion a general skirmish
took place with the citizens, who pursued the Benedictines
with clubs and missiles and drove them back to their
cloister walls.

In answer to a new citation from the privy council, the
magistrates declared that they had done their best to
restrain the populace, but without success — an unfortunate admission, for now the emperor commissioned an out-
sider, Maximilian of Bavaria, to see to the protection of the
Catholics in Wörth, and, of all persons, to Maximilian the
task was most welcome.  He had had the same bringing up
as his brother Ernest, and was possessed with the same
zeal for the cause, and with a great ambition for the House
of Wittelsbach.  Moreover, his ability was undoubted; on
the abdication of his spendthrift father, in 1598, he had
undertaken to restore the ruined finances of his land, and
had succeeded so admirably that he was later able to furnish invaluable pecuniary aid to his own party.  When
Maximilian's envoys appeared in Wörth to demand an
assurance that the Catholics should not be further mo-
lested, a popular tumult arose and the commissioners were
forced to make a hasty exit; in the meanwhile a number
of Protestant estates had remonstrated against the interference of the emperor's court and encouraged the magistrates of Wörth to resist its mandates.  Maximilian induced
the emperor to declare the city in the ban and to intrust the
fulfilment of the sentence to himself; he was all prepared
for the emergency, and held in readiness an army of six
thousand men.  Utterly defenceless, the city surrendered
at once, — December 16, 1607, — whereupon the Bavarian
troops garrisoned the market-place, and erected a gallows.
Wörth was then treated as a spoil of war; it was completely recatholicized, and, in addition, regularly pawned

to Bavaria until the costs attendant on its overthrow should have been paid. Its very name was changed to Donauwörth, and the words, "City of the Holy Roman Empire," were formally erased from its seal.

An atmosphere heavy with storm pervaded the Diet of Ratisbon, which met at the time of these events. If Maximilian of Bavaria really believed, as he wrote to the Pope, that he "had done not a little to establish the authority of his Imperial Majesty in the Holy Empire and to inculcate respect and obedience toward him," he was to find himself strangely mistaken. The very first proposition brought forward by Archduke Ferdinand, to raise a standing army for the protection of the Hungarian frontier, met with an unbending opposition; the second, to make the renewal of the Peace of 1555 A.D. conditional on the restoration of all church lands appropriated since 1552, drove the Protestants to desperation. The only political body that could in any way have brought about a peaceful settlement of the difficulties disbanded in confusion. The importance of the moment was not misconceived; a number of Protestant estates at once proceeded to organize the so-called "Union," of which the Palatine elector was to have the guidance. Its term of duration was to be ten years. Its avowed purposes were, to defend the lands, person, and rights of each individual member, and to obtain redress for the wrongs of the party. There had been nothing like it since that unfortunate Smalkald League, which had come to such an unhappy end some sixty years before; but this time Saxony remained aloof. The Catholics, for their part, were not behindhand in marshalling their forces. Under the leadership of Maximilian of Bavaria,— the only German prince who was to keep his life, his lands, and his policy through all the long horrors of the Thirty Years' War,—an association known as the "League" came

The Protestant "Union" and the Catholic "League."

into being.   The Emperor Rudolph did not join it; on the
one hand it may have dawned upon him that his position
placed him above parties; on the other, Maximilian distinctly did not want him, preferring to play the first rôle
among a host of small ecclesiastical princes.

The
Emperor
Rudolph II.
For a time it seemed as if the question of the Cleves inheritance, of which we shall treat in another connection,
would precipitate the great struggle which all felt to be
approaching; but the murder of Henry IV. of France by
Ravaillac turned aside the danger, and when the storm did
break it was elsewhere — in one of the hereditary kingdoms of the Hapsburgs.   In bringing about the catastrophe
the peculiarities of the heads of that house played a considerable part, and to those peculiarities, as well as to the
general policy of the Hapsburgs at home, it is needful to
turn our attention.

Rudolph II., eldest of the many sons of Maximilian II.,
and emperor since 1576, possessed no merits likely to endear him to posterity, save that he extended his protection
to learned men like Kepler and Tycho Brahe.   An ardent
lover and collector of antiquities, he filled the great palace
on the Hradchin in Prague with every kind of precious
work of art, and spent his time in the midst of his treasures,
delving into astronomy and also into necromancy.   In
character he was suspicious, yet easily deceived, shunning
the influence of strong men while falling under that of
menials, bigoted to the last degree, yet occasionally forced
to place himself in the power of men whom he knew to be
heretics.   His indecision and vacillation were almost beyond belief; time and again, for a period extending over
nearly twenty years, he negotiated with the Spanish king
for the hand of his eldest daughter, Isabella, and when at
last Philip, in despair of seeing the poor princess safely
provided for, gave her to Archduke Albert, Rudolph con-

sidered himself deeply wronged, and allowed the thought
of vengeance seriously to influence his policy.

In his later days Rudolph was afflicted with attacks of
insanity; he thought that his enemies were constantly pursuing him, and that magic arts were being used against
him. More and more did he withdraw from the public gaze;
there were times, even amid the most important happenings,
when it was impossible either for foreign envoys or for
privy councillors to obtain an audience. If the emperor
did occasionally show sufficient energy to send representatives to the German Diet, he expressly omitted to give them
full powers; they were to write to him for instructions,
and often pending the weightiest decisions, interminable
correspondences had first to be spun out between Ratisbon
and the Hradchin. At last the bow was bent too far; a
family conclave, headed by the Archduke Matthias, met
to discuss the state of affairs, and to see what could be done
with this sick man who could neither live nor die, who
clung so fast to a power that he was completely incapable
of exercising. As the breach widened, Matthias was driven
into a union with the nobles and cities of Hungary and the
two Austrias, while the emperor himself drew around him
the estates of Bohemia, — for the most part Protestant, —
which were jealous of the part played by the other Austrian dependencies, and proud, too, of having their city of
Prague the imperial residence. Fairly driven to the wall
by the successes of Matthias, who had now been chosen
king of Hungary, and frightened by the insistence of his
own adherents, Rudolph in 1609 issued the famous instrument of toleration known as the Royal Charter of the
Bohemians. It granted free exercise of their religion to
all persons. The Protestants were to have their own consistory or governing body, the members of which were to
be called "defensors." They could call together general

The "Royal
Charter"
of the
Bohemians.

assemblies representing the Protestants of the whole kingdom.    There were restrictions indeed, in the form of supplementary treaties, that were soon to prove most galling, and
to bring about a vital issue.    These related mainly to the
right of building new places of worship, and provided that
in the smaller territorial holdings the will of the lord of the
land was to be respected, and no churches built without
his permission ; whereas on the royal domains the Protestants might erect such structures as they needed.    But a
bitter dispute soon arose as to the meaning of this technical term, "royal domains."    Did it also include the ecclesiastical estates of which the clergy had the usufruct, but
which were administered by the crown?    It was pointed
out that the kings had not hesitated to draw revenues
from these lands, and even to pawn them for their own
uses.

The
bigoted
Ferdinand
of Styria.

Rudolph's concessions to the Bohemians had called forth
a strong Catholic opposition, heads of which were the
chancellor Sdenko von Lobkowitz, who to the last refused
to place his official seal on the " Royal Charter," the judge
Jaroslav von Martinitz, and the burgrave of the neighboring fortress of Karlstein, Wilhelm von Slavata, the last-
named all the more intolerant for being a renegade from
the cause he now combated.    But a still more inveterate
and implacable enemy of all concessions was Duke Ferdinand of Styria, whose chances were good of one day succeeding to the crowns of Bohemia and the empire, as his
uncles Rudolph and Matthias were both old and childless,
and their brothers Albert and Maximilian were willing to
cede their claims.

Never had the Jesuits had a more devoted pupil or a
more pliant tool than Ferdinand.    Of somewhat stunted
intelligence, but with a passionate love for reciting prayers,
for confessing his sins, and for scourging his own body,

his guiding principle was religious intolerance. He had once made a pilgrimage to Loretto, and had solemnly sworn on the altar of St. James to extirpate the hated creed of Protestantism. In his own domains he had succeeded so well that, in the year 1603, at Easter and at New Year, forty thousand came forward to confess their errors, — the official lists are still preserved, — while thousands more, who refused to abjure, were sent into exile.

The relations, meanwhile, between Rudolph and his powerful brother Matthias were undergoing many phases. Twice there were outward reconciliations, once, in 1610, with every pomp and ceremony. But at the very time when both parties agreed to disband their forces, the emperor was maintaining troops in Passau, which, he claimed, had been levied for service in Julier, but which, as he said, could not be dismissed until their arrears of debt had been paid. Dreams and visions now led him to make a new attack upon Matthias; astrologers had foretold the complete downfall of the latter. The Passau troops, ostensibly in mutiny for their pay, descended upon Austria. Matthias quickly reassembled his army and drove them back, but not until they had inflicted much harm. They then turned to Bohemia and even captured a part of the city of Prague, their successful progress causing Rudolph more and more to lay aside his mask. Now was the time, he thought, to become master of the Protestant estates, and to annul their hated charter. But the Bohemians were already on their guard, and had summoned Matthias to their aid, receiving from him reënforcements to the number of twenty-five hundred men. Rendered all but a prisoner in his own splendid palace, Rudolph was forced to call the Diet that was to pronounce his own fall. In vain he sought to delay the proceedings that he might the better make capital out of the general dis-

Rudolph and Matthias.

union. The first point insisted upon was that Matthias, as the choice of the Bohemian people, should be made king of that land. On the day of the pompous coronation Rudolph hid in the farthest corner of his park, lest he might hear the cries and rejoicings.

**The death of Rudolph.** His imperial dignity still remained to him, and he sought to use this for the coercion of his brother and the regaining of his lost lands. No step was too extreme for him to take ; he was willing now to reverse the century-long policy of his house and to throw himself into the arms of the Protestant Union, nay even himself to turn Protestant and, old and decrepit as he was, to marry the widow of the Palatine elector. But who could now trust to the weather-vane policy of this half-crazed intriguer? His prayers, his commands, his threats, were no longer of any avail. Full of gall and bitterness, he was on the point of setting out from Prague, to try at least to circumvent the election of Matthias as his successor on the imperial throne, when a sharp attack of illness put an end to his life. Without opposition Matthias became emperor.

**Ferdinand becomes king of Bohemia.** Various circumstances combined at this time to make the Holy Roman throne anything but a bed of roses. The ordinary machinery of government had ceased to act. At Matthias's first general Diet the Protestant estates formally declared that they would be bound by no majority vote in matters pertaining to religion, taxation, justice, or the prosperity and safety of the fatherland. On the eastern borders of the Hapsburg lands was a rebellion of the Prince of Transylvania, who was supported by the might of Islam. As to the Bohemian Protestants, among whom the fiercest storm was evidently brewing, Matthias, even had he wished to keep his compacts with them, would have found it a difficult matter. He himself was tottering to his grave.  His chief adviser who, we are told, "thought, spoke, wrote, and acted for him," was the former imperial chancellor, Melchior Klesl, clever, industrious, and not unmerciful, but scenting in heresy the mother of rebellion, and desiring above all things to overthrow or evade the Royal Charter.  But beyond and above all this, it was becoming necessary to regard the wishes of the probable successor to the throne, that Ferdinand of Styria whose bigotry and whose predilection for Jesuit practices have already been noted.  Indeed, Matthias, warned that there was danger of having his house thrust aside at his death, now devoted his efforts to having Ferdinand acknowledged king both of Bohemia and of Hungary.  He met with much opposition, but by sparing no means of coercion at last attained his object.  In vain, at the Diet of 1617, the Bohemian estates attempted to have it stated in the protocol that they had " elected," and not merely "accepted " him as their king — a far-reaching difference, since those who had elected could also depose.  They did indeed succeed in procuring from the new king a confirmation of all the rights and privileges of the land, including the Royal Charter; — with regard to the ratification of this latter instrument, the Jesuits had given him a special dispensation, in case he should be unable otherwise to obtain the crown.

The achievement of the royal dignity in Bohemia was a great victory for the house of Hapsburg, all the greater because the public mind was agitated at this time by what the Protestants considered an unwarrantable breach of this same Royal Charter.  In the little town of Braunau, which belonged to the domain lands of a Benedictine monastery, the inhabitants, aided by contributions from Protestants in Germany, had built a new church of their own.  The abbot of the monastery ordered it closed on the ground

The affairs of Braunau and Klostergrab.

that the land was not royal domain, and Matthias approved the act. Inasmuch as almost identically the same thing occurred in Klostergrab, on the lands of the Archbishop of Prague, there was reason to suspect a far-reaching hostile plan of operations. Meetings of the defensors were hastily called and protests rained in upon the emperor from every quarter; but Matthias, far from yielding, only inaugurated new and harsher measures. The judges were clothed with new powers that they might challenge the titles of Protestant landholders, and Martinitz went so far as to command his subjects, under penalty of eighty thalers, to attend confession in a Catholic church.

It cannot be denied that there were arguments on both sides in this matter of the Braunau and Klostergrab churches; but whatever the true merits of the case, the emperor and the Catholics determined to carry their point with a high hand. Citizens of Braunau who refused to hand over the keys of their church to the abbot were seized and put in prison, — a step which gave rise to a riotous demonstration. In Klostergrab, the Protestants, for fear of worse evils, were forced to help in tearing down their own building.

The throwing of the stadtholders from the window.
The whole of Bohemia was by this time in a ferment, and the defensors, headed by Count Matthias von Thurn, called a general assembly of Protestant delegates at which the fiercest and bitterest denunciatory speeches were held. In Thurn's mind there was already ripening the project of ridding the land of the whole hated dynasty of the Hapsburgs; some one decisive act was needed to make the breach irreparable; consciously or unconsciously, as many persons as possible were to be concerned in the plot. When the Emperor, through his stadtholders, or deputy governors, declared the assembly at Prague treasonous, and forbade a second one that had already been summoned,

Thurn decided to carry out his plan. He had determined on the death of two of the stadtholders, the old enemies of his party, Martinitz and Slavata; they were to be disposed of in a manner commonly associated in the minds of the Bohemians with great national crises.

Ostensibly for the purpose of consulting about a new communication just received from the emperor, Thurn led an armed band of nobles to the council chamber of the castle of Prague; they filled not only the chamber but the halls as well, and blocked the stairway. Slavata and Martinitz were singled out and made to undergo a summary trial. The chief charge, enforced with fierce invective, was their opposition to the Royal Charter in 1609. Facts were adduced that roused to frenzy all who were present. A rush was made for the two stadtholders, as well as for their innocent secretary, Fabricius; they were dragged to the window and hurled to the ditch, some seventy feet below. "Jesus! Mary!" shrieked Martinitz, as he fell. "Let us see," said some one, "if his Mary will help him." "By God," he cried a moment later, "his Mary has helped him!" It seemed as though a miracle had happened.

The deed that took place in that room at Prague was one of the most important and irrevocable acts in the whole of German history; it was the official signal for the opening of the great Thirty Years' War. It is true the intended victims escaped without serious injury, their heavy wadded cloaks and a convenient dunghill helping to soften the fall. But none the less the die had been cast, the Rubicon crossed, and all the elemental passions of Europe roused into life.

The news of the uprising in Prague reached Matthias at Vienna and Ferdinand in Pressburg, where he was preparing for his coronation as king of Hungary. The emperor and Klesl were inclined to use conciliatory

The outbreak of the war.

measures; but Ferdinand, who hurried to the capital, rejoiced at the opportunity for inflicting a never-to-be-forgotten punishment upon the Bohemians. Nothing was to stand in the way of his vengeance. Klesl, on account of his tortuous policy and his slowness in making levies, was seized by stratagem and sent as a prisoner to Innsbruck. No heed was paid to the opposition of Matthias, who is said to have bitten through his bedclothes for very rage. Ferdinand's general, Count Buquoi, took the field at the head of twelve thousand men.

The Bohemians, for their part, lost not a single day in setting up a provisional government, with thirty directors, ten from each state, at its head. One of their first acts was to banish all Jesuits from the land, and to confiscate their property. An army was quickly raised; although the fatal error was committed of not putting its financial support upon a proper basis, and the plundering of its own lands was at times an absolute necessity. Great hopes were placed on foreign aid, and the Duke of Savoy, who was talked of as a possible successor to Ferdinand, actually did send the redoubtable Mansfeld at the head of two thousand men. Thurn, who was appointed commander-in-chief of all the forces, made it his chief aim to gain over the remaining Austrian dependencies, and, after a successful march into Moravia, turned his forces against Vienna. Matthias in the meantime had paid his debt, long overdue, to nature; dying, it is said, of fright at the turn events were taking. Thurn was not able to enter the capital, but within the walls were Protestant sympathizers, who gave Ferdinand momentary reason to fear for his personal safety. His confessor found him one day stretched before a crucifix. "If it be God's will, then let me be destroyed in this struggle," he said to the terrified father. He was obliged to submit to an interview with the rebels, in which the respect due to his rank was completely forgotten, one of the delegates going so far as to seize the button of his coat. Only the approach of a royal regiment rescued him from his position and caused his visitors to slink from the room. The condition of things in Bohemia suddenly recalled Thurn.

The movement begun at Prague affected the sea of European politics much as the casting of a stone disturbs quiet waters. The ripples first felt in the Austrian dependencies widened and spread until they reached the most distant lands, first Savoy and the Palatinate, then central Italy, Spain, and Flanders, Bavaria, and Saxony — not to speak of Transylvania, whose ambitious young prince, Bethlen Gabor, aided by the Porte, thought the time favorable for aiming at the crown of Hungary. *Protestant and Catholic allies.*

Ferdinand's first thoughts turned to the Pope, Paul V., who granted him a monthly subsidy, and handed over to the Catholic League, which reconstituted itself for the present emergency, a tithe on all church benefices in Italy. Philip III. of Spain, though almost bankrupt, was spurred on to the impossible by Ferdinand's ambassador, Khevenhiller, who threatened him, — recovering as he was from a well-nigh mortal illness, — with the terrors of the Last Judgment, should he allow the Protestants to conquer and so many souls to fall into hell fire. The most efficient ally was Maximilian of Bavaria, head of the Catholic League, who was bound, however, that a high price should be paid for his aid. Austrian lands were placed in his hands to cover all possible loss or expense, while Ferdinand promised him, should the rumor prove true that the Elector Palatine intended to accept the throne of Bohemia, that the dignity of his electoral office should be transferred to Bavaria.

To this latter possibility, the election of the Count Palatine, everything was now pointing.   The Bohemians had called together a diet to ratify the recent proceedings, and had solemnly dethroned Ferdinand, causing a list to be read in the assembly of all the sins he had committed in the past twenty years.   The three estates, nobles, knights, and citizens, had voted separately for his fall.   There had been talk of choosing John George of Saxony in his place, but some had objected on the ground of his drunken habits, others because of his coolness and indifference to the whole burning question.   The fact that he was not chosen to an office he would never have accepted, added to the circumstance that the leading Bohemian patriots were Calvinists, then drove this cantankerous prince over to the side of Ferdinand, whom he helped to elect as emperor.

Well would it have been for the handsome, knightly, young elector of the Palatinate, had he possessed some of the worldly wisdom of his Saxon colleague.   The Bohemians now offered him their crown simply because he was their last resource.   They counted on his powerful connections, for he was head of the Protestant Union, and his wife was the daughter of King James of England.   But, although he did hesitate for a time, he finally accepted, failing to realize that no one of the greater princes in Germany, whatever his religious convictions, could ever submit to the uniting of two electorates in one hand, and that, however friendly the people of England might be to his enterprise, the relations of James I. with Spain precluded the possibility of help.   Others saw matters more clearly ; the elector of Cologne declared that Spain and the House of Austria would rather sacrifice everything in the world than give up Bohemia, and that a twenty, thirty, or forty years' war was in prospect.   He joined with Treves and Mainz in a warning letter which declared that the originators of such bloodshed and destruction would be

pointed at by the finger of history, so long as the world
should stand.

Gathering together the riches that his ancestors had The
"winter
king." stored in Heidelberg, and followed by his beautiful English wife, Frederick set out for Prague, where he was
received with the greatest enthusiasm. His youth, his
agreeable countenance, his tall, slender form, made a most
favorable impression. As he approached the capital, he
was met by a magnificent procession of the different guilds.
Fifty thousand guldens had been spent for his reception —
a significant fact, and one casting a glaring light on the
levity of the Bohemians, when it is considered that want
of funds was daily causing a wretched loss of life in the
army, the patriotism of many of the nobles having ceased
at the door of their treasure rooms. At the coronation,
which took place almost immediately, thousands of coins
were scattered among the people, and a fountain ran wine
for more than an hour. When Pope Paul V. heard of
these happenings, he declared that the new monarch was
entering a foul labyrinth that would surely lead to his
own destruction. "He is but a winter king," said the
Jesuits, sure that his reign would not last a year.

And, indeed, a worse marriage of interests than that of
this frivolous boy with the doomed nation that all Europe
was combining to crush, could scarcely be imagined. He
had not the tact, even, to try and keep the favor of his
new subjects. Disapproving of their form of worship,
which laid more stress on outward symbols than the Calvinism of the Palatinate, and sympathizing with his court-
preacher, Scultetus, who declared that "he could not teach
the gospel in the midst of accursed idols," he sacked their
cathedrals, and had their images, altars, and valuable works
of art hewn down with the axe. His wife, for her part,
offended the people by her foreign customs, and especially

by the shockingly low cut of her dress. The general discontent increased from day to day; the nobles harped on
their rights, and the story is told that once, when Frederick called them to council, they answered that it was
against their privileges to get up so early. The fact is
certainly not easy to explain or excuse, that at the moment when the fierce battle was going on, which decided
the fate of Bohemia for generations to come, Frederick
was quietly seated at dinner within the walls of Prague,
and knew nothing until fugitives told him that all was
over.

The battle
on the
White Hill.

Maximilian of Bavaria had intrusted the command of
his numerous and well-organized forces to Baron Tilly, a
Netherlander, who had shown his bravery and capacity
in the Turkish wars. Frederick's general-in-chief was the
Prince of Anhalt, under whom were Thurn and Hohen-
lohe. The armies, when they met on the White Hill, a
few miles from Prague, were not so unequal in numbers,
but how different was the general spirit and courage!
Frederick had hoped at one time to gain the aid of England, France, Venice, and the half of Germany, but
nothing but disappointment had met him in all directions.
The Protestant Union declared that it could only act in
case the Palatinate itself were to be directly attacked, and
even ceased to pay the salary which Frederick had drawn
as its head. The young king's only subsidies were drawn
from Holland, his only useful allies were Mansfeld, the
Savoy commander, and Bethlen Gabor, the uncouth prince
of Transylvania. The army, then, that opposed Tilly was
ragged, unpaid, and altogether lacking in discipline; in
vain Frederick had mortgaged his jewels and the silver
from his table, and had wrung money from the Jews and
the Catholics.

The battle on the White Hill was fought and lost within

the space of little more than an hour. The Bohemians had the advantage of position, but all the daring, all the religious fervor, were on the side of the enemy. Their battle cry was "Holy Mary," the incentive to their decisive charge was given by a saintly monk, who blessed their banners, promised them the intercession of the mother of God in case of death, and thoroughly inspired with his own spirit both leaders and men alike. Anhalt, on the contrary, had relied on a calmness and courage of his troops which had failed them in the hour of need. At the very first charge they had fired wildly, and had become seized with a hopeless panic. Immediately after the defeat, Frederick consulted with his generals as to the possibility of holding Prague, but both Anhalt and Thurn had lost faith in their soldiers, and accused them of treason and cowardice; the signal was given for retreat, and Frederick and his wife left Bohemia, amid the curses of their subjects. His kingship had, indeed, vanished like the melting of winter snows.

Ferdinand, meanwhile, in Vienna, was listening to *Te Deums* and other special services. His preachers had pointed out that the gospel for the day when the battle was fought included the words, "Render unto Cæsar the things that are Cæsar's," while a Capuchin monk chose for his text the Psalmist's words, "Thou shalt chastise them with a rod of iron, and break them in pieces like a potter's vessel." Buoyed up by the consciousness of a righteous cause, the emperor initiated a political and religious reaction almost without a parallel. All important privileges relating to the Bohemians were placed in a box and sent to his palace; the parchment on which the Royal Charter was written shows to this day the savage cut that he made through its centre. The Bohemian throne was pronounced no longer elective, but hereditary, and the

*The subjugation of Bohemia.*

lands of all persons in any way tainted with rebellion were declared *in misericordia regis*. Courts were instituted with new and utterly unheard-of forms of procedure, evidences of evil intent being taken as a proof of the most serious charges. Not many were executed, but thousands were exiled, and the rest deprived, not only of political and religious freedom, but also of the right to speak their own language, and of the bare means of subsistence as well. Out of regard for his ally, the elector of Saxony, Ferdinand at first tried to spare the Lutheran as opposed to the Calvinist clergy; they were even told that they might keep their wives if they would speak of them in public as their cooks. When all such seductive arts had failed, and the Lutherans still persistently refused to turn Catholic, they too were banished in a body. Unremittingly, relentlessly, the reaction was carried through; the population quickly fell from 4,000,000 to less than 800,000, and Slavata reckoned that 30,000 families had wandered into exile. Starvation and torture were regular means of coercion, and in many districts there were quartered, on the refractory, bands of dragoons who in bitter mockery went by the name of angel makers.

The confiscated lands of the Bohemians.

The confiscated lands were sold to the highest bidders and could be bought for a mere song. It was by happy purchases at this dismal auction that the inscrutable Wallenstein laid the basis of his great fortune, whole cities at a time being handed over to him. To Ferdinand's credit it must be said that he afterward made partial repayments to some of those whom he had dispossessed, but whom he considered less guilty than the rest; yet the extraordinary charge is only too well founded that he made such payments in coin that he had expressly ordered debased to one-fourth of its face value, and that in reality contained but one-tenth of pure metal. This is not the least ugly of all the dark transactions of these times. The government itself, intending to defraud its helpless subjects, was in turn the prey of a band of forgers, who, with their nearly worthless coin, bought in great quantities of the vacant lands, at nominally one-fourth, and actually one-tenth, of their already depleted cost. Not until a later generation did the whole of this unsavory matter come to light, and the descendant of one of the coiners was fined a million guldens. For us, the value of the whole Bohemian episode lies in the light it throws on the character of Ferdinand II. He had more difficulty in putting through his bigoted will in Germany, but his attempts were to be just as untiring and equally sincere.

# CHAPTER XVIII

### THE CAREER OF WALLENSTEIN, THE INTERVENTION OF FOREIGN POWERS, AND THE PEACE OF WESTPHALIA

LITERATURE: Same as in last chapter, with the addition of Ranke's *Wallenstein,* Droysen's *Gustavus Adolphus,* and Woltmann's *Geschichte des Westphälischen Friedens. Erdmannsdörfer, Deutsche Geschichte, 1648–1740,* and Ritter's work covering the same period give résumés of the results of the Thirty Years' War.

Absurd demands of Frederick V.

THAT a war which had originated in a private quarrel of the Bohemians should soon have spread to all parts of civilized Europe, was owing to two circumstances: first, that the dethroned Winter King so conducted himself as to justify Ferdinand II. in rigorously proceeding against him; second, that the emperor had made a promise to the Bavarian elector, which he could not fulfil without awakening violent opposition.

At a moment when his hold even on his own hereditary lands was growing precarious, Frederick of the Palatinate imagined that he would still be considered a dangerous pretender to the Bohemian throne. He offered to submit, but under what conditions! The Bohemians were to be amnestied, and also to be confirmed in their right of election and in the free exercise of their religion; the emperor was to make good the back pay of the soldiery that had just fought against him, to assume certain debts of Frederick, and to give him in addition a small gratuity or perhaps a yearly pension. The only answer to such representations was the hurling of the greater ban of the empire at this "rebel and traitor." Spanish troops under Spinola had

450

already quartered themselves in the Palatinate, and had taken several towns; they were now reënforced by a portion of the imperial army under Tilly, the victor of the White Hill. The rest of Ferdinand's forces were kept busy in Hungary against Bethlen-Gabor. Frederick, indeed, was no longer so helpless as he had been in Bohemia. Mansfeld, who was far from Prague at the time of the great battle, had managed to escape with a considerable part of his troops. He would gladly have taken service with Ferdinand had the latter listened to his demands; but failing this, he devoted himself with real ardor to Frederick's cause, marching to the Palatinate with some fourteen thousand men. A no less important ally was the cousin of Frederick's wife, Christian of Brunswick, administrator of the secularized bishopric of Halberstadt. He was moved by a love of war which can only be described as bloodthirsty; by knightly devotion to the ex-queen, whose glove he wore on his helmet, and in whose honor his banner bore the device, "All for God and for her;" and, finally, by a well-grounded fear, that the reactionary policy of the emperor would eventually deprive him of his principality.

In one direction, indeed, from which he had a right to expect the most aid, Frederick was doomed to disappointment. The Protestant union, which had been founded in 1609 in view of just such an emergency as this, proved utterly unreliable and useless. Discord marked its deliberations, terror seized its individual members, and when, in the spring of 1621, an ultimatum was put to it by Spinola, its very existence came to an end. Out of its ruins, however, came succor for its former head, inasmuch as the Margrave of Baden-Durlach, commander of twenty thousand men, disapproving of the action of his colleagues, placed himself unreservedly at Frederick's disposal. The latter's forces had now swelled to some fifty thousand; a few

Frederick's new allies.

victories would have drawn to his banner a number of wavering princes, and a respectable balance might have been maintained even against the combined forces of Austria, Bavaria, and Spain.

Disasters for Frederick's cause.

But, save the one victory over Tilly at Wiesloch, where the imperial commander lost two thousand men, there came nothing but crushing disasters. The Margrave of Baden had tried to storm Tilly's camp upon the heights above Wimpfen, and for his own defence had drawn up his wagons after the manner of an old Hussite fortress. A fierce charge of the Spaniards under Cordova, and the accidental explosion of the margrave's own powder magazines, turned the well-fought day into a signal defeat. A similar fate met Christian of Brunswick at Höchst. This did not yet mean that all was lost, for the armies had retired from both fields in some kind of order; but Frederick now fell a victim to the well-meant interference of King James of England, who had endeavored of his own accord to mediate with the emperor. The emperor's preliminary demand had been that Frederick should lay down his arms and dismiss both Christian and Mansfeld, and this James now persuaded his son-in-law to do. The generals took service with the Dutch, whose long truce with Spain had run out in this same year, and met Cordova in the indecisive battle of Fleurus. Christian lost his arm, which had to be amputated; but he sent word to the Spanish commander-in-chief, Spinola, to note well that the other was still uninjured; *Altera restat* was the motto he engraved on one of his coins.

The Palatinate given to Maximilian of Bavaria.

As for Ferdinand, far from concluding peace as James of England had expected, he allowed Tilly to proceed without interruption to the subjugation of the whole Palatinate. Heidelberg was taken and cruelly plundered. Maximilian of Bavaria, as head of the Catholic league, took possession of its magnificent library, and sent it off to Rome to become a part of the Vatican collection. This ambitious prince, who, after years of careful management, had brought order and system into the Bavarian administration, was now casting lusting eyes, not only on the electoral dignity, but also on the newly conquered lands. He had a bill of costs to present to the emperor; it proved so enormous that Ferdinand was under the necessity of either forfeiting the Austrian lands that he had pledged, or of acceding to the new demands. The bestowal of a Protestant electorate on a Catholic prince: that was a feat that had never yet been successfully accomplished! Maximilian, however, insisted on his claims and was ably seconded by Pope Gregory XV., who was full of proud plans for increasing the power of the holy Catholic church. Spain, on the other hand, objected; she knew better than any power in Europe what war meant, she saw that to utterly crush the count palatine meant to prolong the struggle indefinitely, and that the English friendship must be forfeited should Philip IV. help to rob the son-in-law of James I.

Even Ferdinand II. hesitated to settle the matter by simple imperial rescript. From the beginning of the previous century custom had sanctioned the occasional calling together of a supplementary or deputy diet. Such a delegation now met at Ratisbon in December, 1622, to listen to the emperor's proposals; but the fierce opposition that arose, even on the part of some of the Catholics, caused him seriously to modify his intended measure. He no longer dared now, openly and unconditionally, and for all time, to give the electorate to Maximilian; the Bavarian duke was merely to hold it pending negotiations with Frederick; and he was to resign without a murmur should the former elector "show due humility, ask for pardon, and cease altogether from his machinations." The matter was to come up again for deliberation at a later date; the emperor, in the meanwhile, was to discuss with the electors the question of the rights of the count palatine's children. Even the Protestant Landgrave of Hesse was willing to agree to an arrangement like this, and the investiture of Maximilian took place with all form and ceremony.

But not in vain had Ferdinand been the pupil of the Jesuits. Though assuming for the benefit of the Protestants a yielding attitude, on the very day after the investiture he bound himself to Maximilian by a written agreement, to the effect that the latter should hold the electoral dignity for life; and that he, the emperor, no matter what the electors might determine concerning Frederick's children, would not consider himself bound by their decision.

Indignation at the transfer of the Palatinate.

At the first news of the deposition of Frederick, and the sequestration of his lands in favor of so orthodox a prince, all Catholic Europe was jubilant, and the Pope wrote to Ferdinand that the latter had " filled his breast with delight as with a stream of heavenly manna." But soon to the blindest eye it was evident that a storm was brewing that might shake the power of the Hapsburgs, and thus of the church, to the very foundations. Mansfeld and Christian of Brunswick appeared in North Germany, supplied with gold from England and Holland. The Lower Saxon Circle, one of those organizations for mutual defence of which ten had been formed in 1500, mustered its own army and determined to oppose the emperor, should he interfere with the North German bishoprics. Scattered here and there, their little principalities afforded to the party that held them obvious coigns of vantage.

The court of England by this time had changed its policy and was filled with hatred of Spain. The young

Prince of Wales, the future Charles I., had gone to Madrid incognito to look at his intended bride. Her religious intolerance, and the general stiffness and pride of the court, were such that the match came to nothing, and the young suitor returned home with disgust in his heart for the whole connection. The efforts of the English minister, Buckingham, brought about instead a marriage with Henrietta Maria, the sister of Louis XIII. of France. In this latter country Richelieu had just come into power, and he, although persecuting the Huguenots at home, was willing enough to encourage Protestants abroad to fight against the Hapsburgs. The Spaniards, by interfering in a local quarrel, had taken the Swiss Valtelline, as well as the province of Bormio; by which conquests the house of Austria had opened up direct communication between its German and Italian possessions. This Colossus of a house of Hapsburg was overshadowing Europe, and Richelieu, though not yet prepared for open war, was glad to furnish subsidies and diplomatic support to those who were anxious to begin the struggle.

James I. of England bestirs himself.

During this the last year of his life, the English king made up in some degree for his former lukewarmness in the cause of continental Protestantism. He bestirred himself right busily to form a coalition, that should wage war for the direct purpose of restoring to the count palatine his hereditary domains. The Dutch were easily won over; they had always sympathized with Frederick, had offered him an asylum, had paid him subsidies, and had only been prevented from doing more by reason of their own isolation.

Two other powers in Europe, Denmark and Sweden, were friendly to the cause, but England was placed in an awkward predicament of having to choose between them. Not only were Christian IV. and Gustavus Adolphus personal rivals, but in this very matter of the continental war

Treaty of the Hague with Christian of Denmark.

the policy of the one differed materially from that of the other. Christian both as Duke of Holstein, and thus member of the Lower Saxon Circle, and as uncle of the palatine electress, had his own interest in the struggle; he was, however, in every way, a pygmy compared to the Swedish king. Gustavus Adolphus, whose splendid talents had carried Sweden through glorious years of war and peace, insisted that should the struggle be begun, it should be with a large army and with ample funds; his demands, both on England and on Protestant Germany, were very high, though not higher than to a far-seeing eye the exigencies of the case demanded. But James I., and, on his death, his young successor, preferred the more modest plan of campaign of the Danish king. With him in December, 1625, Charles I. concluded the treaty of the Hague, and Gustavus Adolphus devoted all his energies to his own Polish war, and refrained from interference in Germany.

Wallen-
stein.

In spite of errors of judgment and of sins of omission on the part of his opponents, the emperor Ferdinand was at this moment in an extremely difficult and dangerous position. The sums extorted from the Bohemians had been squandered on churches and on Jesuits; the treasury was empty; to oppose the various forces that were springing up in all directions there was only the army of Tilly. Spain was occupied elsewhere for the moment, while Bethlen Gabor was making ready to help the Protestants.

It was natural that in such an emergency Ferdinand should seek assistance wherever it was most easy to obtain. Then it was that the man came to the fore who was to occupy the thoughts of his fellow-men, and to dominate his age to a rare degree — a mysterious, elusive genius, not thoroughly good but certainly not thoroughly bad. The character of Wallenstein is the more difficult to judge because of his own inveterate caution and reticence; it was his rule never to commit to paper anything that might compromise himself. Everything that we know about his motives is at second-hand, and verdicts vary according to the standpoint.

Born in Bohemia of Protestant parents, and subjected to various religious influences, Wallenstein finally counted himself a Roman Catholic, but was never fanatical or intolerant, unless it served some special turn. Superstitious we may call him, for dreams and portents largely influenced his actions, and the popular study of astrology occupied much of his time. Kepler once took his horoscope and told him that he was destined for great things; no less a person, he declared, than Queen Elizabeth of England had been born under the same constellation. With the stars in their courses in his favor, possessed of an ambition that recoiled before no step toward his own advancement, Wallenstein progressed rapidly in his military and civil career. His first wife, Lucretia Neckish, brought him a considerable fortune; after her death he looked for a connection that would afford him influence and high social position, and found it in the house of Harrach. With a sword that was always at the service of the Hapsburgs, he had risen by the year 1622 to be the highest commanding officer in Bohemia.

*Early years of Wallenstein.*

At the time of the great sale of lands confiscated from the Protestants, Wallenstein had been far and away the largest purchaser; the domains of the "Prince of Friedland," as he was now called, covered the whole of northeastern Bohemia. One can judge of his wealth from the homely fact that in one year alone the beer monopoly within his boundaries brought him a revenue of sixteen thousand guldens. And excellently and economically did he manage his estates; even when busy with his army in field, he is known to have sent directions about the proper food for swine, calves, and foals, and to have recommended a particular treatment for sick hens. Not altogether un-important details these, when we remember that, later, his chief occupation was not fighting battles, but providing food and clothing for immense armies, many of his supplies coming from his own lands.

Ferdinand's arrange-ment with Wallen-stein.

The arrangement was unprecedented, which Ferdinand, in his hour of need, made with Wallenstein. The latter was to raise and equip an army of twenty-one thousand men at his own expense. Once fairly in the field, the emperor was to undertake the pay of the soldiers; but they were largely to subsist by levying contributions on the lands through which they passed. The commander-in-chief, besides his regular yearly compensation, was to have as his perquisite the ransoms of all ordinary prisoners and a share of the booty, and in addition to this, he was en-dowed with political, almost sovereign, rights. He might make treaties with territorial lords, and even, if need be, grant concessions with regard to their religion.

Tilly and Wallen-stein.

Ferdinand little knew as yet the man with whom he had to deal, else how could he have ordered him to consult on all important matters with Tilly, the general of the league forces? The two were as opposed to each other as fire and water. Wallenstein, as he soon showed, meant to raise the ordinary prose both of war and politics to a higher plane. Protestants were as welcome in his army as Catholics, Walloons and Croats as Germans, desperadoes as honest men. His original twenty-one thousand men were growing into many times that number, and he quartered them on the lands of friends and foes alike. In Tilly's head, on the other hand, were no great political plans; he was a brave, plain soldier and a devout Roman Catholic of the intolerant and prosely-tizing kind. As the faithful henchman of Maximilian of Bavaria, his one object was to fight battles and reduce Protestants to submission. To him fell the good fortune of routing the king of Denmark in the fierce battle of Lutter, whereas Wallenstein could only point to a skirmish with Mansfeld at Dessau on the Elbe, and a long pursuit of the Savoy condottiere into Bohemia, where Mansfeld had hoped to unite his forces with those of Bethlen Gabor.

It was Mansfeld's last campaign ; Bethlen, induced by the laxness of the coalition in sending him promised subsidies, made his own peace with the emperor; Mansfeld withdrew, but fell sick on the way. Whatever his faults, he was accustomed to face his enemies; and now, confronted with death, he armed himself to the teeth, girded his sword at his side, and insisted on being held in a standing position until the breath had left his body. The cause that he had espoused seemed again likely to fail, for England and France had fallen out with each other, and the Danish king, chased to the utmost limits of northwestern Europe, had little hope but in submission, and finally, in 1629, concluded the Peace of Lübeck. *Mansfeld's death.*

Wallenstein's whole method of procedure had by this time raised up for him many and violent opponents, chiefly among the members of the Catholic league. What was his purpose in levying this enormous army? What was the need of it now that practically no enemy at all remained in Germany? Ferdinand himself in the days preceding Mansfeld's death had been puzzled and annoyed at the conduct of his general; he desired more activity and less recruiting, and he sent his chief minister Eggenberg to confer with Wallenstein at Bruck on the Leitha. The revelations made in this interview had fairly taken away the breath of the minister, who returned in haste — as Wallenstein's warmest adherent — to acquaint his master with the real trend of the new policy. *Wallenstein's plans for Ferdinand.*

The imperial authority, it seems, was to be established not only over a few rebellious estates like the former elector of the Palatinate or the city of Magdeburg, which refused to accept a garrison, but over all princes and subjects alike. As Wallenstein later expressed himself, the emperor was no longer to be a mere image, an ornament in the general structure. For this it was necessary that he should have a large and well-trained army, one indeed that should be the terror of all Europe. These forces were not to be wasted in petty undertakings, nor was it wise by employing sectarian measures to make the task more difficult. One reason for employing Protestants in the army and for giving them some of the best offices had been to emphasize the superior and impartial position of the nation's head.

Ferdinand heaps honors on Wallenstein.

Ferdinand, for a time at least, was completely won over to these ideas. Even the tolerance towards the Protestants seems to have met with his approval. Never before or since has there been in Germany such a military despotism as was now established. The army reached the enormous total of one hundred and thirty thousand — an incredible number if we consider that each man was more highly paid than are the soldiers of modern times, and that, according to the peculiar custom during these thirty years of war, thousands of women and children were allowed to follow the camps and to add their maintenance to the general expense. The requisitions were burdensome in the extreme; Wallenstein himself, who tried to spare the country as much as possible, and did everything in his power to see that the harvests were properly sown and reaped, wrote to Ferdinand with regard to some of the northern provinces that they were thoroughly ruined, that the inhabitants had taken to eating cats and dogs, and that suicides were frequent.

Yet while the dream lasted Ferdinand could not do enough for his loyal champion and defender. Privileges without end were heaped upon his head. He had formed a plan for winning the Hanseatic towns and gaining for them a monopoly of the trade with Spain. Ferdinand accordingly appointed him "general of the whole imperial armada and of the Baltic and the North Sea." His principality of Friedland was raised to a dukedom, and permission given him to issue coins bearing his own image. He might appoint not only the lower officers of the army, but the colonels and captains as well. His pay was increased threefold, a measure which was to have retroactive force for the past three years. And all this was nothing to the final concession which even Ferdinand hesitated long before deciding to grant. The emperor by this time was millions in his great subject's debt. Wallenstein, supported by Ferdinand's Jesuit councillors, to whom he offered free play in his coveted new domains, proposed the expulsion of the Protestant dukes of Mecklenburg, and the handing over of their lands to himself in lieu of all other claims. It would be a good thing, it was argued, to make a severe example of a few rebellious princes. "I only wish," wrote Wallenstein to his field marshal Arnim, "that the Duke of Pomerania would also prove disloyal."

The "Duke of Friedland" was now an independent sovereign in all but name, with lands stretching far along the Baltic coast. The magnificence of his mode of living beggars all description. In his suite were two hundred and twenty-five chamberlains and stewards, pages, lackeys, and Jesuits; one thousand horses were needed for their use. For his further ambitious schemes it was necessary that he should have more towns upon the seacoast, and he summoned the citizens of Stralsund to receive an imperial garrison within their walls. When the inhabitants refused the request, preferring to withstand a siege, he is said to have remarked that he would have the city, even though it were fastened by chains to the vault of heaven. Here

*Wallenstein's lordly doings.*

finally, however, he met with the first check in his military career, and was obliged to raise the siege on account of the aid which Danish and Swedish ships brought to the garrison.

It may well be imagined that not only the members of the league, but all the electors as well, had now become thoroughly alarmed at Wallenstein's doings. Already in 1627 a convention at Mulhausen had sent a vehement protest to the emperor, declaring that the electors themselves would take measures for "saving the sore-oppressed fatherland from final ruin." Since then, utterances had been reported to the Duke of Bavaria which roused him to the pitch of frenzy: Wallenstein intended to dissolve the league and make the imperial throne hereditary; the electors were to be made to stand on their good behavior; indeed, there would never be peace in Germany until one of them should have his head taken off and placed at his own feet; after Ferdinand's death he, Wallenstein, would make himself master with the title of " Emperor of the West." Probably the truest of all these rumors was one to the effect that Wallenstein meant to make the ruler of Germany as absolute as the monarchs of France or England. And had Ferdinand supported him, the means were at hand to have secured success.

The "Edict of Restitution." But on this none too firm emperor there was now being brought to bear a pressure that he could not withstand. To his request that his son be chosen as his successor during his own lifetime, the electors turned a deaf ear — this finally broke his resistance. He told the representative of the Archbishop of Mainz "so truly as he desired to see God's face," he did not mean to detract from the liberty of the electors; and that if any of his subjects made the attempt, he would order his head cut off. He wrote to Wallenstein that the authority and supremacy of the imperial house were at stake, and that a large part of the army must be dismissed.

This order was in part obeyed, but the appearance of a large French army in Italy in connection with the war for the Mantuan succession, gave the general a pretext for further levies. Of far more lasting importance was the emperor's change of policy, brought about by this same pressure, in the matter of religious toleration. Without consulting Wallenstein, he put his hand to the most radical and dangerous document that has ever been issued in all the long course of German religious history. The question over which, for three-quarters of a century, diets had deliberated and courts of justice had wrangled, was now to be decided by a stroke of the pen. The cruel reaction that had taken place in Bohemia was to be attempted in Germany, and Ferdinand hoped that Tilly and Wallenstein would be his willing instruments. The strongest attack that had ever been made on the work of Martin Luther was now in progress; but the nemesis was under way.

The act known as the Edict of Restitution, which was published in March, 1629, declared roundly that all ecclesiastical property which had come into Protestant hands since the Treaty of Passau in 1552, might now be reclaimed, and that Catholic priests should replace all Protestant holders of bishoprics. Nor should these new bishops be bound by that old, unrecorded declaration which purported to have come from the emperor Ferdinand I., and required toleration for Protestant subjects. To make the rags and tatters of the Augsburg Peace of still less avail, it was now expressly stated that the terms of that instrument had only applied to Lutherans, and that "other sects" were to be excluded from its advantages.

What a complete revolution was here intended will be seen from the fact, that the Protestants at this time held two former archbishoprics, twelve bishoprics, and five hundred abbacies, the revenues of which for two generations had been put to

public uses in the different states.  The Palatinate and Hesse,
moreover, were full of Calvinists, to which faith belonged
also the elector of Brandenburg.  One might possibly
think that such a general edict was meant as a mere threat
or political card, but such was not the case.  Ferdinand
was deadly in earnest, and he set to work at once to seize
churches and monasteries, and to build Jesuit colleges.  A
part of the spoils was to go toward the payment of the
army.  Goslar was fixed upon as the seat of a central
Catholic university, which should spread its influence in all
directions.

Dismissal
of Wallen-
stein.

Wallenstein disapproved of the edict and refused to help
in carrying it out; but little enough could he do, for his
own hour had come.  The princes and electors met together at Ratisbon in June, 1630, determined not to part
without first having achieved the "Friedländer's" fall.
Well might this struggle be called the greatest diplomatic
victory of the century.  Ferdinand's throne was tottering;
Richelieu, whose envoys were present, had offered, if need
be, to throw France's influence into the scale in favor of
having Maximilian of Bavaria declared emperor.  At last
Ferdinand yielded, and emissaries were sent to acquaint
Wallenstein with his fate.  He took the news calmly; he
had read it in the stars, he is reported to have said.  The
army, it was determined, should be reduced to thirty-
nine thousand, the forces of the league to twenty-one
hundred.  Tilly was to be commander-in-chief.

Landing of
Gustavus
Adolphus.

But by this time the Edict of Restitution had called
upon the stage the "strong man armed" who was to
keep the house of German Protestantism.  The "Lion of
the North" had crouched and sprung.  It was known,
indeed, at Ratisbon at the very time of Wallenstein's
dismissal, that the Swedish king had landed on the coast
of Pomerania; but men were utterly unconscious of what

that fact signified. "We have a new little enemy," the emperor is reported to have said good-humoredly in his broadest Viennese dialect. The officers of his chancery consulted their maps to find just where Sweden lay, while the Catholic princes prepared to enjoy a new division of territory, should any one be so foolhardy as to join the northern adventurer.

Wallenstein, indeed, would have known better than to underrate this danger. As "general of the Baltic and the North Sea" he had found his plans crossed at all points by the intervention of the Swedish king, and had assiduously promoted the Polish war so as to keep his enemy occupied. He had even conceived a project for striking at Sweden's trade, by building such a canal between the two bodies of water as has only been completed in our own day.

It was, in very deed, a man of extraordinary ability who had now stepped into the arena of German politics. Gustavus Adolphus, a descendant of the great house of Vasa, had come to the throne of Sweden in 1611 as rival of his Catholic cousin, King Sigismund of Poland. A mere boy of seventeen, but with keen perceptions and thoroughly trained by a watchful father, he had found himself the inheritor of three foreign wars, and of what seemed like civil anarchy. In twenty years of unremitting endeavor he had made Sweden's name thoroughly respected abroad, and had brought order and enterprise into her internal affairs. He had quelled the rebellious nobles and had made them submit to taxation. As for the Swedish army, he had completely remodelled it; combining the various disorderly squads into regular regiments, and arming these with muskets instead of spears and pikes. He uniformed and disciplined his troops, and otherwise prepared for the great tasks he had in hand. The Russians were pushed so far back from the Baltic that, as he told his estates, they would

*Early years of Gustavus Adolphus.*

now find it hard to "spring over the little stream." By
the terms of a peace with Poland, concluded in the year of
the restitution edict through the timely aid of Richelieu,
he gained temporary possession of a number of Prussian
ports.   With his "dominion of the Baltic" thus secured
in the East, with his hands free for new enterprises, his
next thought was to gain points of vantage on the German
coast.   The cry of the Protestants appealed strongly to his
sympathies, but equally strongly to his political aspirations.

Reception
of Gustavus
Adolphus
on German
soil.

Gustavus Adolphus's first reception on German soil was
anything but encouraging.   Even the Duke of Pomerania, though he loathed the imperial garrisons that held
his fortresses, lacked courage to welcome the deliverer, and
only yielded to compulsion.   Months passed before any
power, save the cities of Magdeburg and Stralsund, made
common cause with the Swedes.   With some it may have
been a matter of national pride, but the majority were
influenced by the fear of Tilly's army.   A convention of
Protestant estates did take place at Leipzig in February,
1631, but the proceedings only reflected the weakness and
timidity of the summons ; an assembly that avowedly met
for the "furtherance of peaceful negotiations," and that
expressed its "friendly confidence" in the Catholic powers,
was not likely to accomplish much.

Treaty of
Bärwalde.

The first care of the "Lion of the North" was to rid
Pomerania of the imperial garrisons ; his second, to send
an officer to Magdeburg to organize a systematic plan of
defence, and also to announce the speedy coming of relief.
Napoleon Bonaparte once declared that these early operations of the Swedish king marked him for one of the
greatest generals of any age.   Nor were the diplomatic
achievements of less importance.   By a treaty with France
he secured a large subsidy without in the least compro-
mising his dignity.   Richelieu had tried to patronize this

half-barbaric prince, whose father had owed his throne to the mere will of the people; he had wished Louis XIII., as " King by the grace of God," to take precedence in the wording of the document, and also to have a voice in the plan of campaign. But Gustavus had asserted himself right royally; in one copy of the Treaty of Bärwalde his name followed, in the other it preceded, that of the French king; while the only concessions he made, related to the treatment of Catholics, and the possible neutrality of the league.

Unfortunately for the besieged city of Magdeburg, Gustavus could not move from his base of supplies without first securing the allegiance of the two chief Protestant powers of the North; but two such wavering and unstable princes as George William of Brandenburg and John George of Saxony would have been difficult to find. John George's chief claim to distinction lay in his ability to consume immense quantities of wine, while the Brandenburg elector was urged in vain by his brother-in-law to declare himself either his friend or his enemy, to be one thing or the other, hot or cold; but at any rate to adopt *mascula consilia*, to show that he was a man. Gustavus finally drew up his army before the walls of Berlin, and pointed his cannon at the city—a step which caused the elector to send his mother and all the princesses to beg for mercy, and finally to appear himself and conclude an alliance. He was to deliver up the fortresses of Spandau and Küstrin for the duration of the war, and to pay a monthly subsidy. A passing cloud was cast over the reconciliation, by the fact that when the Swedes fired salvos of joy to celebrate the peace, they forgot to remove their heavy charges, and some damage was done to buildings in Berlin.

So long had these negotiations lasted, that Gustavus had seriously thought of abandoning Germany to her fate;

Negotiations with Brandenburg and Saxony.

The fall of
Magdeburg. had he so wished he could, strange as it may seem, have
joined hands with Wallenstein, who made a proposal to
that effect. The worst result of the delay was the fall of
Magdeburg; day after day, in hourly hope of his coming,
the little garrison of three thousand had held its own
against ten times that number, commanded, too, by such
experienced generals as Tilly and Pappenheim. When the
city at last was taken by storm, the inhabitants, determined
that a point of such great strategic importance should not
be of service to the enemy, applied the torch to their own
houses, — an act for which posterity has given the unenvia-
ble credit to Tilly, who is represented even in engravings
of the time with the flames of Magdeburg as a background.
Of the whole great city, one of the proudest in Germany,
there only remained the cathedral and some fifty houses.

The battle
of Breiten-
feld. For Gustavus, indeed, from the moment of his treaty
with Brandenburg, the whole horizon had begun to brighten.
The queen of Sweden landed in Pomerania with fresh
troops; while from England came reënforcements to the
extent of six thousand men. And the emperor's own action
now drove John George of Saxony to abandon his neutrality; for Tilly was ordered to try the same manœuvre that
Gustavus had practised against Brandenburg, and to force
the elector to a decision at the cannon's mouth. Tilly
gathered all his forces at Eisleben, and put the point-blank
question; but inasmuch as at the same time Saxony's
demand for a reversal of the restitution edict was cate-
gorically refused — the emperor declaring that he would
uphold it until not a shirt was left to his own back — the
decision fell out not to Ferdinand's, but to the Swedish
king's advantage. On the 11th of September, 1631, the
treaty was signed, by which eighteen thousand Saxon soldiers were added to the twenty-eight thousand of Gustavus.

Tilly now turned the whole fury of his attack against

Leipzig, which, unfortified and undefended, was obliged to submit to an immense indemnity, and to accept an imperial garrison. But Gustavus, with his combined army, was close at Tilly's heels, leaving him only time to intrench himself outside the city in the strongest position he could find. With his troops drawn up in a solid phalanx, ten men deep, with the cavalry on either wing and artillery in front, after the old approved fashion, Tilly awaited the enemy's attack.

Not only Tilly, but the whole German people as well, experienced that day a mode of warfare that was entirely new. In the Swedish army all was action and change; cavalry and infantry had been trained to supplement each other at every point. Instead of in dense battalions that trusted to mere weight of onslaught, the vanguard were drawn up in divisions only three men deep, the two front rows kneeling, the third standing, so that all could fire at once. In the rear was a large reserve which, in point of fact, won this battle of Breitenfeld. In spite of Tilly's superior position, in spite of the panic which seized on the Saxons and drove them, together with their elector, into mad flight, Gustavus, by a brilliant manœuvre, carried the day and almost annihilated the imperial army. From eighteen to nineteen thousand men were killed, wounded, or taken prisoners; the whole of the artillery and some ninety standards fell into the hands of the Swedes. A shout of triumph went up from Protestant Germany, and a news-leaf of the day points out in glowing words how the victory was due to God's counsel and the Swedes' undaunted courage, to justice and a good cause. The loss of Magdeburg was gloriously avenged. As no other army of any size was in the field, the road lay open to the possessions of the Catholic league, as well as to the emperor's hereditary lands.

Absolutely the only hope, now, for Ferdinand and the

Catholics, lay in the recall of Wallenstein. But the services
of the great man were difficult to obtain; all the more so,
as Ferdinand's first thought was merely to associate him in
the command with his own son. The wound to Wallenstein's outraged dignity was far from healed; the emperor
should learn, he said to Arnim, what it meant to "affront
a cavalier." He would rather, he declared to an emissary
of Ferdinand, be sent to hell than resume the command.
No, indeed, he would not take it, though God Almighty
should ask him in person. All the grain on his own lands
he removed as far as possible from the clutches of the imperialists. He did his best in these days to come to an
agreement with Gustavus, and had the latter been able to
give him eleven thousand men, he would have struck a
blow at the heart of Bohemia. In judging him for these
intrigues, it must be remembered that, in his own mind at
least, he was as free to make alliances as any other prince;
as free, for instance, as Maximilian of Bavaria, who was
even now a protégé of Richelieu's. Wallenstein had bought
his duchy for hard cash; no debt of gratitude was due to
any one.

At last, finding that Gustavus would not give him the
desired troops, Wallenstein gave way to the emperor's
pressing appeals, and agreed to "take an interest in the
imperial army." Office or pay he did not want, but he
would raise an army of forty thousand within three months,
and the emperor might then intrust the command to whom
he pleased. When the time came, as there was no one
else of sufficient prestige to keep the motley troops in order,
he yielded still further and agreed to take the field, but
only in return for dictatorial, almost royal rights. Wallenstein was to be the sole head of all the imperial armies in
the field and, save through him, the emperor himself was
to give no commands; the latter was to promise expressly

to pay no heed to anything that his father confessor or any other of the clergy should choose to say against his general. An equivalent was to be given for Mecklenburg, until such time as the Swedes should have been dispossessed; and two independent Catholic sources, a papal nuncio and a Spanish envoy, agree that Ferdinand promised Wallenstein the first electorate the latter should be able to conquer.

Meanwhile the Saxons under Arnim had taken Prague, — whence Wallenstein had no difficulty in dislodging them, — and Gustavus Adolphus in an uninterrupted succession of triumphs had marched through the "Priests' Lane," the great row of bishoprics on the Main and Rhine. Like one of the old mediæval emperors, at his headquarters in Mainz he received embassies from all over Germany. During these days of splendid repose, negotiations for peace were entered into, which are interesting as showing the conqueror's projects and his ultimate programme for Germany. For himself he claimed, in addition to a strip of territory along the Pomeranian coast, a sort of protectorship over all German Protestants; services like his, he declared, were not to be rewarded with a few months' pay, like those of any common mercenary. The restitution edict was to be annulled, and complete toleration granted; while not only was the former palatine elector to be reinstated in all his lands and dignities, but matters in Bohemia, Silesia, and Moravia were to return to the standpoint of the year 1618.

On the refusal of these terms, Gustavus resumed his victorious progress; his object being now to penetrate to the heart of Bavaria. The old wrong done to the city of Donauwörth was righted, when, after a two days' bombardment, the Catholic garrison laid down their arms. Tilly, with the remnants of his army, then tried to block the way

Triumphs of Gustavus Adolphus.

at the crossing of the river Lech, but was wounded in the skirmish, and was carried to Ingolstadt to end his life. Just a year after the fall of Magdeburg Gustavus passed in triumph into Maximilian's capital of Munich, and at his side rode that same unfortunate Winter King who owed such a debt of hatred to the Bavarian duke.

The battle of Lützen.

But already Wallenstein, having cleansed Bohemia of the Saxons, had answered the appealing call of his former enemy; joining his forces with Maximilian's, he drew up his army in the neighborhood of Nuremberg, where Gustavus was intrenched. He meant, he said, to show the Swedish king, in turn, a new mode of warfare: it was that of passive resistance. Nothing could budge him from his position, though supplies for both armies grew scarcer and scarcer, and starvation bred disease. In this long game of delay he proved the master, and Gustavus, after a fruitless attempt to storm his ramparts, withdrew his troops. But when Wallenstein turned against Saxony and began ravaging the elector's lands, Gustavus followed him hard and fast, and came upon him near Leipzig. The neighborhood that had witnessed the great battle of Breitenfeld was now to see another similar sight. The fierce encounter at Lützen proved another victory for the Swedes, but it cost them dearer than a dozen ordinary defeats. Their idolized leader had never hesitated personally to face the greatest dangers; at the passage of the Lech he had even done his own reconnoitring, and once, unrecognized, had culled valuable information from one of the enemy's own pickets. Now, anxious to wipe out the repulse at Nuremberg, he seemed almost to court the most exposed positions. Riding into the very midst of a regiment of cuirassiers, he was wounded in several places and fell from his horse. Over his dead body his Swedes, led by the young Duke Bernard of Weimar, fought like very tigers; even the invincible Wal-

lenstein was repulsed with the loss of his best officers, of
thousands of his soldiers, and of the whole of his artillery.
The corpse of Gustavus Adolphus was removed to Wolgast,
where an immense train of mourners followed him to the
grave; there followed, too, an invisible procession of
ruined hopes and lost possibilities. In all probability the
death of the man in whom he had put his trust, broke the
heart of the fugitive palatine elector; for the unfortunate
Frederick breathed his last before the lapse of a fortnight.
It might have comforted his last hours, could he only have
known that his children would receive back their inheritance, and that his daughter's son would one day wear the
crown of England.

As for Wallenstein, after the battle of Lützen he re- Oxen-
mained strictly on the defensive, devoting himself to the stierna's
task of reorganizing his shattered army. On those of his difficulties.
subordinates who had been lacking in bravery, or had in
any way neglected their duty, he inflicted the severest
punishments, no less than eleven officers being put to death
like common criminals. The difficulty of procuring cannon,
not to speak of new recruits, delayed matters for several
months.

During this time the Swedes, led by Bernard of Weimar,
were able to reconquer the whole of Franconia — which was
afterward given to Bernard as a separate duchy, dependent on the crown of Sweden — and also to occupy the
lower Palatinate and parts of Swabia and Bavaria. The
supreme direction of Swedish affairs, was given by the
state council at Stockholm to the chancellor Oxenstierna,
who, indeed, let fall many of his former master's projects
for the Protestant cause, but clung tenaciously to the idea
of securing for his country a fitting reward for all her pains
and sacrifices — such compensation, he claimed, "as kings
and princes, not as shopkeepers, are accustomed to give."

Oxenstierna's designs, including as they did his own continuance as leader of the German Protestants, were hampered by the attitude of the Elector of Saxony, who, although he had subordinated himself to a great king, was not minded to obey an ordinary nobleman. The elector's private desire was for a speedy cessation of hostilities; "better," said Arnim in his name, "the worst kind of a peace than the best kind of a war." But if the struggle must be continued, he, John George, was the proper head for his own countrymen. So bitter was the controversy, that the question of leadership was tacitly waived, and Saxony took part in the subsequent events as an independent third party.

With the smaller Protestant powers, Oxenstierna, in April, 1633, signed the league of Heilbronn, which assured to Sweden a suitable compensation, and gave to himself the wished-for directorship. A war council of seven Germans and three Swedes was to tender him advice, but not restrict his actions. France agreed to continue her subsidies and sent her agents all over Germany to see that the various enemies of the house of Hapsburg should neither slumber nor sleep.

Wallenstein's delays.

By the month of May of the same year, Wallenstein had a well-equipped army of sixty thousand men leisurely encamped in Bohemia and Silesia; but already the old doubts as to his ultimate purpose had begun to arise in many quarters. What was the meaning of this lethargy and of these continued levies, when the whole hostile force in these regions only numbered twenty-four thousand men? Why did he not strike a decisive blow and then hurry to Bavaria, where Bernard of Weimar might at any moment make for Ratisbon, the key to the Danube and to the Austrian possessions? For one thing, Wallenstein miscalculated Bernard's plans, expecting him to invade Bohemia;

he would stake, he said, his honor and his head on the correctness of this judgment. But there was, indeed, another reason for his inactivity. Political schemes, far more than war, occupied his thoughts just now; he held frequent interviews with the Saxon general Arnim, as well as with emissaries of the Bohemian exiles, who were burning to regain their lost possessions. While ostensibly conducting peace negotiations in the name of the emperor, he was striving to bring into effect his own plan for the reconstruction of Germany. If Ferdinand's views should ultimately coincide with his own, well and good; if not, it was to be a question between actual power and lofty prerogative.

From Ferdinand, Wallenstein had not received the Wallenstein's grievances. promised reward for his intervention, nor in other ways had the emperor fulfilled his contract. In spite of all that had been said, Jesuit influences had maintained the upper hand. Spain had conceived the project of setting up an independent army in Alsace to maintain her connection with her Netherland provinces, and the emperor, without waiting for the consent of his generalissimo, had given the required permission. The Viceroy of Milan, Feria, had been appointed to the command; but Wallenstein saw in the whole move an effort to restrict his own absolute power. A still deeper offence was Ferdinand's refusal to make over to him the electorate of Brandenburg, or indeed, to assure him any other equivalent for the loss of Mecklenburg. What Wallenstein had dreamed of, was to found a third great Catholic state in the heart of Germany. The Spanish minister Olivarez had warmly seconded him in the plan, and he had arranged a combination by which, with the lands of the Hohenzollerns for a centre, his territories should stretch from Friedland to Frisia. But the emperor, longing now for a general peace, had dreaded to take so radical a step.

It must not be supposed that Wallenstein's subsequent actions were entirely influenced by a desire to be revenged upon Ferdinand. Much of his conduct must forever remain enigmatical; but enough is known to show that he was far removed from being a common traitor, influenced solely by personal motives. When the plan was broached by Bohemian nobles of making him their king, he quickly repudiated such a "piece of roguery"; when France offered her support to the same end, he broke off all negotiations. It is true he made frequent and unaccountable truces that conduced greatly to the advantage of the enemy; had his aim been perfectly single, he would have struck a crushing blow, and then made his terms.

Wallenstein's treasonable plans.

To Arnim, Wallenstein proposed that the Saxon army should unite with his own, for the purpose of dictating such a peace to Germany as should secure an equal toleration for Catholics and Protestants. All who had been unjustly dispossessed were to be reinstated in their rights. Sweden was to be pacified by being given German districts of importance. Should the emperor prove refractory, he must be intimidated. On a later occasion, in a moment of great irritation, he produced a specific plan for a campaign against Ferdinand, and the Saxon general was despatched to the Swedish camp to win, if he could, the approval of Oxenstierna. These latter negotiations were broken off by Wallenstein of his own accord; either he repented or he feared being thwarted. Perhaps he recoiled before the thought of joining with a foreigner in such an enterprise, and it is certainly significant that, in another interview with Arnim, he declared that no lasting peace could be made until all foreign powers, such as Spain, France, and Sweden, should have been "kicked out" of the empire.

So various, indeed, were Wallenstein's plans, so inscrutable his real aims, that of no power did he win the confidence. Sweden, Saxony, and France were all willing enough to urge him on; but they wished him to thoroughly commit himself, to accept for instance the Bohemian crown, before they could take him seriously. "Question him searchingly and see how far he will go," was the instruction issued to Arnim by the court of Saxony. As for the emperor, he was not at all convinced at this time that events were not pursuing their proper course. But the capture of Ratisbon, which Bernard now accomplished, and Wallenstein's subsequent attitude, brought matters to a final crisis; all that had been needed completely to undermine the great general's influence was one serious military blunder.

How often had Maximilian of Bavaria begged and implored that imperial forces should be sent to his assistance! First General Aldringen, then General Gallas had been stationed not far from the Bavarian frontier; but Wallenstein had instructed each in turn to remain on the defensive. His own firm conviction was that Bernard of Weimar had no serious designs on Bavaria, but by his puzzling marches and counter-marches merely meant to entice away the bulk of the imperial army, and then to fall suddenly on Bohemia. It was here that he made his fatal error; before there was time to render assistance, Ratisbon had capitulated.

Wallenstein's failure to relieve Ratisbon.

Now came a series of incomprehensible moves, on Wallenstein's part, that roused the impatience at Vienna to fever heat. He had at first written that he would march day and night until he had driven back the Duke of Weimar; in a council of war at Pilsen he had announced his intention of taking one hundred companies of the best cavalry and making an instant start. Then quickly came the news that he had renounced the attempt, and would go into winter quarters where he stood. Whether, as he claimed, his act was due to the impossibility of conducting a successful campaign in the severe weather that had already set in, or whether hatred of Maximilian, or other personal reasons, held him back, can never now be ascertained.   In vain Ferdinand expostulated, and asked in any case to be more frequently consulted, lest it might seem that there was "another king in the land besides himself."   In answer to a distinct command to march against the enemy, or at any rate to leave Bohemia, which was being drained dry by the constant contributions, Wallenstein sent a letter, signed by his chief officers, stating that a winter campaign, or even the taking up of winter quarters in an enemy's country, would mean the ruin of the army.   The great general was growing more and more reckless; when Ferdinand gave some simple orders to Colonel Suys, who was stationed in Austria, Wallenstein countermanded them, and released the inferior officers from the duty of obedience.

Wallenstein turns traitor.

By this time Wallenstein's last friends at Vienna had deserted him; his appeal to the army was savagely criticised, and Maximilian of Bavaria openly urged the emperor no longer to be dependent on the freaks, humors, and passions of such a man.   The most active of his enemies was the Spanish envoy, Oñate, who was embittered by the opposition to the army sent under Feria to guard the way to the Netherlands.

The knowledge that his fall was imminent, the determination not to bear quietly a second dismissal, drove Wallenstein into his last and most desperate courses. Flying messengers were sent to the French and to the Saxons to announce that now the mask would really be laid aside.   With feverish impatience, Wallenstein awaited the coming of Feuquière and Arnim, the two ambassadors on whom he had pinned his faith.   He was never to know that Louis XIII. had taken up his cause with enthusiasm, and had sent him an offer to pay him a million francs yearly, from the moment when he should have struck a blow at one of Ferdinand's provinces. The elector of Saxony took time to consult with George William of Brandenburg, and Arnim, also, arrived too late. As for Bernard of Weimar, who was also approached, he refused still to believe in Wallenstein's sincerity.

Wallenstein, in the meantime, had moved his troops around so as to have in his neighborhood those whom he could most trust. Among the higher officers he was absolutely sure of his field marshal, Illow, and of the generals Kinsky and Terzky, the latter of whom was his brother-in-law. He hoped that many more would hold to him for the sake of their own advantage; no one else was so able as he to assure their back pay, and the return of the large outlays made by them for recruiting purposes. When Illow intentionally spread the report that Wallenstein meant to resign, there was an outbreak of grief and indignation, and he was warmly urged to remain. He declared, apparently reluctantly, that he would do so, if the officers would stand by him so long as he remained in the emperor's service, and not allow him to be put upon or insulted. The next day, on the 12th of January, 1634, at a banquet held at Illow's house, when the wine had passed freely, it was determined that this agreement should be committed to writing and should be signed by those present. Each and all thus pledged themselves to stand by their beloved commander, and to " sacrifice for him the last drop of their blood." But even before the guests departed the omission of the clause "so long as he should remain in the emperor's service," was noticed; contentions arose which led to a wild scene, and windows, chairs, and benches were broken. Terzky is said to have drawn his sword and threatened to cut in pieces any enemy of the generalissimo, whereupon Piccolomini, hitherto

*The banquet at Pilsen.*

Wallenstein's warmest friend, and regarded by him with a
superstitious reverence on account of some secret of his
nativity, cried out in his own vernacular, " O traditore ! "

The extent
of Wallen-
stein's
treason.
Even yet Wallenstein cannot be said to have descended
to the lowest depths of treason.   He was false to his emperor, but not false to his country.   He still kept firmly in
view his cherished project of imposing upon Germany a
wholesome and advantageous peace.   For this he labored
to the last ; for this, in part at least, he had sinned.   Four
days before the banquet at Pilsen he confided his plans to
a Bohemian refugee named Schlieff, who afterward drew
up a protocol of what he had been told.   The French,
although their money would be welcome, were not to be
allowed to cross the Rhine ; they were to be compensated
at the cost of the Spaniards in Italy.   The Swedes were to
be given as little as possible, the Palatinate to be restored
to the family of its former owner.   The chief sufferer was
to be Maximilian of Bavaria, at whose cost a number of
restitutions and rewards were to be granted.

The order
for Wallen-
stein's
arrest.
The news of the happenings at the banquet in Pilsen, removed from the court of Vienna its last doubts and its last
compunctions.   It was determined to watch for the proper
moment for informing the officers and soldiers that they
were released from their obedience to Wallenstein ; as yet
three generals only — Aldringen, Gallas, and Piccolomini
— were taken into the emperor's confidence, and told to seize
the person of their commander-in-chief, if possible, and
bring him to trial.   The greatest secrecy was observed in
the whole matter.   An envoy sent by Aldringen to Vienna
to ask for money to appease the soldiers, and, in general,
for further instructions, did not dare to enter the city, but
transacted his business through Oñate beyond the gates.
After the interview, the Spanish ambassador hurried to
Ferdinand, whom he found already in a state of intense

fear and excitement, and wrested from him an order, which was at once conveyed to Aldringen's messenger, that Wallenstein was to be taken, living or dead. The emperor has been charged with rank deceitfulness for continuing, even after this, to correspond, on apparently friendly terms, with the man whose death-warrant he had already issued. It can only be answered that Wallenstein's conduct was equally underhanded. In his letters to Vienna he wrote of his young master, Ferdinand's son, as his own natural successor, and told how glad he would be to raise him in the saddle and then kiss the stirrup and depart. He called his officers together a second time at Pilsen, declared that his only intention was to bring about the longed-for peace, and once more secured their promise of loyalty, on the express understanding that nothing was to be undertaken against the Emperor's person or power, or against the Roman Catholic religion. A protestation to this same effect was signed by Wallenstein and by thirty of his officers, and sent to Vienna. Yet, at the same time, the Duke of Saxe-Lauenburg, in Wallenstein's name, was urging the emperor's enemy, Bernard of Weimar, to advance his troops to the Bohemia frontier.

On one pretext or another the general-in-chief had assembled all his troops at Prague; he was about to set out from Pilsen to put himself at their head, when the news came that the imperial order deposing him had been made public, and had been generally accepted. With a thousand riders, half of whom left him under way, Wallenstein quickly made for the little fortress of Eger, where was stationed one of Terzky's regiments, under Lieutenant-Colonel Gordon, a Protestant Scotchman, whom he hoped easily to win to his side. The cavalcade was joined under way by Colonel Butler and a regiment of dragoons. Butler, a Catholic Irishman of good family, had already become

Gordon and Butler.

convinced that Wallenstein was a traitor, and now sent word to Piccolomini that though he had joined in the march to Eger, he was one of his Majesty's truest and most upright soldiers. Piccolomini ordered him to capture or to kill Wallenstein, and to return with him to Pilsen. Butler had, in fact, obeyed the command even before the letter reached him.

Wallenstein had tried to win over Gordon and his sergeant Leslie by assuring them that Bernard of Weimar was on the way to his rescue; Illow and Terzky later summoned these two, together with Butler, to Illow's quarters and urged them to declare themselves for Wallenstein. They refused; but the two conspirators, thinking the better to persuade them over their wine, invited themselves to dine the same evening at Gordon's quarters in the castle. They appeared accordingly, with Kinsky and Neumann, the latter Wallenstein's secretary, and sat down to a feast in a niche of the great hall. Healths were drunk to the general-in-chief, and especially to his project of ceasing to be servant and becoming master.

The death of Wallenstein.
But, in the meantime, several officers and a hundred dragoons from Butler's regiment had secretly been admitted to the building. The dessert had just been served when, through two doors, they burst into the banquet room with a cry of "Long live Emperor Ferdinand!" All four of the unfortunate adherents of Wallenstein were struck down in a moment; Illow had just time to cry shame upon Gordon, and to challenge him to single combat.

From the castle the soldiers hurried to Wallenstein's own quarters, where an outdoor stairway led directly to his sleeping apartment. His steward met them at the door, and began to chide them for disturbing his master, but with cries of "rogue," "traitor," and "rebel" they broke down the door. As Wallenstein stood there, in his night clothes, leaning against a table, and saw the halberds pointed against him, he opened his arms wide, and bowed as though to receive the blows. The Irish captain Devereux stabbed him squarely in the breast. The long career was ended that had promised so much, and accomplished so little. His murderers gloried in their deed, which, according to the sentiment of the time, was a just and righteous one. They were richly and publicly rewarded by Ferdinand, who confiscated the immense wealth of Wallenstein, and bestowed it upon his own officers and soldiers. The power that had shaken the throne, and seemed about to transform Germany thus melted into nothingness. The original estates of Friedland were given to General Gallas. In the light of future events, of the unexampled misery and wretchedness to which Germany was still, by fourteen years of the most wasting and demoralizing warfare, to be reduced, one cannot help wishing, that the one man who was capable of making head against greedy and insolent foreigners, had continued to control affairs, even at the cost of the legitimate, but thoroughly incapable, Hapsburg ruler. There are things that are worse for a country than a violent change of government.

After the death of Wallenstein there is little in the purely military events of the Thirty Years' War to interest the modern reader. The young Ferdinand, aided by the Cardinal Infant of Spain, recaptured Ratisbon, and inflicted a decisive defeat on Bernard of Weimar at Nördlingen; indeed, to the outcome of this latter battle it may be ascribed that South Germany was to remain almost exclusively Roman Catholic. "It was so bad it could not have been worse," so Bernard announced his own defeat to the Swedish chancellor. Soon afterward, in 1635, the electors of Saxony and Brandenburg withdrew from the war, and concluded with the emperor the Peace of Prague, by which

*The peace of Prague.*

they were to abandon the Swedish alliance and receive in return some few concessions with regard to the Edict of Restitution. Two years later the votes of these two electors turned the scale in favor of the young Ferdinand as king of the Romans, and the death of the old emperor brought him almost immediately to the imperial throne, as Ferdinand III.

France enters the struggle.

The war by this time had entered into an entirely new phase, for Louis XIII. of France had placed himself at the head of the enemies of the house of Hapsburg. After the battle of Nördlingen, Sweden and the Heilbronn league had been willing to pay Richelieu almost any price for his aid, and had agreed to let him have Alsace in return for 12,000 men and a half a million francs. In May, 1635, France formally declared war against Spain, closed a treaty with the Dutch, who were to attack the Spanish Netherlands, and prepared to throw not 12,000, but 132,000 men into the field. It will be seen how this action changed the fundamental nature of the struggle; the religious question was thrust entirely into the background, for the Catholic king had certainly no desire to see the triumph of Protestant tenets. Both France and Sweden were openly fighting for territory, and the chief occupation of their troops was ravaging and plundering Germany.

Bernard of Weimar.

Bernard of Weimar allowed himself to be regularly taken into the pay of the French king; his reward was to be a yearly salary of two hundred thousand francs, a large pension at the end of the war, and, eventually, the possession of Alsace; in addition his army was to be subsidized, and also an agreement made that, in case of his capture, no peace should ever be signed that did not include his liberation. He was treated, however, as a mere hireling, and his thraldom at last became so irksome that he cast it off. His great achievement was the siege of Breisach, where he reduced the garrison to the necessity of slaughtering children and eating the bodies of the fallen. When the surrender of the town became known, he was hailed as a second Gustavus, and the news of his success infused a different spirit into the whole Protestant-Swedish party. All the greater was the gloom cast by his sudden death, and it was darkly hinted that French poison had been at work.

Although Bernard's death afforded a breathing space to the emperor, it did nothing toward bringing to an end this frightful, universal war. The Swedish general, Banér, had meanwhile wreaked terrible retribution upon Saxony for having concluded the Peace of Prague, and had crowned his work by a victory over the elector at Wittstock; but by the end of the year 1637 he had been forced back on Stettin. By this time Catholics and Protestants alike were urging that a diet be called, to settle the differences at home, and to provide for driving out the foreign enemies. Such a diet — the first that had been held in twenty-seven years — met at Ratisbon in 1640, and the chief subject discussed was that of a general amnesty. But from the first, it was all too plain that the worst enemy of peace was the emperor himself, with his exclusively Austrian and Spanish interests. It was in vain that even Maximilian of Bavaria urged him to change his policy and adopt one more national, more German. During the progress of this diet, and by no mere coincidence, there appeared a writing by one Hippolytus a Lapide (in reality the Swede Chemnitz), which aroused intense excitement, and greatly influenced public opinion. It was entitled *On the State of Things in our Roman-German Empire*, was a study on the ultimate source of the supreme authority, and wound up with the crushing conclusion, that the sway of the Hapsburgs had always proved fatal to the progress

The longing for peace.

of the country ; that no remedy could now avail; that an executioner was needed, not a physician !

Banér's attack on Ratisbon.

For a moment it seemed as though that executioner were at the very gates. Banér was suddenly seized with the idea of descending upon Ratisbon, taking captive the emperor, and putting the diet to flight. He encamped on the opposite side of the Danube, and commenced bombarding the city; he intended on the following day to cross on the ice and complete his hardy undertaking. Even in those days of continual surprises this was a feat to set Europe agog ; but it was one that, unfortunately, Banér was unable to accomplish. In the night there came a heavy thaw, the ice broke up, and the golden opportunity vanished forever. Banér withdrew to Bohemia and thence to Saxony, where he died within four months, in consequence, it is said, of his intemperate habits.

One good result the Diet of Ratisbon did finally accomplish : it was decreed that a congress should assemble at Münster and Osnabrück, and at the same time a deputy diet at Frankfort, to see what could be done in the way of a settlement. It was the first faint glimmering of the dawn of peace, though numberless small battles were first to be fought. Banér's place was taken by Linnard Torstenson, the last good general of the school of Gustavus Adolphus. In the year 1642 he marched from Brunswick to the emperor's hereditary lands, took a number of towns in Bohemia and Moravia, then turned suddenly and, joining with Wrangel and Königsmark, settled down before Leipzig. Here, on the very spot where Gustavus Adolphus had gained his first great victory, eleven years before, the imperial forces were again put to flight; according to the commanders, Piccolomini and Archduke Leopold, the whole fault lay with Colonel Mandlot's regiment, which had been the first to run. Mandlot himself,

Torstenson's campaign.

accordingly, and all the superior officers were beheaded; while of the subalterns and common soldiers every tenth man was hung to a tree by the roadside.

The outcome of this second battle of Breitenfeld placed Leipzig at the mercy of Torstenson; but, as imperial reën-forcements arrived, he retired once more to Bohemia, followed by General Gallas, to whom the emperor had given the chief command. The entry of Denmark into the struggle in September, 1643, gave a new direction to events; Torstenson, bidden by the Swedish government to march against the Danes in Schleswig Holstein, cleared that whole province of the enemy, and advanced to the borders of Jutland; while Gallas, sent by the emperor to the aid of the Danish king, appeared in Holstein in the following year.

Of all the disastrous undertakings of this whole period, this campaign of Gallas was about the worst. He had started out with some eighteen or twenty thousand men, but, chiefly, through his own carelessness and hesitancy, — which can only be accounted for by accepting the report that he was daily intoxicated, — he lost all but two thousand, as many falling on the march as in the engagements at Magdeburg and Jüterbog. The remnant turned up finally in Bohemia, where they joined a new army which had been raised by the emperor's own personal efforts, and placed under the command of Hatzfeld. Torstenson defeated Hatzfeld in the fierce battle of Jankau, and Ferdinand III.'s very throne seemed in jeopardy. By the end of the year 1645, Wrangel, Torstenson's successor, had in his hands the whole of northern Bohemia and a chain of fortified places extending as far as the Danube.

During all this time, French armies had been fighting with equal zeal, but with varied success, on the Rhine and Neckar, as well as in the Spanish Netherlands, where they had gained the truly magnificent victory of Rocroi. They

Shifting alliances.

had been defeated at Tuttlingen and Freiburg, had then
made extensive conquests, such as Spires, Mainz, and
Worms, only to receive a crushing defeat at Mergentheim
in the spring of 1645, when Mercy and John of Werth
practically annihilated the infantry of Turenne. A few
months later the blow was returned at Allerheim, in the
immediate neighborhood of Nördlingen, where Mercy fell,
vainly trying to retrieve the lost day.

Apart from the military events, this last period of the
Thirty Years' War is remarkable for the frequent and
sudden changes of allegiance on the part of almost all the
powers concerned in the struggle. Only France, Austria,
and Sweden stood consistently to their colors; Denmark and
Transylvania proved but fitful participants; Spain, weakened by internal troubles and by the loss of her fleet in
Dutch waters, could render little aid in Germany, the new
elector of Brandenburg, Frederick William, who came to
the throne in 1640, made a truce with the Swedes, and
allowed them free passage through his lands; the Duke of
Würtemberg was a secret friend of the French, and accepted a pension from them, while the Saxon elector entered
into a strange agreement with the Swedes, by which he gave
up Leipzig and Torgau, but was allowed to send regiments
to the emperor's aid.

The cam-
paign
against
Maximilian
of Bavaria.
It remained to be seen what test the loyalty of Maximilian of Bavaria would withstand, and on him, now,
French and Swedes alike turned and concentrated their
attention. Wrangel, Torstenson's successor, had marched
from Bohemia to Thuringia, thence north to the Weser,
where he had taken Höxter and Paderborn; he now united
at Fritzlar with Turenne, and together they started off by
the most direct road for Maximilian's dominions. They
took Donauwörth, but were forced to retire from Augsburg,
returning, however, on a plundering and ravaging expedi-

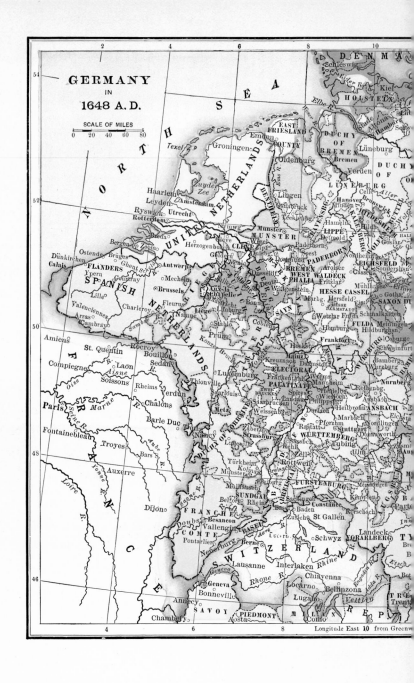

GERMANY
IN
1648 A.D.

SCALE OF MILES

0   20   40   60   80

NORTH SEA

DENMARK

Schleswig

HOLSTEIN

Kiel

Hamburg

DUCHY OF BREMEN

Lüneburg

Verden

Bremen

DUCHY OF LÜNEBURG

Celle

Hanover

Minden

Brunswick

HILDESHEIM

Goslar

EAST FRIESLAND COUNTY

Emden

Oldenburg

Lingen

Osnabrück

RAVENSBR.

Hamelin

Texel

Groningen

Zuyder Zee

Haarlem
Leyden
Utrecht
Ryswick
Rotterdam

Amsterdam

UNITED NETHERLANDS

Bergen op Zoom

Breda

Herzogenbusch

Cleve
Wesel

MUNSTER
Münster

Lippe

Soest

Paderborn

Dortmund

PADERBORN

Arolsen

WALDECK

Cassel

EICHSFELD

Erfurt

Gotha

SAXON DU.

Dünkirchen
Calais
Ostende
Bruges
Ghent
Antwerp
Mechlin

FLANDERS
Ypren
Courtray
Lille

SPANISH
Brussels
Fleurus

NETHERLANDS

Valenciennes
Charleroy
Arras
Cambray

Charleroy
Namur
Liège

Aix-la-Chapelle
Bonn

CLEVE

Düsseldorf
Duisbg.

BERG

SAYN

BREMEN
WEST PHALIA

HESSE CASSEL

Marbg. Hersfeld

FULDA
Fritzlar

Schmalkalden

Coblentz

Wetzlar
Homburg

Hildburghsn.

Amiens

St. Quentin

Laon

Soissons

Rocroy
Bouillon
Sedan

Luxemburg

Prüm

Frankfort

Höchst

Mainz

ELECTORAL
PALATINATE

Bamberg
Würzburg

Nürnberg

Compiegne

Rheims

Verdun

Metz

Thionville

Saarlouis

Saarbrucken

Kreuznach

Frankenthal
ZWEI
BRUCKEN
Landau

Darmstadt

Worms

Mannheim
Heidelbg.
Wiesloch
Philippsbg.
Speire

Rothenbg.

Augsburg

ANSBACH

Nördlingen

Paris

Chalons

Verdun

Weissenbg.

Heilbronn

Durlach

Rastatt

Pforzhm.

Marbach

Stuttgart

WÜRTEMBERG

Donauwörth

Eichstet

Bar le Duc

Nancy

DUCHY OF LORRAINE

Zabern

Strassburg

Kehl

Sasbch.

Tübingen

Ulm

Fontainebleau

Troyes

Auxerre

Bar s.

Türkheim
Kolmar
Münster

Lützelstein

Schlettstadt

Breisach

Freiburg

Rottweil

Zell

FURSTENBURG

Memmingen

Kempten

Dijon

SUNDGAU
Belfort
Rheinf.

Mühlhausen

Säckingen

Basel

Constance

BADEN

St. Gallen

Rorschach

Landeck

VARLBERG

FRANCHE
Besançon
Vallengin
COMTE
Pontarlier

Neuburg

BASEL

Zürich

Baden

Lucern

Schwyz

TYROL

Doubs R.

Berne

Berne

SWITZERLAND

Rhine R.

Neuenburg

Lausanne

Interlaken

Chiavenna

Geneva

Rhone R.

Locarno

Bellinzona

Veltlin

Annecy

Geneva

Bonneville

SAVOY

Chambery

Lugano

PIEDMONT

Aosta

MILAN
REP.

Trent

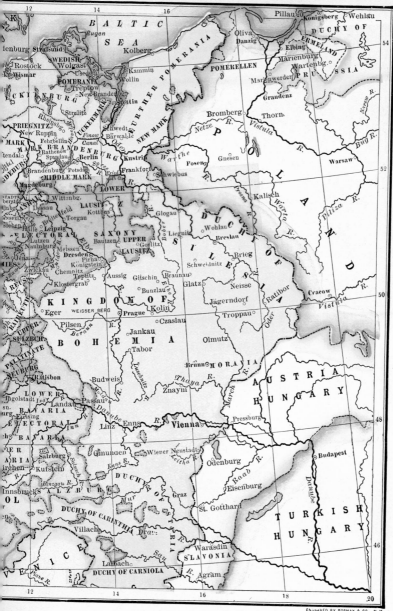

BALTIC
SEA

Rugen

Pillau Königsberg Wehlau
Oliva
Danzig
Elbing
Mårienburg
Marienwerder
DUCHY OF
ERMELAND

PRU
SS
IA

lenburg Stralsund
Rostock
Wismar
SWEDISH
Wolgast
POMERANIA
Treptow
New Brandenb
Stettin
Kolberg

Usedom
Kammin
Wollin

POMERELLEN

FURTHER POMERANIA

Graudenz
Thorn

Strelitz

UCKERMERK
Schwedt
Bärwalde

NEW MARK

Bromberg

Netze R.
Vistula R.

Rheinsberg

PRIEGNITZ
New Ruppin
Fehrbellin
MARK
BRANDENBURG
Berlin
Kustrin
Frankfort
Schwiebus

Finow Canal
Oder

Warthe

Gnesen
Posen

P O L A N D

Warsaw

MARK
MIDDLE MARK
Magdeburg
Spandau
Rathenow
Potsdam
Brandenburg
LOWER
Wittenbg.
LAUSITZ
Kottbus
Torgau
SAXONY
UPPER
LAUSITZ

Schlesien
Spree
Eide

Wörta R.
Prosna R.
Pilita R.
Kalisch

Glogau
Wohlau
Breslau
DUCHY OF
SILESIA

Dessau
Leipzig
ELECTORAL
Lutzen
Naumburg
Meissen
Dresden
Pirna
Königstein
Bautzen
Görlitz

Bober R.
Liegnitz
Schweidnitz
Brieg
Neisse

Cracow

Chemnitz
Teplitz
Zwickau
Klostergrab

Aussig
Gitschin
Braunau
Glatz
Jägerndorf
Ratibor

Oder R.
Vistula R.

Eger
WEISSER BERG
Prague
Kolin
Czaslau
Jankau
Tabor

KINGDOM OF
BOHEMIA

Pilsen
Beraun R.

Olmutz

Troppau
MORAVIA
Brünn

AUSTRIA
HUNGARY

UPPER
SULZBCH
PALATINATE
NEUBG
Ratisbon
Budweis
Znaym
Thaya R.
March R.

LOWER
BAVARIA
Landau
Passau
Danube R.
Linz
Enns
Vienna
Pressburg

Ingolstadt
Ensing
ELECTORAL
BAVARIA

Isar R.
Inn R.

Salzburg
Kufstein
Gmunden
Wiener Neustadt
Odenburg
Budapest

Innsbruck
SALZBURG
DUCHY OF
Graz
Raab R.
Eisenburg
Danube R.

DUCHY OF CARINTHIA
Villach
Drau R.
St. Gotthard

TURKISH
HUNGARY

VENICE
Laibach
Warasdin
SLAVONIA
Agram
DUCHY OF CARNIOLA

ENGRAVED BY BORMAY & CO., N. Y.

tion, that brought them to the gates of Munich. Almost all Bavaria was in their hands, and in January, 1647, they took Bregenz, whither all the treasure and supplies from the rich Swabian monasteries had been brought together for safe keeping. Maximilian, for the moment, was in despair; he had long been listening to tempting offers from France, and he now signed a treaty by which the enemy was to vacate Bavaria in return for some Swabian fortresses. In vain had the emperor tried to deter him from this step; the elector showed that he meant his defection seriously, and when John of Werth tried to hurry with the remnants of the Bavarian army to the emperor's side, Maximilian declared him an outlaw. After a few months, however, Maximilian found that the new alliance did not bring him the peace and quiet for which he longed. The aging prince, who, directly and indirectly, had been the cause of so much evil, was under the ban of a bitter retribution from which there was no escape. The renewal of his allegiance to the emperor brought down upon him, in 1648, a fresh attack of the Swedes and French. It came to a sharp battle at Zusmarshausen, where the imperialists and Bavarians lost two thousand men, and the strong-box as well, that contained all the pay for their troops. Completely *hors de combat*, the imperial general, Gronsfeld, withdrew to the extreme eastern boundary of Bavaria, and Maximilian fled to Salzburg. The enemy rioted at will in his cities, villages, and castles, until at last, in the summer, John of Werth and Piccolomini appeared with a new army and drove them from the Inn to the Isar, eventually compelling them to cross the Lech.

Ferdinand's spirit by this time was almost broken. During the long negotiations at Münster and Osnabrück, his ambassador, Trautmannsdorf, had stood out bravely for what he deemed his master's rights. The events of the

The end of military operations.

war had changed his policy from time to time, and had greatly delayed the work of peace. But of late the defeats had been growing too frequent, and now a Swedish army under Charles Gustavus of Pfalz Zwiebrücken, the new generalissimo and future king of Sweden, stood at the gates of Prague. The Hradschin and the whole quarter surrounding it had been taken, and the immeasurably rich art collections carried away; but, in consequence of the stubborn resistance of the city proper, a temporary truce had been signed. At this juncture the news came that the last signature had been affixed to the treaty of peace; the war ceased where it had begun, under the walls of Prague, after having made the rounds of Europe.

The settlement of boundaries at Münster.

The double assembly that sat from 1644 to 1648 — the Catholic powers at Münster, the Protestant at Osnabrück — brought forth finally an instrument of peace, which deservedly ranks as a landmark in European history. It shows the end of one whole era and the beginning of modern times. It settled three questions of cardinal importance : What were to be the future boundaries of the continental states? What balance could be struck between two faiths that had hitherto fought each other to the knife? and, lastly, What was to be the future of Germany?—Was an emperor to be able to inflict upon it again such miseries as it had just been through?

The boundary problem was solved by giving to Sweden, besides an indemnity, the bishoprics of Bremen and Verden and the half of Pomerania, includings a trip on the eastern bank of the Oder, which placed the control of that stream and of all the bays and islands at its mouth, in Swedish hands. France's share was — in addition to Metz, Toul, and Verdun, which she had practically owned since 1552 — Alsace with Breisach, the Sundgau, and the right of garrisoning Philipsburg. The Rhine was thus the new boundary from the Palatinate south to Switzerland. The religious differences were settled on the basis of the Peace of Augsburg, each ruler enjoying "autonomy," being allowed, that is, to decide for himself what form of faith his subjects should follow. Germany was to continue nominally an empire, within which, however, each state was to enjoy the utmost possible degree of independence.

But what bald statement of results can possibly convey an idea of the stirring issues that were joined, and the diplomatic victories that were won and lost at Münster and Osnabrück? Ten whole months were spent in settling preliminary questions alone: such as, what powers should be admitted to the Congress; what matters should be treated; whether the papers and authorizations of individual members were in order; and what should be the rules of precedence.

The emperor had fought hard to have the empire represented at the Congress as a unit, and also to have matters which pertained solely to the internal welfare of Germany reserved for a German diet. But the Hapsburg character was too well known, and German diets, in which Catholics were apt to predominate, had hitherto been none too successful in settling religious differences. It is perfectly true, this calling in of foreign powers to sit as judges between the throne and its princes, was a humiliation such as no other of the great powers of Europe had ever been under the necessity of enduring. It was to avoid such a contingency that Henry IV. had dragged himself up the frosty slope of Canossa, and had stood barefooted, like a beggar, before Gregory VII. But now there was no remedy. Wallenstein might have helped matters; Ferdinand III. could not. By the will of Sweden and France, accordingly, each petty state was instructed to send its own ambassadors; therewith Germany's fate was sealed. The different

*The triumph of the petty states.*

principalities and little republics, the number of which reached to nearly three hundred, claimed, and obtained for themselves, the right to coin money, raise armies, and close alliances, besides the privilege of being consulted in matters of general government. Without their consent, the emperor might not declare war nor make peace, nor even order the building of a fortress, save on his own lands.

Etiquette.

Questions of etiquette played a great part in the Congress and led to interminable disputes, nor, absurd as they seem now, were they then without real significance. It was but one step from denying a man his due equality, to turning a deaf ear to his just demands. Disputes as to first visits, seats in the hall of assembly, titles and other marks of distinction, all received the most serious consideration. The papal nuncio demanded the loftiest place of all, nor would the imperial envoy sit on a level with the ambassador of France. The latter again was obliged to yield to the Venetian representative, who insisted, when leaving him after a visit, on being accompanied the whole way to his carriage, and not merely halfway down the path. No sooner had this weighty matter been decided in favor of Venice, than the Netherlands put in a similar claim. The right to be called "your Excellency" was urged and disputed at infinite lengths by this and that envoy. On certain such matters the French and the Spaniards failed to come to any other agreement than that, with their whole suites, they should avoid each other on every public occasion.

Close bargaining.

The difficulties as to these mere questions of form were but the mildest prelude to the haggling and bargaining, the recriminations and obstructions, when it came to active business. Each of the powers concerned had placed its demands many times higher than there was any possibility of realizing. Many months passed while Sweden was being screwed down from her ruinous demand of a twenty million indemnity to an ultimate five million. Originally, too, she had claimed for her queen a vote in the German college of electors, and the possession of all Silesia, the apple of Ferdinand's eye. The emperor, on the other hand, had done everything to save the fortress of Breisach from falling into the clutches of France. He had even suggested levelling it to the ground. But Mazarin was inexorable; not in vain had he bribed the greater number of the German princes. Nor could Ferdinand himself now afford to relinquish the proffer of the French cardinal's good offices in paring down the demands of Sweden.

Of all the clauses of the peace, none was more ambiguous than the one relating to the French frontier. The nature of the rights to be enjoyed over Alsace, and especially over the ten free cities of the empire that lay within that province, were couched in such ambiguous terms, and hedged in by so many restrictive and mutually negatory clauses, that either party might consider itself the actual possessor. Full sovereignty was to be granted to France, *saving the allegiance due to the empire!* It is believed now that this vagueness was in part intentional; though few could have dreamed of the evils that were to arise in the next half century, when a French king, with very decided views as to the benefits of absolute ownership, was to take the matter in hand. *The French frontier.*

As might have been expected, the hardest questions of all to settle, proved to be those concerning religious toleration, and the restoration of lands appropriated by the one church or the other. Around the old provision known as the *reservatum ecclesiasticum* a whole diplomatic battle was waged; it was finally decided to retain the measure, but to make it as applicable to Protestants who turned Catholic as it was the other way. In any case, the convert to the other faith must renounce his former holding. Long did *The Bohemian exiles.*

Sweden and the German Protestants hold out for a return to the state of things that had existed at the very beginning of the war. The Swedish government had practically pledged itself to restore their lands to the thousands of Bohemian refugees who had done good service in its ranks; but here the emperor remained firm — his minister Trautmannsdorf, who was acting in his name, declared that not even the miseries of a Stockholm prison could reduce him to consider such a proposal. Nor would it have been possible, with the best of wills, to reverse all that had been done in these thirty years. The most that Ferdinand would grant for Bohemia was, that those who had been driven out since 1630 might have their lands restored.

Important measures.

For the empire at large it proved an even more difficult question to fix upon this so-called normal year whereby to test the title to property. Back of the Edict of Restitution the emperor was willing to go, but not back of that arrangement by which the upper Palatinate had been given to Maximilian of Bavaria. That would have brought Ferdinand once more to the condition of owing Maximilian the immense debt for which his father had pledged his Austrian possessions. By way of a compromise the year 1624 was finally chosen. The question of providing for the heirs of the Winter King, was solved by giving the lower or Rhine Palatinate to the young Charles Louis, for whose benefit an eighth electorate was then created, the arrangement to lapse with the extinction of either line.

Toward the end of the term of session, as the emperor, in consequence of his severe defeats, grew more and more pliant, a number of important measures were rushed through the congress without delay. The elector of Brandenburg was the successful promoter of a plan for placing Calvinists, once and for all, on the same plane as the orthodox Lutherans; and he gained his point, even though Saxony, self-centred and bigoted to the last, bitterly opposed the measure.

Altogether, the sentiment had gained ground that there must be mutual toleration in every way. Though the rulers might choose the form of faith, they were bound to give dissenters a period of th ee years in which to dispose of their property before emigrating, and they were compelled to exercise consideration in many ways even for those who remained. In Bohemia, Moravia, and Austria, indeed, Ferdinand made no lasting concessions. He felt, and perhaps rightly, that Protestant communities would always side with his own enemies, and he was determined not to have them in his neighborhood. In Silesia he gave permission to build Protestant churches in certain specified towns. *Mutual toleration in religious matters.*

Before the congress separated it gave its sanction to some important political changes that had long been accomplished facts, such as the independence of Switzerland and the Netherlands, and then struck a decided blow at the prestige of the Roman church. Although the extreme Catholic party was furious at the concessions to the Protestants, and Pope Innocent X. questioned the right of founding an eighth electorate without his sanction, the instrument of peace declared expressly that no contradiction on the part of the church or of any secular power should interfere with its validity. The Pope accordingly condemned the Peace of Westphalia, as a predecessor had once condemned the Magna Charta. *Papal condemnation of the peace.*

With the signing of the great treaty on the 24th of October, 1648, the long reign of terror in Germany was brought to a close. No wonder the jubilations knew no end; no wonder that the poets of the time broke into song like so many liberated birds. Paul Gerhard, the best of them all, gives fervent thanks to God that the noble word of peace and joy has sounded, and that the murderous spear and *Ruin and demoralization caused by the war.*

sword are to rest unwielded; but he cannot forget his country's ruined castles, her cities heaped with foul rubbish, her fields that are like tangled thickets, her graves so full of heroes. And, indeed, over large portions of the land there hung the desolation of the Dead Sea. It has been proved that many of the countless details of horror that have come down to us are exaggerated, are tinged with a melancholy desire to make things seem worse than they actually were. But even the most sober statistics show that men and women were reduced to the state of the lowest animals, that cannibalism was rife in various quarters, that morality was an unknown quantity. What better evidence of the utter lawlessness of the soldiery can be wanted than the famous order of General Banèr to his officers to treat the nobles, burgomasters, and other notables (from whose forced contributions he hoped to grow rich) with kicks and blows and insults of all kinds, "like dogs, slaves, and serfs!" Recruiting for the army had become the merest mercenary speculation; robbers and criminals of all kinds had flocked to the camps, where alone in the whole length and breadth of the wretched land a semblance of plenty could be found. Here, after a victory, soldiers could have been seen strutting about in gaudy clothes that had been found among the booty, or revelling with the bestial crowd of camp-followers. Toward the end of the war the proportion of these had assumed truly hideous dimensions, at the battle of Zusmarshausen, in 1648, there were present on the side of the emperor thirty-four thousand combatants and one hundred and twenty-seven thousand women, children, and useless men!

Evil results of the war. The loss of life, due directly to the war, has been placed by the lowest estimate at one-third of the whole population; some districts were turned into such total deserts that the most heroic means had to be taken to repeople them. A local diet in Franconia gave permission for every man to have two wives, and forbade any one under sixty to become a monk. A blow was struck at various industries from which they did not recover for a whole century. The grand old Hansa came to its death in these days ; the exports of Danzig amounted, in 1619, to over a hundred thousand tons, in 1659, to a little more than five hundred. Had the potato not come into use at this time as an article of food, the general misery would doubtless have been even greater. The demoralization of the people at large is shown in various ways, in the decline of art, of literature, and of learning, but above all in the senseless aping of the foreigner. Each little court tried to copy Versailles, and spent the money that should have gone to healing the wounds of war, in senseless luxury ; the language becomes almost another tongue, so interlarded is it with French phrases ; questions of etiquette now regularly play a prominent part in the discussions of the diets. Shall the ordinary princes sit on red or, like the electors, on green chairs ? Shall their lackeys wear gold or silver lace? Shall their wives be asked to take a *fauteuil* or merely a *tabouret?* At a great festival held at Nuremberg in 1650, to celebrate the progress of the measures for carrying out the different agreements, it was five hours after dinner was announced before the unfortunate guests could be seated in the proper order.

Then, indeed, at this historic feast, be it said to their credit, they thoroughly enjoyed themselves. Piccolomini, who had previously been serenaded at his house by fifteen hundred boys on hobby horses, was one of the most prominent men present ; but Wrangel was also there, and many of the generals had stood over against each other in the field. Like young schoolboys, they engaged once more in a rollicking game of war, chased each other round the table, and then perambulated the town, until their colonel laughingly dismissed them, with the reminder that peace had been declared.

*Childlike rejoicings.*

# CHRONOLOGICAL TABLE[1]

| A.D. | | PAGE |
|------|---|------|
| 9 | The battle in the Teutoburg Forest. | 4 |
| 375–568 | The wandering of the nations. | 11–13 |
| 481–511 | *Clovis, the Merovingian:* founds the Frankish kingdom by conquering Syagrius (486), the Allemanni (496), the Visigoths (507). Is converted to Christianity (496). His sons conquer the Burgundians, Thuringians, Allemanni, and Bavarians. | 13–16 |
| 481–752 | Civilization of Merovingian times. | 16–21 |
| 687 | *Pepin of Heristal:* by the battle of Testry, unifies the Frankish kingdom. | 22 |
| 715–741 | *Charles Martel:* administers the Frankish kingdom, furthers the feudal system, protects St. Boniface, and (732) turns back the Arabs. | 23–25 |
| 741–768 | *Pepin the Short:* assumes the royal crown (752), wars with the Lombards, makes gift of Pentapolis to the Papacy. | 25–26 |
| 768–814 | *Charles the Great:* conquers Lombards, Bavarians, Saxons (772–803), Avars; is friendly with Popes Adrian I. and Leo III.; is crowned emperor by Leo III. (800); organizes the administration; encourages learning and art. | 26–38 |
| 814–840 | *Louis the Pious:* divides the empire (817); seeks to appanage Charles the Bald; wars with his sons; does penance at Soissons. | 38–40 |
| 840–843 | Sons of Louis the Pious at war; coming of the Northmen; Treaty of Verdun (843) between Louis the German (d. 876), Charles the Bald (d. 877), and Lothar (d. 855). | 40–44 |

[1] This table contains some facts that are not in the text.

A.D.                                                                PAGE

855–888        *End of the Carolingian Empire:* Lothar II.
               (d. 869); Treaty of Mersen (870); deposition of
               Charles the Fat (888).                              44–45

887–899        *Arnulf of Carinthia,* king of Germany: con-
               quers the Northmen (891).                           45

899–911        *Louis the Child:* formation of stem-duchies;
               civilization in the monasteries.                    45–48

911–918        *Conrad of Franconia.*                              49

919–1024       SAXON KINGS AND EMPERORS.                           49–75

919–936        *Henry I.:* conciliates the heads of the duchies;
               makes military reforms; conquers the Hunga-
               rians (933).                                        49

936–973        *Otto I., the Great:* treatment of clergy; impe-
               rial coronation (962); dealings with the popes.     49–53

973–983        *Otto II.*                                          53

983–1002       *Otto III.*                                         53–54

1002–1024      *Henry II., the Saint.*                             54

1024–1125      THE SALIAN EMPERORS.                                54–75

1024–1039      *Conrad II.* (Burgundy joined to the Empire,
               1032–1034).                                         54

1039–1056      *Henry III., the Black:* holds council at Sutri
               (1046) and deposes three popes. Leo IX., Pope
               from 1048–1054, strengthens and reforms the
               Papacy.                                             54–58

1056–1106      *Henry IV.:* decree of Pope Nicholas II. regard-
               ing papal elections (1059); abduction of Henry
               in Kaiserswerth by Anno of Cologne (1062); the
               Normans as allies of the Papacy; rebellion in
               Saxony (1073–1075); Pope Gregory VII. (1073–
               1085); deposition of Gregory (1076); penance
               in Canossa (1077); Rudolph of Swabia, anti-
               king (1077–1081); Herman of Luxemburg, anti-
               king (1081); Henry crowned emperor by
               Clement III. (1084); Henry in Italy (1090–
               1097); Pope Urban II. preaches crusade (1096);
               Conquest of Jerusalem (1099).                       58–71

1106–1125      *Henry V.:* crowned emperor by Paschal II.
               (1111), who is forced to confirm the right of in-
               vestiture; attempt to end the struggle at Council
               of Rheims (1119); Concordat of Worms (1122).        71–75

A.D.                                                                    PAGE

1125–1137    *Lothar of Saxony:* crowned emperor by Innocent II. (1133); gives the North Mark to Albert
the Bear (1134); Bernard of Clairvaux and
Norbert founds the Cistercian order.                    76–77

1138–1254    THE HOHENSTAUFEN KINGS AND EMPERORS.       77–121

1138–1152    *Conrad III.:* struggle with the Guelphs;
Henry the Lion gives up Bavaria and receives
Saxony, but (1156) receives back Bavaria minus
the East Mark, which becomes the duchy of
Austria; Conrad's crusade (1147–1149).                  77–78

1152–1190    *Frederick Barbarossa:* crowned emperor by
Adrian IV. (1155); subdues northern Italy
(1158–1162); Pope Alexander III. (1159–1181);
Frederick's triumph over the Pope spoilt by pestilence in Rome (1167); defeat at Legnano, at
the hands of the Milanese (1176); Peace of
Venice (1177) with Alexander III.; fall of
Henry the Lion and subdivision of the duchy
of Saxony (1180); Bavaria comes to the Wittelsbachs (1180), but Styria is joined to Austria;
Peace of Constance (1183) with the Lombard
cities; great Diet at Mainz (1184); marriage
of Henry VI. with Constance of Naples and
Sicily (1186); crusade of Frederick (1189–
1190).                                                  78–90

1190–1197    *Henry VI.:* crowned emperor (1191); holds
Richard of England captive (1192–1194); con-
quers Naples and Sicily (1194).                         90–92

1198         Double election (Philip of Swabia and
Otto IV.).                                              92

1198–1208    *Philip of Swabia:* murdered by Otto of Wittelsbach.                                               92

1198–1215    *Otto IV.:* crowned emperor (1209) by Innocent III. (1198–1216); under the ban (1211);
conquered by Philip Augustus of France at
Bouvines (1214); died (1218).                           92–93

1215–1250    *Frederick II.:* founding of the Franciscan
and Dominican orders (1216–1223); Frederick       93
crowned emperor (1220); goes on crusade
(1228–1229); the Sachsenspiegel (c. 1230); con-

A.D.                                                                    PAGE

quest of Prussia by the Teutonic Order (1231–
1283); killing of Conrad of Marburg (1233);
Frederick at war with the popes and the Lom-
bard cities (1237–1250); defeat of the Mongols
at Liegnitz (1241); Council of Lyons (1245) —
Frederick deposed by Innocent IV.; death of
Henry Raspe, anti-king (1247); William of
Holland, anti-king (1247–1256).                          93–100

1250–1254    *Conrad IV.:* Rhine Confederation (1254).

1254–1273    *Interregnum:* Double election, Richard of
Cornwall and Alfonso of Castile (1257); Charles
of Anjou conquers Naples (1266); defeat of
Conradin at Tagliacozzo (1268).                         100–101

1100–1300    *Age of Chivalry:* influence of crusades; increase in power of the church; the Inquisition
in Germany; duties, ideals, and training of a
knight; the tournament; trial by combat; de-
votion to woman, decline of knighthood.                 102–121

1273–1437    KINGS FROM DIFFERENT HOUSES.

1273–1291    *Rudolph of Hapsburg:* battle of Dornkrut
against Ottocar of Bohemia (1278); investiture
of Hapsburgs with Austrian lands (1282); end
of Christian rule in the Orient (1291); false
Fredericks.                                             122–126

1291–1298    *Adolphus of Nassau:* battle of Göllheim
(1298).                                                 126

1298–1308    *Albert of Austria:* dealings with the electors;
Pope Boniface VIII. (1294–1303); Pope Clem-
ent V. (1305–1314); Albert murdered by John
the Parricide (1308); Babylonian captivity of
the Papacy in Avignon (1305–1376).                      126–133

1308–1313    *Henry VII., of Luxemburg:* unsuccessful interference in Italy; crowned emperor in Rome
(1312).                                                 127–129

1314         Double election (Louis IV., the Bavarian,     and
and Frederick III., the Fair, of Austria).             133–134

1314–1347    *Louis IV., the Bavarian:* struggle with Pope
John XXII. (1316–1334); the *Defensor Pacis* of
Marsilius of Padua (1323); Brandenburg falls
to the Wittelsbachs (1323); crowned emperor

A.D.                                                                    PAGE

in Rome (1328); Pope Benedict XII. (1334–
1342); assembly of electors at Rense (1338);
the Tyrol won for Bavaria by marriage of
young Louis with Margaret Maultasch (1342);
Pope Clement VI. (1342–1352).                          134–145

1314–1330    *Frederick the Fair:* the Swiss defeat Leopold of Austria at Morgarten (1315); Frederick
defeated and taken prisoner at Mühldorf (1322).   134–138

1346–1378    *Charles IV.:* chosen in opposition to Louis
the Bavarian; struggle with the Wittelsbachs
on account of Brandenburg; founding of the
University of Prague (1348); the Black Death
(1348); persecution of the Jews; Günther of
Schwarzburg as anti-king (1349); imperial coronation in Rome by papal legates (1355); the
Golden Bull (1356); crowned king of Burgundy
at Arles (1365); founding of the University of
Vienna by Duke Rudolph IV. (1365); second
Italian expedition (1367–1369); Charles acquires
Brandenburg (1373); election of Wenceslaus as
king of the Romans (1376); founding of the
Swabian League of cities (1376); outbreak of
the great schism in the church (1378), Urban VI.
in Rome, Clement VII. in Avignon.                     146–164

1378–1410    *Wenceslaus:* battle of Sempach (1386); Sigismund, brother of Wenceslaus, becomes king
of Hungary (1387); deposition of Wenceslaus
(1400).                                                               164–166

1400–1410    *Rupert of the Palatinate:* campaign against
Milan (1401–1402); Council of Pisa (1409) de-
poses Benedict XIII. and Gregory XII., elects
Alexander V.; founding of the University of        166–167
Leipzig, after defection from Prague (1409);          and
battle of Tannenberg between Teutonic Order      205–206
and Poland (1410); three emperors.

1410–1437    *Sigismund* (also king of Hungary): the Holy
Veme; the Teutonic Order, its development and
decline; battle of Tannenberg (1410); civic
life; Hanseatic League; Brandenburg given
to Frederick of Hohenzollern (1415); Council

A.D.                                                              PAGE

of Constance (1414–1418); deposition of Pope
John XXIII. (1415); burning of John Huss
(1415); election of Pope Martin V. (1417);
Hussite war (1420–1431); battle of Tauss (1431);
Saxony given to the House of Wettin (1423);
Council of Basel (1431–1449); the Prague
Compactates (1433); Sigismund's coronation
as emperor (1433); battle of Lipan (1434);
Sigismund recognized as King of Bohemia
(1436); Pope Eugenius IV. (1441–1447) trans-
fers Council of Basel to Ferrara (1437).          167–221

1438–1740     THE EMPERORS OF THE HOUSE OF HAPS-
              BURG.

1438–1439     *Albert II.*

1440–1493     *Frederick III.:* Concordat of Vienna with
              Pope Nicholas V. (1448); invention of printing,
              by John Gutenberg; Frederick crowned em-
              peror (1452); conquest of Constantinople by
              the Turks (1453); Austria becomes an arch-
              duchy (1453); Pope Pius II. (Æneas Sylvius)
              (1458–1464); Matthias Corvinus, king of Hun-
              gary (1458–1490); Peace of Thorn (1466);
              Teutonic Order in bondage to Poland, West
              Prussia a part of Poland; Charles the Bold, of
              Burgundy, fights battles of Granson, Murten,
              and Nancy (1476–1477); Maximilian of Austria
              weds Mary of Burgundy (1477); death of Mary
              of Burgundy (1482); birth of Luther (1483);
              division of Saxony between the Ernestine and
              Albertine lines (1485); election of Maximil-
              ian as emperor of the Romans (1486); division
              of the Hohenzollerns into the Brandenburg
              and the Franconian lines (1486); elector Fred-
              erick the Wise of Saxony (1486–1525); Bohemia
              and Hungary have the same king — Vladislav
              (1490); heritage treaty with Austria (1491);
              discovery of America (1492).                221–227

1493–1519     *Maximilian I.:* Würtemberg becomes a duchy
              (1495); Diet of Worms (1495) establishes per-
              petual peace, imperial Chamber Court and "com-

mon penny "; wars of Maximilian in Italy and
against France (1496–1517); marriage of Philip,
Maximilian's son, with Joanna of Spain (1496);
Maximilian's war with the Swiss cantons (1499);
Diet of Augsburg establishes *Reichsregiment*
(1500); Maximilian takes title of "Roman emperor elect" (1508); Erasmus, *Praise of Folly*
(1509); Reuchlin's feud with the Dominicans of
Cologne (1510); Pope Leo X. (1513–1521); Francis I. of France conquers Milan by the battle
of Marignano (1515); the *Epistolæ Virorum Obscurorum* (1515); Luther posts his theses (1517);
Philip of Hesse (1518–1567); Luther's hearing
at Augsburg (1518); Duke Ulrich of Würtemberg driven out by the Swabian League (1519);
disputation at Leipzig (1519); German life on
the eve of the Reformation.                         227–263

1519–1558   *Charles V.:* Luther's three great writings;
the burning of the papal bull (1520); the Diet
of Worms condemns Luther (1521); war against
Francis I. (1521–1525); Francis taken prisoner
at Pavia (1525); Peace of Madrid (1526); death
of Sickingen and of Hutten (1523); Pope Clement VII. (1523–1534); the Peasants' War (1525);
John, elector of Saxony (1525–1532); Prussia
becomes a secular duchy under Albert of Brandenburg (1525); Torgau League (1526); first
Diet of Spires (1526); Ferdinand, brother of
Charles V., becomes king of Hungary after the
battle of Mohacs, in which Louis of Hungary
falls (1527); war with Francis I., which ends
with the Peace of Cambray (1527–1529); sack
of Rome by imperial troops (1527); second
Diet of Spires, the Protestants (1529); Disputation of Marburg (1529); Vienna besieged by
the Turks (1530); Augsburg Confession (1530);
Ferdinand elected king of the Romans (1531);
founding of the Smalkald League (1531); death
of Zwingli at Cappel (1531); religious Peace of
Nuremberg (1532); John Frederick, elector of

A.D.                                                                PAGE

Saxony (1532–1547); Ulrich of Würtemberg re-
covers his duchy (1534); the anabaptists in
Münster (1535); war with Francis I. (1536–
1544); Peace of Crespy (1544); Brandenburg
accepts the Reformation (1539); opening of the
Council of Trent (1545); Pope Paul III. (1534–
1549); death of Luther (1546); Smalkald
War (1546–1547); battle of Mühlberg (1547);
Maurice becomes elector of Saxony (1547); the
"Interim" (1547); League of Protestants with
Henry II. of France (1552); Maurice turns
against Charles V. (1552); treaty of Passau
(1552); death of Maurice (1553); religious
Peace of Augsburg (1555); abdication of
Charles V. (1555); death of Charles V. (1558).    263–394

1558–1564    *Ferdinand I.:* struggles of Protestants and
Catholics for supremacy; Calvin (1509–1564);
Calvinism in Germany; Augustus of Saxony
and Frederick III. of the Palatinate; the crypto-
Calvinists; the Council of Trent (1545–1563).    394–415

1564–1576    *Maximilian II.:* Ignatius Loyola (1491–1556)
and the Jesuits in Germany; the Protestants
lose ground.                                          415–421

1576–1612    *Rudolph II.:* the struggle for the Cologne
bishopric (1582); the reform of the Calendar
by Gregory XIII. (1582); Maximilian I., duke,
and afterward elector, of Bavaria (1598–1651);
the affair of Donauwörth (1606–1607); the
Protestant Union (1608); the Royal Charter of
the Bohemians (1609); beginning of the Cleves-
Julier question (1609); death of Henry IV. of
France (1610); John George, elector of Saxony (1611–1656); Rudolph and Matthias.          421–438

1612–1619    *Matthias:* Ferdinand becomes king of Bohemia (1617); affairs of Braunau and Klostergrab
(1618); Prussia falls to Brandenburg by inheritance (1618); outbreak of Thirty Years' War
(1618); Bohemian period of the war (1618–
1623); the councillors thrown out of the win-
dow (1618).                                            438–441

A.D.                                                                    PAGE

1619–1637    *Ferdinand II.:* George William, elector of
             Brandenburg (1619–1640); election of Fred-
             erick V. of the Palatinate as king of Bohemia
             (1619); battle on the White Hill (1620); Fred-
             erick's electoral vote given to Maximilian of Ba-
             varia (1623); the Saxon-Danish period of the war
             (1625–1629); Wallenstein (1583–1634) defeats
             Mansfeld at Dessau (1626); Tilly defeats Chris-
             tian IV. of Denmark at Lutter (1626); Wal-
             lenstein besieges Stralsund (1628); edict of
             restitution (1629); Peace of Lübeck with Den-
             mark (1629); dismissal of Wallenstein (1630);
             landing of Gustavus Adolphus, king of Sweden
             (1611–1632) (1630); destruction of Magdeburg
             (1631); Gustavus Adolphus defeats Tilly at
             Breitenfeld (1631); death of Tilly (1632); re-
             turn of Wallenstein (1632); death of Gustavus
             Adolphus at Lützen (1632); League of Heil-
             bronn (1633); murder of Wallenstein (1634);
             battle of Nördlingen (1634); Peace of Prague
             (1635); Swedish general, Banèr, conquers at
             Wittstock (1636).                                        441–484

1637–1657    *Ferdinand III.:* campaigns of Bernard of
             Weimar and of Torstenson; Frederick William,
             Great Elector of Brandenburg (1640–1688);
             assembly at Münster and Osnabrück (1644–
             1648); Louis XIV. (1643–1715); the Peace of
             Westphalia (1648).                                       484–497

# INDEX

Adalbert of Bremen, 61.
Adolphus of Nassau, 126.
Adrian I., Pope, 29.
Adrian IV. and Frederick Barbarossa, 79, 83; death of, 84.
Æneas Sylvius Piccolomini, 222; becomes Pope Pius II., 227.
Agnes, Empress, 58.
Agricola, John, 382.
Alaric, 12.
Alberich, 52.
Albert of Austria, 126; murder of, 127; conflict with the electors, 131; and Pope Boniface VIII., 132.
Alcibiades, Albrecht, of Culmbach, 374, 389–390.
Alcuin, 36.
Aldringen, General, 477.
Aleander, 277, 299, 305; papal legate, 284.
Alexander II., Pope, 60.
Alexander III., election of, 84.
Alexander VI., 240.
Alexius, Greek emperor, 91.
Alfonso of Castile, 100.
Alessandria, 87; change of name of, 89.
Alsace, rights ceded to France, 493.
Alva, Duke of, 376, 378, 380, 381, 405.
Amiens, Peace of, 350.
Anabaptists, 308 ff.
Andreæ, James, Dr., 409–410.
Angilbert, 37.
Anglo-Saxons, 12.
Anno of Cologne, 61.
Antwerp, 195.
Aquæ Sextiæ, battle of, 4.
Aquila, 298.
Ariovistus, 4.
Arminius, 5.
Arnim, embassador of Wallenstein, 478.

Arnulf of Carinthia, 45.
Augsburg, the hearing of Luther at, 257; Luther's flight from, 258; confession of, 360; Diet of, 1547 A.D., 382; Diet of, 1555 A.D., 391; religious peace of, 392–394.
Augustus, elector of Saxony, 401; bigotry of, 404; and the crypto-Calvinists, 406; breach with the Palatinate, 407–408; establishes a norm of faith, 409; harms the Protestant cause, 426.
Austrasia, 22.
Avignon, the popes at, 203.

Babylonian captivity, the, of the Papacy, 133.
Banèr, General, 486.
Barbarossa, Chaireddin, 367.
Barbarossa, Frederick, accession of, 78; difficulties with Milan, 79; personality, 79; and Adrian IV., 79, 83; enters Rome, 1167 A.D., 85; crusade and death of, 90.
Barcelona, Peace of, 351.
Bärwalde, Treaty of, 466.
Basel, Council of, 217; opens, 217; Sigismund at, 218; Council of Schism in, 220, 221; and the seven electors, 225; frustration of, 226; reforms, 226.
Bavaria, Jesuits in, 422.
Benedict IX., Pope, 55.
Benedict XII., Pope, 142.
Benedict XIII., 205, 206, 213, 214.
Berengar of Ivrea, 51.
Bergen, 195.
Bergen book, the, 409.
Berlichingen, Götz von, 325.
Bernard, St., of Clairvaux, 77.
Bernard of Weimar, 473, 474; in French pay, 484; death of, 485.

Besant, the Saracen, 104.
Bible, Wulfila's translation of, 10.
Bicocca, battle of, 335.
Black Death, the, 151.
Bockellson, John, of Leyden, 328, 331, 332.
Bohemia, civil war in, 219, 220; subjugation of, 1621 A.D., 447–449.
Bohemian refugees, 494.
Boniface VIII., Pope, 132; death of, 133.
Boniface IX., Pope, 204.
Boniface, Saint, 24; furthers letters, 25.
Bonnivet, 335.
Bora, Catherine von, wife of Luther, 342.
Bourbon, constable of France, 335, 336, 347; death of, 348.
Bouvines, battle of, 93.
Brahe, Tycho, 434.
Brandenburg, electorate of, becomes Protestant, 369.
Brant, Sebastian, 236; *Ship of Fools*, 236.
Braunau, 439.
Breitenfeld, battle of, 469.
Brunhilda, 16.
Bucer, Martin, 298, 364.
Bundschuh, 250, 283.
Buquoi, 442.
Burgundy, 22.
Butler, Colonel, 481.

Cæsar, 4.
Cæsarea, 89.
Cajetanus (Cardinal de Vio), 256, 257.
Calendar, reform of, by Gregory XIII., 429–430.
Calixtus II., Pope, 74.
Calvin, 374; and Luther, 398; *Institutes of Religion*, 398.
Calvinism, 397–399; severity of, 399.
Calvinists, 464.
Campeggi, 341, 342, 358.
Canossa, penance at, 67.
Cappel, battle of, 364.
Carlstadt, 314; at Leipzig, 260, 261, 311.
Casimir, John, of Pfalz-Lautern, 408, 410, 426, 427.
Catherine of Aragon, 350.
Celestine III., 91.
Cellini, Benvenuto, 348.

Centenarius, 6.
Chamber Court, 429.
Charles of Anjou, 101.
Charles the Bald, 39.
Charles the Bold, 229.
Charles the Fat, 44.
Charles the Great, military achievements, 27; conquests of, 27; and Adrian, 29; subjugates the Saxons, 28; and Pope Leo III., 30; coronation of, 31; and the *missi dominici*, 33; his capitularies, 34; his zeal for learning, 35; and his paladins, 36; and the beginning of art, 37; death of, 38; canonization of, 106.
Charles Gustavus, Swedish king, 490.
Charles I., of England, 455.
Charles IV., election of, 144; personality of, 146; piety of, 147; against the Wittelsbachs, 148; accepts the false Waldemar, 149; and Rienzi, 157; and Petrarch, 157, 158; Italian expedition, 158; and Gregory XI., Pope, 162, 163; acquires Brandenburg, 163, 164.
Charles V., 333; youth of, 265–266; rivalry with Francis I., 267–268; wins the election, 270; electoral compromise of, 271; coronation, 272; feeling to Martin Luther, 278; delivers dictum at Worms, 282; wars with Francis I., 334–339; marriage of, 345; enjoys the sack of Rome, 349; crowned emperor, 351; at the Diet of Augsburg, 358–362; at Ratisbon, 376; at Ingolstadt, 377; flight from Innsbruck, 387; abdication, and death, 391.
Christian of Brunswick, 451, 452, 454.
Christian IV., of Denmark, 455, 456.
Christine, wife of Philip of Hesse, 371, 389.
Cities, unsanitary condition of, 182; administration of, in the Middle Ages, 183, 184.
Clair-sur-Epte, Treaty of, 42.
Clement IV., 101.
Clement VI., 138, 144.
Clement VII., 205, 339; attacked in St. Peter's, 348; surrenders, 349.
Cleves heritage, the, 434.
Cleves-Julier, William of, 369, 373, 423.

Clovis, 13; conversion of, to Christianity, 14–15.
Cnipperdolling, 332.
Cognac, League of, 339.
Cologne, struggle for, in 1582 A.D., 424.
Columbanus, St., 17.
Communes, Italian, 80; royal rights in, 81.
Compiègne, Diet at, 40.
Conrad, of Jungingen, 177.
Conrad, Poor, 250.
Conrad of Marburg, 109, 110.
Conrad I., 49; and the church, 50.
Conrad II., 54.
Conrad IV., 101.
Conradin, execution of, 101.
Conradins, false, 125.
Constance, Peace of, 1183 A.D., 89; council of, 209.
Constance of Sicily, 90, 91.
Constantinople, fall of, 1453 A.D., 264.
Copenhagen, plundering of, 1368 A.D., 200.
Craco, Dr., 407.
Crespy, Peace of, 373.
Crusade, the second, 77.
Crusades, influence of, 103, 107.
Crypto-Calvinists, 406–407.

Dante, and Henry VII., 128.
Danzig, commercial decline of, 497.
Decretum Gratiani, 78.
Defensor Pacis, the, 139; success of, 140.
Denk, Hans, 327.
Djem, 239–240.
Donauwörth (or Wörth), religious disturbances in, 430–433, 488.
Dorso, heretic hunter, 110.
Dress, extravagance in, 247.
Dürer, Albrecht, 285, 307.
Dusentschur of Warendorf, 331.
Dyle, battle on the, 45.

Ebernburg, the, 297.
Eck, John, 260–262.
Edict of Restitution, 463–464.
Edward III. of England, 143.
Einhard, 17.
Electoral college, 130.
Elizabeth, St., of Thuringia, 109.

Empire, Holy Roman, founding of, 32; extent of, 32; decline of, 228.
Enzio, i. 98; capture of, 100.
Erasmus of Rotterdam, 233; Praise of Folly, 236; attacks Luther, 285; and Hutten, 303–304.
Ernest of Bavaria, 423, 424, 427.
Eschenbach, Wolfram von, 108, 114.
Eugenius IV., and the Council of Basel, 220, 221; death of, 226.

Feiken, Hille, 331.
Ferdinand, brother of Charles V., 269; elected king of the Romans, 341; 350, 355, 387, 393; and the council of Trent, 412–413.
Ferdinand of Styria, 436–437; becomes king of Bohemia, 438–439.
Ferdinand II., gives the Palatinate to Maximilian, 453–454; issues Edict of Restitution, 463–464; dismisses Wallenstein, 464.
Feudal System, beginning of, 23.
Field of Lies, 40.
Fiescho, Sinnibald, 98.
Flagellants, the, 152.
Fontenoy, battle of, 42.
Francis I., 350, 369; as candidate for the imperial throne, 267–268, 270; wars with Charles V., 334–339; capture of, 336; captivity of, 337; death of, 382.
Franks, 12, 13.
Fredegunda, 16.
Frederick of Austria, 208.
Frederick the Fair, and Louis the Bavarian, 129, 135, 138; capture of, 130; liberation of, 137.
Frederick the Wise, 270, 304; and Luther, 305–306; death of, 319.
Frederick II., Emperor, 93; personality of, 93; crusading vow of, 94; marriage of, 94; and Gregory IX., 95; crusade of, 95; papal accusations against, 96; crusades against, 97; captures prelates, 97; deposition of, 99; death of, 100.
Frederick III., Elector Palatine, Calvinism of, 400–405; death of, 408.
Frederick III., Emperor, accession of, 221; character of, 222, 223; apathy of, 223, 224; 229.

Frederick V., Elector Palatine, 444; chosen king of Bohemia, 444; offends the Bohemians, 445; declared in the ban of the empire, 450; death of, 473.
Fredericks, false, 125.
Freiburg, battle of, 488.
Freidank, poet, 108.
Frisian Law, poetry in, 21.
Fritz, Jost, 250, 316.
Frundsberg, 335.
Frundsberg, George von, 346–347.

Gabor, Bethlen, 443, 446, 451.
Gallas, General, 487.
Gebhard, Paul, 495.
Gebhard Truchsess, Archbishop of Cologne, conversion to Protestantism, 424–427.
George, Duke of Saxony, 261, 312, 341, 368.
Gerard the Great, 197.
Germans and Romans, 9.
Ghibelline, 77.
Glapion, 300.
Golden Bull, the, 159–162.
Göllheim, battle of, 126.
Gonzaga, Ferrante, 384.
Gordon, Colonel, 481.
Granvella, 373.
Gratius, Ortuin, 237, 238.
Gregory of Heimburg, 222.
Gregory VI., Pope, 56.
Gregory VII., accession of, 61; pretensions of, 63; at Canossa, 67; straits of, 69; death of, 70.
Gregory IX., and Frederick II., 95; death of, 98.
Gregory X., Pope, 122.
Gregory XI., Pope, 162, 163.
Gregory XII., 205, 206, 213.
Gregory XIII., 426.
Gregory XV., 453.
Gronsfeld, General, 489.
Guelph, 77.
Guild merchants, trials of, 187, 188.
Guilds, trade, 185; activity of, 186.
Guiscard, Robert, 59.
Güns, siege of, 366.
Gunther of Schwarzburg, election of, 150; death of, 151.

Gustavus Adolphus of Sweden, 455; landing of, 464; early years of, 465; reception on German soil, 466; negotiates with Saxony and Brandenburg, 467; triumphs of, 471; death of, 472.
Gutenberg, John, 234.

Hague, Treaty of the, 1625 A.D., 456.
Hans of Küstrin, 374.
Hanseatic League, beginnings of, 189; membership and extent of, 190; products traded in, 192; "courts" of the, 194, 195; war with Denmark, 198, 200; decline of, 201, 202.
Hapsburg, Rudolph of, 123.
Harmony of Creeds, the, 410.
Heidelberg University, founding of, 197.
Heilbronn, League of, 474.
Helfenstein, Louis, Count of, 320, 326.
Henrietta Maria, English queen, 455.
Henry (son of Frederick II.), 110.
Henry the Lion, 88.
Henry of Plauen, grand master, 179; captivity of, 180.
Henry Raspe, 100.
Henry I., 49.
Henry II., 54.
Henry II. of France, joins German princes, 387.
Henry III., 54, 56.
Henry IV., abduction of, 60; character of, 61; submissive letter of, 62; banning of, 64; at Oppenheim, 65; in Spires, 66; ultimatum to, 66; at Canossa, 67; second banning of, 68; death of, 71.
Henry V., and Paschal II., 72; and the investiture, 72; extorts concessions, 73.
Henry VI., marriage of, 90; character of, 91; Sicily falls to, 91; death of, 92.
Henry VII., personality of, 127; in Italy, 128; Dante and, 128; death of, 129, 134; Clement V. and, 134.
Henry VIII. of England, 339, 350, 368; death of, 382.
Hildebrand, monk, 58.
Hippolytus, a Lapide, 485.
Höchst, battle of, 452.

Hohenaltheim, synod of, 50.
Holzschuh, Dietrich, 125.
Homburg, battle of, 62.
Honorius II., Pope, 60.
Hubmaier, Balthasar, 327.
Hussite, Luther a, 263.
Hussite War, 214–217.
Huss, John, at Prague, 209; and Archbishop Sbynek, 210; goes to Constance, 211; abandoned by Sigismund, 212; burning of, 212, 213.
Hutten, Ulrich von, 289 ff.; early
years, 290; as a writer, 291; against
Ulrich of Würtemberg, 292; against
the Papacy, 293; in danger, 296;
estrangement from Luther, 298; and
the Diet of Worms, 299; degenerates, 300; and Erasmus, 303–304;
death of, 304.

Illow, 479.
Indulgences, theory of, 242.
Innocent II., 76.
Innocent IV., 98.
Innocent VII., 205.
Innocent VIII., 239.
Inquisition, the, in Germany, 108; end
of, 111.
Interim, the, of Charles V., 382–383,
385.
Iodocus of Moravia, 164; elected em-
peror, 167.
Isabella of Portugal, 345.

James I., of England, 455.
Jankau, battle of, 487.
Jesuits, 415, 418–421.
Jews, the, attacks on, 153; legal status
of, 153; practise usury, 154, 155;
massacres of, 155, 156.
Joachim II., elector of Brandenburg,
369, 381.
Joanna the Insane, 229.
John, elector of Saxony, 344, 354, 364.
John Frederick of Saxony, 367; and
Philip of Hesse, 372, 376; fights for
his electorate, 378; capture of, 379–
380; in captivity, 384; release, 388.
John George of Saxony, 474.
John Henry of the Tyrol, 143.
John of Luxemburg, death of, 145.

John the one-eyed and one-handed,
110.
John XII., Pope, 52; deposition of, 53.
John XXII., Pope, 135; conflict with
Louis of Bavaria, 136; deposed, 140.
John XXIII., 206, 207; promises to
abdicate, 208; flight of, 208; arraign-
ment of, 209.
Joust, the, 116.
Jubilee, institution of the, 204.
Julius II., 240.

Kadan, Treaty of, 1534 A.D., 367.
Kaisersberg, Geiler von, 236.
Kaiserswerth, 60.
Kammergericht, 230.
Kepler, 434.
Kinsky, 479.
Klesl, chancellor, 442.
Klostergrab, 440.
Knight, duties of, 112.
Knighthood, a general order of, 111;
preparation for, 116; discomforts
of, 120; decline of, 121.
Knighting, ceremony of, 115.
Kranach, Lucas, 285, 384.

Landfrieden, 230.
Landsknechts, 232–233.
Lannoy, 336, 338, 347.
Lautrec, 334, 351.
League, the Catholic, 433.
Legnano, battle of, 88.
Leipzig, disputation at, 261–263.
Leo III., Pope, 30.
Leo IX., Pope, 56; zeal of, 57; death
of, 58.
Leo X., 240, 255; objects to Charles
V.'s election, 266; death of, 334.
Letters of Obscure Men, 238.
Liechtenstein, Ulrich von, 120.
Limes or Pfahlbau, 8.
Lithuania, raids into, 177; Christian-
ization of, 178.
Lobkowitz, Sdenko von, 436.
Lombard cities, German claim to, 78.
Lombard League, 87.
Lombards, 12.
Lothar, king of the Romans, 76.
Louis the Bavarian, and Frederick the
Fair, 129, 135; coronation as em-

peror, 140; growing unpopularity of, 141; submissiveness of, 142; opposition to, 143; death of, 145.

Louis the Child, 45.

Louis the Pious, accession, 38; marriage with Judith, 39; end of his reign, 40.

Louis XIII., of France, 455, 484.

Louise of France, 352.

Loyasa, 358, 359.

Loyola, Ignatius, 415; early training, 415–416; spiritual exercises of 416–417.

Luther, Martin, 251, 318; journey to Rome, 251–252; his humility, 255; at Augsburg, 257 ; flight from Augsburg, 258; and Miltitz, 259; and Eck, 260; finds himself a Hussite, 262–263; to the Christian Nobility, 272; writings of, in 1520, 273; papal bull against, 274–276; summoned to Worms, 277; journey to Worms, 279; reception in Worms, 280; first hearing, 280; second hearing, 281; and Frederick the Wise, 305–306; carried to the Wartburg, 306; return of, to Wittenberg, 312–313; and the Peasants' War, 314 ff.; view of peasants, 321 ; organizes the new church, 342; marriage of, 343; consents to marriage of Philip of Hesse, 371; and Philip of Hesse, 372; death of, 373; and Calvin, 398.

Lutter, battle of, 459.

Lützen, battle of, 472.

Luxemburg, house of, 127.

Lyons, Council of, 1245 A.D., 99.

Madrid, Treaty of, 1526 A.D., 338.

Magdeburg, surrender of, to Maurice of Saxony, 386; burning of, 468.

Mainz, festival at, 1184 A.D., 102.

Mandlot, Colonel, 486.

Manfred, 101.

Mansfeld, General, 442, 446, 451, 452, 454; death of, 459.

Marburg, disputation of, 1529 A.D., 357–358.

Margaret of Austria, 352.

Margarete von der Sale, 371.

Marienburg, building of the, 175.

Marius, battles of, 4.

Marozia, 52.

Marseilles, siege of, 335.

Marsilius of Padua, 138.

Martel, Charles, and the Arabs, 23; seizes church lands, 24.

Martin V., 214.

Martinitz, Jaroslav von, 436, 441.

Mary of Burgundy, 229.

Matilda, Countess, 67, 70.

Matthias, Archduke, 435; and Rudolph, 437; death of, 442.

Matthias, John, of Haarlem, 328–331.

Maultasch, Margaret, 143.

Maurice of Saxony, deserts the Protestants, 374–375; invades electoral Saxony, 377 ; 381, 385; heads revolt, 386; death of, 390.

Maximilian, elector of Bavaria, 432; overthrows Wörth, 432; 433, 443; is given the Palatinate, 452–454; campaign against, 489.

Maximilian I., wars in Italy, 229; marriage with Mary of Burgundy, 229; personality of, 230; wild projects of, 231; inventions and reforms, 232; death of, 263.

Maximilian II., son of Archduke Ferdinand, 385, 396; political schemes, 402; attitude to Spain, 405; death of, 408.

Meckbach, chancellor of Magdeburg, 428.

Melanchthon, youth of, 286; in Wittenberg, 287; and Luther, 288–289; 318; and the peasants, 322; at Augsburg, 320; 364, 371; disloyalty to Luther, 383; 385; changes Augsburg Confession, 400.

Melander, 371.

Memmingen, peasants at, 318.

Merovingians, power and riches, 16; decline of, 17; administration, 18.

Mersen, Treaty of, 44.

Metzler, George, of Ballenberg, 320.

Milan, difficulties with Frederick Barbarossa, 79; submission of, in 1158 A.D., 80; overthrow of, 82.

Milanese, sufferings of, 86.

Miltitz, and Luther, 259; and Tetzel, 259.

Minorites, the, against the Pope, 137.

*Missi dominici*, 33.

Mohacs, battle of, 350.
Mohammedans, culture of, 103.
Monasteries, civilization in, 46.
Morone, 339.
Mühlberg, battle of, 379.
Müller, Hans, 315–316.
Münster, anabaptists in, 327–333; congress at, 489.
Münzer, Thomas, 310, 314, 316, 319–320; downfall of, 324.
Music among the Germans, 21.

Nations, wandering of, 11.
Naumburg, assembly at, 401.
Neustria, 22.
Nicholas II., Pope, 59.
Nicholas V., antipope, 141.
Nithard, historian, 42.
Nonnenmacher, Melchior, 321, 326.
Normans, coming of, 41.
Normans, settlement in Italy, 59.
Novgorod, 195.
Nuremberg, religious Peace of, 366.

Octavian, 52.
Odoacer, 12.
Œcolampadius, 298.
Onate, Spanish envoy, 478.
Ordeal, the, 19.
Ottocar of Bohemia, 124.
Otto I., 49; and the clergy, 51; and the popes, 51; imperial coronation, 52.
Otto II., 53.
Otto III., 53.
Otto IV., emperor, 92; under the ban, 93.
Oxenstierna, Swedish chancellor, 473.

Pack, Otto von, 353, 354.
Parsifal, 113, 114.
Paschal II., Pope, 72; renounces investiture, 73.
Paschal III., antipope, 85.
Passau, Treaty of, 387–388.
Pataria, the, in Milan, 60.
Paul II., 239.
Paul III., 368, 375, 412.
Paul V., 445.
Pavia, synod of, 1160 A.D., 84; siege of, 335; battle of, 336.

Peasant, condition of the, 246; oppression of, 248–249.
Peasants' War, 315 ff.
Pepin, son of Charles Martel, becomes king, 25; donation of, 26.
Pepin of Héristal, 22.
Pescara, 336, 339, 340.
Peter of Danzig, the, 191.
Peter de Vigne, 100.
Pfefferkorn, 237, 238.
Philip Augustus of France, 93.
Philip of Hohenstaufen, 92.
Philip, landgrave of Hesse, 319, 344, 353, 361, 364; double marriage of, 370–373; arrest of, 381; release, 388–389.
Philip, son of Charles V., 385.
Philip III., of Spain, 443.
Piccolomini, 479, 497.
Pisa, Council of, 1409 A.D., 206.
Pius II., Æneas Sylvius, as Pope, 227.
Pius IV., 411.
Pliny, 4.
Poictiers, battle near, 23.
Prague, university of, 147; Compactates, 219; peace of, 1635 A.D., 483.
Prayer brotherhoods, 245.
Printing, invention of, 234.
Protestants, origin of the name, 355; lose ground, 428.
Prussians, subjugation of, 174.
Pythias of Marseilles, 2.

Ratisbon, Diet of, 1608 A.D., 433.
Reichshofrath, 429.
Reichsregiment, 230, 277, 340; end of, 303.
Relics, collections of, 244.
Renaissance, 233–234.
Reservatum ecclesiasticum, 393, 493.
Reuchlin, John, 233, 237, 238; repudiates Luther, 286; educates Melanchthon, 286.
Rense, meeting of electors at, 142.
Richard the Lion-hearted, 91.
Richelieu, 466.
Robber knight, the, 182.
Rocroi, battle of, 487.
Rohrbach, Jacquelein, 326.
Roland, banner-bearer of Charles the Great, 27.
Romans and Germans, 9.

Rome, siege of, 1527 A.D., 347; sack of, 1527 A.D., 348.
Rothmann, Bernard, 327–328.
Royal Charter, 435–436.
Rudolph of Hapsburg, election of, 123; personality of, 123; struggle with Ottocar of Bohemia, 124.
Rudolph of Swabia, 68.
Rudolph II., chosen king of the Romans, 408; character of, 434–435; and Matthias, 437; death of, 438.
Rupert of the Palatinate, Emperor, 166; death of, 167.

Sachs, Hans, 285.
Salic Law, 19; punishments under, 20; poetry in, 20.
San Germano, Treaty of, 94.
Saxons, rebellion of, 62.
Saxony, division between Albertines and Ernestines, 230; duchy of, becomes Protestant, 369; electorate of, invaded by Maurice, 377.
Schärtlin, 349, 376.
Schism, the great, 204; end of, 213.
Schonen, 195, 196, 197, 198.
Scultetus, 445.
Serralonga, 257.
Sforza, Duke of, 369.
Sicily falls to Henry VI., 91.
Sickingen, Franz von, 295; his feuds, 294–295; won for the Reformation, 295–296; in pay of Charles V., 300; last feud, 301; death of, 302.
Sigismund, Emperor, personality, 167; faults, 168; death of, 170; enters Constance, 207; gives safe-conduct to Huss, 211; abandons Huss, 212; peregrinates Europe, 213; at Basel, 218.
Silvester, Pope, 55.
Simon, 55.
Simons, Menno, 332.
Sixtus IV., 239.
Slavata, Wilhelm von, 436, 441.
Smalkald League, 363, 364; end of, 377.
Soissons, penance at, 40.
Spalatin, 263, 298, 305.
Spinola, 450, 452.
Spires, Diet of, 1526 A.D., 344–345; Diet of, 1529 A.D., 354–356.

Squire, the, 116.
St. Benedict, rule of, 46.
St. Gall, saint, monastery, 18; plan of, 46.
Steelyard, the, 193.
Stephen IV., Pope, crosses the Alps, 26.
Storch, Nicholas, 310.
Störtebeker, Hans, 191.
Strabo, 4.
Stralsund, Peace of, 1370 A.D., 201; besieged by Wallenstein, 461.
Strassburg, oath of, 42.
Stübner, Marcus, 310, 314.
Suessa, Thaddeus of, 99.
Suleiman, 366.
Superstition, 243.
Susa, 87.
Swabian League, 317.
Switzerland, war with, 229.
Syagrius, 13.

Tacitus, 4; the *Germania* of, 5 ff.
Tagliacozzo, 101.
Tannenberg, battle of, 178.
Tartars, invasion of Germany by, 97.
Tauss, battle of, 217.
Tersky, 479.
Testry, battle of, 22.
Tetrapolitana, 360.
Tetzel, John, employed to sell indulgences, 252; methods of, 253; writes counter theses, 255; and Miltitz, 259.
Teutoburg Forest, battle of, 5.
Teutonic Order, moves to Prussia, 173; subjugates the Prussians, 174; administration of, 175; degeneration of, 177; poverty and ruin of, 180; secularization of, 353.
Theodoric, 12.
Theses, the ninety-five, 254.
Thorn, Treaty of, 1466 A.D., 181.
Thurn, Matthias von, 440, 446.
Tilly, General, 446; imperial commander, 452, 464; at Breitenfeld, 469; death of, 472.
Torgau Compilation, 409.
Torstenson, General, 486.
Totilo, versatile monk, 48.
Tournament, the, 117; the church and, 118.
Trent, Council of, opening, 374, 411–414.

Trial by combat, 119.
Tuttlingen, battle of, 488.

Ulfila or Wulfila, 10.
Ulrich of Jungingen, 178.
Ulrich of Würtemberg, 292, 316, 365, 367.
Union, the Protestant, 433, 451.
Urban II., Pope, 70.
Urban IV., bull of, 175.

Vandals, 12.
Varus, 5.
Veme, the Holy, procedure of, 169; decline of, 170.
Venice, Peace of, 88–89.
Verdun, Treaty of, 43.
Vergerio, papal legate, 368.
Victor III., Pope, 70.
Victor IV., antipope, 84.
Vienna, Concordat of, 224; siege of, 1529 A.D., 352.
Visigoths, 12.
Vladislav, of Hungary, 350.
Vogelweide, Walter of the, 106.

Wagenburg, the functions of, 216.
Waldeck, Franz von, Bishop, 328, 330.
Waldemar, of Denmark, 198, 199, 200.
Waldemar, the false, acceptance by Charles IV., 149; investiture of, 150; abandons claims, 151.
Wallenstein, buys lands, 448; first called to command, 456; early years, 457; arrangement with, 458; and Tilly, 458; his plans for Ferdinand, 459; honors heaped on, 460; his lordly doings, 461–462; dismissal of, 464; recall of, 470; unaccountable delays of, 474; grievances of, 475; treasonable plans of, 476; fails to relieve Ratisbon, 477; turns traitor, 478; extent of his treason, 480; death of, 482–483.
Warbeck, Perkin, 231.
Wenceslaus, Emperor, 164; deposition of, 165; death of, 215.
Werth, John of, 489.
Westphalia, Peace of, 490–495.
White Hill, battle on the, 446–447.
Wiesloch, battle of, 452.
William of Holland, 100.
Winrich von Kniprode, 176.
Wisby, 195, 196, 198.
Withold, Lithuanian prince, 215.
Wittenberg, anabaptists in, 311.
Wolsey, Cardinal, 269, 350, 351.
Wordinborg, Peace of, 199.
Worms, Council at, 64; Concordat of, 74, 75; Diet of, 1495 A.D., 230; Diet of, 1521 A.D., 276–277, 280–283; edict of, 284, 341.
Wörth (see Donauwörth), religious disturbances in, 430–433.
Wrangel, General, 488, 497.
Würzburg, oath of, 85.

Zapolya, John, 350, 354.
Ziegler, James, 346.
Ziscka, John, 216.
Zusmarshausen, battle of, 489.
Zwickau, 310.
Zwingli, Ulrich, and Hutten, 304; 318; differs from Luther, 356–357.